VADER TIME

Story of a Modern Day Gladiator

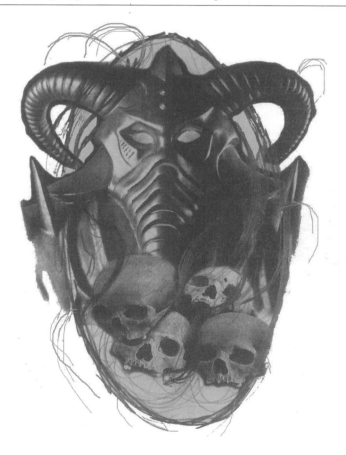

Leon White
with Kenny Casanova

VADER TIME: Story of a Modern Day Gladiator

ISBN: 978-1-941356-08-1

Printed in the USA

TABLE OF CONTENTS

FOREWORD - BY MICK FOLEY

I had a unique problem in the spring of 1993 for which there was really only one solution. I had become a babyface, a good guy, for Ted Turner's World Championship Wrestling (WCW) a few months earlier, and things were going fairly well with one exception; it was difficult for me to get sympathy from the fans. As a heel, a bad guy, I'd been portrayed as a guy who thrived on pain, maybe even liked it - which helped create a very interesting wrestling villain persona. It did not,  however, make for a terribly sympathetic portrait as a good guy.

I requested a meeting with WCW booker Dusty Rhodes, and together we came up with a plan to combat the sympathy problem. Quite simply, I would wrestle Big Van Vader. Two matches, twenty stitches, a broken nose, and a memorable ambulance ride later, my sympathy problem was a thing of the past. Vader had cured it.

It was almost impossible not to feel a sense of sympathy for an opponent of Leon White during his career as Vader. To me, he was the most believable, most talented "monster" wrestler of his generation. No one was better at being the immovable object, that impenetrable wall, than Leon White. Eventually - if you worked hard enough, and if it was in the interest of doing business - the object would move and the wall would crumble in spectacular, athletic fashion. But if you were his opponent, he'd make damn sure that you were the very best irresistible force you could possibly be - or he'd eat you alive. The price you paid to be the best you could be against Vader was high, but the rewards for going places you didn't know you could go (until he helped you get there) were even higher.

At the time of writing this book, Leon White has not yet secured his spot in the WWE Hall of Fame.

Every year fans wonder if Leon White will finally, one day, be inducted into the WWE Hall of Fame, and every year, most of those slots are filled by wrestlers who didn't draw a fraction of the money, or contribute to the wrestling business on nearly the level that Leon White/Vader did.

I'm not belittling the importance of the WWE Hall of Fame. Indeed, being inducted was one of the personal highlights of my career. As we head into another year wondering if Leon White will finally be inducted, let me put forth my criteria, by which Leon/Vader is worthy not only of induction but of consideration as one of the greatest, most influential superstars of his generation.

1) He drew more money, with a wider variety of opponents, for different promotions, on a global basis, than just about any of his contemporaries. Basically, until WWE tried to fix something that wasn't broken, Vader was money everywhere he went.

2) He brought out the best in his opponents. Vader "paid it forward" by bringing out the very best in some of the greatest stars of his time, and of all time.

3) His matches stand the test of time. No matter what trends the business may go through, Vader's believable brawling, combined with his impressive athleticism will never go out of style.

4) He was able to turn a 6'4, 300 pound maniac with a love for pain into a sympathetic underdog.

So... *who's the man?*

Read on for your answer ...but I think you already know.

CHAPTER ZERO - EYE-POPPING EXPERIENCE

WHAPPP!
Something metal smacked me in the face.
As I was walking up the ring stairs to perhaps one of my biggest matches ever, something hit me harder than I had ever been hit before.

There was blood even before the bell. I could taste it in the back of my throat. I reached up and felt the looseness of the cartilage inside my nose. In my head, I could hear the shards crunching and grinding together under my fingers, over the dulling roar of the 80,000 plus screaming fans.

"Yep. It's broken," I thought.

Everything went fuzzy. The audience sounded like they were underwater. I went into a little box of solitude for a moment, then snapped out of it and got back to my feet.

It was February of 1990. I was climbing into the ring at a Japanese wrestling fan dream show; NJPW (New Japan Pro Wrestling) versus our rivals, AJPW (All Japan Pro Wrestling). On this particular "super card," I was about to face one of the toughest bastards ever, Stan "The Lariat" Hansen.

To add to the stress of doing the very best job I could to represent our banner, I had heard rumblings that Stan might not be happy that he had to walk out to the ring first. In Japan, it was perceived that they always saved the best for last, as far as entrances were concerned. So I am assuming that Stan was upset that he was called to come out first.

Some people in the locker room were saying that Stan Hansen, one of the biggest drawing names in Japan ever, wouldn't like being looked at as the challenger, and he might be pissed because of the order of our entrances. I knew he probably didn't like coming out first, but I had no idea to what extent. I didn't think about it much at the time, though. Maybe he was right, but it didn't figure it would make sense to take it out on me. I didn't call the shots.

Before the match had even started and before knowing what had even hit me, I had to stop and get my bearings back. He hit me so hard, I barely knew where I was!

It was dark. Wrestling shows back then didn't have the crazy lighting like they do today, although NJPW had some. I looked around dazed for a moment. I looked directly into a light and then at the indistinct shadow of a cowboy in the ring who was waiting for me.

Hansen would later say that it was an accident because he didn't see me, but who the fuck knows? All I know is that before I had stepped into the ring between the ropes, Hansen swung a bull rope with a cowbell tied to the end of it and it hit me square in the face.

That little "accident" didn't sit well with me. Now, Hansen often told people that he was legally blind without his glasses. Whether that was true in this case or not, it didn't matter. Before the bell rang, I decided it was my turn to strike back with my own false start penalty. I walked right over to Hansen's corner and gave him the receipt for his stupid cowbell. I slapped him so hard I knocked the cowboy hat right off his head.

I was beyond pissed. After throwing a few more stiff shots and a few more receipts for the collapsed nose that was hanging off my face, the timekeeper said screw it. He shrugged and rang the bell. We started going right after each other, with shoot punches – real man shit.

Now, at this point in my career, I was on my way up, and Hansen was just was past his prime.

Although Hansen was considered one of the stiffest guys in the business, I was around 380 pounds and benching about 600. After hitting him with even more stiff shots for what he did to what was left of my broken nose, he went into defensive mode and was ready to retaliate.

We traded some really tough shots. I was coming out on top, and we moved over to the corner. That is when it happened.

Stan took his thumb and gouged it as deep as he could into my eye.

I heard a wet snap.

Something wasn't right. Everything went blurry again and then the cotton-mouth kicked in. The hair stood up on the back of my neck. I felt nauseous. My shoulders, the back of my neck and my underarms all instantly broke out into a cold sweat.

I grabbed him in an arm bar down on the mat.

"You fucked my eye up, Stan!" I said. As Hansen worked his way back up out of the move, I felt my eye get worse. I had been hit in the eye before, but this was different. I felt a pressure pushing down on my cheekbone under the mask.

I carefully touched the area around the injury, and it was then I realized what happened. Rather than to freak out, I decided to remain calm.

I pushed the palm of my hand hard against my face and tried to wriggle the greasy mound back into the hamburger-like meat hole in my head. It burned like hell sliding in. Quickly, I mashed it in and the eyeball slipped over the swollen lid. There was a slight suction as it the skin-flap positioned it into place.

I prayed that my eyelid, wet with all that eye-junk and goo, would do the best job it could to hold my eye in place for the rest of the match and not unravel and fall out on the floor. Once it was mostly in, I felt more at ease knowing I could continue the fight.

I reached up and took off my mask to show the entire Tokyo Dome that my eye had *popped out of its socket.*

Fucking sick.

It was only barely in place. I already had a broken nose, but if that wasn't enough, it now looked like I had a raw, slimy testicle hanging out of the side of my head.

I didn't panic. I didn't scream at Stan. I didn't scream for the ref. I didn't scream for a medic. What could I do? There is only one thing I could do. *Finish the match.*

I didn't think about the injury. I didn't think about the six operations it would eventually take to fix vision impairment and lazy eye. I only had one thing on my mind.

The show must go on."

It was Vader time.

I drove with one headlight out for another twelve and a half minutes until the bell rang. It was brutal, but that didn't matter.

You know what? I made it to the end of the match.

Yep. It's
Little Van
Vader.

CHAPTER 1 - STRAIGHT OUT OF COMPTON

Vader fans may have felt that being announced as coming from the Rocky Mountains had a big, tough, rugged sound to it, but I am really from an even bigger and tougher city, with an even bigger reputation. *I was born and raised in the city of Compton.*

Even though my mother was tougher than nails back then, and still is, before I was born, there were some health concerns during her pregnancy. My mom is a really small lady standing at about 4'10" with a tiny frame. When she was carrying me, she blew up only in her midsection like a giant balloon.

Two months before I was scheduled for my big debut, she was rushed to the hospital. As she waited in the room, the doctor grabbed my daddy and pulled him out into the hall.

"Listen, Mr. White," he said. "We don't know what you both have in there, but we do know this: it is big, very big, and it needs to come out, right now!"

There was no room left in there for me to grow. I was just too big for her. The thinking was that if they did not induce labor when they did, I might have killed my mother when she gave birth. After only seven and a half months of term, my mom was wheeled into the delivery ward at the Saint Francis Hospital in Lynwood, CA.

I was a big baby. I made my debut at almost 11 pounds and 24 inches. Of course, I didn't get that from my mother. The bigness gene that would eventually help turn me into one of the biggest big-men in wrestling comes from my daddy's side. My grandfather was a big red-headed guy at 6'6. My father was around 6'4, as well.

Compton is not known for producing giant Caucasian red-headed men. However, the Compton I grew up in wasn't an urban all black neighborhood at all, like the rest of the world today may see on TV, or in the movies. Just for the record, I didn't know Dr. Dre. I didn't know Easy-E. The only Ice Cube I knew of was the occasional one in my glass of water.

Back in the 60s when I was growing up, the big city of Compton was probably 60/40 mixed. It wasn't really run down anywhere, yet. In fact, my Aunt Virginia had an exceptionally nice house right in the heart of Compton, right near our place. Her home was really beautiful. It was a very nice Victorian with a slate roof and crown molding. We used to go over there for hours and play.

My father used to commute to work every day on the Long Beach 7 Highway. He passed Compton College heading towards San Pedro to get to a place called "Todd's Shipyard." He was a hard worker, for sure, and could do just about anything with his hands.

Before that, my daddy was a WWII vet, who at one point had one of the most dangerous jobs in the world. When still with the armed forces, he was a Navy diver that worked as an underwater welder. With an average death rate of around 17 percent, this occupation could be considered one of the most deadly professions out there, even today. Even after all the technological advancements made today, an average of three out of 20 underwater welders die every year on the job.

After the underwater work dried up with the Navy, he moved on to vehicle repair. Getting away from the water welding sounded like a good idea to my mom because it meant less risk of electrocution. My dad liked the idea of living, too.

The next chapter of his career taught him a whole lot about engines, but it also beat up on his body. Eventually, my dad left the service and started a muffler shop and it did really well at first. So well, they opened a second location.

The way they fixed vehicles in the 1960s may seem a bit archaic by today's standards. If a truck needed structural work, or say a muffler, they would dig a pit in the ground and have their guys crawl down into it. They would drive the vehicles over the hole and people would work lying down with their hands up in the air.

Even though there was no water and less chance of electrocution, my dad always came home a crinkled mess. Dripping sweat and dirt right down into his eyes all day also didn't help conditions. Being a big and tall guy at 6'4", crunched up in a trench made it tough work, day in and day out. It's no wonder he often came home with a few drinks in him, to boot.

One day after work, he told us that he crawled out of his hole that day and said to a buddy of his, "I've had just about enough of this. There has got to be a better way." He told us he was going to figure out how to make his work day easier unless it killed him first.

That night, he told us not to bother him and he disappeared into his bedroom. He put pen to paper for a few hours and drafted up an idea that would save his back. The next day, he returned to work with a plan that, little did he know, would revolutionize the way people worked on cars.

"Instead of lying down, why don't we just raise the car up?" my father, Arty Allen White, said – who they affectional called "Art."

His plans did just that. Falling back on his welding and mechanical experience from the Navy, my dad invented an electric auto hoist that would lift the vehicle so you could stand under it and do all your work on the underside of vehicles.

No more lying down. No more pits. His co-workers were impressed. You could just stand there and reach out in front of you, cut the muffler and then you were done! It may not sound like much to most today, but it was a real game changer at the time.

My dad's hoist is the same one that eventually ended up in muffler garages around the world. His invention brought everyone a lot of backache relief, but his invention actually didn't bring our family any money. Sadly, he didn't know the value of what he had created.

Two rich guys eventually came over to our place to talk business. They had heard about my father's invention and wanted to know more about it. I knew something was up when I sat down to dinner with the two guys in shirts in ties. They had weird looks on their faces, but they got what they came for – and that wasn't a free dinner. By the time they left our home that night, they had bought the rights to Dad's plan for a few thousand dollars. Soon after that, the shirt-and-ties mass-produced the lift and sold it all around the world. They instantly became millionaires.

While our family didn't make much money off of his invention, we were able to capitalize on the initial success of the invention. The first hoist at my father's shop allowed for much quicker work to happen and people came from miles away just to see it happen.

With all the success of the muffler shop, our family was able to move to a better home. From the money that the business made, we ended up living in a pretty decent suburb outside of Anaheim for a time. Because of this, I ended up going to Bell High School on the outside of town, rather than Compton High.

Before high school, life was relatively pretty safe where we lived. I'm not sure of a really nice way to say this, but as time progressed, a lot of the "better-off" families started to leave Compton and the areas surrounding it.

During my middle and high school days, I remember watching a number of my younger childhood friends pack their bags and say goodbye. Before our very eyes, the city crept onto us. Our area slowly transformed from quiet suburbia into more of an inner-city type neighborhood. That change quickly turned my world into a pretty rough place to grow up.

Before I had graduated, everything had changed. I had to learn how to live differently, by means of survival. Put it this way, I learned that if you wanted to live where I did, you had to earn it.

You grew up fast if you grew up in Compton. You either got good at fighting fast, or you got good at running fast. To be honest, I had to get a little good at both.

TOO BIG, TOO FAST

Being big in Japan would come later. I was first big in middle school. Come fourth grade, I really started growing. I felt a little socially awkward early on. Heck, for most of my time in school, I was a misfit because of my size. I didn't always recognize it, however.

One morning, I remember my daddy got up early like he always did.

"Get up, Leon," he said. He stuck his head into the bedroom and yelled at the top of his lungs, "I'm waiting!"

Now at 5:30 a.m., most kids would get a little angry and roll over, but not this kid. This wakeup call was one of my favorite things in the world. Maybe it was an excuse to cook a bunch of grub up for himself, or maybe he was actually just trying to bond with his kids. I don't know.

What I do know is my daddy loved to cook breakfast and I loved to eat it.

One of my earliest, fondest memories is of me walking down the hall, being pulled magnetically by the smell of crispy goodness in the air. The scent of smoky bacon had a way of doing that to me. It also had a way of opening my eyes and waking me right up.

Every other morning or so, my daddy figured cereal was not enough. He wanted protein. He would cook bacon, eggs, sausage, pancakes, grits, waffles, you name it. He wasn't selfish either when it came to food. He would cook any damn thing you wanted.

On one particular morning that I remember vividly, he already had a massive spread waiting by the time I made it to the table.

"What do you want, Leon?" he asked, pushing an empty plate in front of me.

I looked around and couldn't make a decision. I was a kid in a candy store and wanted to sample everything.

"I'll take it all," I said.

"All of it?" he laughed. "Okay, then. All of it, it is."

As a joke, my father dumped the whole serving bowl full of eggs onto my plate. He had mixed some cheese and other stuff in it as he usually did. It was a whole shit-ton of food.

Up for the challenge and trying to show off, I picked up a fork and went to town. I polished off that whole dozen of eggs. Then, I added a waffle, a pancake and a whole bunch of salty meat.

My dad watched me pounding my breakfast down like an animal, and he couldn't believe his eyes. He did the math. I ate more eggs than I was years old. Then, I went back for seconds.

"Thanks, daddy," I said licking ketchup off of my fingers when I was done. "That was great!" Fuller than usual, I got up and stretched. My gut flopped out a little bit over my pajama bottoms.

My dad took a close look at me. I was about 8-years-old, but I was a foot taller than everyone in my classes and at least 50, 60, or even 70 pounds heavier. My daddy scratched his head. He felt like an enabler with all his cooking and decided he needed to take action to make up for his sins.

"Boy, we gotta do something. You're different than the rest. You are just getting too big, too fast," he said. "After school today, we are going to have to get to working on that."

I went to school that day and his words kept replaying in my head. All through class, I wasn't listening to the teacher, but rather thinking about what my daddy said. For some reason, I just didn't see it.

Was I really that different?

I remember looking around the room a little more. I tried to pay more attention to the actual body sizes of the other kids to try and see what my father saw in me. Sitting in class all morning didn't really offer much of a comparison for my personal case study, but after class was to be something else.

The bell rang.

I noticed that when I walked down the hall, all the other students were stepping out of my way, a little out of instinct, even though there was plenty of room. After that observation, I remember intentionally walking towards a line of oncoming people traffic, and nobody stayed in my way. I was the proverbial Moses parting the Red Sea and nobody wanted a part of me.

I remember walking right up to some of the other kids and trying to compare our sizes. There was no comparison. I was in the 4th grade. All of my classmates were about 80 to 90 pounds, but I looked twice their size!

Just as he had promised, when I finally got home from my case study at school my daddy was waiting. We jumped into his station wagon and headed straight toward the Pop Warner football field.

As we pulled into the lot, I looked out on the green. I could smell the cut grass in the air from the cracked open window. I could hear the sound of shoulder pads hitting each other. Kids were wearing helmets and running some drills. It all looked pretty exciting to me.

My dad walked over to the coach, a tiny Italian guy with a whistle around his neck. They shook hands and my dad pat me on the shoulder and said something about the exercise doing me some good.

"How old again did you say your boy was?" The coach shook his head in disbelief. He looked me up and down really slow. "God damn. If you didn't already tell me, I would assume he was ten or eleven." He scowled. "I'm sorry Mr. White, but this monster of a boy you got here will just about kill everyone else his age."

"Does that mean he can't play?" he asked.

The coach paused and looked me up and down again like a piece of meat. "He is going to have to play in the next age bracket up. Maybe even two brackets."

"Well, did you hear that, Leon?" my dad said. "That's good news."

"But he is going to have to lose 20 pounds to do even that," the coach added.

He let me out on the field to get a taste though, before I left.

Those kids beat the snot out of me. I remember my first hit. It felt like somebody had run me over and kept on going. When you are an eight-year-old boy, three or four years of age difference was a heck of a lot on the gridiron.

After that day, I wanted to get better. I cut down on the massive breakfast buffet a bit and kept at the football. I dropped about 20 pounds. After some more hard work running around in the yard and playing with some of the neighbors, I was allowed to play. I eventually got on a level playing field with some kids who were probably about four years older than me.

GETTING TOUGH

My dad was a little rough around the edges. When he left the first time, I was around 8 years old. It made it hard on all of us, but I still wanted to be more like him. There was less money and less authority, for one. There was also less protection in a city that was becoming more and more volatile. It made it pretty hard for Momma, but she managed. I remember when he was still around though, one night, my dad took my mom out to the pub for some drinks.

I was sitting on the couch like I normally did, watching some Star Trek with my sister, Kathy. She was about 13 and I was 11, but I towered over her, of course. Now, I'm not a Star Trek nerd with ears on or anything, but I remember getting into it at the time. There was like this big intergalactic battle royal going on.

We were watching a pretty elaborate fight scene. A bunch of weird Martians and Klingons had tag teamed up I guess to invade the Enterprise. I was excited to see my favorite, Captain Kirk, knowing he was about to have none of that shit.

Spock was dropping bastards with his "Vulcan Nerve Pinch" finisher. Sulu broke out his nun-chucks and popped off Tribbles like Bruce Lee. They were doing pretty well holding off the aliens, but then a bunch of lizard people showed up.

Just as all hope seemed to be lost, Captain Kirk did a run-in on the deck. He didn't use his phasor gun and he didn't have a sawed-off baseball bat. He used what he knew best to beat Martian ass, his Kung-Fu fists.

I was on the edge of my seat and then, all of a sudden, BANG! We heard a loud noise. Something fell and broke in the other room. We were two young kids and scared.

We didn't have a Dolby Surround Sound system. That kind of thing didn't even exist yet. I knew it had to be bad news.

My sister looked over at me, "Did you hear that?"

"Yeah," I nodded. "Stay here, Kathy."

My adrenaline was already pumping from the space rumble on TV. I was ready to fight anyone, anything I could find. I snuck around the corner ready to do some Captain Kirk Kung-Fu chops of my own and then it got real; very real.

Someone was breaking into one of the bedrooms.

My heart dropped. I stopped at the doorway and ducked back out of sight. I looked around for a weapon, but I realized that all the real good stuff was in the kitchen where I couldn't get to because I would have to both pass the invader and leave my sister. I peered around the corner to get a better look at who I was going to have to fight.

"Nobody is going to get into our Enterprise," I thought.

Just beyond the doorframe, I saw it was actually three dudes sneaking in our window! This one guy dressed in dark clothing was reaching outside the window to help in the next guy. And behind him, there was another guy pushing the middle guy in.

It is funny the way you think like a kid. I wanted to be just like Captain Kirk from Star Trek, but I ended up being more like the cowardly Doctor Smith from Lost in Space.

I froze.

Rather than fighting to protect my spaceship and even more importantly my little sister, I turned around and hightailed it back to the living room as fast as I could to offer heroic advice.

"Run!"

She froze. I knew she was probably not preparing to fight, she was scared. Since she was not going to go into beast-mode and fight like Uhura, I grabbed her hand and pulled her out of the living room and to the front door.

When we ran out of the house, I slammed the door behind me. We ran as fast as we could and when I looked back, I saw that the first guy come out our front door and was chasing after us with bad intentions.

Kathy tripped and fell, and I pulled her back to her feet. Then, the two other henchmen came running straight at us from the side of our house.

Fortunately, there was a big, old, fat guy that lived next to us sitting on his porch. He was a bit of a hillbilly, but he wasn't dumb. He immediately saw what was going on.

It was good for us that not only did he love food, but he also loved guns.

"Hey!" he yelled. "What's going on over there?"

He flashed something at the two guys and they scattered. Then, the guy behind us disappeared, too, but we didn't know where he went for sure.

The hillbilly came running over to us, as the real Captain Kirk.

"Did you see where he went?" he asked.

"No sir," I said, sucking back a sob, trying to look more like a man and less like the coward who had just been chased out of his own home.

"Go in the house," he said, motioning to his place. "I'll go take a look." He headed over to our place and started poking his rifle into the bushes. He didn't have to tell us twice. In less than a minute, we were in with Mrs. Hillbilly eating cookies and milk.

By the time the cops came, the invaders were gone. The robbers didn't realize that someone was home and weren't looking for a gunfight. My dad's friend, the neighbor, rushed off. He knew where my parents were and brought back my father.

My dad grabbed my wrist. I could smell the hard medical stench of whiskey on his breath. His nose was red from the alcohol, and his ears were red, too. That meant that he was pissed. He was clearly mad that would-be robbers had robbed him from his drinking time. He walked me into his bedroom.

"Look in there," he said.

My father pushed me into his closet and pulled aside his hanging clothes. Just behind his nice never-worn church suit, there was a shotgun leaning against the wall with a small box of shells on the floor.

"Now Leon, I showed you how to use this, already. Right? You know what to do if this happens again, right?"

I nodded.

"Good," he said.

And then he didn't skip a beat. My dad went to the garage, grabbed a hammer, and selected a few pieces of scrap wood. He boarded up that window in record time. Then, he left us again to go finish his beer at the pub before it got warm.

So Kathy and I went back to the couch ready to watch Star Trek again, but this time with a box of shells on my lap.

"If he comes back, will you shoot him?" She asked me.

"I sure will," I said.

BOWLING

Later on when I was in Junior High, I started hanging out at the bowling lane. I became a pretty good bowler at a young age and really had fun doing so every weekend.

One Saturday morning while waiting for a lane to open, I went over to the billboard where people posted things for sale and odd jobs needed around the community. I saw a posting from the bowling alley, itself.

PART-TIME DISHWASHER NEEDED: 11pm-7am.

I got excited thinking about the possibility. I figured working for the bowling alley would help me get my hands on some much needed money and also give me the opportunity to bowl even more!

I was so big that when I applied for the job, they really couldn't tell how old I was. They just didn't think I was still in Junior High and too young for that kind of shift, so I got the job.

I knew well enough that I wasn't supposed to be working that late, so I didn't tell anyone. My father was in and out of our lives at this point anyhow and he wasn't really a factor. My mom had taken on a second job. They both had no idea.

In fact, nobody knew I was working a job.

Every night, I would say good night to anyone who cared and go back to my room. I would just gimmick things up in my bedroom so it looked like I was sleeping. You know, I would do the classic pillow thing under the sheets to make a sleeping body. Then, I would just sneak out and head over to "All Night Bowling."

I would work hard all night to make some money and maybe bowl a couple of games. At the end of my shift, I remember I would punch out, then lock myself into the bathroom for a few minutes. I would just wash my face and go right to school.

At school the next day, I know I must have smelled like the dishes and food sitting in my math class, or whatever. I knew maybe some of the girls didn't like it, but along with the fast food fragrance at least I had a little money in my pocket.

I did this job on and off for a couple of years. The weeknight shifts were kind of slow and I often got to bowl a lot then, but the weekends were just crazy. I could bowl free and that was great, but the $2 an hour wage wasn't so great, so I had to improvise. I was young with a hell of a lot of energy, and I learned real fast how to make more money by working the crowd. What I would do is play off their empathy.

When the place got really busy, I would run out of the dining hall with the bucket and try to look horribly overworked. I would rush around and try to grab everything as fast as I could like I was super backed up in work. It always worked. The weekend bowlers would feel bad for me and tell their wives to tip me extra. That normal $2 an hour extra in tips easily became $5 to $10 from the right crowd.

One particular night, I was working the night shift and I was soon to be reminded that I was not working in a bowling lane on the set of Happy Days. I was working in Compton, CA.

The last bowlers had left and there wasn't any real work to be done. I heard a voice behind me. It was Gus the old bartender.

"Hey, kid. We are going to close up, early. You can head home."

Now, I looked up at the clock. It was only 4 AM, and I yawned. He was right though, the lanes were all empty and it was pretty much a ghost town. I really didn't like the idea of walking home in the dark this late at night, but I really had no choice. They were going to lock the place up soon, and I wasn't going to be able to go over to school this early because it wouldn't be open.

I started my way home. I was walking pretty steadily down the sidewalk and probably spooking myself out. I started whistling to try and kill the silence, but it didn't really help much.

As I was walking, I heard something in an alleyway and freaked out a little. I started walking faster.

I laughed to myself, "It was probably just a cat."

Then, I heard something behind me. There was a humming sound. It was a beat up sedan pulling up on me slowly.

The car followed me for a few blocks, so I decided to alter my route. The car followed, too. I switched up my route again, and so did the car. This continued for a few more minutes.

I looked back like I was trying to scratch my chin on my shoulder and saw that two men were looking right at me.

Eye contact.

I started moving a little bit faster, without being obvious. The car pulled over and slowed to a stop.

"Finally," I thought.

I heard the doors slam shut in the distance. I turned around a corner and figured it was over. I looked back. "Nobody, see? They must have just made it to their destination," I figured.

Thinking I was stupid to get scared like that, I continued on into a darker-lit section of the block. Then, I turned around one more time, just to make sure and I noticed that two figures were coming around the corner behind me.

The two guys were walking behind me, slowly at first, so I sped up. They sped up. I ducked down an alley. They ducked down the alley right behind me.

At this point it was obvious. They were on my tail. Now, I don't know what they were after, but at 4 AM it couldn't be good at all. I knew they had evil intent.

I took off in a full sprint, running up a small hill in a bit of a residential area. I turned around and they were still right there, closing in on me.

I dodged a trash can. They dodged a trash can. I jumped a fence. They jumped the fence. We were in a full-fledged chase.

This is where my football training helped me. I tried zigzagging throughout the yards. At first, I may have only gained a few yards lead but it seemed to work.

Eventually, I gained quite a bit of ground by using some running techniques from football plays and it worked.

It took some work, but they gave up.

I finally lost them.

It was about 4:30 in the morning or so, and I had to sneak back into my house.

I pulled the blanket up over my head and hid under the covers. I heard my heart pounding under my chest.

As you can tell, Compton just wasn't the easiest place to grow up in.

THE FIRST DATE

I knew that the dishwashing smell on my body had possibly turned off a number of potential early attempts at love. After that scary night walking home from the bowling alley, I made an even worse decision for my love life; I quit my job. Having no income at all would have really hurt my chances with the ladies, so I knew I had to step up my game. With no girl in sight to spend the little bit I had saved on, I decided to make a move.

My first real crush came along while I was still a junior in high school. I had been eyeballing this real cute Cuban girl named Bobby for some time. I had first noticed her in the hallway at school, and she had that clean fresh smell to her. Not that all the other girls smelled dirty or anything, she just had that little something extra. You know when a girl walks by you and you can smell a faint bit of perfume in her hair as she passes by? Anyhow, her smell was better than bacon; it was love at first scent.

Even though I was a big guy in school, I was still kind of shy with the women. Standing out and being different made things difficult. I didn't want to go out on a limb and risk rejection. Then, not only would I be the big kid, but I would be the big loser kid who got rejected. I didn't know how to approach any girl, let alone a girl of the caliber of Bobby.

I remember before I had the courage to ask her out, I had her schedule all figured out. I would rush home every single day as fast as I could. What happened was, each and every day, Bobby would pass my house on her way home from school. If I could get ahead of her and to my house early enough, I could get to the side window and watch her walk the whole length of the sidewalk towards our house. As she was passing our house, I would then shift to the front window so I could watch her pass directly in front of it, then rush to the opposite side to watch her walk away.

After a few weeks of doing this, my older half-brother on my mom's side, Jimmy, decided to try and figure out what was up.

"Who is she?" he said, watching me peering through the venetian blinds.

"Huh?" I replied, trying to pretend I was normal and not some kind of stalker. "Who?"

"The girl."

"What girl?" I asked trying to play dumb.

He knew I was playing dumb. He saw me more than once run into the house as fast as I could, rushing straight to the window blinds. I had to! When she walked by my house, I needed to see that jiggle. She had all the right curves in all the right places if you know what I mean. She was gorgeous.

"Come on!" he said. "You can't bullshit a bullshitter!"

"Okay, okay," I admitted.

"Look," he said. "You want to try and make a go after her? I'll loan you my car, then you can bring her over by the park and go parking!" he laughed.

Eventually, after some coaching from my brother, I got the nerve up to ask her out. My brother made good on his car offer and told me to bring her out someplace to eat, first.

Not having all that much left from the bowling savings, I decided to bring her somewhere cheap but romantic, I brought her to the "Queen Mary Church Ham Dinner."

I showed up to pick Bobby up in my brother's sweet ride. It was an old-school station wagon that looked like something out of the Chevy Chase *Vacation* movies. I was wearing one of my dad's jackets and ties and had just enough money in my pocket for two plates of scrumptious ham.

We had an awkward dinner. We barely talked. I commented on how good the mashed potatoes were. She agreed. I asked her if she wanted more green beans and then served her some like a true romantic. That was all pretty good discourse, I figured, and I was hoping she was finding me attractive in my daddy's clothing.

My brother's words kept coming into my head. "If you want to make out with her, you are going to have to talk to her! A girl isn't going to give you anything if you just sit there like a clam."

I tried to think about more to say, but nothing. All I could think about was wanting to leave so I could try to get that "first kiss" opportunity.

I pictured Jimmy watching our lack of conversation and imagined him saying, "Come on, Leon! Romance! Tell her she is pretty, or has nice eyes or something. Anything!"

I know. My game was pretty lame. I mustered up the courage to ask, "Would you care for another dinner roll?"

"No thanks," Bobby said. She shook her head.

"You want to go to the park then?" I asked randomly.

"Okay," she said.

Things must have gone well enough without much talking, however, because the park was Compton's version of Happy Days' "Inspiration Point" and she agreed.

Though I would have liked to stick around for a piece of chocolate cake, a piece of ass sounded even better. A little kissing after dinner was the perfect dessert. At that age, who would have thought that there was something better than cake?

So there I was, making out like the Fonz in my brother's car. For the first time, I felt really cool, really manly, like Arthur Fonzerelli. I was behind the wheel. I was wearing a tie. I was high rolling and big pimping.

We are going at it, hugging and kissing, and I was licking her whole face pretty much when all of a sudden…

THUMP! THUMP! THUMP!

A dastardly homeless man was in front of the car, slamming his hands on the hood and cock-blocking me.

I sat up and looked at him dead in the face. His eyes looked like fire, but glassed over like a zombie. The guy was insane. He looked like a skinny Charlie Manson with rabies. He was kind of hippy-like, too, like a cross between Cactus and Dude Love with a long straggly beard and a large gold ring in his ear.

Bobby tried to turn around to see what the sound was, but I pushed her down under towards my lap out of view. "Okay," she said.

"Stay down," I said quietly. I didn't know if the crazy guy had seen her or not, but I didn't want him to see her.

I continued to keep eye contact with Zombie Manson. One thing growing up Compton-style taught me was to never look away. The moment you do that and you're dead.

I reached slowly behind the seat and then opened the door, all the while, keeping my eyes on the prize.

"Where are you going?" she whispered.

"I'll be right back," I said. I got out of the car with a sawed-off baseball bat.

By the time I made it to the front of the car, the homeless cock-blocker disappeared.

I guessed he had finally run off. I let down my guard for a second. I walked around the hood and figured I must have scared him off. Then, out of nowhere, he pounced on me like a cat out of the bushes.

After knocking me down, we rolled in the dirt and threw punches. I was dazed. As I came to my senses, I looked up and Manson was making a mad dash for the passenger side's door. He was trying to get to Bobby.

I thought I was tough, but this was the real deal. Back then, we had forced integration of school buses. We had early stages of the Bloods and Crips traveling on the same ride every morning on the way to school. If a fight broke out, I always had back up. I always had my tag team partners to fall back on. However, on this particular night, there was nobody to tag in.

The Fonz was laying down on his back at Inspiration Point and there was no girl on top. In fact, some uncool jive turkey was about to steal his girl and his ride.

Adrenaline rush.

I knew I had to man up. I jumped to my feet and yanked him out of the driver's seat before he could close the door. Before he knew what hit him, I buckled up my fist and "Biffed" him in the face like George McFly fighting for his girl's honor.

The bearded warrior went down hard. I watched as he hit the ground and decided I wasn't going to let him get up again.

I picked up my bat and beat the dog shit out of him.

I hit him in the face. I hit him in the ribs. Then, I held the bat high over my head like Conan the Barbarian and swung that motherfucker straight down into his ballsack.

He curled up into a ball and then fell limp.

When he stopped moving, I jumped in the car and took off. To be totally honest, I don't even know if he was alive or not when I left. But after that, I found some courage.

PARTS DISTRIBUTER

Bobby and I dated my last two years in high school. We got along great but we never talked about that again. The one or two times we got close to mentioning it, we went back into awkward ham dinner mode.

Bobby was great, but as most of you know, girlfriends cost money. I didn't have a job anymore, so I started hanging around with a bad bunch to make ends meet.

By this point, my dad was totally gone and my mom was working crazy hours to make ends meet. We were having a hard time paying the bills and I took to drastic means to help feed us.

Our gang of misfits was pretty much held together by a common thread; football. These were the same guys who always had my back, so it only made good sense to make them my business partners.

None of us had a pot to piss in, so we decided to start going into business for ourselves. We started stealing things. First off, we would go in mom-and-pop stores and distract the cashier while one of us would rob the place blind. Eventually, we graduated to stealing bigger ticket items, like motorcycles.

Motorcycles were great money because we could easily drive up to a target and wait until the coast was clear. Then, we would just drive up next to it, throw it into my buddy Petey's van and bring them over another buddy's house to break down for parts.

One of the smooth-talking guys in our posse set up business arrangements with a number of different bike shops and a few salvage yards who would pay top dollar for our parts. He told them all we had "overseas connections" to get pieces cheap as distributors. I'm sure they knew it was bullshit, but they were happy to do business with us, nonetheless.

It would have been nice to just sell these places the whole bike for even more money, but we were smart. We all agreed that if we got greedy and tried to do that, we would eventually end up getting caught.

As smart as we were, however, I was a horrible thief. The few times I tried to provide the parts myself for the business, I would practically shit my pants. Eventually, I gave up trying and left that part of the job to the professionals in our distribution company. I just felt too guilty. Although I could never really do any of the stealing part myself, I was able to make it okay in my head to act as a lookout or a parts salesman. I also rationalized that my actions could help feed myself and my family.

We would always sell everything except the one piece that would get us into trouble; *the frame.* The frame had serial numbers and serial numbers had a paper trail. We always threw the frame away with the serial numbers so that nobody could ever trace anything back to us. Then, we would go dumping in the middle of the night.

At the end of a busy week at the "distribution center," we would often take like five or six of the naked frames and throw them into the back of Petey's van. Since I didn't do a whole lot of the heavy lifting when it came to the acquiring part of our parts company, I was often placed on garbage duty. That meant I had to find a place to dispose of the stuff that could get us into trouble.

At first, I was lazy. I would drive the van out into a residential area and then throw the frames off a bridge into the water. But then I started having nightmares that someone was going to find those frames and then come and find us.

I eventually decided to drive the frames out as far away as possible to try to eliminate anyone from figuring out where they came from if found. The whole ride, I would always think I was going to get pulled over and then arrested for smuggling contraband. I would drive as far out of town as my nerves could handle and then throw the frames in an unsuspecting McDonald's dumpster.

After the dump, I remember often reaching in the dumpster frantically to try and bury the evidence in McGarbage so that my dump would go unnoticed.

I'm embarrassed I had anything to do with this, but it did help us feed ourselves and our families. I remember filling my fridge with groceries for a whole month from my share of one Harley we came across once, alone.

After Petey's van broke down, we had to get creative. Yamahas became an easy target because one of those boys figured out how to unplug the starter cable and just stick a piece of foil in it to make it start. Then, one of us would get on and fly out of there for dear life. For a time, we would bag up to three Yamahas a week. Then, one of the guys got caught. That really slowed down the business.

After the parts company fizzled, we had even less to concentrate on and keep us busy and we started to get into more fights. One of my boy's brothers got shot in a fight, so I started to think carefully before just swinging a fist after that. My general rule of thumb was usually if I could run, I would try to run first before fighting. You never knew what you were going to get. But the run rule didn't always happen.

My saving grace was getting into the gym and staying in the gym for the sake of football. After working out with some guys much older than me, I got into some real training and learned how to really work out. It paid off in record time. My football game got much better, and people started to notice. By the end of my senior year, almost 40 different schools tried recruiting me!

White
otball, ELAC,

Leon White
Var Football; All City
Letterman Colorado;
Univ. Business

Sam Whitta
CSF, UCLA

GUEST PASSAGE – DAVE LOGAN

He was a complex man. Big Smile plastered on a bigger body. Fierce, yet sensitive. Combative but compassionate, and if he considered you a friend, brother you were a friend for life. Even in college, Leon White was already bigger than life. His personality matched his physical presence.

We first met in the summer of 1973. We both were highly recruited athletes that picked the University of Colorado to attend school and play football. The team had gathered in Boulder in August to prepare for the upcoming season. There were lots of alpha dogs and youthful testosterone in the room that day.

Leon approached a small group of guys I was standing with. He shook hands with all of us, me last. As Leon introduced himself to us one by one, I was struck be his enormity and his shock of red hair. He patiently worked his way down the line and finally extended his massive right hand to me. I had huge hands, his were every bit as big.

"I'm Leon White from Compton, you can just call me Baby Bull". He quickly moved onto the other soon-to-be teammates.

"Did he just say Baby Bull?" one of my teammates asked?

"Yup" I responded. "That's what he said."

Over the next three years, my roommate, Don Hasselback, (NFL QB, Matt Hasselback's dad) and I became fast friends with "Bull." Sometimes I'd take both to my parent's house for the weekend in Denver. Bull would always hug my mom like he'd known her since birth. Weekend fun and really good home cooking aren't a bad thing when your 19 and 20 years old. On the field, Bull was as talented as any big man I ever played with. He was 6'2, 275 pounds, powerful and explosive with almost super human strength. I saw him do a backflip from a standing position many times. He was freakishly athletic.

I'm convinced that if not for a devastating knee injury, Bull was headed for a 10-year NFL career. He was that good. But the NFL's loss was Professional Wrestling's gain.

Before he was "Vader", world-wide celebrity and star, he was just Leon, "The Baby Bull."

CHAPTER 2 – FOOTBALL CAREER

Born and raised in Lynwood, California in 1956, I was thrown into Pop Warner football early on. Football was in my blood. Right away, I enjoyed the athleticism of it all. I also found that the performing aspect, the playing in front of a crowd, was something that really motivated me. Hearing the audience cheer for you, trying to push you further to do the "impossible" was really something. It is hard to describe, but the power gained from all that energy can really help make something happen. At an early age, I learned to love being an athlete in a competitive full-contact sport and also learned to love feeding off a large audience.

A little later, I captained my high school football team in 1972-73, playing both offensive and defensive lineman. There, I earned city, state and national honors.

I was 270 pounds in Bell High School and had a great number of players on my team. My high school football coach, Owen Hahn, knew that a law eliminating the forced bussing segregation was coming. He enlisted an assistant coach who was a former defensive tackle for the LA Rams.

Harold Daniels, a black coach, was just the street credit we needed. Harold was 6'8, 360 pounds. He drove our little, pretty, beach boy coach, Owen Hahn, to the hood for scouting. Together, they went to some of the rougher areas and hand-picked a whole bunch of diverse, great athletes. This was great because it meant that I got to work with some of the best ballplayers in the area.

There are a lot of good football states, but I have to say, I was lucky to be in California when I was. Just in sheer numbers, LA had over 600 high schools to pick the very best from to build their teams. Typically, the All-American team was the one everyone wanted to play for. However, regionally, the "All LA team" was even tougher to make because of the huge pool of players they could select from. We played some really good football because of it. If you were on the All-Los Angeles team, that represented the best high school football players in America, bar none. I often got into passionate arguments with people from Texas because they'd just get upset. We had more people to pick from in LA so we got better football players, overall.

So at Bell High, I was an All-American. Even at this young age, I began to learn that there were politics in sports that needed to be dealt with. In high school, being All-American was cool, but there were guys on the All-American team from say South Dakota who didn't belong. You would look at some of the players and say,

"Wait a minute. That guy couldn't even start on my high school team. How the hell did he make the team?"

The All-American is a boat-load of politics. Because it's spread out all over the country, the team that I was most proud of making was actually the "All-Los Angeles" team.

I HAD FOOTBALL

Life continued to get tough for my family. By this point, my dad was long gone. Our family of four was living in a beat-up, two-bedroom apartment with some bad plumbing and thin walls. My mom was working two, sometimes three jobs trying to make ends meet. By the end of the day, she was often too tired to interact with us, let alone try and hold us together.

With my father gone, I had nobody to learn from. I started picking up some real bad habits on the street as a "ghetto kid" and I knew it. I was rolling with a bad bunch. We stole things, we beat up people, we partied a lot and we generally didn't care much about anyone but ourselves.

Most of my friends found too much time on their hands and no real skills to get by. Without jobs to earn some kind of income, most of the people I knew started dabbling in drugs and then transitioned that into becoming full-fledged drug dealers themselves. It was too easy.

I knew and associated daily with tough gang members, the Black Panthers, and a pretty bad-ass Mexican gang. Luckily for me, by the time I got to this point in my life, I did have something that stood me out from the rest.

I had football.

When I had my chance to make the jump from high school to a number of different colleges that were looking at me, I decided the best thing for me was to get as far away from the Compton area as possible.

I looked at football as being my way out of a lifestyle that was clearly the beginning of what could have been a downward spiral for me. Football was a good outlet for me, and to put it mildly, football probably saved my life.

All my early friends from this period that I spoke about are dead now.

COLORADO BUFFALOES

I was in high demand. I was recruited to a lot of big time schools. I got scholarship offers from Notre Dame, Oklahoma, South Carolina, you name it. I eventually choose Boulder,

Colorado, mostly because it didn't at all look like Compton. I fell in love with those mountains and wouldn't trade them in for the concrete and LA streets any day.

One of the things that helped me select Boulder was their style. Boulder pulled out all the shots and was playing my game from day one. I was at a recruiting party. We were all hanging out and getting to know each other to see if it was a good fit. We had a nice little barbecue going on at one of the player's houses. Music was playing. We were all having a good time, and I went over to grab some more beer.

Pretty girls were running around and they had a keg of beer. One girl was there trying to pump out some brew, but finding some difficulty. Earlier, I had already put the moves on this cute blonde girl and this was a perfect opportunity to play the hero.

"Hey babe," I said. "Let me get that for you."

"Oh, thanks," she said, handing me the cup.

As I went to retrieve her some more of that frothy adult beverage, I saw something familiar reflecting off a window onto the keg. I turned, knowing exactly full-well what the blinking lights were coming from.

"Uh oh, the cops!" I yelled to the crowd. I didn't stick around. It was every man for himself.

I dropped my cup where I stood. The beer splashed up on my legs, but I paid it no mind. I made a mad dash for the woods. In three seconds, I was over that fence and I was gone.

I ran through the brush and found myself waist high in a pricker-bush. The thorns were short but hurt like a son of a bitch. They tore at my sides and also at my legs. A few branches flew up towards my face, but I pushed them down. Once I felt I was far enough away from the danger, I stopped.

I waited about five minutes until the coast was clear. I didn't really hear any commotion, however. Rather than hearing sirens, I heard something else.

"Leon?!" one of the recruiters yelled. "LEON!"

I snuck back up to the fence I had just hurdled over and peeked cautiously through a hole.

A few of the guys were standing there looking confused.

"Where'd Leon go? What's going on?" they said.

One of the other recruiters could see me and pointed my way. "Look!" he said, gesticulating at me through the panes. Then, he slowly pointed over to one of the other players.

Two police officers were also standing there with their arms folded, trying to look as mean as possible. Then, the senior offensive lineman who was throwing the recruiting party moved towards the cops. He threw his arm around one of them and they all laughed.

"You can come out, Leon."

I'm not going to say the police stopped by just to drink beer with us, but it certainly looked that way. Let's just say they just wanted to "check and make sure everything was okay."

Wow. This is pretty good.

I hopped back over the fence with beer on my leg and thorns in my ass. One of the officers even poured me a fresh cold one as a replacement.

I knew this was the place for me because it was entirely different from what I grew up around in Los Angeles.

I was an offensive and defensive tackle in high school, but I loved playing defense. However, I knew my future was playing o-line. I started at three different offensive line positions at the University of Colorado. I was extremely proud to start on CU's 1975 offensive line, which was considered to be one of the best in Colorado's history, even to this day. I was called one of the best in college football history, and consensus All-American and All-Big Eight at guard and center from 1976-77. I was also a pre-season All-American at tackle before my first knee injury. But I didn't let that setback hold me back. I was made co-captain later that year and was also voted the outstanding lineman of the 1977 Hula Bowl, East-West Shrine Game and Japan Bowl.

THE FOOTBALL DRILL

One of my best friends in college was a guy named Tom Perry. He was a big, skinny, lanky guy with a black father and a white German mother. He was also on the Colorado Buffaloes football team but looked more like a basketball player at about 6'4 and 255 pounds. We met in college training back in 1976 and we really hit it off. We sparred in a lot in drills together, with him as a defensive linebacker and me on the offensive line. We did a lot of gym time together, as well.

After a year or so of really pumping the iron, he finally started to put on some muscle – about 25 pounds worth or so. With me busting his ass as his gym buddy, in no time, he was benching almost twice the amount he could when I first met him.

So one day, we were playing one of our rivals, a real good team in Lincoln, Nebraska called the Cornhuskers. The other team was turning it up hard, when all of a sudden, Tom charged the other line. He and another player collided head on. It was very loud and a pretty brutal collision, and I knew it wasn't going to end well. The two of them hit so hard that Tom's facemask flew clear off his head.

The other team called timeout. Their player was laid out cold and stretchered off the field. Despite the fact that we totally needed him, our coaches made the call to take Tom out of the game, too.

Tom staggered off the field and over to the benches. He vomited a long rope of clear liquid behind the bench and looked for some water. After that, Tom dropped hard next to me.

"You ok, buddy?" I asked.

He said, "Yes," but his eyes were telling a different story.

I leaned in. His eyes were bloodshot and not dilating properly with that deer-in-headlights look on his face. He was one of the best players we had, and I know he wanted to get back in there, but shouldn't. He was all messed up and he knew it.

"Tom, I know what the coaches are going to say. Don't do it," I said.

Tom shrugged. He was clearly off his game and dizzy. He wasn't right, but I knew they were going to throw him right back in there, even though he wasn't ready.

The training coach came up to us and was sort of half-checking Tom's vitals. He was standing in front of us with a concerned look on his face. The crowd was cheering and coach shook his head to someone else looking on, just outside of my view.

I didn't need to look behind me. The other coach was behind us and I heard him clear as day say "I don't care. Get him back in the game."

Tom looked at me and nodded. He pushed his helmet back on and headed out.

We were down a few points and Tom did it. His defense set us up for a major play that got us back on the board.

He helped put us over the top, but at what price? He played for a full hour with bloodshot eyes that turned crimson by the final play.

We jogged off the field the winners that day.

Back in the locker room, I was in the shower getting cleaned up and saw Tom was stumbling over his own feet. I didn't think much of it, but then Tom got dressed on the bench next to me and kept leaning over on my shoulder. He couldn't support his own weight.

A few minutes later, Tom went to get his sneakers out of the locker and he fell to the floor. His body started convulsing. I thought he was dying. He turned white right in front of me.

The coaches came swarming over.

"What the hell?!" one yelled. There was a hard gasping sound, followed by choking and gagging. Tom swallowed his tongue right there on the locker room floor in front of us.

I cradled his head, "Come on guys! He needs air," I said in a panic.

I remember looking at him, trying to get him to make eye contact, but that wasn't happening. Tom was in his own world, shaking and gasping to breathe. All I could see was a red crust around the rims of his eyes.

"Tom look at me!" The only thing I could think was, *Tom is dying! Tom is dying!* ...and I wasn't too far from the truth.

The coaches surrounded us and took over. Everyone was in hysteria and they pushed me out of the way, while Tom's body continued to flail like a fish out of water. Finally, the team doctor showed up. He pushed his way through the jerseys and parted the sea of onlookers.

"Tom. Tommy," he said, attempting to check for vitals. He stuck his fingers in his mouth and tried to fishhook his tongue away from his throat. Tom gagged. It wasn't working.

Then, the doctor used a finger to pry open one of Tom's eyelids. His eyes weren't bloodshot. They were straight up blood red and glassy.

"What's wrong?" one of the coaches asked.

"We have to drain the bleeding in his head immediately," he said. "There is heavy internal bleeding and blood is essentially drowning his brain."

The head coach and the doctor disappeared to the office.

Tom continued to twitch. We all watched not knowing what to do, in shock, for what seemed like an eternity. When the doctor finally returned, Tom was looking really bad.

"Drag him over by the wall socket," he said calmly.

Nobody moved.

"Now!" he demanded.

One of the practice coaches grabbed him and pulled him violently toward the cinderblock wall.

It was then the doctor revealed why. He had returned with a Black & Decker drill that he was hiding behind his back. The cord was too short, and they struggled once again to move the twitching body closer to the electric.

Let me back this up again. Think about that. *The doctor was holding a power tool.*

It was then that I realized, he was looking for a place on his head to drill a hole.

Nobody said anything. The silence was deafening, all you could hear was the saliva in Tom's swollen mouth failing to swallow and a few other players gasping as well. They were leveled at the sight of a crude, filthy drill targeted at their teammate's head by the hands of a trained physician. I mean, he was a doctor after all, and must have known what he was doing, right?

It was a good thing for Tom that the Colorado Buffaloes hired MacGyver to be the team doctor. This Doctor Frankenstein moment gave us a new meaning for the term "football drill."

Without a second to spare, he plugged it in and was pulling the trigger. He immediately spun a small hole in Tom's head to drain it out. Then, he parted his hair to both sides to see if he could see the excess blood.

The thought was sickening. To hear the "grinding of bone" sound was worse than any visit to a dentist. It made my stomach drop and left me light headed. I remember blocking my ears and closing my eyes like a little kid who didn't want to eat his vegetables. I was nauseous at the thought. I wanted to puke.

The hum passing my ears is a doctor drilling a hole directly into Tom's head with a screw-bit!

The whole time this was going on, I couldn't help but think that the coach who forced Tom to continue playing while injured was just a selfish asshole. I really wanted to go over and drill him once in his head with a right hook.

Luckily for us, this particular team doctor was a smart guy and actually knew what to do.

Tom, needed that doctor like he needed a hole in his head.

Just like when you bump your knee and it swells, Tom bumped his brain. The brain swelling, also called an edema, was his body's response to a head trauma injury, as a result of continuing to play after the hard, head-on collision.

Usually, with say a knee injury, the swelling happens quickly but is simple to treat with some combination of rest, ice, elevation, medication, or removal of excess fluid.

However, your brain is an altogether different beast.

Brain swelling is far more difficult to treat and can quickly cause serious problems - *including death*. Your brain is critical for overall body function, but the thick protective skull that protects this vital organ leaves practically no room for the brain to swell.

The swelling of Tom's brain had increased pressure inside his skull and made everything stop working correctly. This "intracranial pressure," was a tightening that preventing blood from flowing inside Tom's brain and out. It was depriving the oxygen Tom needed to do very normal, fundamental, vital things like swallow and breath.

If this had gone on much longer, Tom would have died.

After the drilling stopped, almost immediately, right before our very eyes, the convulsions stopped. Blood trickled down the side of Tom's head and down his neck, but he stopped flopping around.

It was obvious, *the draining worked.* Tom opened his eyes and wiped his mouth with his wrist. He tried to talk but choked on his dry mouth. He started coughing, again, but it was clear things were better.

The doctor and the head coach threw him in the van and headed out to a hospital in Omaha. Because I couldn't jump in the van with them, I hitched a ride with one of the other players. We followed behind the makeshift ambulance driving almost 100 mph the whole way.

I remember the trip well. We didn't speak for almost a half hour. When I wasn't saying prayers for Tom under my breath, I was thinking about what I was going to do with the coach who made Tom go back into the game out of the selfishness of wanting to win.

Fortunately, I didn't need to seek vengeance on Tom's behalf. When we made it to the hospital, Tom had stabilized and was doing well.

Tom never played football again.

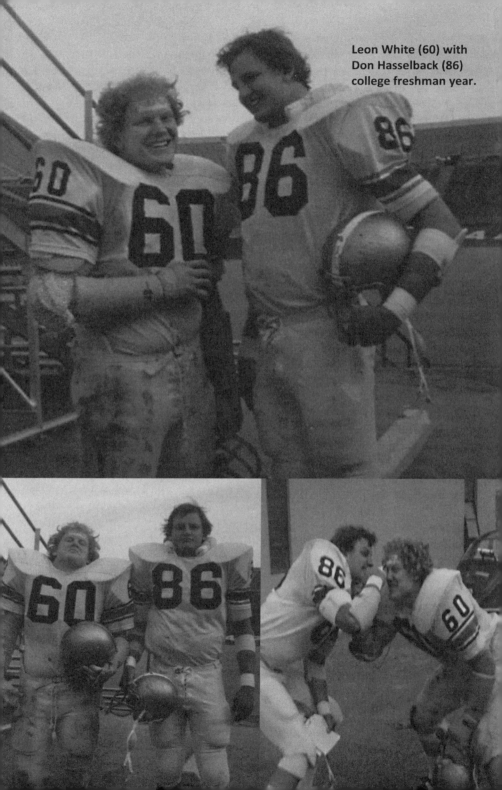

Leon White (60) with Don Hasselback (86) college freshman year.

ALL-AMERICAN IS A PRICE TOO HIGH

While the football doctor did help Tom on that one particular grim, cringe-worthy day, team doctors weren't always engaging in the most sound-of-mind practices for the long haul. His short-term-minded decisions often caused the key players some problems down the road for a quick fix in "the now."

What the doctor did with one of my injuries cost me my NFL career before I even stepped foot on their field.

After working out one day on the field, I had a burning sensation in my right knee and upper leg. It was stiffening up on me fast and it almost felt like it was cracking each time I took a step. I knew something was up, so I went in to see the team doctor. After some tests, he determined correctly that I had injured my patellar tendon.

The patellar tendon is a ligament that connects two different bones together, the bottom of the kneecap (patella) to the top of the shinbone (tibia). Being that it is attached to the quadriceps muscles in the front of your thigh, they all work together to straighten the knee and straighten your leg.

Although anyone can injure the patellar tendon, it seems to happen more to those who play running or jumping sports. My injury was pretty small. We caught it early, before it was a complete tear which would have been a completely disabling injury.

Later on, I learned that all they needed to do was sew up the small hole (called a rent) that I had developed and just take some time off to let it heal. However, whether it was a decision of the coaches again to keep me playing, or a bad decision by the doctor, I do not know. Some kind of politics was going on behind the scenes where they wanted me to not get the operation. They wanted me to play the season out.

What was maybe for the good of the team was not for the good of my long-term best interest. Rather than to have the smaller operation that could have sat me out for the rest of the season, the doctor decided to inject me with Cortisone.

So he began the treatments of injections directly into the tendon, just six weeks before the NFL draft, which was something I was being considered for and the coaches knew it. They wanted me to do well in the final games for our team. Maybe they had good intentions, or maybe they were just being shortsighted and wanted their team to do well. Again, I do not know.

Cortisone may have been okay if it were being shot into the area around the injury for absorption, however, injecting it directly into the tendon itself is something you are not supposed to do. I didn't know any better and was being misadvised. The injections before each game further weakened the tendon even more and the rent (tear) got bigger and bigger as I played hard on a bad wheel. Eventually, the injections caused the tendon to rupture.

This injury was life-altering for me. If I had just had the operation, I would not have had the injury.

When it ruptured on the field, I knew it, right away. It felt like it exploded inside my leg and I could no longer bend it. They stretchered me off the field that day and I went right to the hospital.

I remember staring up at the ceiling as they pushed me down that sterile hallway.

My football days are over.

When I finally saw the hospital doctor he asked me what kind of medications I was on. I told him what we had been doing for the rent and he just shook his head.

"Cortisone being injected into the tendon itself is very, very bad," he said. "He should have never been doing that to you."

I felt like I was betrayed. Just like Tom, I felt like they drove me as hard as they could to get as much mileage out of me as possible for the team. Then, after the season, I figured they were just going to trade me out for a newer, younger-model race car.

I was told I would not be able to do much of anything after the rupture. There was some worry that I may not even be able to walk. I was an All-American, yeah, but at what cost? The team chewed me up and spat me out before I could even make it to the big leagues.

The courts agreed. I actually sued the team doctor and won.

THE NFL

I got injured, but I didn't let that hold me back. Having been a high school All-American and a two-time college All-American, and having played in so many high-profile games, I was able to do what many great college players only dream of.

I put on an NFL helmet.

In 1978, I despite my setbacks, I was drafted by the Los Angeles Rams as their first pick in the third round.

The Rams saw something in me from my college football achievements. It really meant something in that they were still bringing me in, knowing I was injured. I was still rehabbing a ruptured patella tendon, an injury that most coaches would have considered a career ending. However, because of my outstanding college record, the Rams decided my potential was worth the investment.

Being on the injured player list, I had time to recoup around some of the best in the business. There was this one really great player there at the time, Rich Saw. He was a center and had that position locked up. I wanted to be like him, and his influence pushed me to become even better than I was before.

In my NFL days, I started eating better and got in great shape. For me, 290 pounds was light and I was becoming even faster than I'd been in my high school days. I had good legs and good strength and was putting up about 535 pounds on the bench.

Feeling better towards the tail end of my first year, the Rams made the playoffs. It was just kind of ironic and even a blessing for me that an opening came about. The starting center guard became injured. I was given the green light and they activated me. I came off of the injured-reserve list at the best possible time, *to play in the playoffs!*

Our team then did what most players only dream of, we made it to the Super Bowl. I actually got field time and was able to play against the Pittsburgh Steelers.

So on January 20, 1980, at the Rose Bowl in Pasadena, California, we made history. We broke a Super Bowl attendance record of 103,985, and it was also the first time that the Super Bowl was happening in the home market of one of the participants.

Super Bowl XIV was a close game for the first three quarters. We led 13–10 at halftime. I got my Super Bowl time on the field. Nothing fancy, but I'll tell you what, feeding off that crowd? There was nothing like it in the world.

Steelers quarterback Terry Bradshaw was on fire. He was a machine. He connected with Lynn Swann on a 47-yard touchdown pass and changed the momentum. The Steelers ended up defeating the Rams 31 to 19, becoming the first team to win four Super Bowls in six years.

We didn't win, but that didn't matter to me. *I played in the freaking Super Bowl.* I got a Super Bowl ring, and I was already a winner the moment I stepped out onto the field.

I played some more for the Rams and got to play against the NFL Hall of famer Randy White. I had a really great game against him. I shut him out for three quarters with absolutely no tackles and no sacks.

I didn't have a very long NFL career, however. I was forced to retire after only a couple of seasons due to a re-rupturing that damn patella.

In a very unimportant game, I planted my leg to the right and let my guard down for just a second, and that is all it took. I saw a flash in my peripheral vision as a player on the opposite team forced his helmet up under my jaw.

I saw stars and went down.

"Whoa," I looked around when I came to.

Everything was watery. I literally didn't know where I was and I didn't know what hit me. Coming back to reality, I swallowed hard to try and clear my cottonmouth. I lifted my head and tried to sit up. I couldn't see my leg.

"Where did that go? Where is my leg?" I thought in a moment of panic.

It was still there, however, just not where it usually was. My leg had buckled up under me in a sickening 90-degree-angle. It was turned over to one side underneath me.

Now, I had pictured myself making a 15-year-career out of playing football and maybe starting a family and then becoming a football coach someday after that. I really didn't expect my sports career to be cut so short early on after finally making it into the NFL. After re-injuring my patellar tendon, I found myself back in the same familiar hospital.

They told me it was possible that I would never walk again.

The crippling injury threat was back. I knew my days on the field were officially gone. My biggest hope was that I would at least walk again someday on my own, without any help from a wheelchair or cane.

The doctor told me there was some hope, still, but they were going to have to actually replace a large portion of the tendon.

I was lying in the hospital bed and heard someone coming into the room. I was excited at first thinking it was my sister. It was lonely in there, being able to go pretty much nowhere and see pretty much no one for six days. However, when the team's general manager came around the corner, my heart dropped to the floor.

I knew the team manager wasn't there to just give me some balloons and a box of chocolates.

"I'm sorry, Leon," he said. "I think it is in our best interest to go in a different direction."

I looked at him, then looked away. It was officially over.

"I know it's not what you want to hear right now, but we want you to know that we were thinking about you," he said.

It was clear he had done this before. At the same time, he was giving me his well-wishes, he was giving me my release and had really come to give me a settlement on my contract, so I was no longer an expense.

More obstacles.

I had almost a dozen surgeries on my right leg after the day the NFL decided to trade me away for a better race car. With so many operations, I had to work really hard to get back into walking shape let alone ready for the next chapter of my life.

So, how does one make it from wheeling around in a wheel chair to arguably becoming what some consider one of the greatest super heavyweight wrestlers in history?

The answer is, "overcoming obstacles."

OVERCOMING OBSTACLES

Fortunately for me, unlike many narrow-minded athletes, I had invested in a good backup plan that many others couldn't have been bothered with.

I made good and sure that I was set to graduate with a bachelor's degree in Business Administration (and a minor in Sociology) before playing for the Los Angeles Rams.

During my time at the University of Colorado, I worked hard on the field and I worked hard off the field *in the classroom.* My business degree from Colorado helped when things didn't pan out for me in the NFL. I did well enough in school that I was able to make an easy transition, but I didn't know exactly what I was going to get into, I just knew I had to start the next chapter of my life.

I can't recommend this formula enough to anyone who is wanting to be a professional athlete:

You absolutely have to have a strong backup plan, because "living the dream" doesn't last forever. "Living the dream" usually lasts far less than the actual backup plan will.

I was at a major crossroads in my life. My NFL career was over and maybe I was starting to show some stages of depression. Now, once a person leaves the NFL, you pretty much leave all of your NFL friends behind. This includes your drinking buddies. I am not sure if it is because they look at you as being a failure or someone with less money, or whatever, but my drinking partners from the Rams really didn't have time for me anymore. This was probably a good thing for me in hindsight.

My old high school buddies were still living in South Central LA which, by this point, had gotten even worse. I called them a few times with the intention probably of drinking, but we only really talked on the phone. I realized with all of them, nothing had changed. They were still up to their destructive ways and I could see it. I made a conscious decision not to fall into my old ways, again. I didn't want to get back into that environment anymore.

I was growing up.

Boulder and LA were opposites, and I realized that LA was no longer the right place for me. At a crossroads in my life, I was the type of individual who could have gone either way at that point. I knew that it would force me to seek happiness elsewhere in my life, and I was worried about falling back into old habits. Boulder, therefore, would be a much safer place for me to live.

I knew I needed to move back to Boulder, however. I needed to sell the duplex that I had purchased. What I forgot to mention earlier was that with my signing bonus I became the proud owner of a beautiful four-plex where I was living in a ground-level. It was a perfect three bedroom apartment that also had three other sections I could rent out in the back. At the time, it only cost $150,000 and the income property paid for the mortgage and the taxes easily. I was living there for free.

After a short period of time, I eventually sold the duplex. This was the exact moment I realized I could make some good money in real estate. With the money, I made from selling the duplex I was headed back to beautiful Boulder, CO. This is where I would start the new chapter of my life.

My life was changing. There, I eventually met my wife and mother of my child, Debra White. I bought a few cheap suits and ties and started to put my college degree to use. I took the real estate exam and passed it in six weeks. Selling houses was a new opportunity for me, and I took it very seriously.

The real estate business showed good potential. It was competitive and good money if you were good at it, but it was much slower than being a professional athlete longing for field time. It didn't take me long to get bored. Dealing day in and day out with cranky women who wanted a certain color carpet and tiles just wasn't my cup of tea. Dealing with those snotty bitches made me want to put something in my glass that was a little bit stronger than Lipton.

I did a lot of quick work in realty that first year or so. I sold 15 houses. I built a car wash called "The White Wash" in Longmont, CO. I built a few town homes. It sounds like things were going well for me after such a career-ending injury and maybe it was, but for some reason I was miserable.

I was making great money for a single guy, but I was getting out of shape and I felt like there was still a lot left in my body. I was kicking myself for not trying to tap into that athletic potential. It really bothered me.

I started picturing myself just getting old, and being a crotchety old shirt and tie, at that. I hated that vision.

I continued on the next year. I had money saved up from a large bonus and money I saved with the Rams. I speculated on some more homes. I invested in some good raw property, developed it and built some more homes on it. I was playing real-life monopoly.

I drive around some of those homes I built today and they're all still standing. Actually, I often pass one of them in particular; my old home, the one I built where my son was eventually born. I sometimes go out of my way to drive by it and remember the good old days. That house has really blossomed and I wonder what would have happened if I had stayed there and lived in that life. I wish I still owned that house, but I am not sure it is only because of the way the house looks, or rather the more simple life I could have had.

I often wonder, if I had that choice to do over again, would I switch from real estate to wrestling? Knowing what I know now, I am not so sure I made the right decision. Because 31 years later and 20 world titles later, I'm very beat up and life is pretty hard.

GETTING BORED

I continued to get bored after the NFL.

I was getting even more fat and sloppy because I was making some very good money. With money, I could eat like a king any night of the week, and I did just that.

I was doing well with business. I met my wife through the lawsuit I had involved with over my leg. She meant the world to me. I started becoming a "suit and tie," living the grown up life and making good money. Everything was now great, but the problem was, something was still missing. One night, I was sitting in my nice apartment paying bills, and it hit me. *I didn't like being a suit and tie.*

Maybe I was starting to show some early stages of depression. I don't know, but I started finding myself thinking about drinking a lot.

Now, once a person leaves the NFL, you pretty much leave all of your NFL friends behind. This includes your drinking buddies. I am not sure if it is because they look at you as being a failure or someone with less money, or whatever, but my drinking partners from the Rams really didn't have time for me anymore. This was probably a good thing for me in hindsight. My old high school buddies were still living in South Central which, by this point, had gotten even worse. I called them a few times with the intention probably of drinking, but we only really talked on the phone. I realized with all of them, nothing had changed. They were still up to their destructive ways and I could see it. I made a conscious decision not to fall into my old ways, again. I didn't want to get back into that environment anymore.

I was growing up.

Boulder and LA were opposites, and I realized it the first time around that LA was no longer the right place for me. At yet another crossroads in my life, I was the type of individual who could have gone either way at that point. I was just starting out in a new, possibly good career for me, but I wasn't happy. I knew that it would force me to seek happiness elsewhere in my life, and I was worried about falling back into old habits. Boulder, therefore, would be a much safer place for me to live.

I was finally thinking ahead and thinking smart for a change. Rather than choose the wrong path and lose everything, I sold the four-plex and almost doubled my money.

I know I made the right choice to leave LA when I returned to Boulder.

CHAPTER 3 - TRAINING FOR THE RING

Life was kind of plain, but it was an honest living. I felt good about where I was, but something was still missing.

Then, one day, I was working out at a gym, and I was spotted by a man who remembered me from my college football days. He came up to me and patted me on the shoulder.

"Hey, man. You're Leon White!" he said.

"That's right," I said, finishing a heavy set of weights to shake his hand. I hadn't been recognized for some time and it was nice again to feel appreciated.

"I heard about your injury, man, that sucks," he said.

"Yeah. Thanks, man."

"You are still a powerhouse," he said pointing at the big weights. "Maybe you could get into pro wrestling or something. It would be a shame to waste that."

I laughed a little as he walked away, but then started to think about what he said. "Maybe he is right," I said to myself. I was pushing up almost 550 pounds on the bench. I knew all of this hard work to get to this point should be able to transition into some kind of income for me other than just the boring regular suit and tie job lifestyle I was living.

I then really started watching wrestling on TV. I had always been a bit of a fan, but then Saturday mornings became different for me. I watched everything I could. I started to eventually study it, almost like my film room days in football.

Based out of Denver, our channels aired AWA Wrestling with Stan Hansen, Jerry Blackwell, and some of the bigger guys. One of the big individuals who really caught my eye was Bruiser Brody. Occasionally, we would also get some wrestling programming on our channels from down south. With the early WWF, I remember seeing André the Giant now and again. He was always a treat to watch!

I don't think there was any particular individual that turned me on to the sport, but rather the whole idea in general. I liked the idea of wrestling being both athleticism and performing while entertaining a crowd. I felt like there were some connections for me with how I approached football and that also made wrestling interesting to me.

My first thought was, if I wanted to get noticed by a potential wrestling promoter, then I needed to get bigger. I knew I already had the strength, but another 75 pounds or so would set me aside from the rest. With the size, strength, athleticism, and my NFL experience, I figured a wrestling promoter couldn't say no and this formula would be a sure-win for a career in the ring.

I continued to train like a fool. For some reason, I thought size was really what I needed to succeed and then I started eating everything in sight. I switched gears to a powerlifter diet and, in no time, I got bigger alright. At this point, I was benching just under 600 pounds.

Once I figured I was ready, I did some networking and made a few calls and finally found a promoter from Denver with the AWA named Gene Reed. He knew who I was, and I think the NFL experience put dollar signs in his eyes. I planted a few more seeds of curiosity, and he told me he was interested. By the end of the call, he said he wanted to take a look at me the next time they were in town, though we didn't really set an official date or anything.

Fast forward about two weeks later. I was on my way to the gym when I noticed in the morning paper that an AWA show was coming to The Denver Coliseum.

"TONIGHT… Brody! Blackwell! Scott Hall! Curt Hennig! All coming to Denver, Colorado."

"I know where I am going tonight!" I said. I was excited.

I hit the gym hard but cut some of the time from my workout. If I was going to make a good first impression, I needed to look good.

About this time, I felt I was ready to make a monster of an impression. I was 6'4, 325 plus pounds, benching 600 and squatting close to a thousand pounds. My claim to fame in the local gym was I could jump press (a push-up military press behind my neck) somewhere in the area of 365 pounds about 12-15 times.

Around dinner time, I got decked out in the best tough guy clothes I could put together to try to make an impression. Wearing a Stetson hat and badass cowboy boots to make me look even taller, I journeyed over to the scene and I was ready.

I walked up right up to the locker room door behind the Coliseum, ready to demand a job. I stood a few inches away from my future.

Um… About twenty minutes later, I finally got the guts to open the door.

Once inside, I had officially rushed the AWA locker room.

The term "kayfabe" is an important thing in wrestling. Though it is used in many ways, it generally has to do with protecting the secrets of wrestling from someone who is not in the business. I quickly looked around the kayfabe locker room. One wrestler was putting together the finishing touches on a fake pair of brass knuckles made out of tape and a toilet paper roll. Another couple of guys were planning out the finish of their match. They would be fighting each other in less than an hour.

Back then, promoters would always split up "the good guys" from "the bad guys." That meant they would make good use of venues with two different un-adjoining locker rooms and use a separate locker room for the heels, and a separate locker room for the babyfaces (fan favorites.) Opponents were not supposed to see each other before a match, but this layout, however, was not withholding the image that a wrestling fan was supposed to imagine behind the curtain.

Allowing a fan to storm into a locker room was the very last thing that wrestlers would allow. As a fan, this was also a good way to get your ass handed to you by a wrestler acting in under the doctrine of "trying to protect the business."

I looked around. Guys were drinking and playing cards. Just as I started taking it all in, I was shoved into a locker hard.

Before I knew what hit me, there was a massive cloud of hair in my face, and all I could smell was stale beer breath. A hand parted those wiry, wisps of hair and I found myself entranced. I was in a Bruiser Brody stare down.

"What are you doing in my locker room?!" Brody yelled.

"I'm here to get a job," I said coldly.

Brody started breathing hard. I had learned the rules of survival from my days in LA that if you looked away, you showed weakness. So I just stood there, toe-to-toe, with a scruffy-looking Viking who wanted to kill me.

Brody moved closer.

I didn't move but I could see from my peripherals that this was becoming an event for the rest of the boys. A number of colors flashed around the sides of my head to see what was going to happen next. Just passed Brody's huge head, I recognized one of the color shapes. It was Curt Hennig who came running in, but not to break things up. He was there for his ringside seat for the main event in the locker room.

I didn't want to fight Bruiser Brody; *I almost wanted to ask for his autograph.* I mean I idolized this guy. The way he moved on TV. The power. The intensity. Brody was "the man." However, he was the "the man" to me and I idolized him in part because he was a total killer in the ring. But if I had to square up with him to make a name for myself, that was what I had to do. Until then, I continued to swallow back my fear and stare that monster in the eyes.

I mean, I knew that Bruiser Brody was a legend. He was a real smart guy who called all his own spots, and I had heard he was someone who no wrestler or promoter would ever mess with.

I didn't show it at the time, but I just about shit my pants.

Promoter Gene Reed finally heard the commotion and rushed on to the scene. He parted the sea of wrestlers and came between the two monsters in front of him. "Who is this?" he asked, seeing the possible eyeballing confrontation about to turn into a physical one.

I didn't speak. I couldn't speak. If I said anything, it could be misconstrued as a weakness, or a means to get out of the stare down. Saying anything and breaking focus could also mean, "Please help me out of this mess I am in." I did not want to do anything that could be mistaken as a cry for help. Coming unannounced had made an impression and I felt like my foot was almost in the door. So I just stood there and I continued to stare down one of the biggest names in the game.

I am not sure if Gene just flat out recognized me from the NFL, or just took a guess, but it was a good thing for me that he figured out who I was. "Are you Leon?"

I nodded, just barely.

"He's okay, Frank," he said to the angry face behind the bush of a beard.

Brody didn't budge.

"HE'S OKAY, FRANK!" Gene repeated.

There was another moment or two of awkwardness before we both slowly backed down and averted our focus to Gene. Brody finally nodded. He circled over to his pile of clothing then walked by me towards a door, brushing into my shoulder intentionally like a schoolyard bully.

Gene exhaled. "I actually do need to talk with you. I just didn't think it would be here in the locker room."

"Awe shucks," Curt Hennig said at the missed opportunity. "Ok boys, move along. There is nothing here to see."

As the dust finally began to settle, Brad Rheingans walked up into the scene. Brad was an NCAA Division II champion in 1975 for North Dakota State University. He was also on the 1976 & 1980 Olympic wrestling team. He was pretty well-respected. "This is Leon White?" he asked Gene.

"Yes sir," I said.

Brad shook my hand and Greg Gagne too. "Gene told me about you," Brad said.

"I hope good things."

Brody got another glance in and walked away with some of the other big guys who were actually on the card.

"Let me get a pen and your number before something bad happens," Brad said laughing. "It would be a shame if your jaw was wired shut before I could get your contact info."

Gene laughed. I gave Brad my phone number and he patted me on the shoulder.

"I have a camp starting in two weeks. Be there."

BRAD RHEINGANS

I remember my first day well. I was excited to get to Brad's invitation-only school and didn't know what to expect. There was a little cheesy Las Vegas-style hotel with a weekly rate just down the street from where we would be training. I pretty much checked in, threw my bags on the bed and rushed off to Brad's place.

I felt my heart beating on the way over there and stopped to pick up a gallon of water. I remember swallowing hard from a bad case of nervous "cotton mouth" I was developing because I knew Brad was the best. I did my homework. I had learned that Brad was the real deal. He was a great amateur wrestler with an Olympic background. He was a recognized coach of actual Olympic champions. In addition to coaching top name wrestlers throughout his Olympic wrestling career, Brad Rheingans also trained a number of the biggest names in professional wrestling at the time. If I was no good, he would know it in an instant.

Looking back today at his entire body of work really is impressive. Some of his well-known students included Curt Hennig, Curtis Axel, Jake Roberts, JBL, Rick Steiner, Tom Zenk, Nailz, The Nasty Boys, The Beverly Brothers, Jerry Lynn, The

Patriot Del Wilkes, Scott Norton, Don Frye, and even the UFC & WWE crossover star, Brock Lesnar.

To say I was excited to be a part of his camp would have been an understatement, but I knew I had to play it smart. I didn't just rush in there that day without taking any precautions. After that almost-altercation with Bruiser Brody, I knew I needed a reinforcement to have my back in case anything got out of hand.

I brought my friend Greg Boyd with me, a former Denver Bronco who was also interested in getting into wrestling. We both pulled up at about the same time and it was comforting to know I had an ace in the hole.

THE FIRST DAY OF SCHOOL

I walked into Brad's backyard where he had a beautiful swimming pool and a nice Jacuzzi, however, the key word is "had." The place where swimming holes had been was filled in with cement to provide a level playing field for exercise equipment and a ring.

"What a shame," I said to myself, thinking that the property might be worth less now without a pool. "I could go for a nice dip."

It was pretty hot out that first day. I could feel the sun beating down on the back of my neck and the sour stickiness on my skin. We had already broken a sweat before we even did one thing.

I walked over to talk with one anxious student who was doing pushups waiting around for the class to start.

Brad showed up. He didn't look at all as intimidating as he may have looked to some on TV. He, for one, was a heck of a lot smaller in person than I thought he looked from his pictures, and he was pretty dressed down wearing beat up sweat pants.

Everyone got into the ring. Brad jumped in with us and gave us a little speech.

I don't remember all the words, but it was the typical inspirational speech. The general idea was that if you want to make something happen, then you have to work hard to get there. You know. He talked about how nothing is handed to you in this business.

We started running some simple drills. We hit the ropes. We learned the basics on how to fall without hurting ourselves. It was all helpful stuff, but I really wanted some action. I figured the best way to really make myself known was to start throwing my weight around and manhandle some people, so I started sizing people up and nobody much seemed like a real threat.

After an hour of drills, Brad gave us a break for a drink.

"Ok guys," Brad said. "I need you to pair up."

Strategy. Rather than to just pick out a partner, or grab Greg Boyd and put on a show to make us look good, I decided to show Brad who the real boss was.

Just like my episode with Brody, I wanted to make an immediate impact. I sized him up and made a game plan. I knew Brad was a good hand, but he was a heck of a lot smaller than me and I knew I was much stronger. I figured if I threw my actual trainer around a bit, he would get word back to Gene Reed and the AWA on how tough I was. That would make me one step closer to getting a job.

We locked up. I did pretty well for about 10 to 15 seconds or so until Brad had enough. He used my own weight against me and slammed me into the shithouse door face first.

My mouth started to bleed and, before I knew it, Brad was pushing my face right down towards the bowl. My face was in pain, but that wasn't the worst. The worst thing about this moment was the last guy in the outhouse didn't flush.

A burger-sized turd was stuck in the funnel that led down to the open septic tank. It was so close to my face I could almost taste it through my nose.

I don't know whose nasty dump that was, but from that moment on, I decided that dealing with Brad's shit was better than dealing with bad shit in a porta-potty.

When I retreated back to the line, I learned my first and maybe most important lesson of them all. I learned a lesson about respect. I learned *Brad was in charge.*

After day one, I didn't mess with Brad anymore. I went right into yes-sir-no-sir mode and did whatever he wanted. In return, he trained me pretty well. I did countless drills to learn the basics and gained a whole lot of respect for all the different moves and reversals I was learning about wrestling.

The days were long. At night, I was hitting the gym extra hard to make more of an impact in the ring.

One day at the end of a very grueling training session under the hot sun, Brad slapped me on the shoulder and said, "Oh, by the way. Work on getting a tan the rest of the day. The bosses are coming tomorrow."

So I did just that or at least tried. Being a bit of a ginger, tans usually came out like burns for me. I do remember actually trying to get a tan that afternoon, so I could look like a real "professional wrestler."

I think I showed up to class the next day with second degree burns and the initial stages of Melanoma skin cancer.

Anyhow, just as Brad had promised, Verne and Greg did, in fact, come over and watched us at the training center. I knew they had big shot roles, but they didn't really act like it. They were both really nice to everyone.

They started by asking us some individual questions and then watching us in the ring doing moves.

I knew they were impressed by my size, but I decided to dazzle them in another way, so I came up with a plan. I wanted to illustrate to them that I was a big man who could also move.

I had learned that high-flying moves were easy for me, even as a big man. They were just something that I was always capable of doing even though very few other 375 pounders could do them with ease. As an NFL football player and an All-American in college, I always aspired to be the most athletic guy on the field, then all the other things seemed to just fall into place.

While training, I made sure to throw as many high dropkicks as I could while I was in the ring. I watched Verne immediately say something to Greg, so I added some high-risk moves off the top.

Because of my intensive weight training regimen and athleticism, those moves were things that I could do. I figured because other big guys aren't doing them, maybe I should. I figured right.

I guess they were one of the things that made me unique as a big man in the eyes of a promoter. I thought it added to my character's ability to entertain and I think they did, too. After some pretty intense training, Verne went over and talked a little to Brad, then came over to me and asked me when I was available.

As far as my buddy Boyd was concerned, he was exactly who I needed there with me for confidence at the time. He was always the best dancer in the club and he had really great rhythm, but the moment he got into the ring, we learned that he became too mechanical and stiff. Wrestling wouldn't work out for him. (He wrestled a few years here and there. He even went to Europe with me for Otto Wanz at one point, but never really went anywhere.)

Brad must have seen potential in me as I made it in the ring quicker than most. Not only that, but I was treated a little better. I didn't have to start out in the smaller territories working for the little promotions. I went right into one of the biggest promotions America had to offer – the AWA.

BUILDING MOMENTUM

After Verne saw me in training with Brad, it all happened very fast. I remember going to Las Vegas for a television taping that would soon air in Denver. We had a really hot audience that night, wrestling in front of a sold-out crowd. Their energy set the tone for me. I was finally in my element.

Talk about throwing me under the bus, however. For my first match, I actually had to wrestle Bruiser Brody that night. I remember very little of the match, and maybe that is a good thing. Maybe I have little memory of my debut because it was a horrific beating that my mind wanted to black out. I don't know. What I do know, however, is how it felt afterwards. It hurt like hell.

The idea that I didn't have to pay any dues and I didn't have to work smaller promotions first was something Brody, like most people, didn't like. Brad loved high-caliber athletes, and I was considered one of them because of my NFL experience. However, being a favorite of his didn't go unnoticed from the boys in the back. Not only did I step right into a television spot, but I was also playing by different rules that the others didn't.

While most of the undercard wrestlers on the roster had to endure the frigid cold winters that Minnesota had to offer, Gene Reed didn't make me live there like he did with all the rest of the boys. Gene allowed me to continue to live in Boulder, Colorado and actually flew me into matches in whatever area we were touring in.

Now, I'm not saying that I was special or anything at this point, nor did I act like it. In fact, maybe only Gene Reed, the guy who signed me, thought I was because Brad taught me well and I knew I was still green. However, the special treatment is probably what led me into some heat with the boys early on.

The heat I had with the boys wasn't my only problem. Whether it was fate, whether I was being tested by the powers-that-be, or whether the booker just didn't like my special deal, the rookie year that was mapped out for me was tough. Nobody took it easy on me. Nobody was there to really show me the ropes like a new guy needed. I was on my own.

Nine times out of ten, I would look at the card taped to the locker room wall and see the same thing. I would see the same name opposite mine and that name was synonymous to one of the toughest, stiffest, most hardcore wrestler of that time - *Bruiser Brody*.

Bruiser Brody (TOP RIGHT), Stan "The Lariat" Hansen (TOP LEFT),
The Midnight Rockers, Marty Jannetty & Shawn Michaels (BOTTOM LEFT),
Crusher Jerry Blackwell (BOTTOM RIGHT)

CHAPTER 4 - AWA

As a crossover athlete who competed in the Super Bowl, Verne Gagne had a lot of faith in me and wanted to see me succeed. The American Wrestling Association was running about 25 shows a month at this time and Verne started me out getting about half of them. I didn't get a contract guarantee, but nobody did back then. A wrestler's pay was always a portion of the gate calculated by your position on the show.

From 1985 until around 1987, I went by the moniker Leon "The Baby Bull" White. I liked the "bull" part because it was my nickname from football, but the "baby" thing kind of bugged me. That part of the name was Verne's idea though and I was just starting out, so who was I to say no?

My very first match had no real reason or rhyme and was set up simply because of my size. It was with Bruiser Brody; the very same guy I stood up to when I crashed the locker room before my training. Let me tell you, that first bout was one of the most painful things I have ever done in my life.

Before Verne decided to just put me into a regular program with Brody, he put me all over the card; bad guy, good guy, tag team, whatever they could to figure out what would click for me. All the while, I didn't know that I was starting to get a bit of a rep from the boys in the back for the special treatment.

I was trained by one of the best. I could run the ropes well and could perform the moves, but still, a lot of the guys didn't want to work with me. I thought I didn't have the trust factor. That may have been part of it, but that wasn't entirely it. Someone has since told me that, when I was green, it was a classic case of, "I didn't know my own strength."

A body slam from me was like, "getting drilled through the mat."

Some of the boys started telling Verne that they didn't want to work with me. They said that my timing was all off and also that I was "too strong." They were worried that I might end up hurting someone by mistake.

The last straw was Verne hearing feedback about me after being thrown into some tag matches with the Fabulous Freebirds. When Terry Gordy thinks you are too stiff, there is probably something wrong.

I came off the ropes and hit Michael Hayes with a clothesline at the wrong time in the match that he wasn't expecting. On top of that, the clothesline that I threw was thrown as hard as I could. I was so new at the game that I thought certain things were still supposed to happen at full force, so they looked good.

Verne knew something had to change.

Before long, Verne called me in to sit down with him in the office.

"Leon, we need to change things up," he said.

I remember my heart racing. I knew a few of the guys didn't want to work with me, so I thought I was being fired. I remember looking around the room a little, in an uncomfortable silence. *Damn, I failed. It's all over. It's back to selling houses.*

"I'll try harder," I said. "Just give me another chance."

"We aren't cutting you, not yet," he said. "I think you just need a mentor. From now on, we want you to work with Bruiser and do whatever he says."

BRUISES FROM BRODY

The idea behind moving to a series of matches with Brody was to get me some psychology, some time with another big man who could help show me the ropes. I think Verne really was hoping that I would learn some timing and also learn how to lighten up a little in the ring. However, Brody wasn't the best guy they had to teach me how to lighten up. In fact, giving me this mentor had the inverse reaction.

The beatings I took from Bruiser Brody made me further believe that most of the moves were supposed to be stiff. The way he hit me made me think that aside from the characters and personas, *the wrestling part was real.*

Back in the '60s, '70s and even some of the '80s, many trainers didn't smarten guys up until their first matches or so. A guy like Kamala as a rookie was working $10,000 battle royals and didn't even know that wrestling was fixed yet, trying to collect on the money! Not smartening up wasn't the case with how Brad taught me. I knew that the promos, the feuds, and the finishes were all entertainment. But for some reason, I thought professional wrestling, the actual moves were supposed to be more athletic and physical than they actually were.

Now, add Brody to the learning equation. I mean if you are taking Brody clotheslines every night that feel like you are getting hit by a car full of bricks, you are probably going to believe *that is what a clothesline is supposed to feel like.* To a green wrestler's mind trying to absorb everything possible, Brody's style made me think that wrestling was supposed to be stiff.

In our first six-week program, Bruiser Brody did teach me a lot about timing. I learned that if I really needed to do some work at home, or something that called for picking something up off the ground, it was probably better to do that before a Brody match rather than after.

Looking back, it's possible that Verne was testing me. It's possible that he asked Brody to hit hard to see if I could take it. This is what some wrestling camps do to weed out the garbage. It's also possible that Brody was still mad that I stood up to him in that locker room, or was trying to teach me a lesson on his own. I don't know. What I do know was his matches really hurt.

Brody eventually eased up a little from those first few matches. I think he finally figured I wasn't going anywhere and then decided to try to help me learn. The first thing he did was he taught me how to work a crowd. He taught me how to really play with their emotions. He showed me how to make fans root more for the babyface and how to make them hate the heel even more by slowing things down and making the moves more important.

He also taught me how to sell big like a big man should. If I didn't give the proper facial emotions or body language to show that something hurt, he would just lay in harder so it actually did.

"Argh!" I'd bellow after being put into some kind of crazy-ass submission.

Brody would wrinkle up his face under the beard and say under his breath, "No good. Not believable." Then he would stretch the hell out of me, ten times worse than before.

"ARGGGHHH!"

"There kid," he would say. "See the face you are making now? That's what it should look like!" He would chuckle a little at the thought of inflicting real pain. "Good, kid."

Most of our matches were still pretty much the same though – brutal. The hits were hard. The moves were snug. The pain was long. The recovery was longer.

One match I remember, however, was a little different.

I remember coming into the locker room. There was already tension in the air. A few of the boys were clearly staying out of the way and off to the side, kind of minding their own business. It was pretty clear I had walked in right after words had been exchanged.

Brody looked like hell. His face was red and he was breathing out of his nose like a bull. He was walking away from Verne and Jerry Blackwell and made his way to the opposite corner where his bag was. The show hadn't even started and he was already taking his gear off.

It was clear that something went down, probably about money, and Brody decided not to wrestle that night. The problem was, if that were so, that could mean I was going to lose a payday, as well.

I decided to try to talk to him.

I pulled him off to the side and tried to convince him to work the match for me. He didn't say anything, at first. But he listened. I pleaded my case and eventually, I think I got through to him when I explained that I really needed the money, as my wife and I were thinking that we might have a baby on the way. That humanized me, and Brody saw it.

"Okay, kid," he said. "I'll do it for you."

I could smell the alcohol through his beard. It was so strong that it smelled like paint thinner. I knew he had quite a buzz on already and I wasn't sure how that was going to affect our match, but I guess the booze didn't matter. Our matches together hurt the most anyhow, so what did I really have to lose?

I made it to the curtain and they announced me out first. I got to the ring and was happy because I knew at least I was going to get paid that night. Then, I waited. Then waited and waited and waited some more.

"What's the hold up?" I asked the announcer.

"I guess they can't find Brody in the back?"

"Great," I thought, not knowing if we would actually have the match, after all.

A few minutes or so and we got the thumbs up from behind the curtain. A weight lifted off of my shoulders. Ken Resnick was doing the ring announcing that evening. He re-announced me, again and then finally, after much delay, announced my opponent.

"...And now without further ado, he is from Santé Fe, New Mexico. He stands 6 feet, 6 inches tall. He weighs in tonight at 307 pounds, here is King Kong Brody!"

The wild mess of curly, unruly hair wisps came barreling our way.

As you may or may not know, Frank Goodish, aka Bruiser Brody, was always announced as "King Kong Brody," while wrestling under the AWA banner. The reason for this was simple. Another AWA wrestler, Dick the Bruiser, did not want to relinquish the "Bruiser" moniker to anyone working for Verne. I never thought much of it at the time, but sometimes the boys would still slip up and call Brody "Bruiser Brody," while cutting AWA promos.

As a side note, eventually, the name change had further recourse when King Kong Bundy made his way to the AWA. He then had to be called "Boom Boom" Bundy, because of King Kong Brody. For Brody, at least his name change kept a mean connotation. "Boom Boom" sounded more like the name of a stereotypically loose woman on a bad '70's sitcom, but I digress.

Anyhow when Bruiser Brody finally got to the ring, he immediately twisted over his wrist with his palm in the air and started up his gimmick.

"Huss! Huss! Huss!" he yelled. He snorted with every breath like a wild man.

Boy, I'll tell you, I don't know what it meant, but it made me not want to run into him in a dark alley.

It was quite a sight; him doing that random wrist-holding thing yelling, "Huss! Huss! Huss!" at the audience at the top of his lungs. It sounded almost like a warrior in the midst of a savage, barking war cry.

The audience was just as clueless as I was, but the "huss" thing was contagious. Sometimes audience members would yell it back at Brody and it would become a "Battle of the Husses."

At this particular event, he just kept barking at the fans and was getting a really good reaction, so he figured "why stop?" The bell hadn't rung yet, so he just stepped over the rail and jumped into the audience.

He was in full huss mode.

He hussed it up at one fan and then heard another fan behind him doing it back. Distracted, he turned quickly and would then hear another "huss" come from another direction and would run over there to sell that. He kept doing this and doing this until he ended up way up in the cheap seats! I could barely see him up in the stands yelling, "Huss! Huss! Huss!" at anyone who would give him some kind of a reaction.

The match hadn't even started yet, but we were almost ten minutes in on hussing alone.

"What the hell is he doing?" I asked the ref.

"Probably trying to work off that 12 pack," he said.

I watched from a distance and leaned on the ropes. I played it up a little and acted confused to members of the crowd. I didn't really need to act though, as I had no idea what was going on.

Brody continued barking at the audience members and eventually turned around and started working his way back down the stands. All the while, he was yelling, "Huss! Huss! Huss!" and breathing deadly vodka fumes on practically everyone's face in the arena.

When he finally got back into the ring, the bell rang to start the match.

He stiffed me really bad with one big boot to the face and went for the pin.

"That's it, kid," he said calling for the finish. "Go home."

And that was it.

The match totally sucked, but at least this time it was not on the account of me. That match was a riot. Easy night. Easy payday. At least I was only stiffed once that night.

Our program continued all over the place. Eventually, I started to really get the timing down of when I should shine and when Brody needed to look good. Fans started eating it up. Due to us going out there and beating the living crap out of each other every night for real. Despite the fact that the moves were really stiff, I honed my skills during this time, and my ring-work improved significantly.

One night Brody called me over in the locker room. "How old are you?" he asked.

I told him. I was really young at the time. After saying it, Brody bugged his eyes out of his head and it looked as if he had seen a ghost.

"Damn, you look like an old man!" he said, over exaggerating with a gaping mouth. "You gotta do something about your hair."

It was true. I was balding a little and it didn't look great, but I really didn't think about it much until he mentioned it. "Well, what do you think I should do? Just shave it all off?"

"Hell no. Then, you might look even older!" Brody laughed and scratched his beard in deep thought. "Look. You can work now. I bet I can get you booked with me down in Texas, but I think you should shave your head in some kind of design to look hip. Maybe like Hawk, with the horns."

"Working Texas would be great," I said. "Okay, let me see what I can do."

I decided to try and get the Road Warrior's blessing to shave my hair into double-horn Mohawks to try and get that booking.

I was pretty scared approaching Hawk in the locker room the next night. He and his partner were huge and I knew they pulled a lot of weight with promoters. I didn't want my request to come off as a mark who just wanted to copy their hero or something, but I also wanted to show him respect.

When I finally got the courage up to approach him, he was painting his face in the mirror. He was just putting the finishing touches on a forehead design when I knocked on the door frame and swung my body around the corner.

"Hey man," I said.

He ignored me a second and continued with his paint. Then stopped.

"What's up, kid?"

"Well, something I have been meaning to ask you, Mike," I said, using his real name to sound more professional. At this point in my career, I did not really know that stage names were totally fine in the locker room.

"Shoot," he said, getting back to his painting.

"Well, um," I hesitated, taking time to choose my words.

Hawk laughed. "What is it?"

"Brody suggested I shaved my head to look a little more hip – like you."

"He did, did he?"

"He suggested a Mohawk but my hair doesn't grow well in the center, so we thought maybe like yours, the double one with the horns."

Hawk stopped painting for a second. He put his paint brush down on the sink and turned around to face me. He looked mad. "Is that so?"

Dammit, I asked wrong! I somehow insulted him, just what I didn't want to do!

"You want to rip me off?" he asked, seemingly looking for clarification.

Oh no! Not gimmick infringement!

I was taken aback and didn't know what else to say, so I shook my head and turned to walk away.

"I'm just messing with you," he said, "Sure man. It's cool."

"You sure?"

"Sure. We won't look the same," he tapped me on the shoulder and went back to his painting.

I was relieved. Neither Hawk nor Animal probably gave a flying shit what I did with my hair. At that point, I wasn't really a name. And he was right, no matter what haircut I got, there was no way I was going to look or be mistaken for Road Warrior Hawk in the ring.

It seemed that my matches with Brody were starting to get a little respect from the boys in the back, finally, as well. That was another thing to be happy about.

I knew it would be hard to look badass if I looked like I was losing the battle against baldness. I didn't want it to look like I would benefit from Rogaine even a little, because people would associate that with being old and would think that anyone could kick my ass. I also didn't want to just admit defeat and shave my head, and go all "King Kong Bundy" on everyone. I needed to look hip. So, I remember staring in the mirror that night with a trimmer I borrowed from one of the boys and a hand-held mirror. I had a PWI magazine folded open to a picture of the Road Warriors to my side, and started buzzing away. As the hair trimmings fell to the floor, slowly but surely it started to come together and I could see it.

Brody never did get me booked in Texas, but his tip did help me improve my brand tremendously for what it is worth. That haircut helped my look and probably helped make me into the name I later became. I have a lot of respect for him and am very thankful.

JERRY BLACKWELL

After taking some horrible beatings from Bruiser Brody for the better part of a year, Verne came up to me and said he liked what he was seeing. The next program I would find myself in was with Crusher Blackwell.

Nicknamed "The Mountain from Stone Mountain," Jerry Blackwell started his career in the 1970s. Despite being a super heavyweight at sometimes almost 500 pounds, Blackwell was a very nimble and gifted worker, able to throw a great standing dropkick! Putting him with me only made sense.

Jerry had seen it all. He had been there and done that and was the epitome of what you would consider a grizzled ring veteran. In the 1980s, Blackwell became a main event star in the AWA. He feuded with guys like Mad Dog Vachon and Hulk Hogan and was given the name "The Rattlesnake," because of his quick speed and aggression in the ring.

Blackwell's career reached new highs just before I got to AWA after Hulk Hogan left to go work for Vince. He wrestled in tons of title matches against AWA champions Stan Hansen and Curt Hennig in 1986 and 1987. Even though Blackwell was Hogan's replacement, he had a different style and was a legitimate bad ass.

Blackwell was known for his ridiculous feats of strength. One of the most famous stunts that he sometimes performed during live interviews was driving nails into 2x4s using nothing but his head. Still paying my dues so to speak, I became a softer target than a nail for Blackwell.

One of the things promoters did to weed out guys they weren't sure about was to really beat on them and to see how well they could endure. It was similar in football, and I knew that Verne was still trying to test me.

Knowing full well that I was being tested kept my confidence down a little in my rookie year. I was still a little too nervous to say much of anything when the strikes felt a little stiffer than they should have been.

What if I was wrong? What if that was how pro wrestling really worked?

I really couldn't afford to lose my spot there in AWA. I can't lie and say I felt all that secure in what I was doing at this point in my career. The way I would approach these fights again was "you give what you take." If they were hitting hard, I would just have to hit them back just as hard.

What I would do is take things one day at a time. Be it Brody, or Blackwell or Hansen, I would just look at each match as yet another obstacle I had to overcome.

STAN THE LARIAT HANSEN

Verne Gagne came to me one night before a show and said, "You've done really well with Brody and Blackwell and you are making us some good money. Now, I want you to start working some with Stan and do whatever he says."

Enter Stan Hansen.

Stan was also known for his hard-hitting stiff wrestling style, which he blamed on his poor eyesight. He would hit someone as hard as he could, then apologize afterwards to them, saying his "depth of perception" was at fault for not being able to pull the punch correctly.

Many people wonder if he was really that blind, or if he just used his thick glasses as an excuse to whoop ass and get over. After all, the harder you hit someone, the better you would look to the fans - then the more you are worth to promoters.

Stan played his gimmick well, however. He was perfect at being a loud, violent cowboy who wanted to fight everybody. His image was emphasized by his great interviews, always appearing in a cowboy hat, leather vest and swinging that bull rope and chewing on tobacco.

Being one of the veterans in the AWA locker room, Stan was respected by all. He was also considered to be one of the most successful and popular gaijins in Japan at this time, maybe finding even more popularity there than in his native country of the United States.

In my early days in AWA, Stan kind of eyeballed me whenever I walked into the room. I remember early on walking into a locker room somewhere and getting that odd feeling on the back of my neck that would make the hairs stand up on end like someone was watching me. Then, sure enough, I would see Stan sitting on a bench, lacing up his boots – but all the while burning a hole through me and my soul with his eyes.

I don't know if this staring thing stemmed from my odd first day of breaking into the business or not. It could have been that because Brody was one of Stan's best friends. Either way, I do think Stan looked at me as a threat; as being another big man. This competitive air would even more evident later on when I would follow his footsteps and take bookings in Japan, myself, however, we would eventually become and always remained good friends.

During my early days in AWA, he made me pay my dues. He stiffed the living hell out of me too, just like Brody. But, boy, I will say this, between all the beatings, Stan really helped me out in understanding timing. After Brody and Blackwell, Stan was the next step and my next mentor. Though I didn't know it at the time, he was preparing me for the next level, the next step in my career that I was working up to.

BRUISER BRODY – A TRUE GENTLEMAN

Well into my wrestling career with the AWA, I started to feel like I was really getting the hang of things. I was no longer ridiculously stiff. People weren't afraid to work with me. I started to really get the courage to lay moves in hard when I was getting hit hard and created the philosophy that you give what you get. However, nothing gave me the courage to know what to do in this case.

Now just as I was a big baby born to my mother, our son was slated to be born and born big. The AWA All-Stars were doing Denver Coliseum that same weekend with a huge super card on Saturday night in my "hometown." I had done the match and agreed to headline it, opposite Bruiser Brody.

From what the doctors had said, it seemed like he would be born probably on Wednesday or Thursday and I would have plenty of time to hit the locker room with a picture and some cigars to pass out. However, that wasn't quite the case. They didn't take into account that my son was going to be "stubborn like a bull" just like his old man.

My wife, Debbie White, went into labor and it was going to be an "Iron-Baby Match" that lasted 44 hours.

Thursday goes by. Friday goes by. Saturday morning goes by. Not knowing exactly when she was going to have the baby, I stayed right by her side, but I had my wrestling gear on hand because I had a friend go pick it up.

Now don't get me wrong. I wanted to see the birth of my son, more than anything in the world. Come early afternoon, a nurse came to the door.

"Mr. White?"

"Yes?"

"You have an urgent call at the desk," she said.

I ducked out of the birthing room, tripping over my wrestling boots by the door and made my way down to the maternity ward front desk, a few rooms down and was handed a phone.

"Leon? It's Gene Reed," the AWA promoter said. "How is everything? Will everything be okay for the match?"

"Yes, it should be. They are saying there is a bit of an issue with the cord, but the doctor thinks that can be remedied through a Cesarean if we have to."

"Oh, I hope he is alright, Leon," Gene said hesitantly. "But I didn't mean that. I meant will everything be alright for you making it to the show?"

I paused.

"Please Leon. Please don't leave me hanging without a main event. The show is sold out," he begged.

I headed back to the birthing room. I sat right beside my wife ready for one of the most important moments of my life and started lacing up my boots.

We were getting down to the clockwork. I hadn't slept for two days and was out of it, to say the least. Being stressed to the gills and pulled in different directions didn't help, either. They said at first that the baby was possibly being choked a bit by the cord. My son was in danger. My wife was in danger. My boss was in danger.

I was wiped out and in dire straits because they all wanted me to make a decision that I just couldn't do.

The doctor was a smart woman though and knew I wasn't of sound mind and body. She decided to just call the match. "Listen, I am trying to think about what is best for all the parties here. Obviously, Mr. White, you making it to a wrestling match is the least of my concerns."

Finally, he was born. There were eventually some issues with being entangled in the umbilical cord, but they worked it out without having the c-section. I was the happiest man in the world. Once I knew that all was good, I was so happy that I picked that doctor up almost into a bodyslam position and spun her around the room. Then, I picked up the apple of my eye and held him. It is still the proudest moment I have ever had in my life.

After Jesse's two-day-long entrance, he was ready for the weigh-in. Now, you know how wrestlers work their height and weight sometimes? I wanted Jesse to be huge. He was a big bastard, but I wanted to give him that little extra added push so I put my thumb on the scale.

"Twelve pounds?!" one of the nurses said. "That can't be right." She tried it again, and this time caught me with my hand on the platform. "Come on, Mr. White!" She knew damn well what I was trying to do. She weighed him one last time and said, "8 pounds and 6 ounces."

"Awe,'" I said, caught red-handed.

After she got the weight right, she went through the fingerprint procedure for the birth record that went along with the birth certificate. She took his little fingers and printed each one. Then she did his feet. When she was finished, she called me over and had me hold out my hand. She pressed his black foot on my palm.

"There you go, Mr. White," she said. "Now you can show that off to your wrestler friends."

She was right. A show I was headlining had already started and, as much as I didn't want to, I had to go.

I had a friend there by the hospital standing by in the emergency ward parking lot with his car all warmed up. My buddy Mark Coahram whom I grew up with some in LA was my getaway driver. I jumped in and he immediately got onto the Denver-Boulder Turnpike. We pretty much broke every rule we had to. We were breaking the speed limit big time to try to get me there. The speed limit was 55, and we were doing almost 100.

When we got there, we pulled up to the front door and the ticket-taker let me right in. I walked through the auditorium to get to the locker room. The show was already more than half over. Intermission had already ended, but I made it in with just enough time for the main event. With about three beers on my breath, I showed the ink on my palm to a couple of the boys in the room. I spotted Bruiser Brody, my opponent for the match, to let him know I was there.

"Hey Brody," I said.

"Congratulations on your kid," he said.

Brody and I already knew what type of match we would have. We would just "call it in the ring." We had worked so many times together in the past when he was showing me the ropes that I knew the deal without having to discuss it with him. All the hits were going to be pretty stiff, and we would pretty much put it together on the fly and call everything in the ring except for the actual finish.

Now, for me, a Brody match was less about preparation and more about post-match rituals. That meant I always needed to allow for a few days or so of healing afterwards. I really liked our matches because we could really tear down the house, but I never much cared about the post-match injuries that would come from working Brody like the sore back, a blackened eye or a banged up face. I was used to it by this point and could always hang with him in the ring, but it always sucked after the fact. Getting clotheslined in the Adam's Apple or the side of the head was a normal thing when you worked wrestlers like Stan Hansen and Bruiser Brody, and when I wasn't just destroying a "jobber," those were the types of matches I was used to having. The only difference on this particular night was, *I was now a dad.*

I wanted to enjoy my first day as a dad and be able to hold my son, not hold an icepack to the side of my face.

"Thanks, man," I said to Brody. "That means a lot to me," I grabbed his huge outstretched paw and shook it.

Brody nodded and continued to shake my hand.

"Bruiser, I know you are already a huge name in this business and I am just starting out, but I have a favor to ask. Tonight's a little different for me this time, my son was just born and I'm anxious to get back to him." I spoke very professionally and serious and I could see through all the hair that Brody seemed to understand.

Brody smiled, "Fair enough." He nodded and gave me a sense that all would be okay.

The stress in my shoulders subsided. "Thank you. So, I'd like to have a good simple match and pretty much just get what I give tonight. Simple lock up stuff and just go from there," I said. Basically, I was saying, "Let's have an easy match, not a pier-six brawl where I get my ass handed to me." I didn't really want to engage in one of the real snug type matches we were used to having together with a new baby waiting for me at home. The typical kick-the-living-shit-out-of-Leon-White matches that Brody usually had with me were fine, but just not this night. I was a new daddy.

"Say no more," Brody said like a true gentleman. He was an old-timer and he knew the deal. He seemed to know that I didn't want to be all beat up for the next few days. "You bet. Let's go out there and have a good one." He patted me on the shoulder and we headed over to the curtains and waited for our names.

The announcer introduced Brody first, who put on the whole show for the audience with the classic "Huss! Huss! Huss!" and everything.

Then he introduced me, as a hometown hero from Boulder, Colorado. "Leon, Baby Bull, White!!!"

I got a huge reaction from the crowd in Denver Coliseum. The air was electric. The audience went crazy. There were probably a few hundred local people who knew me in person that came just to see me and they let me know it. On top of that, many of them knew the baby was either on his way *or already here.*

So to add the icing on the cake, the announcer continued and gave those in the know an update. "And ladies and gentlemen… We want to thank Bull from making it out here to celebrate with all of you. He just came from the hospital. It is my pleasure to inform you all that tonight… Baby Bull wife gave birth to a bouncing baby boy."

I started crying and couldn't stop. The entire audience popped, as I showed everyone the footprint on my hand. This is a moment I will never forget.

People everywhere stood up with the most moving standing ovation I have ever seen on one of the most important days of my life. I looked over at Brody who seemingly nodded in admiration for me under his massive beard, but continued to stay in character but did not attack me. He continued just pacing back and forth, like a leopard, like a hungry cheetah ready to pounce on a victim.

The bell rang. And rather than the usual crazy, savage attack from the monstrous Bruiser Brody, we locked up.

"Bruiser showing respect!" I thought to myself.

One of the biggest and toughest names in the sport was giving me my night. I was on cloud nine. The audience was behind me 100 percent and so was Bruiser Brody if only just for this one special moment.

Then, out of nowhere, Bruiser kicked me in the mouth as hard as he could and cut my lip in half. Dazed, I fell outside of the ring the hard way. He jumped outside, grabbed a chair and nailed me again even harder.

"How's that?" he asked. "Is that what you had in mind?"

To say the least, the match was brutal. I gave it back like usual and we went on to beat the crap out of each other. It turned out we had one hell of a match. Brody had practically killed me once again, beating me an inch from death. In the end though, the ref raised my hand. I was victorious.

After the show, I showered the blood off my face, dried off and got dressed. Rigor mortis started to set in and it already hurt a little to tie my shoes.

As I made my way to my car, a number of fans were there slapping my back and congratulating me. A few of them asked to buy me a drink to celebrate my win, and also the birth of my son. Never to be one to turn down a free drink, I obliged.

I walked over to the bar across the street from the Denver Coliseum where some fans were already collecting. They opened the door for me and I walked into a hero's welcome. I signed a few autographs, but mostly drank my fill of whatever I wanted and smoked some good cigars.

Later, however, something happened that I never thought I would never see. The door swung open and it felt like a scene out of the old west. Bruiser Brody stepped in and came right at me. The fans didn't know what to make of it and neither did I. Hell, I'm not even sure Brody knew what he was going to do at first.

Brody then did something he probably almost never did before; he dropped the character and shook my hand. The fans cheered and Brody bought me a drink that night.

That was one of the greatest nights of my life, but it was also one of the last nights I ever saw Bruiser Brody.

After that, I rushed back to the hospital. I had just wrestled Bruiser Brody with no sleep and was exhausted. When I finally got there to look after my wife and newborn son, I was so drunk and out of it from celebrating that my wife got up and put me in her bed and started taking care of me.

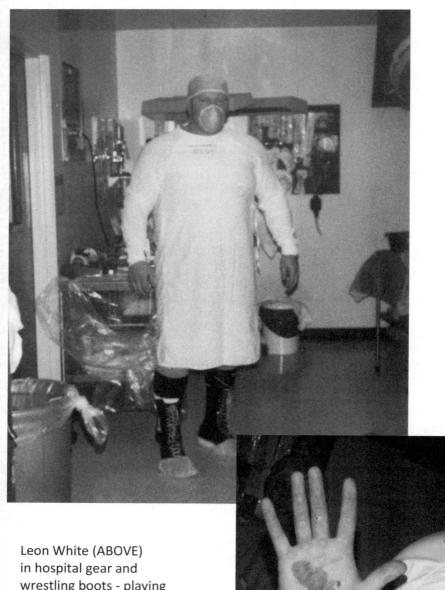

Leon White (ABOVE)
in hospital gear and
wrestling boots - playing
midwife just before an
AWA event.

Baby Bull also stamped
his newborn's footprint
on his hand (RIGHT)
to show the boys back
at the show.

CHAPTER 5 - AWA ROAD STORIES

The American Wrestling Association is where I got my first national exposure. Despite the beatings at hand, I got better and better in the ring working with Brody, Jerry Blackwell, and later Stan Hansen. They calloused my entire body and prepared me for just about any level of pain.

Eventually, I tagged some with Curt Hennig and Scott Hall to learn some tag team psychology. They would tag me in and use me a little and make fine adjustments on the fly. Scott would watch my work and yell instructions from ringside before I would tag out.

"Ok, big man. Don't tag out yet. Show your power!" he would say, refusing a tag from me as his partner. He would point at our opponent and I would go back and do some more. It looked like he was just being cocky and wishing more pain on our opponent, but he was actually teaching me what I should do so I could get a better feel for timing.

Once I got it and understood the formula, Nick Bockwinkel told Verne Gagne that I had come a long way in a short time. People can work around me now and make me look even better, so Verne started giving me more dates.

Verne Gagne promised I would be eventually getting that 20-25 days a month. While we never really approached that, he started using me more. I started making the circuit riding with whomever I could to listen and learn in the car on the way to the shows. It was this way for a good six months, cramming four guys into a hotel room, and we would make anywhere from $50 to maybe $250 on a really good night.

The money was pretty good, so I started investing in better ring gear. I remember wanting to look good so I could try and make even more money from my image. In AWA, the first pieces of the puzzle that would eventually spell "Vader Time" were starting to come together.

SEX SYMBOLS & PRANKS

Around 1983, Bill Watts' territory, Mid-South Wrestling, was down and he didn't know why, so he asked Jerry Jarrett and Jerry Lawler to come up for a show and take notes to give their opinions. He obliged. After the show, Watts took them out to a nice Italian restaurant. They were eating, and Watts asked them what they thought was wrong.

"Where are all the blowjobs?" Jarrett said, nonchalantly pounding some pasta.

"What the hell does that mean?" Watts asked.

"All your wrestlers are big, ugly, tough guys who only appeal to your standard wrestling audience," Jarrett replied, taking another big bite of spaghetti. "If you get younger wrestlers and push them properly, you'll get more girls and kids to come to the shows."

He was right, so Watts brought in Terry Taylor, Magnum TA, and The Rock & Roll Express. In no time at all, ticket sales increased for Mid-South wrestling by almost 30-40 percent! Bringing in The R&R Express was genius because they already had good experience in taking blowjobs. They were already the kings of the rats in Memphis, I heard.

At some point, this same idea made it across the table of Verne Gagne in the AWA. The average wrestling fan was coming to the shows anyhow, but he needed something more to bring in the other demographic.

Girls weren't lining up to see Crusher, a chunky guy who loved polka music, looked like Pat Patterson and sounded like Burgess Meredith. What chick would look at Von Raschke, Dick the Bruiser, or even worse Jerry Blackwell, and find them attractive?

Just before I started wrestling, promoters in the early 80s where just starting to realize that babyfaces needed to look good to girls so that they would sell more tickets to that demographic.

Verne actually had conversations with his younger, good-looking names about the birds and the bees. When he learned the idea that sex sells, he saw his ticket sales go up. He would explain to his younger talent to be flirtier and make all girls think they had a chance with them. He actually encouraged them to go out with as many different girls as possible. This way, they seemed "getable" and would be desirable like real sex symbols. He wanted his top names to appear so sexy that girls would actually fight over them!

None of the better-looking part of the locker room seemed to mind meeting this standard. This boss' request didn't always come without recourse, however. The boys in the locker room often ended up having to cover for each other, because with sex often comes violence.

Covering for the promiscuity of the babyface became an unwritten rule of the game. If you had that one good-looking draw on the same show you were on, more people would buy tickets and that meant you would get paid more, as well.

Enter the Midnight Rockers… Getting their start with AWA, Shawn Michaels and Marty Jannetty fit the sex-symbol bill that Verne was looking for perfectly. However, knowing they were valuable went straight to their heads. This led to spoiled rockstar-like antics that pissed off the veterans and got them all kinds of heat. I remember hearing old school vets like Brody, Hansen and Blackwell discus how they could maybe get away with murder on a guy like Michaels.

"With all the backwoods travelling we do from town to town," one would say, "we could just dump his body off in the middle of nowhere." Another would continue, "If the cops did find Shawn's body, one of his party-girl's boyfriends would probably take the rap."

"He's still a kid," I said, hearing the tail end of a Michaels-hating session. "He is only 21. He will learn his ways on his own, and when he does, lesson learned." However, thinking that Shawn or Marty would quickly outgrow this behavior was actually wrong.

After shows, Curt Hennig, Scott Hall and I would go unwind at the bar. A lot of times, then we would see Shawn Michaels and his partner in crime, Marty Jannetty, show up. They brought out the worst in each other. A younger more reserved Scott would say something like, "It's going to be another rough day at the office," when he saw them come through the door because they would dog on every girl in the joint.

If Shawn thought there was any interest, he would strut right up to a girl like a cocky peacock and start throwing play, even if she was with her boyfriend! Then the next thing you know it, he would pinch them on the ass, or slap them on the tits. He didn't care. *He was Shawn Michaels.* "Ok, wrestler or no wrestler, I'm going to kick your ass!" the girl's boyfriend would say. Then, it would turn into an old fashioned saloon fight with Shawn and

Marty in the middle. Soon, I'd be joining other members of the AWA playing the role of the cavalry.

Eventually, we could predict a fight before it happened. We'd rush through the crowded bar to find Shawn talking to some hoochie with the hot-headed boyfriend right behind him. Early in the game, we showed up too late and the fight would break out. But after some practice, we would rush right over to the angry, butt-hurt boyfriend early and pull him off to the side. Then, we would tell him to relax and point out the other wrestlers in the bar. The boyfriend would then crunch the numbers in his mind, and I would add something like, "It's not worth it man, he's just a flirt. I'll make sure she still goes home with you." After that, Scott or I would then pull Shawn (or Marty) off to the side and tell him to just go hit on someone else.

"Awe, come on man," Shawn would say. "But I want her!"

"Just fuck someone else, Shawn, or you are going to get yourself fucked up," we would say. Most of the boyfriends would then grab their girls by the wrist and leave. Nine times out of ten, the girl would still wink at The Rockers on her way out. The kind of girls the Rockers always went for loved the drama of being fought over. *Bitches!*

Their pranks were horrible. If we were at a school gym with no windows, the Rockers would have someone explain the light controls to them. Then during the show, Shawn or Marty would watch the kids run to the barricades. Once a train of fans was in full motion, they would wait for the most opportune moment, *and then hit the lights.* This would cause the people to bang into each other and literally pile up. When the lights came back on, it always looked as if a tornado came through and threw bodies everywhere. All the while, Shawn and Marty were laughing their asses off at the switches.

On one particular "light prank" night, I remember I was with Jerry Blackwell when everything went black. When the lights came back on, Jerry had somehow spilled a beer all over himself. "Those guys, again!" Jerry said, clearly pissed off. "The Rockers!" Jerry ducked out the curtain to check on the fallen kid who was crying. Once he knew all was okay, Jerry rushed backstage and I followed. By the time he found Verne Gagne, his face was red with anger. "Verne, I want to work one of those assholes. I saw what they did again, tonight. They are going to hurt someone, so I'm going to hurt one of them. Give me a match, right now. They are going too far and need to learn a lesson."

"Come on, Jerry," Verne said. "You can't. We need them."

"It's going to happen," he said. "They are going to the hospital, Verne. Better write them off TV. Whether I hurt them in the ring or not, it's going to happen."

"I'll have a talk with them," Verne said. Without speaking, Vern looked at me, as if asking me to help diffuse the situation.

I nodded to him, to let him know I would try. I decided to give them a fair warning. I saw Shawn in the locker room and pulled him to a side hallway. "Shawn, about the lights tonight…"

"Ha! Did you like that, Leon?"

"Listen. You can't do stuff like that, anymore. You are getting heat in the back, man. They want an excuse to teach you a lesson."

"Thanks for the heads up," he said, rolling his eyes. I watched as the gears in his head spun for maybe a few seconds, then stop. "I'll back off on the lights rib for now because I respect you, but not because I pissed off the old farts."

THE ART SHOW

When The Rockers showed up to an event, they would go right to the front door to see what was "on the menu." They would walk up and down the ticket line to see what little dish they wanted. During the show, they would "order their take-out." Sometimes, they would bump near a girl during a match and tell them to meet them after the show in the parking lot. Other times if they were really hungry, they would have a ring crew guy or security bring a girl back to the locker room and have them "make a special delivery" in a back alley.

I heard a story once where Marty had to start a match without Shawn because he was in the parking lot with a girl. Shawn finally joined his partner five minutes after the match had already started. I guess he made it there just in time for the hot tag, ironically after he just tagged some hot girl!

Every night after a show, the Midnight Rockers always had an after-party. They would always find the prettiest girls you could imagine and invite them back to their rooms as party guests. I don't know what they were partying with, but those girls weren't just drinking Shirley Temples. The guests would often say it was always the same scene; the girls would party hard, probably have some crazy naked wrestling match, and then eventually pass out. Then, the pranks would begin.

The next thing the Rockers got blamed for by the old vets was some really strange and inappropriate "Art Shows." In the '80s, girls groomed a little different than they do today. Pick up any old Playboy and you will see what I mean. It was believed (but never confirmed) that someone in the AWA liked to play tricks on groupies who had the unfortunate mishap of passing out in their hotel rooms. What they would do was remove any of their date's remaining clothes, give them a haircut and then draw faces below their belts with markers. Next, they would drag the girl's body to an unmonitored area in the hotel. They would finally prop them up in a chair spread eagle in all that shaven splendor, so anyone walking by could admire their beautiful Sharpie artwork.

To be fair, both of them vehemently deny having anything to do with putting on the art shows. It still hasn't been confirmed who the actual artists were to this very day. Despite fingers pointing at the shenanigans of Shawn and Marty for this one, there were a lot of other pranksters in the AWA locker room like Curt Hennig and others who could have been the sick hair-removal culprits. At least we know Brutus Beefcake wasn't responsible. He left AWA around '83.

I guess giving The Rockers this push in the AWA really made it difficult to work with Shawn. Our paths never crossed in the ring at this point in our careers, but I certainly would find out later in mine how difficult he truly was to work with.

CURT HENNIG

Speaking of Curt Hennig as being a prankster of sorts, he too majored in the art of the wrestling rib.

At some point, a former heavyweight boxer, Scott LeDoux, became a part of the AWA locker room. Following his boxing career, LeDoux joined the AWA in the mid-1980s as a color commentator and a referee. Those spots were mostly just a lead up for him to eventually participate in a match against Larry Zbyszko at the AWA Wrestlerock '86 card at the Metrodome in Minneapolis.

Verne thought that it would be a decent idea to have a boxer challenge Larry Zbyszko in some "Boxer vs. Wrestler" matches all around the country. While it looked good on paper, these potentially great Boxer vs. Wrestler matches turned out to be some pretty painfully average Boxer vs. Wrestler matches all around the country.

Not to bust his balls too badly because he is no longer with us, but Scott was a bit of a prick.

One night my knee was bothering me. I had a spot early on in the card and then another one just before the main event. During the intermission, I decided to ice it a bit and just relax a little. LeDoux saw me over in the corner nursing my knee and he scoffed.

"You didn't hurt your knee," LeDoux said.

"Excuse me?" I said.

"You just think you're too good to sign some autographs for the kids," he said, seemingly picking a fight for no real reason at all.

"I sign them all the time," I responded. "It's not that at all."

"I'm just saying. You really shouldn't be here if you can't sign an autograph once in a while. That's part of it, you know."

"What the hell do you know about wrestling?" I said. "You would think someone like you would know about the importance of looking after injuries and all, getting your ass beat in boxing all the time."

The boys in the locker room laughed and started to create a crowd.

LeDoux swallowed hard. I don't know why he felt like picking a fight with me. I was minding my own business, and it wasn't like you had to go out to every town during intermission to sign autographs. Feeling that I attacked his pride, LeDoux decided to respond by knocking my NFL career.

"You did great at college, yeah, but you couldn't do shit with the big guys, you were too afraid and lazy," he said looking for a response from the building audience. "That's why you were a failure. You are still lazy! Same thing I'm seeing here, tonight."

Scott Hall, Curt Hennig, and The Rockers joined what they wanted to be a rank-out session, but there was nothing funny about this. Let me get this straight, we were really getting pissed at each other. There was no humor or passive aggressive sarcasm. We were about to throw down and the boys just thought it was funny.

I stood up and got in his face. I think I smelled alcohol on his breath which is probably why he was being such an asshole.

"Okay. A lazy NFL player who is wearing a Super Bowl ring. Okay."

"Lost that one, right?"

"Want to talk losing? Maybe if you had trained harder, you wouldn't have gotten your ass beat by every boxer you got in the ring with," I said. "Let me rephrase that. Maybe you did really work hard. It must have been pretty hard sucking all those dicks to get matches with 8 or 9 World champions. The sad part is, you couldn't beat nobody because you ARE a nobody."

My face was red. Who the hell was this guy anyhow? I shoved him and was waiting for him to throw the first punch so I could break his leg.

Marty Jannetty stepped in between us and tried to defuse the situation. "Look, Scott. I'll sign autographs, for him."

I shoved Marty out of the way.

"You wanna go?" I asked as it looked like LeDoux was preparing for a fight.

"I think you should sign autographs, Leon!" Curt Hennig chimed in, being typical Curt trying to throw gasoline on a fire. I ignored him.

"I fought a REAL boxer before, I'll fight you," I said.

"I'd love to knock you out," he said, taking off his jacket.

"Yeah, because it would be the first time you ever did."

He rolled up his sleeves. The boxer was steaming.

I was preparing to fight dirty as hell. I was in front of all the boys and had to win. Since it was now coming to blows, I felt a lot of pressure to really put up a fight to show everyone that the wrestler would win over the stupid, cocky boxer, anytime. My mind mapped out my attack. I was going to bite his face, punch his eyes, rip his balls off, whatever I had to do to shut that jerk off up.

Just as we were about to lock horns, Scott Hall and Shawn Michaels jumped in for a pull apart and managed to calm us down. It's a good thing that they did because I was sizing him up and I seriously would have killed him.

The next morning, the AWA stars were rushing in typical fashion to get a quick bite to eat because we all had a flight to catch. They had one of those cook-to-order omelet chef gimmicks in the hotel restaurant, which I loved so I decided to make time. There's always time for a western omelet with sausage, right? *Fuckin' delicious.*

At breakfast, I won't lie. I sat down to eat my eggs with Curt and a few of the others and LeDoux came in like an asshole and sat right down next to me. Rather than to go off by himself, he started right in again on me, jaw-jacking again at my own table.

What an asshole.

I thought about getting up and hitting him in the head with the chef's cooking iron, but I wasn't done eating yet so I decided to ignore him. For an athlete, breakfast is one of the most important meals of the day, *right next to lunch and dinner.* The fucking eggs were delicious and, damn it, I wasn't going to let him ruin them for me.

After breakfast, we all rushed out for the hotel shuttle, threw our bags in the back and headed over to the airport.

Curt Hennig was the last one in the van and the first one out. I didn't think much about it at the time, and that is exactly why I should have. When I went to grab my suit case out of the back, I discovered that my bag was stuck to another one. It had been padlocked together perfectly around the handle with Scott LeDoux's bag.

"Oh, booyees!" he said, perhaps doing a Gene Wilder impersonation from *Blazing Saddles*.

I showed LeDoux what Curt did. We both looked over and watched Curt disappear into the airport, rolling his luggage away with ease.

Because it was the beginning of a pretty long tour, both of our bags were heavy as hell. We had to roll them, side by side almost like we were handcuffed together into and around the airport. As luck would have it, we had to go way into the place and walk all throughout the airport just to check in.

Rather than looking like the two guys who were about to kill each other only twelve hours before, we looked like a couple of dipshits almost holding hands.

In the match "Bull Power versus Scott LeDoux," your real winner: *Curt Hennig.*

STAN HANSEN & TAKING THE BELT

I never did take the AWA belt, but I came pretty close. On March 13, 1986, Verne decided I was really showing even more growth and decided to throw me a bone regarding the current AWA Champion Stan Hansen.

"Hey Leon, we want you to work with Hansen again. This time, we want you to have a good showing against Stan and put the spotlight on you even more," he said. "We think you could have a pretty good future."

It still came to me as a surprise that Stan Hansen was the AWA champ in and of itself, let alone the fact that I was getting a shot at the title so early in the game. At the time, I still didn't know why they had selected Stan to be the face of the company in the first place. Now, don't get me wrong, Hansen as a wrestler was on top of his game and he sure was fun to watch in the AWA. He played his character perfectly. However, from a booking standpoint, it seemed that he was the exact opposite of what the AWA needed in a champion – reliable consistency.

Stan was similar to Bruiser Brody in one regard; he was notorious for being "independent" of promotions. When you look back at the great career of Stan Hansen, you think of Japan, but you don't think of any specific US promotion. That is because, not unlike Brody, he went wherever the money was and often pitted different promoters against each other for leverage. In other words, the bouncing around as a free agent so to speak, was strategic but was more self-serving in that it helped himself more than it ever did any promotion. He kept his name alive in different territories and recognizable amongst the fans, but he was never really around any American promotion long enough to really build stories up off of his name.

Because Stan travelled around so much, it just seemed even stranger that he was chosen to become the face of the AWA in the first place. The AWA at that time was a promotion about to take on the WWF nationally, needing consistency in its television markets.

Stan's only loyalty at the time seemed to fall right in line with his strong ties to Japan. It seemed like the only promoter he would do anything for was for Shohei "Great" Baba in All Japan Pro Wrestling.

Stan and I had our match and he made me look pretty good. It honestly was really good exposure for me. It showed the AWA audience that I was a contender now.

After losing that match, however, I honestly wasn't sure how long Stan was going to continue to hold the title. The contrast from, say, a Rick Martel as the AWA champion was striking. Martel was always available to headline every show and was always the main event on all their TV programs. Stan? Not so much. I sort of predicted that he would only be a part-time champ.

In a few short months after our match, I would be proven to be correct in my prediction. Stan Hansen would soon no longer be champion, but not because he would lose the belt in the ring. Stan decided to walk out on the AWA one night in Denver, Colorado and take the belt with him after he was told he was supposed to lose it.

What I later found out was that Verne originally had put the belt on Stan because Giant Baba offered a good deal of money to make the title reign happen. You see, Baba wanted Stan to tour All Japan as the AWA World Champ so that he could sell more tickets for his promotion, AJPW.

Verne agreed that would be good, but then something happened. Verne noticed that Hansen was not making himself available for all the AWA dates. What happened was, Hansen started cherry-picking bookings. He was only accepting high-paying bookings in places like Japan because of the additional spotlight he was getting as the AWA champion. Because of this, it didn't look to Verne like Stan was going to be available enough to the AWA, despite the fact that it was the AWA title that was giving him the exposure in the first place. Verne was concerned about losing ratings to the growing monster (the WWF) and decided to make a tough decision.

Hansen wasn't told beforehand of his fate that night, before making his long way out to Denver. Verne decided that when Stan got to the venue, he would break the news to him that he was going to have to drop the AWA title to Nick Bockwinkel that night.

When Hansen found out, he was pissed. Hansen knew that Baba wasn't going to like these plans and that it would mess everything up for him in Japan. He had already made plans with Baba to defend the belt on the All Japan tour that was set to take place next week.

As many other wrestlers in the locker room saw that night, I watched Stan get right in Verne's face and say "Fuck you," before walking out and taking the belt with him.

Well, asking Hansen to drop the championship right before the tour was probably not a good idea. If Verne could have just waited and let Hansen do his tour for Baba, then Verne would have gotten *the actual physical belt that represented the title* back when Stan returned from the tour. Then, everything would have all been fine. But I think Verne was operating under a lot of stress added from the new competition created by Vince McMahon.

It hit Verne Gagne like a ton of bricks just how bad things were becoming. The WWF was steamrolling over every territory, and it was easy to see that the AWA was in danger. I think Verne recognized this and he panicked. He decided that he couldn't afford to see the AWA title defended outside of his own territory for any extended period of time. That meant for fewer opportunities to print "Heavyweight Championship Match" on the top of his own promotion's cards which could mean less ticket sales.

Verne decided he needed a safe bet. He needed a trustworthy champion, like his son or Bockwinkel, who he could count on not to jump ship and take the AWA championship title belt with him. With all the talent bailing over to New York, Verne could probably imagine Vince McMahon having one of his boys hold up the AWA title and make a mockery of it. (These thoughts are ironically the same thing that probably went through Vince's mind when Bret Hart was jumping ship to WCW and the whole Montreal Screwjob occurred, which we will touch upon later in the book.)

The real slam by the timing of this move was not to Hansen, but rather to Giant Baba. There was nothing to indicate that All Japan was acting in a way that wasn't living up to their part of the deal. Many would argue that he broke his word. At a time when Gagne needed allies to survive, some would say he double-crossed one of the biggest and most respected promoters on the planet. Baba paid good money for the AWA Champion to come to All Japan, and I suspect Gagne never gave Baba a refund.

Worried that Hansen was not going to always be there for the AWA, Verne was attempting to avoid a potential hole in future AWA storylines that could make his product look inferior to WWF's. Verne then ironically found himself with no champion at all to even drop the title. The AWA ended up having to just hand the title over to the number one contender, Nick Bockwinkel, and let him win it by forfeit.

Stan didn't give two shits. He just left the States as planned that weekend with the title and defended the AWA championship in Japan, like he was still champion. He proved his loyalty to Baba and was paid good money for a successful tour. More tours would continue to come Stan's way because of this loyalty for a long time after that.

Stan was no thief, however.

As soon as he made it home, he mailed the coveted AWA championship belt back to Verne – but not before driving his truck over it, several times.

WINNING A TITLE IN THE AWA

So again, I didn't get to hold an AWA singles title, but I did technically wrestle a singles match in the AWA and win a singles title. Do you follow me?

On an AWA house show, meaning one not being televised on national TV, Verne Gagne had me wrestle a guy by the name of Big Otto Wanz for the CWA championship. The CWA title was the main title of a promotion that Otto ran overseas in Germany.

Otto put me over with his title just to pop the American audience. It was sort of like the opposite of a phantom title change, where a promoter puts the strap on someone new and says that the match happened somewhere when it really didn't.

In this case, as a means to get even more excitement out of the crowd, Otto decided to give me his promotion's title just to add the title-defense element to his match with me. That way when Otto lost, there would be even more response from the fans because it was a high stakes bout. They would be happy to see a hated heel lose.

"Phantom title changes" are pretty much just matches that never really happened. This kind of booking practice is used to "fill in the blanks" of a story and has been around for as long as there have been stories in wrestling. Many of you have probably heard that Pat Patterson won a tournament to crown the first ever Intercontinental Champion. However, it was in a tournament that never happened and in a match that never happened. What happened was the WWF just gave Pat the title to run with and said a tournament had taken place so it made sense that he had the belt.

Jerry "The King" Lawler held the Memphis championship something like 28 times! Many of the title changes occurred just to invoke a crowd response and then a "phantom title change" would happen by the next show to reset whatever had occurred on the previous one. This wasn't unusual practice in territorial wrestling promotions back in a day and age when the internet and smart phones didn't exist.

The same time I had my CWA title match with Otto in the AWA, there was a very famous forced phantom title change in the NWA. Rick Rude and Manny Fernandez were the NWA tag team champions at the time. Then, all of the sudden, another McMahon-induced casualty occurred. Rick Rude jumped ship with no notice to the WWF. Scrambling to fix their storytelling, the NWA went through their archives and found an old tape of the Rock & Roll Express beating Rude & Fernandez in a non-title match. This footage was taped months earlier in South Carolina, mind you, but that didn't matter. They just cut new commentary and passed it off as a legit title switch from Spokane, WA where they weren't even running at the time!

A few years later in another weird scenario, the Freebirds lost the belts at a WCW TV taping a few days before they even won them at a PPV.

"Dropping the belts around the horn" was another move where promoters would book the same championship match in every city of a tour. The champ would then lose the belt over and over again in every town on the circuit, just reenacting the same match everywhere to get that great crowd reaction they wanted from a title change. Then at the end of the tour, an announcement was made on TV about the titles changing hand, but with no mention where it happened. Anybody who saw a title change would think the commentators were referring to their town! This would also likely increase ticket sales because anything could happen at your venue.

Back in 1979, Bob Backlund dropped the WWF title in Japan to a guy who would eventually play a major role in my career, Antonio Inoki. This was a huge deal in Japan, but in America, it wasn't even mentioned. Because of this, New Japan wrestling was pissed at WWF and there were major behind-the-scenes political ramifications.

With me winning the CWA championship, I knew going in that the change didn't really count on the books or anything. Because there was no internet, nobody in Germany would ever know it happened. It didn't matter to Otto that I would never get to defend the title in Germany. He would just return to his home country and his fans would never be the wiser. If there were any question, he could have always just used the phantom title change idea and say he won it back again off of me the next night.

Even though nobody overseas would ever really know about me winning the CWA championship that night, the match did count in at least one way. My match with Otto impressed him so much as a German promoter that I would soon find myself flying over to Germany to wrestle for that title for real.

CHAPTER 6 – CWA IN AUSTRIA

Big Otto Wanz worked with me when I was just starting out, but he was by no means an unaccomplished rookie like I was at the time. Otto was an Austrian professional wrestler who had made his debut back in 1978, coming from a strong man competition background. Before what would become an impressive wrestling career, he held several tough man championships and world records for tearing telephone books. He was a really big name across Germany and around the world whose most famous international opponents included Antonio Inoki and André the Giant. Even today, Arnold Schwarzenegger credits Otto Wanz as being a huge influence on his own career.

As a super-heavyweight, Otto wrestled with a big-man style because of his size. I remember one time meeting him at an AWA show. Otto was set to compete in a battle royal where they, unfortunately, didn't have any ring stairs. Otto couldn't easily just jump into the ring. So he decided to just march around and took some shots at a few of the boys. Then, the grizzled veteran turned around and made his way back to the locker room. He never even got in the ring! The boys loved him so much and had so much respect for him that nobody ever told to Verne.

Being a former American Wrestling Association champion, he was well-respected by the people I was working for, so it was a big deal when Otto asked to continue working with me, even after he was set to leave the states and return to Austria. It meant "I had something." It is also important to note that Otto had something, too; he had money.

Verne and Otto did some business together. By that, I mean there was a rumor out there that money exchanged hands. Otto paid Verne $40 grand to be the AWA champion so he could take the title back overseas with him and play it up.

Being the AWA champion meant a lot over in Europe, so it was quite an investment for Otto. Many people behind the scenes thought it looked a little off at the time. Wrestling historians will tell you that Verne had all these giant guys like Hulk, André, and Big John Studd, but there was a short little stint with a shorter guy named Otto; an Austrian guy who won the American Wrestling Association title!

It is an understatement to say that Otto didn't get a lot of mileage out of that 41-day AWA Championship title run. He would plug the hell out of his former-AWA champion status for the rest of his life.

As odd as it sounds, back then, Otto and I really clicked. He liked working with me so much that he wanted to take me back to Europe with him! So eventually, he asked Verne Gagne if I could also work for his promotion, the CWA (Catch Wrestling Association) in Austria and Germany. Otto thought I would translate to some good money for his promotion so he invested in me by adding his promotion to my AWA contract. Behind the scenes, he greased Verne good to not only allow me to leave AWA but also to get Verne to convince me to want to go over to Germany.

They say that Otto then dropped another $30,000 or so on buying my rights from Verne to go over and work for Otto and his promotion, the CWA. Verne knew I wanted more dates so he knew I would be interested in the deal.

"Leon. This is quite an opportunity," Verne said. "Worldwide exposure. And once in Germany, you will wrestle every night of the week and they even have seasons over there. So they will fly you over, and you can actually live there for like 8 months. Then they will fly you home, and then back over again."

I didn't say anything. I was making good money. Verne was using me on all the cards by then. I was in the main event against Brody and Hansen, from time to time. At first, I didn't really like the idea of going to wrestle in some foreign country that I knew nothing about.

"It would mean really good money, Leon," he said. "More than you are making here."

"How much, you think?" I asked.

"About three grand a week."

It didn't take a whole lot of math or more convincing. After that, I was off to the CWA promotion of Germany and Austria.

THE BLUE DANUBE WALTZ

When I got off the plane, one of Otto's guys, Karloff, showed up and had a car waiting for me. Karloff gave me a BMW that could easily drive 170 miles an hour on the Autobahn. The thing was dirt cheap, too.

The place Otto got me was also really something. I was set up in a beautiful guest house, like a bed and breakfast, right on the Blue Danube River. Now, I don't know if "Bed & Breakfast" is really the correct term for this place, but it is the closest thing I can think of.

I was living in a huge mansion of a place with the actual family that owned it who also rented out 8 or 9 other rooms like mine to others. The funny thing is that it wasn't at all like a hotel. It was something else like a hybrid. I had a shared toilet, but my room was locked up, isolated and all mine. The lower level downstairs wasn't a kitchen, but it always had cold beer and sandwiches and customers who would wander by and stop in just for the food.

Now, the really unheard of thing here in America was that my breakfast and dinner were both included in my rent price. If I was hungry, I would just go downstairs and I could eat whatever I wanted and not pay. The only thing I really had to pay for was the beer and let me tell you, that beer was worth its weight in gold and worth paying for at any price.

The downstairs level was sort of like a bar, but a bar where people lived and would migrate into for meals. Anyhow, the food was fantastic and every night, I would have four or five of those big strong Austrian beers and get a buzz on like you wouldn't believe.

The Blue Danube River strip was a party place with beautiful night clubs. I was already with my future wife, but she was back home in the States in Colorado. We weren't married yet and she didn't come over for the first month or so. I mean, I missed her a little, but the absence of the mother of my child made the place that much better. There were tons of sexy women everywhere!

Let me tell you about these women in Austria. They were beautiful, but their taste in men wouldn't indicate that. All I can say is that the Austrian women really loved their men big over there. Being heavy was a status symbol. The bigger the guy is, the more money he must have – *so the more desirable he would be.*

I guess it is an "old country" thing. Back in the castle days, the king would eat and eat all day. Keeping the weight on showed he was wealthy. Slaves and laborers, on the other hand, would be fit and/or thin from having to work all day. Therefore, the financial stability of the fat guy was more appealing to a woman.

This short little "fat guy" was practically 400 pounds, and that put me into King Pimp status for the first time in my life. That's right. For the first time ever, I was a sex symbol. I was en vogue.

That first week or so riding solo could have been like Sodom and Gomorrah for me. If I was there much longer alone, I was surely going to get a woman pregnant. Those Austrian women were so much more sexually forward and mature than American women are. They were unlike any women in the world. I transformed into some kind of high-roller, overnight. I was a big deal with the ladies.

The first night in Austria, I wrestled in a place that also doubled as a pub during the day. Otto always had venders on hand with crazy deals and made perhaps more money selling food and beer that he did with the wrestling.

I was the bad guy, but it was the girls who were giving me the evil eye. After my first match there that night, I got myself cleaned up and just headed around the building to the bar. I'll tell you what, boy, it didn't take long at all. A girl came right over and sat on the bench next to me. I don't know if she was a hungry German or what, but she immediately reached right for MY German sausage.

"Man, it is easy to pick up girls here," I said to myself as she tried to *knock the worst* out of my Knockwurst right there in the bar. Just like their highways, there was no speed limit to how fast they would go. She was practically throwing herself on me and she wouldn't be the last.

So each and every night of that first month or so, it was the same thing. I would wrestle, hit the pub and then hit the sack. I would get my fill of beer and women advances, then wake up early the next morning for some breakfast sausage action and rush right over to the pool.

It was such a weird thing there in Austria. I would enter the scene as the fat guy at the pool and I would take off my shirt. The next thing I knew, girls would flock right to my side and take their shirts off, too! That's right. Random girls would seek me out, sit right next to me and just take their tops off to sunbathe nude, giving me the best seat in the house. And that's not all, either.

Some of those hot sunbathing Austrian ladies would even ask me to put lotions on their backs... *their backs and their fronts!*

Boy, let me tell you. People might say that maybe I didn't like to "do the job," but that there was one job I didn't mind doing.

Quite often, I would tell some of the boys that I would meet them at noon over at the ring. Being the wrestler from America, some of the Austrian guys would look forward to training with me. I was the hand-picked guy with international experience, after all. The thing is, even though I would promise to be there, I almost never managed to make it happen. I can only imagine that one of the wrestlers waiting for me might say to another looking at his watch, "Hey man. Where is Leon?

"He is over at the pool again. I don't know why."

"Must really like swimming, I guess."

When my wife finally showed up, it was a good thing. As soon as Jesse was old enough to fly at around five weeks old, she dropped everything and came to be with me in Austria. Once she was there, she got a real taste of what the business was like. I remember her saying that we were "living like circus people," and she was right. I had my own trailer and when we were on tour, we were living out of it in a different city every night.

That trailer was hell too, I'll tell you. It wasn't built for a guy like me. I couldn't even get through the narrow walkway to the little bedroom area in the back. I was just too big. So what we did was switch out the living room space with the bedroom, and I just never went back there. That was life in Austria, in and out for almost two and a half years living like gypsies.

I remember one night, we were shooting promos at a venue. My wife was entertaining the baby. She kiddie corner to where they were filming me in the ring, sitting on the mat with Jesse. While I was being filmed, Jesse decided it was time to take his first steps, when he started heading right for me. That's right. My kid's first steps were in a wrestling ring.

SOME BULL
One of the first things Otto did was toughen up my name. Verne had called me "Baby Bull," borrowing from my college football nickname "Bull" that I was already known for. "Baby Bull" as a moniker, however, I didn't like very much. Keeping "Baby" was something Verne wanted to do to help get me over as a fan favorite, but I thought it really weakened my image as a professional wrestler. Babies weren't tough. They were the exact opposite. Otto also agreed "baby" made me sound green or weak. With me coming in as the big, bad, American rule breaker, people may not think I was so "big and bad" if they read my name on a poster and could imagine me fighting in a diaper.

Otto wanted to build the promotion around me and make me into a big tough monster. He changed my nickname to Leon "Bull Power" White and off we went.

The audience ate it up. They really hated me.

The wrestling wasn't hard out there at all. It was a cakewalk. I didn't get my ass beat up and handed to me by Otto either like I always did with Brody and Hansen. In fact, there was even less of a need for rest holds because of the breaks. European matches had built in breaks designed right into the construct of their rules. Their pro wrestling bouts had a number of rounds that were like 4 minutes of wrestling and then one full minute off for a water break, much like the way the matches worked in boxing.

There was an established CWA rule, however, where a wrestler could by no means interact or lay a finger on his opponent between rounds during the break. If he did so and was caught, he would be fined heavily. Otto and I decided to use it to our advantage and to *actually make more money.*

Looking for a way to supplement my income overseas, I developed a pretty neat way to make an extra bonus in my weekly salary that could earn me a few extra thousand dollars a show when done correctly.

I was the big, bad American foil to Otto and German fans hated me just simply because of where I was from, so when I was able to pull a fast one on him, they would just hate me all the more. As the bad guy, what I would do is sneak over to Otto's corner behind the referee's back a few times and tease getting a cheap shot in on Otto. By the time I actually did it, the place would be on fire with rage.

I can't explain how angry they would get. It really was white heat; red heat meant they hated you, white heat meant they wanted to kill you for real. The audience would get so pissed at the moment I finally hit Otto behind the ref's back. It was always like no other moment on the show. To make matters worse for the fans, the referee would never see what I was doing, and I would not get fined for my actions.

I would do this same cheap shot thing two or three times between rounds and each time, the referee would never see it. Finally, between the last two rounds when the referee would appear to not be looking, Otto would sneak over to my corner to finally get his turn at a cheap shot on me.

The crowd would then cheer, but their response would be a dead giveaway to the ref that something outside the rules was happening. The referee would then see Otto in the act of revenge, and he was the one who would get caught and fined.

The next part was great. It always worked because of the type of people who were in the audience. The Germans and the Austrians were both proud people, full of ego. And if you got a couple of stiff beers into them, they would be even more ready to stand up for whatever they believed to be right. After Otto had been caught for his cheap shot on Bull Power, the referee would then whisper and motion to the announcer to make a statement.

The announcer would shake his head and then make a reluctant announcement. "Due to the unsportsmanlike conduct of Otto Wanz, he will now be fined one thousand marks for his actions. If this fine is not paid, he will be disqualified, lose the match and is in danger of being suspended indefinitely."

The audience booed.

They threw cups in the ring after hearing that Otto was to be fined for his actions. They screamed in horror at the injustice before their eyes. The announcement of the fine would particularly infuriate the male population in the audience who would then want nothing more than to help Otto come out on top.

Who needs a Kickstarter or GoFundMe campaign? A plant in the audience was also never needed to get the crowdfunding ball rolling, speaking in German of course. Like clockwork, one fan would always stand when the light bulb flickered above his head with a bright idea: Perhaps to impress his woman he would reach into his pockets and yell, "I will help pay that man's fine!" That is all it took and it worked every time. After the first donation, another fan would immediately stand up to also flaunt his riches in front of his girlfriend or wife. He would then yell, "I will help too!"

Taking advantage of the German ego was easy. After the first two or so, we would then have the timekeeper shrug and then pass around his hat. Fans would run up to the front row from all over the hall and practically empty their wallets in the hat.

The one thousand marks fine would be easily paid in full in a matter of moments, but who was counting? Most often times we would extend the 1 minute break between the final rounds to 5 or 10 minutes so we could collect three, four, or even five thousand marks to pay off the fine.

At the end of the match, Otto would win, but we were really both winners. We would dump out the timekeeper's hat onto the locker room floor and split the money.

We did some great business there. CWA was operating out of what looked like a giant circus tent, and by the way we were working the audience, I guess you could say there was a carnival-like aspect to it. Some would think that there wouldn't be a substantial amount of money to be made at such a venue, but there really was. The tickets were high and people were paying it. One of the hottest crowds was at a show on the gorgeous Blue Danube strip which had a great tourist attraction element to it that commanded money. Some people came there just for the hotdogs alone to watch the show. The location was perfect and we made a lot of money there.

March 22, 1987, is an important date for me. It marks the day that I REALLY won my first major championship, the CWA World Heavyweight Championship, and this time it counted. Otto was getting older and having some health issues, so he decided to take things a little easier. Being impressed with my work, he gave me the honor of ending his reign of nearly nine years with the CWA title and trusted me enough to allow the title to change in the United States.

I defeating Otto Wanz in my own neck of the woods, Denver, Colorado.

After that, I held the title for about four months, before making good on my promise to drop it back to Otto on July 11 in Graz, Austria. In December 1987, I participated in a tournament, for "The Bremen Catch Cup" in Germany. There I defeated Rambo in the finals, to win my first major tournament.

After winning that cup there in Graz, a tourist of sorts made his way to the ring. He had watched me at the show and what I didn't know at the time was that the strange Japanese guy who was sticking out in the German crowd like a sore thumb, was also there more than just for entertainment. *He was scouting me.*

Masao "Tiger" Hattori was a very well-known referee in Japan and he was on a mission. After the show, he stopped by and Otto let him into the locker room to see me.

Tiger waited until he had me alone and then shook my hand. "It looks as if you are doing well here. We have a mutual friend of ours that recommends you to Antonio Inoki who says you could make good money at a tour over in New Japan."

"Inoki?"

"He has an offer for you."

CHAPTER 7 – BIRTH OF BIG VAN VADER

Tiger Haitori the famous ref said, "When you are done with Otto, you should come over for our January tour that Inoki is setting up right now. He wants you for 20 weeks."

"Wow, 20 weeks? That sounds great," I said, excited as I was only a few years in with the wrestling business. Then, it hit me. "Oh Tiger, I'm sorry. I wish I knew of this before. I already accepted a deal with Baba. I couldn't go if I wanted to, now."

Before this chance meeting, I had already reached out to Stan Hansen over at All Japan. He pulled some strings to get me on my first AJPW tour that was to last about five weeks and, at that time, you couldn't go and work for the competition. Working for the other promotion was highly frowned upon, if not even legally against the contract that you signed.

So, I had to politely refuse. I originally had talked to my wife about the All Japan Baba deal and we both agreed five weeks was pretty long in itself, let alone 20, because of our current situation. We wanted me to be home more with the new baby and all.

Tiger wasn't taking no for an answer. He called me back a day or so later. When he told me the amount of money they would likely be offering for me, he said I simply could not refuse.

"Wow," I said to Tiger on the phone. "It sounds like someone really likes me over there."

The person most instrumental in bringing me into Japan was Masa "Mister" Saito. He was really whispering into the ears of Inoki at New Japan and telling them I was perfect for some mysterious "tour" they were planning. I considered it a great honor to be recommended by Saito. Being an American wrestler who they considered tough enough to compete in Japan was quite a compliment.

You see, in Japan at that time, they wrestled in a strong style that Americans were not used to where all the moves were executed really snug. Getting the nudge from Masa Saito was a compliment to me, as he himself was one of the toughest men in the sport.

He truly was a badass.

Saito's first match out of prison was for the AWA. This came immediately after the legendary debacle of when he and Ken Patera threw a giant rock through a McDonald's window for not serving them late at night. Saito's first match back win the ring was in a six-man tag against Scott Hall, Curt Hennig, and myself. Saito was tagging with Larry Zbyszko and somebody else, I'm not sure exactly who it was.

Wrestling Saito was like trying to wrestle a moose. Punching him was like punching a cement wall. It actually hurt your hand. He was very well built.

I remember the very move that impressed Saito. I gorilla-pressed Saito up in the air and held him there. I held him there forever. Then, I turned to each side of the ring so everyone could see him really well before I slammed him down hard to the mat. He thought the whole image of the move must have looked spectacular to the crowd, and it was one that would go over very well in Japan. This sequence of moves essentially got me my job in New Japan, leading to the birth of Big Van Vader.

After the match, we had some drinks together and he told me about how he was getting ready to go back over to Japan now, after being let out early for good behavior. I felt bad for him because it seemed like Ken Patera was the real instigator, but if you are driving the getaway car when someone robs a bank – you both go to jail.

Saito said, "I was in the wrong place at the wrong time, and knew the only way out would be to do everything they said."

He played it cool and only did a very small portion of his sentence. We got to talking about his future plans and he told me about leaving to work for Inoki soon in New Japan.

"I will put in good word for you," he said.

I just had no idea he actually would.

Fast forward a couple of years to Germany. I hadn't heard or thought of Saito for some time when Masao "Tiger" Hattori randomly showed up to Otto's wrestling promotion for our first meeting.

After that phone call, Tiger got permission again to come and watch some more of my matches for a whole week. I guess Tiger told Otto it was for the possibility of booking me when I had some down time from Germany. I'm not sure "down time" was actually Tiger's real plan, but it pulled the competition aspect out of it, so Otto was more than happy to help me get some more work.

Another night after a show, Tiger caught up with me again, this time in person.

"So, did you get to speak with your wife?"

"Yes, Tiger and it looks real good," I said. I was still skeptical, however, as to why they were doing so much to bring a virtual no-name talent in, like myself. They were really bending over backwards. "But let me ask you this, why me?"

"Inoki sent Saito from Japan back to the AWA. He looked for you for some time," he said. "Saito described you and Inoki thinks you are perfect for this tour and has some big plans," he said.

It was true. I had moved over to Germany and must have just missed his return.

"Big plans. Okay, well, if you think you can make it happen."

"Done," he said. After one call from Tiger, he finished brokering the deal to get me out of the five-week contract with AJPW for Giant Baba.

THE CREATON OF BIG VAN VADER

Eventually, I finished up in Germany and found a break in the schedule. I promised Otto I would return, and I was off to Japan. Once I arrived for the All Japan tour that was being offered to me in 1987, Masa Saito told me there was also another offer on the table, so I hopped in his little car and took a ride to NJPW's training facility. Saito brought us up into Antonio Inoki's office, owner of NJPW and also one of the largest, most respected name wrestlers ever to wrestle in the country and the world.

Antonio Inoki was huge in Japan. He was nothing less than legendary. He had been undefeated for 8 years at this time. His popularity made him like the Japanese version of the early WWF Hulk Hogan. Fans around the world knew him from his famous fight with Muhammad Ali, which broadcasted to 34 countries and reached an audience of an estimated 1.4 billion people.

Inoki was a smart man, but he knew that his very long reign was starting to go stale with the audience. He knew that "winds of change" were happening and his competition was closing the gap. NJPW was still doing very well, but Giant Baba's AJPW was becoming the hotter promotion by pushing diversity.

Baba was bringing in guys like DiBiase, Brody, Hansen, Snuka, the Ortons, and the Funks. Some of Baba's cards were 50/50, featuring half Japanese workers and half other wrestlers from around the world. The Japanese wrestling fans were eating Baba's booking formula up. It was very rare that you would see anyone who was not Japanese walking on the street, so seeing just a different race alone in the ring was special.

Inoki decided he needed to shake things up to continue to see success. Now, I didn't know it at the time, but Inoki had already created a plan to do just that. He wanted to cast the right person to take on a new role that would ultimately reshape his entire promotion. The idea was to create a new "super wrestling villain" who would be larger-than-life and practically unbeatable. To make this happen, Inoki decided to create the over-the-top character out of a cartoon.

For the first sketches of what "Big Van Vader" would look like, Inoki brought in a very popular artist named Go Nagai, who was known for his Japanese manga comic books. Strangely enough, this was not Nagai's first venture in creating a likeness for a professional wrestler. Nagai was also the same artist that drew a character in one of his books that would be used for the likeness of Jushin Thunder Liger. (See Nagai below with Liger, today.)

Go Nagai's backstory for Big Van Vader was inspired by different elements of Japanese mythology. He cobbled together two different fables of folklore that people who grew up in Japan might recognize. This created an awesome mythical character.

The "Vader" part of the name came from the story of a Samurai warrior named "Wada," which also meant "father." Wada Yoshimori had great strength and once defeated the "Lord of Hell" to open a pathway to heaven with his son Asahina Yoshihide. ("Wada," coincidentally, was also the same name-source that George Lucas used for his main villain in Star Wars, Darth Vader, meaning the "Dark Father.")

Big Van Vader's backstory had him connected to the gods, not unlike Hercules of Greek mythology. In this case, however, Vader was a feared Samurai warrior from an ancient Japanese tribe. During this time, if two towns had a dispute, they would take their very best fighters and leave them off on a little deserted island for a fight to the finish. This way, the whole village then didn't have to fight each other in war, losing many people in battle. Each town just simply sent one person; their very best to represent them. The two warriors would then fight day and night, non-stop, in a "last man standing match" scenario until only one man survived. Whoever won the battle determined which village won the dispute. Then, the warrior returned to his village and was looked at as a hero.

Vader was the very best of these village warriors. He won every time. The last time around, Vader fought his final battle for 72 hours straight, overcoming every obstacle his competitor threw his way. However, there was to be no winner. Both warriors ended up dying at each other's feet. This "Samurai Island Battle" that Go Nagai used for Big Van Vader was most likely borrowed from the famous "Musashi Miyamoto Duel" that took place on Ganryu-jima Island. Antonio Inoki recalled hearing similar stories like that as a child and loved Nagai's twist on it. He was sold on having an unstoppable samurai in the ring that would only be stopped by death, so after buying the likeness from the comic book creator, it was on. *It would soon be Vader Time.*

Inoki had his sights on bringing in a big American man to take on a live action role depicting this 5th century Samurai Warrior. Two wrestlers that Inoki initially looked at to fill play the part of Big Van Vader were the Ultimate Warrior and Psycho Sid Vicious. These options didn't pan out so Masa Saito stepped in to help him in casting. Saito explained that I was perfect and would be even better than the other two options. Inoki bought it, and they decided to bring me in for a meeting to offer me the gimmick.

We shook hands, and Inoki sat me down.

"Let me show you pictures of who we will call, *Big Van Vader,*" said the translator.

First, he showed me the cartoon rendition of the character put together from Japanese folklore. Then, he showed me some rough sketches of the character they were asking me to portray. He explained that Big Van Vader "as a professional wrestler" would have a black wrestling mask and be very evil and mysterious. Finally, he showed me the designs for a massive, elephant-like metallic headpiece that shot fire.

It was nothing short of awesome.

To add the icing to the cake, Inoki said, "You know Leon, this is extremely important for New Japan. We are talking about making you unstoppable. You would be the new number one person in the company, even above me."

He was willing to give up his eight year winning streak to help create his vision of Big Van Vader.

Can you imagine a brand new character, a virtual nobody, coming in at the height of The Rock's career and beat him out of nowhere? When you talk about Hulk Hogan, Steve Austin and The Rock in America, Inoki in Japan was the same thing and hadn't been beaten in almost a decade. That is the kind of popularity that Inoki had at this time.

I looked at the vision he had for me. It was perfect, and I knew it could take me to the next level. He then offered me, still a rookie, mind you, even more money than Baba was offering and 20 weeks' worth of paydays! I really wanted the money because the wife and I were planning on building a house back in the States.

"I would love to do it, but I'm afraid I'm already under contract with All Japan," I said.

I wasn't trying to negotiate at all with them. I had to still honor my first contract with Baba, and he had a clause that allowed him to extend my contract at the end of the five weeks.

Now at this point, Baba and Inoki rarely worked together. They were competitors, after all, but I guess I was to be a rare case and an exception to this rule. Apparently, the Japanese do business a little different though from time to time. Some kind of money was traded behind the scenes and a talent trade went down. I was officially in the NJPW and I was officially about to become "Big Van Vader."

RIOT IN SUMO HALL

It was December 27, 1987. New Japan Pro Wrestling had a sold-out show that night in the world famous Sumo Hall, in Tokyo, Japan. The night had finally come for the debut of Big Van Vader.

I was booked on a show at Sumo Hall and hanging out in the locker room as usual with no assignment. Essentially, I was just being paid to be there, in case I was needed. I didn't know what was about to happen when Inoki called me over to speak with him.

I was ushered into Inoki's dressing room by one of the young boys and I laughed a little. There, I saw what may have seemed odd to some out of context, but it really wasn't. Inoki had another one of the young training wrestlers putting his socks on him. This was a way to teach them respect. Inoki smiled back, then got serious, quickly.

"This is what I want," Inoki said. "I want you to just rush in after my match. Punch me in the face just as hard as you can. Now, I don't want you to knock me out, but I want you to break my nose and cut my lip, whatever you need to do. You are a monster."

We hadn't talked in a few weeks about it, but it was finally time.

It was Vader time.

He wanted a monster and that is what he was going to get. I nodded.

"It is very important now how you go out there. It is very important how you handle yourself in the ring to make sure this works," he said.

"I understand," I said, nodding my head.

After a winning a hard match with Riki Chōshū, Antonio Inoki tried to catch his breath as I got ready to shift gears into attack mode.

In Japanese, my new manager, Takeshi Kitano, Introduced me as being, "The New Crown Jewel of The Puroresu Gundan Stable."

The audience gasped.

Before Inoki could even breathe after a hard-fought victory, we were doing the unthinkable – we were demanding a match from their already exhausted hero and we were demanding it to happen now.

Antonio Inoki was a proud man. He was known to never back down from anyone and had to accept.

The match started. I charged him and attacked. There was already a bit of commotion coming from the usually silent Japanese audience.

My first couple of punches were not very stiff. I was still new in New Japan and probably lacked a little confidence to bring the beating on the promotion's owner who was paying me. I think Inoki sensed this and urged me to hit harder.

"Shoot," Inoki said, over the building roar of the huge Japanese audience. "Shoot fight!"

Big mistake.

I knew in order to give him what he wanted, it was going to really hurt, but I complied.

Inoki himself was known for his "bitch slap." Fans, politician and celebrities still today line up for miles to have Inoki slap them in the face in his signature insulting maneuver. What I threw was no bitch slap. I hit him so hard that it hurt my hand. It probably hurt my mother's hand, too. I could really throw a right. After the right hand connected, I threw a left in his face, too.

Boom! Boom! BOOM!

…and then an uppercut.

Inoki looked dazed. I pushed him into the corner and decided to check on him.

"You okay?" I asked.

"Yes," Inoki said. "More shoot!"

He wanted more, so I continued to beat the hell out of him, just as he wished. After all, he was the boss. I clubbed him in the face. Then, I gorilla pressed NJPW's hero up high for all to see.

I threw him out of the ring, then went out to get him. I followed up with a sweet "Davey Boy Smith-style hang time" suplex and a powerslam. I was still pretty green and hadn't really perfected the Vader arsenal of assault yet, but it didn't matter.

"You okay?" I asked.

"Yes," he said, maybe with a little less passion than the first time. "More!"

Inoki wasn't a big guy, but he was a very skilled fighter, trained in the martial arts. He was a shoot wrestler that could have grabbed a hold of me at any time and broke my wrist or broke my ankle, but he showed absolutely no offense. He wanted me to look like a monster. He was passing the torch to me. He just kept taking the shots.

"You okay?" I asked.

No answer.

"You okay?" I asked again.

"Oh man," Inoki said.

After the third time of checking in on him with some of the hardest punches I could throw, there was a long pause. What was supposed to be a six or seven minute match lasted only about three before Inoki called for the finish.

"Take home," he finally said.

I finished destroying him, and the match was over.

After the match, however, we decided to further the onslaught to add insult to injury. The fans watched in horror, as I continued to beat on Inoki in the corner after the bell had already sounded. They rang it again a few times, just for good measure.

The fans were pissed. It was white heat, man, real anger. Antonio Inoki had already competed in two brutal matches before this fight and they couldn't believe that a crazy unknown monster was now continuing to make a statement by pounding on their fallen hero.

Next, all the young boys stormed the ring. Then, one at a time, I tossed each one of those "young boys" out onto each one of their "young boy" heads.

Now, we knew that the audience was not going to like it, but we had no idea to what extent of dislike we would get. Usually, Japanese fans are very reserved, but not on this night. I ended an 8-year streak in the most horrible way they could imagine. This action led the Inoki fans to riot. They wanted blood; *my blood.*

If you ever saw the opening credits for ECW, there was a clip where the fans threw all their chairs into the ring during a Terry Funk and Cactus Jack match. In Sumo Hall, there are no chairs. The arena had elevated risers, like steps, and the fans sat on each riser on pillows. So, there were no wooden or steel chairs that fans could throw in the ring. However, the creative Japanese fans were so pissed that their hero was defeated in such a disrespectful fashion that they created a new weapon.

Now everyone in Japan smoked, so they literally lit their seat cushions on fire and flung them at me like Frisbees. It looked like hell was blazing all around me.

I looked at the ref, Masao Tiger Hattori. "Is this like some kind of tradition, or are these guys really mad at me?"

"No. They are really mad, and we need to get you out of here, and now!" Tiger replied.

If having to dodge dozens of fireballs wasn't enough, a fury of fans began to storm the ring. Fortunately for me, security held them off just long enough to usher me in the right direction. I sidestepped a massive pig-pile of pissed people just in time. I fought my way out of the arena, dodging flying sodas and ducking flaming pillows.

When I finally made it back to the locker room, I was alive and I was ecstatic. It was the Super Bowl all over for me again, but this time I had won and had found a winning gimmick at the same time.

Saito ran up to me and cut my celebration short. "You got to get out of here. Fans are going to be back here in the locker room at any minute and they want your ass."

I grabbed my gear and jumped in the car.

The monster, Big Van Vader, was born.

After the riot we started and the burning of the cushions, NJPW was immediately banned by the owners of Sumo Hall; its home arena. The ban lasted two full years and wasn't rescinded until 1989. But that didn't matter. For close to four years, despite the fact that we were not in Sumo Hall, we were sold out everywhere, no matter where we went.

The plan worked. Business picked up and Inoki was then able to afford more names from overseas. This allowed us to compete with All Japan Pro Wrestling. Both of the big promotions did really well.

Inoki and I made great money together, and it wasn't always from me beating on him.

If you ever wondered how I got that big scar on my upper left arm, it was of course in a match with Antonio Inoki. We had a spot planned outside the ring where I was attempting to hit him with a ring hook, with Inoki reversing it. The timing of the swing was a little off, and he wailed me in the arm with it. It was supposed to hit flat, but it spun and nailed me with the point, just right. It flanked me right open like a butterfly shrimp, and I needed 52 stitches that night to close it up.

THE BIG HELMET

One thing that really got me over in New Japan was my mysterious look. After my debut, I added a black spandex mask with red lightning bolts that matched my tights, but that was only a subtle touch. The first thing they really noticed was the mask I wore over the mask, the big helmet.

Inoki had a huge Samaria Warrior elephant head-like helmet made for my entrance that shot steam. It stood about a foot above my head and made me look like a cybernetic machine. When I first saw him take it out of the box, I didn't really know what it was – but I already knew I liked it. I had never seen anything like it in wrestling and knew it would set me apart from all the rest.

Antonio Inoki explained that the helmet was supposed to resemble the battle armor that a certain Samurai warrior once wore. Inoki's creation was funny, though, because it was an attempt to materialize ancient Samurai armor based on pictures from a kid's anime cartoon. The cartoon's depiction, however, was an overly-exaggerated mockup of real historical armor. If the armor was proportionately real, nobody could have ever fought in it and its weight probably would have flattened the fighter's head!

My big iron helmet had a head piece, two shoulder pads, and a chest/back protection plate. It looked like the top portion of an elaborate Transformer-like suit of armor, but more evil. Because it was built off of stylized cartoon drawings, it was both ancient and futuristic-looking at the same time.

It wasn't just a costume, either. If anyone asked, I always told them that it was a magical mythological god that blew smoke. In reality, it was a pretty complicated contraption. It had eyes that lit up. It had two CO_2 tanks built in underneath and a motorized engine system in the back that shot up colored steam. It also had a wireless microphone set up so I could talk to the audience over the intercom in the arena while wearing it on my way to the ring. It was almost like a remote controlled robot that did stuff.

In order to animate it and bring it to life, Inoki assigned one of the wrestlers, Black Cat, to go incognito ringside at every show. Black Cat did a great job getting as close to the helmet as possible to use the remote without being noticed by the fans.

It was a really big piece of equipment, and fortunately for me, I didn't have to lug it around to every show with me. The NJPW ring crew kept it on their truck and always had it waiting for me before the curtain. They were great about it. The only interaction I ever really had with it was the few minutes before my entrance when I needed it.

Before my match, one of the young boys would take the helmet out of its custom box and wheel it over to me. They would then test it out to make sure it was working for me. In the event that Black Cat wasn't available, I would sometimes have to show whoever the helmet handler was for the night a quick remote lesson if needed. But normally the ring crew had everything under control and I just needed to slam that bad boy on.

I'll tell you what though, just wearing that helmet was tough. You could see straight on, but that was about it. There were no peripherals. You couldn't see to the left and you couldn't see to the right. The blind spots that the mask created were a big problem for me in Japan, especially because of the rough character that was supposed to be underneath.

Despite the fact that I had decent security with me on my way to the ring, little Japanese kids hated my gimmick. They would run up to me as fast as they could while I was wearing the helmet and I couldn't see them. Nine times out ten, the security guards couldn't see them, either.

Then, out of nowhere, these little 12 or 13-year-old kids who were all into karate would jump me. It was typically a dark arena with no security rails. They would kick me in the knee and kick me in the back of the legs – all because they didn't like Big Van Vader. They really hated the character and more than once, my leg would buckle from a little punk trying to be Bruce Lee.

Those little bastards hated me. They would try to kill me for just coming to the ring, and I hadn't even done anything yet! It wasn't even just their kicks that got to me. Sometimes they brought foreign objects.

One time I remember all too clearly, I was walking to the ring hamming it up while in character, when all of the sudden… ZAP!

My knee gave out.

Through the opening in the helmet, I got a glimpse of a tiny, rag-headed kid making off in the audience laughing his ass off. He made eye contact with me and I knew he did it. What I didn't know however was what had hit me so hard at the time. Just before the kid disappeared into the swarm of 20,000 plus fans, the little bastard held up his weapon to show me.

"You little shit," I said under my breath, rubbing my knee. I took a shot to the leg from two sticks connected with a chain.

The kid swung one of the clubs over his head like a helicopter before flying off into the stands.

Really? Fucking nunchucks?

I didn't complain, however. It was part of the job. A couple of shin bruises were small prices to pay, but boy, those hurt like a bitch!

HELMET CEREMONY

I treated the big helmet like it was alive and had a mind of its own. It lit up. It blew smoke. It made noises. It did stuff, so I treated it like it was an entirely separate identity from myself.

I created a whole pre-match ceremony with the helmet. When I would remove it from my head, I would present it to the crowd and let them I know I was going to try my hardest for them in the ring. I would then make this rattlesnake-like noise, "hasa hasa hasa hasa," to simulate an evil sound that would often happen before a death scene in a horror movie.

Normally, the ceremony went well as planned. First, I would set down the helmet in the ring in front of me and then motion to the people to get them going. I would start a fight chant in the ring and build up momentum. Most often once they had seen the gimmick, the fans would get behind me and then finally smoke would shoot up and the audience would pop.

However, once in a while things wouldn't come off as planned. I would get the audience all hyped up for the smoke and just when it was time - nothing would happen. At first, this anti-climactic blooper-reel finish of the ceremony made me look like a giant asshole. Eventually, after this happened a few times, we came up with a backup plan to go with for when the steam didn't shoot off on the first fire.

Since it was a separate entity, I would just blame the lack of smoke on the helmet. I would turn around and walk away from it like I was disgusted and throw my hands back at it like it was someone who sucked and let me down. I would walk away from it like, "Damn you, you didn't shoot for me so I am done with you." Then, Black Cat, the time keeper, or whoever would hit the remote button again a second time. When the steam finally fired, it looked as if the helmet finally fired just to spite me.

Inoki was very pleased with my work. He had a duplicate helmet built and he gave it to me. It was an awesome gesture on Inoki's part as I am sure the helmet cost him a pretty penny. I still have it today.

I used the replica a number of times in WCW and also for some other promotions. From time to time, I take it out to some autograph signings, but it's really too hard to deal with. It is a real pain in the ass to transport and it doesn't often see the light of day because of that. It costs about $150 just to get it onto the airplane.

BIG IN JAPAN

The Big Van Vader character took off as a money-making gimmick from day one. The Japanese people really ate it up.

Antonio Inoki's idea worked. He credited and thanked me personally on more than one occasion for helping to make himself and NJPW more popular, in light of All Japan really taking off.

Once they had me in the role of Vader, Inoki started selling out arenas where they never did before. Vader was selling literally thousands and thousands more in ticket sales for New Japan. Angry fans wanted to see him lose.

Big Van Vader was a success!

The other NJPW wrestlers started getting in line to face me. I was like the centerpiece and others would surround me in a circle, each eventually taking a turn to challenge me. We built the promotion around wrestlers trying to take down the unstoppable monster. Though I didn't know it at the time, the same cornerstone idea would follow me to other Japanese promotions at various times in my career. We would do it again in All Japan for Baba, and yet again in NOAH for Misawa later on in my career.

Three of the guys that were on top of the game in NJPW before my time over there were Inoki, Chōshū and Fujinami. They were "the hot three" at the time and when I came in, they seemed to step aside for me and I am eternally grateful.

There was a bit of a rivalry between the three of them, but they would never come out and talk about it like you might see people do in the States. They were very private. They never talked badly about each other when I was working with them, though I know there was some professional jealousy going on.

I was fortunate enough to work with each one of them. I will say that there was a heavy responsibility that had fallen on my shoulders to have classic bouts with each one of them, and though it was hard work, I brought the best out in each one of them. All three consider our matches together the best of that year and tell interviewers even today that I was one of their best opponents, which is a great honor.

One of the reasons why I can attribute having the best matches with "the hot three" is that I always did my homework. In other words, being the heel, I always called a big portion of the match. What I would always do before a big event is request tapes of my opponent weeks before the show and I would just sit in my room and study them, just like a film study in football.

I took the matches very seriously, as I did my gimmick. I would study tapes of whoever I was fighting and would take notes. I draw a line down the middle of the paper and would make a T-chart. I would then attempt to make a top 10 list of every move they could take and a top ten list of every move they should give. My notepad would only indicate the best of the best custom catered to the move sets of the individual I would face. It was a list of moves that I thought they could do well to a wrestler my size and also a list of moves I thought they would take well from me, according to what I had seen from the footage. Then during our matches when I had to call something, I would only select from the best-of list that I had created for Inoki, Chōshū and Fujinami.

One time after a match, I remember Chōshū coming up to me in the locker room. He smiled. He shook my hand and gave me a congratulatory hug. He said, "Vader. How do you do it?"

"Do what, buddy?" I asked.

"How you read my mind?" he laughed. "You know everything I would want to do and then call it exactly where I would do it!"

I would just smile. I didn't want to give away my secrets.

A DIFFERENT STYLE

One thing that I noticed from wrestling a lot in Japan was that the ring psychology was different than I was used to seeing in the States. Most of the time, in matches for AWA or even in matches for Otto, there was a basic formula. The babyface would start out ahead in the match and then they would fall back and have to sell for the heel for a period of time. After this, there was typically some kind of comeback. This wasn't the case in Japan.

What I noticed right away was it was more like anything goes. The regular mindset from the Japanese professional wrestlers as a whole was, "Let's just go out there and entertain." It is interesting now that in today's modern professional wrestling, the idea of ring psychology has seemingly since flipped; now Japanese wrestling has caught on to that traditional American formula more so and seems to sell a whole lot while American wrestlers are selling like Japan was back then.

One thing that Inoki was really impressed with in choosing me for the Vader gimmick was my conditioning. Not only could I keep up with some of the fastest guys in the sport, but I could actually on occasion blow up guys like Masahiro Chono and

Fujinami and make them more tired at the end of a match than I was at almost 400 pounds.

I really kept to myself while in Japan. I did hang out a bit with an English wrestler named Tony Sinclair, however, whom I had met and worked with a lot in the UK.

I really enjoyed working with the greats like Chono, Muta, Sasake, Hase, but at that time I never saw much in Shinya Hashimoto. The time that I was over there with him, he generally was out of shape and smoked cigarettes. Back during my time around Shinya Hashimoto, I remember he was very concerned because, at one point, Inoki came to me and told me he was thinking of letting him go.

I hadn't really kept all that much in contact with him since then, but I know he worked hard to clean up his act. Since I worked with him, I know Hashimoto became quite a big box-office draw in Japan during the 1990s, and he later died in 2005.

IWGP CHAMPION

The IWGP Heavyweight Championship is the main heavyweight championship of the New Japan Pro Wrestling (NJPW) promotion. The acronym "IWGP" stands for NJPW's governing body, The International Wrestling Grand Prix.

On April 24, 1989, at Battle Satellite in The Tokyo Dome, I competed in an eight-man tournament for the vacant IWGP title.

After winning that final match against Shinya Hashimoto, I was declared the new IWGP Heavyweight Champion. Boy, I'll tell you, I was on top of the world. This was a great feather in my hat. I was the first non-Japanese reigning wrestler to hold and defend the IWGP Heavyweight Championship. This was a huge honor for me and a huge advancement for my career.

That title meant everything. It instantly gave me credibility all over the world and my phone started ringing with all kinds of offers. People wanted me to endorse products and clothing and everything from all corners of the world.

I became a major part of the heavyweight scene, trading the belt around to help get some guys over. I lost the title to "Russian Suplex Master" Salman Hashimikov. Then, he dropped the title to my old rival, Riki Chōshū. After that, I defeated Chōshū to become the IWGP Champion, once again.

For me, this championship title run was fantastic. I flew first class from Denver to Seattle, Seattle over to Tokyo and I enjoyed the rides over there. If you were IWGP champion, you had a bed and you had a TV and they chauffeured you around everywhere with basically a seat that you could fold back into a bed. They fed you three or four times out there and you could have a glass of wine and relax, so the trip didn't bother me at all.

Now, when I was flying coach, it was a whole different thing; cramped seats, arm-rests poking in my sides. People don't realize it, but a big guy in coach is torture! I didn't have any of that as champion. They would pick me up at the airport from first class and bring me to one of the best hotels money could buy. And that's it. So, I would just go to bed that night and then, perhaps, possibly be "rudely" awakened the next morning to get the best almost no-strings-attached massage you can imagine.

What a way to start the day.

Antonio Inoki was the man. He would find the best Shiatsu masseuse in the area possible, you know, one of those girls who could do wonders on your back and then take off their shoes and walk all over you in the right places? Anyhow, they would just randomly show up unannounced in my hotel room and Shiatsu the hell out of me, free of charge. I never knew when this was going to happen, but boy let me tell you, I liked that kind of surprise. I could be just hanging out and minding my own business and then all of the sudden, knock, knock, knock... *Shiatsu!*

My days were perfect in New Japan. I wake up, would work out and then get ready for my match later in the day.

NEW JAPAN TOUR BUS

They next day after a show, the bus would come and pick me up to bring me to the next tour date. The NJPW bus was a big, luxurious limo bus with all the trimmings. It had everything, but it was made for the average-sized Japanese male at the time. So they did have all these little small chairs in there, but none of those were for me. For me, they took two of the chairs out and put one big red cushioned one in. It was essentially the IWGP championship throne.

For me when I sat in it, I felt like King Vader. It was also a soft, big recliner and I loved it. I often just sat back and looked at a magazine or sipped on an adult beverage. I could sleep, or do whatever in that throne. The other thing about it was it symbolized respect. The Japanese were very thoughtful in this way.

Before my match, all they wanted me to do was relax and think about my opponent and how the match should unfold, on the ride over. After the match, it was the same thing. They would have cold beer on the bus and, again, it was even more relax time because I just worked.

There was no need for driving, no need for me to have a real car. I was treated like royalty. It wasn't a good life. It was a fantastic life! I often wonder why I ever left.

What happened was, I got injured and distracted by a huge name; one I looked up to watching on TV myself as a younger guy, Dusty Rhodes. Though I'll cover this shortly, in a nutshell, Dusty and Jim Ross saw my tapes and wanted me at any cost. Jim Ross called one night and said, "We're going to pay you this much money," and it was real good money, too. The thing was, it had to be a lot of money to get me to leave such a good deal.

If Japan said you were making $100,000 a year over (and I was making way more than that,) they meant that was what you would net after Japanese taxes. They always paid the tax money for you on top of what they quoted, so you would get the $100 grand plus another 20 percent on top of that. This was an even greater deal for me because I was traveling. Then, I would bring that 20 percent foreign tax credit back to America with my salary and not have to pay on it. American taxes worked out to be, I think, like 32 or 33 percent – so I only ended up having to pay about 12 percent on all the money I brought home.

It was a pretty good deal, and it's not a loophole; it was completely legal. It was in their constitution. You can't be taxed twice so if they are including and covering that 20% over there, I can't come back and have to pay another tax on top of that.

Looking back if I could do it again, I would have a pretty tough decision to make. I could have very well just stayed in Japan and forgot about WCW and America altogether.

CHAPTER 8 - WORLD TOURS

I quickly started to learn that each country is different as far as wrestling was concerned. Each country had its own wrestling style, period. There are some things that go over very well in some countries that just would not do as well in others. This was important for me to keep in mind because the Vader World tour was now hitting many continents.

If I was in Europe, my wrestling style would be different than it is in Japan. If I was in Mexico, my wrestling style would have to be different than it was in the AWA. You just have to figure out which style works where.

At the time, it seemed that my default wrestling style was best suited in Japan. This, of course, I would attribute to me "serving hard time" in the ring with Bruiser Brody and Stan Hansen. In Europe and Mexico, my aggressive style was fine but other than those, I will admit, I was sometimes accused in other countries of being too stiff.

Simply enough, I learned I needed to adapt. It became apparent to me that I needed to work a certain way in one company and another way in another company. That all goes back to my point of having to adapt to your environment. Sometimes, I would actually pay a promotion's workers, early on, to meet up with me for some instruction. I would have them then show me the differences in the area and get me up to speed for that particular country.

Then, once I thought I had a country all figured out, I would learn that some of the promotions within a particular country had their own take on the style, to make things even more confusing. Later on down the road in the big leagues, I would find that my wrestling style was borderline in WCW and in WWF, it was considered entirely too stiff, overall.

It didn't matter all that much, however. Most promoters booked me because of the style that I brought with the character and would adjust to the differences I brought, accordingly.

EUROPE & MEXICO TOURS

Right after winning the IWGP title again for the second time, Otto in Germany was barking down my door. You see, both Tiger (the ref) and I had promised that I was to only work the NJPW tour and then return to CWA to do more for his promotion in Germany. I was really taking off in Japan, but I couldn't say "no" to Otto. He really helped put me on the international map when I really didn't have much of anything going on.

To make things even more interesting, Otto had me travel from Japan to Europe. He wanted his fans to see Bull Power return and take on Otto Wanz in a rematch for the CWA World Heavyweight Championship.

I didn't know it at the time, but doing this favor for my old friend Otto had also generated even more exposure for my growing worldwide brand. I won that CWA match, and as a result, grabbed yet another feather for my hat. I was then holding the Heavyweight Championship of two separate organizations at the same time.

The magazines immediately jumped all over this.

I'll tell you, with business picking up in both New Japan and CWA, I continued to travel back and forth between Japan and Europe to defend both of my titles. The schedule was grueling and it seemed I was quite often living my life jumping on a plane every night of the week.

MEXICO

Come November of 1989, I got a call from Carlos Mienes. He was a promoter in Mexico with the Universal Wrestling Association. He had a reputation from the boys in Japan as being a really good guy who both treated and paid his talent very well. He told me he had learned of my success in NJPW and really wanted to see a piece of the Big Van Vader action in the UWA. Then said the magic words; I am willing to pay very well to make a Mexican tour happen.

I accepted. I remember hanging up and going down the street to find a good Spanish dictionary so I could try and brush up on my Spanish. Only a few pages in and I soon realized that any of the language I had once learned was pretty much gone. Since high school, the closest thing I came to speaking Spanish was when I was ordering a bunch of Mexican food, but I guess that didn't count.

Therefore, I knew I was going to need a translator. I didn't know the language very well, but I knew someone in Japan who did; *Hiroaki Hamada.*

Hamada was one of the first dojo trainees at New Japan Pro Wrestling. When New Japan entered into an agreement for a talent exchange with Mexico's Universal Wrestling Association, Inoki decided that at 5'6, Hamada would be a perfect fit for the smaller traditional Lucha Libre wresting style. He was right.

Little Hamada's career really took off in Mexico, almost to legendary status. Back then starting out, he was first known as "Little" Hamada, but little didn't do him justice with all that he was accomplishing. Mexican fans and promoters soon more appropriately changed his name to Gran Hamada, meaning *The Great Hamada*.

Hamada was already booked in Mexico and was more than happy to help me out. Having Hamada as my Lucha tour guide was just priceless for me. He broke me in and showed me all the little Lucha nuisances in the ring and offered quite a bit of psychology suggestions, as well. He showed me how to mesh my wrestling style with their Lucha style. My Mexican mentor from Japan really helped me further my career by keeping the ball rolling.

At the end of our first tour of Mexico together, the feedback was immediate. Carlos Mienes took Hamada and me out for a great Mexican dinner.

"First off, I want to thank you, Hamada, for producing the monster like you did and being able to control him like you did," Carlos said. "You were right. He is drawing incredible money for us. The Mexican fans are really eating it up."

Hamada bowed in his seat and smiled at me. It was then I realized, Hamada was probably the one who referred me to Carlos and actually helped get me the booking in the first place.

"And Big Van Vader, I can't thank you enough for such a great tour. I am impressed at how well you have been able to adapt to our style so quickly. For all your hard work to make this happen, I now want to sweeten the deal for you, as a show of our thanks."

I looked around expecting to see some pretty Mexican waitress holding some trays of margaritas or something, but there were none to be found.

That was not what he meant. Carlos went on to tell me they wanted to finish things off for the tour by having me defeat their champion, El Canek, and win the coveted UWA World Heavyweight Championship. He did this knowing fully-well I was about to fly home.

Carlos was offering to let me run with their belt outside the company, as long as I would return in one year to give them the belt back and put over El Canek, once again as champion. It was a no-brainer. Of course, I accepted, and then I even got to drink some margaritas, too. What a great night!

Carlos' move made me become the first and only man to hold three major world heavyweight titles on three different continents at the same time. Carlos and the guys at the UWA were great and let me hold their belt for almost a year as their champion, as I continued to work matches all over the world. In doing so, their promotion's name was mentioned everywhere and it really helped them promote their brand, as well. It was real "win-win" for both of us.

With some huge hype in Mexico for a year about our rematch, I eventually made good on my promise and returned. I dropped the title back to El Canek on December 12, 1990, with no regrets. It was good business all around and helped both of us out tremendously.

GOING IN THE LITTLE ROOM

When you started reading this book, I set you up to feel what it was like when I faced Stan Hansen at an AJPW versus NJPW super card show in February of 1990.

Again, what they wanted me to do was to go in the ring after Stan and then do the whole helmet ceremony. Stan was more of the vet than I was, so I knew he was not going to like coming out first. The promoters didn't care and they also didn't understand.

I told them Stan wasn't going to like that and wouldn't just stand there while I played around with my gimmick, but they were persistent and I told them that I would try anyhow.

I didn't even make it in the ring and he hit me between the eyes with a cowbell on a rope. Hit me so hard fluid came out my ears and I started hearing a ringing that wouldn't go away. Hansen broke my nose.

Now think about this for a second when someone implies wrestling is fake; football players leave the game when they get injured. We don't. We continue.

When you get hit that hard, you go into like a "little room." Everything gets quiet. I could see the audience of almost 100,000 people there waiting to see a fight, but I couldn't hear them. It sounded like I was under water. I had been in this room before, however, and I knew what to expect. I knew how to handle being in that room now probably better than anyone. (You forget, I had practice. I had to wrestle Bruiser Brody for the first six months of my career!)

So I calmly went into that little silent room and then came back out of that little room, knowing exactly what I had to do. Without losing my cool, I set my helmet down safely over to the side and got in the ring, then, *I smacked the living shit out of Stan as hard as I could.*

I guarantee you, nobody had ever hit Stan like that, and he didn't know what to do. Maybe part of me was showing that I was no longer the rookie that he and Brody threw around the AWA ring. I don't know.

I took a step forward, and Stan pushed referee Tiger Hattori aside. He kept trying to make it look like he was going to lock up with me, but he was really trying to thumb me in the eye. He decided to try and spoon my right eye out of its socket with his thumb.

The eye stayed intact for the time being, but he spiked me right in the corner of the eye one time and man I couldn't see. It felt like I had been stabbed in the eye. From the blur, I could just barely see Stan through what looked like a red and blue explosion of stars. Then my ears started ringing louder and even more blood-snot was pouring out my nose.

I stopped and stood there like that. I went back into that room.

When I finally came back to reality some 45 seconds after the spike, I walked up to Stan and clubbed him as hard as I could again, directly in his ear. So the big fight's on again and I'm punching him. I'm drilling him, over and over.

BAM! BAM! BAM! BAM!

Stan got back in the corner. I was really taking it to him. I slowed for like one second and that was all it took. I was guarding on my left, expecting the right hook and forgot he was a leftie.

WHAM!

Stan had achieved his goal. He had weakened my orbital socket. Like many wrestlers go to work on a body part in the ring, Stan had done the same thing, but in this case, it wasn't an arm or a leg. It was my eyeball.

We traded some more blows and then finally we locked up. Stan seemed to give himself to me so, I figured he was done trying to shoot with me.

Okay, enough of that, then. I guess we are going to work the match now.

I started to take him to the mat in an arm bar. Figuring we were good to go now and that he was ready to work, I let my guard down, but he wasn't done. Stan was only playing possum. One quick thumb was all it took.

Bop!

That sucker popped right out. You couldn't see it at first because the mask was on, but it fell right out of my eye socket and was only being held in by my eyelid.

"Stan, you popped my eye out, you fucking prick!"

I took my mask off, and there was a big moment of surprise for the fans. They had never seen me pull my mask off like that, so they knew something was wrong and I meant business. There was a moment of awe, but then the response was two-fold. The cameras zoomed in. My right eye was drooping out of my head like a pair of slinky peeper glasses you might have had as a kid, only with one eyelid over it.

It looked like a scrotum of a man with one nut.

I pushed my slimy eyeball back into my head from under my bruised eyelid. Luckily for me, that lid was so swollen that it held it in until the match was rendered a no contest.

After that, I found myself in an ambulance rushing to a Japanese hospital. I didn't know if I had a dead eyeball inside my head, or what. I couldn't see anything because my eyelid was ballooning and swollen shut. It was mushy to the touch like raw hamburger.

Once I made it to the emergency room, I was told by the doctors that I had risked serious injury by shoving my eye back in by myself and continuing the fight.

They did some tests on it. After some close inspection, they readjusted it the best they could as a temporary fix for the night.

As a result of the injury, they had to do two separate operations on my face; one on my nose and another on the orbital socket area around my eye. First, a metal plate had to be surgically placed under my eye to hold everything into place. Then next, I had to have some reconstructive surgery done on the pancake that I was calling a nose.

A few weeks after the eye operation, the eye finally healed enough so we could take another look at it. I remember them taking the bandage off. It was all crusty feeling and gross, but I could see some light, as blurry as it was. They had me do some muscular tests on it and I was somewhat relieved. *It still worked.*

"I can see!" I said to the eye specialist.

He did a few more checks on my sight and then we realized it wasn't going to be over that easy.

It worked, but it wasn't working right.

After the first eye operation, I could open and close my right eye, but it would just keep looking straight. What had happened was, when the eye came out, the cord got stretched so that the muscles couldn't pull on the eye tight enough to get it to look from left to right and up and down. They had to go in there and operate again to recalibrate the cords, like the alignment on a car, so that everything worked together correctly. It took another 6 times before they got it right.

People ask me today what I think about Stan Hansen. Believe it or not, we are all good! As crazy as that may seem, Stan Hansen asked for forgiveness and I forgave him. Because of that match, we upped our interest around the world. We decided to turn a bad into a good and we certainly made good money by allowing promoters to book us and to continue to work together.

I even had the pleasure of inducting him into the WWE Hall of Fame, Class of 2016. I did so wearing a pair of those slinky glasses minus one eye, to boot.

VIRAL VADER VIDEO

Again, my popularity was happening at a time that predated the internet. There was no way to see just whatever you wanted. News got around quick that some wrestler in Japan had an eye fall out of his head during a match.

It was a game of telephone in that people had heard the story and added facts to try and fill in the blanks. Diehard wrestling fans became bloodthirsty and just had to see it. Soon after, an underground VHS video tape of the match started to circulate that instantly made me into a legend.

There was nothing else on the tape. I would argue that this clip became one of the first viral videos, even before there was YouTube and social media. People started copying that footage over and over again and shared it with all their friends.

It wasn't just fans. Promoters everywhere would see it too then offer to book Stan and me all over the world. So, Stan and I took the show on the road. We started to oversell arenas everywhere. Yes, we had an unfortunate moment but we moved beyond it, both professionally and personally. I still think very highly of Stan.

Little did I know, the underground tape of that match was also gaining some attention from a mainstream promotion. Somebody liked what they saw on that tape and decided they wanted me so bad that they were willing to change their exclusivity rules in order to get me. They were prepared to allow me to work for them whenever I wanted, while still being the IWGP Heavyweight Champion and an active competitor in NJPW, and also a competitor in other areas over the world.

This major promotion was World Championship Wrestling.

GUEST PASSAGE – BY JIM ROSS

I was first made aware of Leon when he was starting out as the "Baby Bull" for Verne Gagne in the AWA. I saw him on ESPN, as I recall, noting that athletic, super heavyweights are hard to miss. I remember thinking to myself, "Leon White is one freak of an athlete."

From what Leon says today about how he ended up in WCW, he believes that I must have somehow later got a hold of a certain Japanese video tape making the rounds. True story. This same tape had the now legendary match of Vader against Stan Hansen, where he practically got his eye knocked out of his head. Folks, remember this was in a time when there was no internet or WWE Network. As a wrestling fan when I heard about this horror show of a fight, I immediately put my feelers out to find that footage so I could see it for myself.

I finally got a hold of that tape and, let me tell you, it was certainly worth the wait. That match instantly turned me into a Big Van Vader fan. I loved it. I loved the brutality. I loved the physicality of that match. It lived up to the hype and everything I had heard about it. It personally made me a believer.

As a talent scout for WCW, I also believed that our American fans would embrace the intensity of both of them because the Vader-Hansen matches were already becoming classic in Japan. I also pictured how well-received a rematch of that competition could be and how both wrestlers alone would look in a WCW ring.

After a few calls, I reached out to both men. The way I pitched it was we were offering them the chance to earn good cash and to also base out of their homes in the United States. Turner was a great landing spot for them both, and I really stressed that we knew how to utilize the both of them best.

Once Vader agreed and finally appeared in the United States in full character, we knew right away that his look and persona were going to translate very well on WCW television. Leon was a rugged, athletic big man who was everything and more that we had envisioned. He was even more than we had hoped for. After that, we only wished that we had signed him earlier in his career - as wrestling in the Japanese style typically shortens careers more often than not.

Immediately after bringing him into Turner, I had absolutely no concerns about how his Japanese wrestling style would translate to the American wrestling audience. None to any degree. My only concern at the time was the possibility that some of the "boys" might be reluctant to physically engage with Leon. Some actually did voice their concerns and bitch about his physicality, or "stiffness," but when they did, I would always come to his defense and just say, "Well, pro wrestling isn't ballet."

Vader proved to become truly one of the best big men in the history of the business.

CHAPTER 9 - COMING TO AMERICA

Around 1990, I really started to catch on with the Big Van Vader gimmick in different major promotions around the world. All the wrestling magazines loved me as "the man holding more heavyweight championships in different continents than anyone." The imagery of the larger-than-life wrestler dominating matches and the crazy helmet was something that they just couldn't get enough of. The contrast of a typical Japanese wrestler in the ring next to me really made for some good pictures.

We contacted Bill Apter, one of the most highly-revered wrestling journalists of all time, and he confirmed that my new look was something they really liked in the office at the time. Bill Apter (and great photographers like George Napolitano) knew that fans liked "different." They decided to use the very different, exotic and menacing pictures of Big Van Vader to help sell their magazines around the world. It worked.

"The first time I saw Leon as non-Vader in the AWA, he just looked tough. He needed a way to make him stand out from the other guys," Apter said. "Then one day, our photographer Koichi Yoshizawa called me up raving about the new look! The Big Van Vader persona did just that. He became a trademarked monster. We ran him in American mags pre-WCW, despite the fact that nobody knew who he was because his new look translated perfectly through his photos."

I was picking up a large cult following in the States of people who were interested in my career overseas because people were intrigued by this gimmick they only knew about from the magazines. American promoters started to notice.

The timing for all of this was perfect. It was as if the moon, the stars and the planets all aligned to allow Big Van Vader to be seen everywhere. I was already getting international exposure in Apter magazines, and their Big Van Vader pictures were acting like commercials, urging fans everywhere to see my matches.

While still working heavily in Japan, someone gave that underground VHS tape to Jim Ross back in the states. Jim Ross was, in fact, a commentator, but also a talent scout and a point guy for new talent. Ross always liked to "keep an eye out" for new talent (pardon the pun,) so when he heard about an urban legend of "an eye falling out of someone's head during a match," he already couldn't wait to witness the footage.

Again, this was before the internet. Back then, you couldn't just do a Google search and find anything you wanted. There was no YouTube or WWE Network at your fingertips, ready to show you any match you wanted. Fans had to actively seek out other fans and trade tapes by mail – *snail mail!* If you wanted to see a particular match, especially a foreign one, you had to work hard to find it and then wait. So, just like a number of diehard fans around the world, Ross finally got to watch the much-shared tape of our cross-promotional bout. He saw the eye-popping incident in all its gory glory. Maybe the anticipation of not being able to see it the moment he read about it helped, I don't know, but either way, Jim Ross was sold immediately. That tape put an "urban legend" status under my belt that made me look valuable.

I am forever grateful to the Apter magazines and Jim Ross for his WCW endorsement because once I had the attention of World Championship Wrestling, the ball started rolling fast. It didn't matter to them that I was still under contract with New Japan. Big Van Vader would soon be coming to America.

"I wanted to bring a new level of intensity and physicality to the promotion that, until then, didn't exist," Jim says today about the situation. He wanted the Vader he saw in Japan and he was determined to get it.

I was still under contract with Japan, but WCW was calling, asking me to moonlight. There was big money in Japan, but possibly bigger money for a top spot in America.

Jim Ross must have really wanted to sign me. The kind of contract that they gave me to start was not a normal one by any means. It couldn't be because of my situation. They knew that I had obligations with New Japan, but were totally fine with letting me work there first.

WCW was fine with me working for another promotion as a first priority in order to at least have a piece of me whenever I was in the States. This was perceived to be an investment for them that they hoped would pay off later on. They told me they eventually wanted to offer me a fulltime contract after my obligations with NJPW were up.

I accepted. The plan was, during my downtime and days off from Japan, I would fly back to America for some high profile matches and work for WCW. I was still the IWGP Heavyweight Champion and an active competitor in NJPW, but I was also to be introduced on WCW television. This was pretty much unheard of.

Now, I still had a load of stuff going on in Japan, so I didn't think it could even happen when Jim Ross first contacted me. I was surprised that being second fiddle was totally okay with WCW. But they agreed to a lucrative deal that allowed me to both continue my career in Japan and moonlight in WCW at the same time.

FIRST BOOKING IN WCW

Upon my first shot with WCW, I didn't yet get to work with arguably the best booker ever, Dusty Rhodes. He was over in WWF doing a brief spot with them, but upon his return, he would, in fact, end up booking me the best in my entire career.

Around this time, there were a handful of guys on the book. Jim Herd was running the show. He had Ric Flair, George Scott, and Ole Anderson all helping out at different times, as needed in creating the matches. WCW management agreed that I looked different they needed to treat me like a monster. In WCW, that meant I would be established in squash matches where I could "guzzle people up."

My first match in WCW was against Tom Zenk, on July 7, 1990, at The Great American Bash. (For those of you who might remember, this is where Sting worked an awesome five-star match, pinning Ric Flair with a small package by countering his figure-four leg lock in the main event.)

They really made me look great in my WCW debut. Dusty wanted me just annihilate Tom Zenk in under two minutes. Tom had no offense at all; one dropkick which I no-sold.

I wasn't with them full time yet, so it was really something to get a match like that at the time. That meant WCW really had faith in me.

Actually, all of my appearances until around 1992 were under a special circumstance contract with WCW. My unusual WCW agreement stated I would wrestle for them whenever I was available in the States, while still being under contract for New Japan.

My debut match was like a teaser of things to come for the WCW audience. Here I was, a champion from another promotion, and I was being permitted to destroy their talent! That almost never happened. Jim Ross and others in the locker room went out of their way to congratulate me for my first match that night. The consensus was they liked what they saw.

I was very different from what they were used to. I wrestled different and I looked different.

THE AMERICAN VADER HELMET

Starting fresh with WCW, I decided to use the big helmet that Inoki gave me as part of my entrance. I knew that it was very unlike anything American wrestling fans had ever seen on American TV and that it would really help me get over. However, there were a few problems with using it as part of my persona.

Now the mask that I wore in New Japan belonged to New Japan so they kept it. However, the extra one that Inoki had built for me was an exact duplicate of the first one - meaning the circuitry was also exactly the same, as well. This was problematic for me initially because my helmet was mechanically-based on Japan's metric system. In order to use it in the States so it would charge properly, it would be necessary to do some custom electronic adjustments on the interior. Eventually, I found a movie prop guy that was up for the task, but even just locating him was a difficult process, in itself.

The helmet also needed someone to transport it to and from shows and also trigger the smoke at the appropriate times. In Japan, the helmet handler was usually a wrestler named Black Cat that Inoki had provided. In WCW, I didn't have such a provision and honestly didn't want to incur the headache myself. That thing was a heavy royal pain in the ass to transport and maintain. So, I called WCW and cleared it with Jim Herd's office to hire someone on weekends to operate the helmet as an expense. They approved it.

Enter Steve Harms.

Steve was a guy who had an interesting skill set. He was a sportscaster for the ABC affiliate in Denver, KMGH-7. He also did some announcing in WCCW for Fritz Von Erich and some referee work in AWA for promoter Gene Reed. I knew him from my AWA days as Bull Power White and figured he would be right for the job. I gave him a call, fortunately enough for me, he was available. He was a good man, who I believe was really only accepting the gig to give me a hand and help me get over.

Steve was to be paid $350 a night as well as the rental, which incidentally had to be a van to transport the Vader helmet and its huge case. The only time a rental wouldn't be needed was when I was to be booked on a Friday, Saturday, and Sunday. Then, we would be able to transport the helmet on the ring truck. However, we would find out soon enough that we needed access to the helmet anyway for charging purposes and would eventually need to get a rental anyhow.

I know I had a reputation for being a bit of a loner, but Steve often traveled with me and often drove the van for me as well. We had most of our meals together and I can say that it was fun to be around him, and he was supportive in a stressful time for me. Like many other wrestlers, my professional mindset was based on insecurity, as you never knew when they would be done with you. I can imagine that sometimes the pressure of maintaining my position in WCW, as well as two or three promotions at once, was too much, but Steve was always there for me in the first part of my WCW run. He helped me accomplish fine-detail goals that I couldn't have achieved without him.

For one, Steve will tell you that the whole helmet-charging thing was a nightmare.

The remote-control-triggered smoke was CO_2 gas that had to be loaded into two small canisters built into the shoulder pieces, but airlines wouldn't let us fly with the canisters already loaded. Because of this, in each town, we would have to go on a wild goose chase to look for new CO_2. Before every show, Steve would have to go and find a new place that could fill the canisters for us. Steve would often find companies that had the CO_2, but then we would have to actually go there with the helmet to check and see if they had the means to fill our tanks. More times than not, these companies simply did not have the right equipment or fittings to deliver the gas to the custom canisters inside the helmet.

Finally, after much trial and error, we started going to the local Pepsi or Coke bottling plants where we found they had better means of filling our tank.

The first time Steve controlled the helmet for me was at the very first appearance of Big Van Vader in WCW against Tom Zenk. My debut would also mark the first appearance of the big helmet and the Vader helmet smoke ritual.

While I was getting ready for my first WCW pre-match rituals, Steve was back in the corner of a locker room somewhere, engaged in a new ritual of his own; testing the gimmick to make sure the remote control would work properly upon command for the first time on WCW pay-per-view television.

We worked it out so just before my entrance, Steve was going to make his way to the ringside area with the remote beneath his jacket or whatever, so he could handle the controls perfectly. He needed to be pretty close to somewhere less than 25 feet away from the helmet or so, or else it wouldn't work.

Silence before the storm.

Before I came through the curtain I put the big helmet over my black masked face. (This was before I started wearing the leather strap mask.) I could hear my breath and even my pulse echo in the neck of the helmet and when my music hit there was silence.

I remember today taking a deep breath before turning the character on in my mind for the first time in America.

There was a really long ramp that led straight into the ring without incline. As I made my way out, the fans in Baltimore took one look at me and were in awe. Before this, nobody came to the ring with a massive prop to this magnitude and they popped for it even more than the fans did in Japan. When I came out to the ring for the first time on American soil in that helmet, I got just what I needed. The fan response was even better than I had hoped for!

I stomped down the aisle very deliberately and turned just a little bit to see their faces. Even though I could barely see, I could see that I scared the holy hell out of a handful of kids just beyond the barricade. I smiled under that cybernetic elephant armor as they all went running back into the cheap seats for their mommies.

As they introduced me from "parts unknown," I stepped in front of the WCW ring for the first time as a monster. I did the whole, "hasa, hasa, hasa, hasa" pre-match Vader helmet smoke ritual thing on the ramp, and it was unbelievable. I looked around to breathe it all in. I saw looks of terror from many and people gasping. The look of the American audience's faces was far different than I had remembered seeing in the AWA.

I knew they bought it right away, more so than they ever did with Bull Power.

"This character is going to be big here!" I said to myself.

I took off the huge helmet and stood it before me and at precisely the right time, I crossed my fingers and waited for Steve to set off the controls.

"Please, God," I said, remembering the failed attempts of misfiring CO2 chambers in New Japan that left me red in the face with embarrassment. "Let there be smoke."

...And there was smoke.

I walked around the huge ramp to the ring again where I did my "Samurai warrior ritual" as they called it on TV.

About the commentary again, fortunately for me, the people watching at home on pay-per-view got to hear the legendary Jim Ross put me over as a monster.

"There is nothing connected to that odd apparatus that he was wearing - with the steam shooting from it," he said. "At 399 pounds, Vader is one of the most sadistic and physically intimidating athletes I have ever seen!"

After the Vader helmet had shot smoke and was done, I swung my helmet around again for added dramatic effect, then handed the helmet down to Steve.

"That was awesome, Leon!" he said with hands outstretched towards me up on the long ramp connecting to the ring. "Congratulations! You have arrived!"

Steve took the helmet backstage, packed it up and waited for the end of the match.

Our planning worked perfectly. The same formula pretty much happened everywhere we went after that and continued to meet great success apparent from the crowd's reaction. We would do the whole ritual gimmick and then we would be off again to the next town.

Steve and I did this same thing over the course of about six months. Eventually, I think, it was taking up too much time and while the money was a nice bonus for Steve, it wasn't at all enough to make him want to stay out on the road and I don't blame him.

After Steve had enough, I understood. I knew he had really only taken the gig in the first place to give me a hand in introducing the gimmick.

After Steve was gone, WCW looked for someone else within to take over the responsibility and make sure the helmet ritual would continue to happen. They tried to use different guys on the remote control gimmick and they all worked out okay, but that wasn't really the hard part. The difficult part was the logistics. Getting a van and having to lug that thing around everywhere still had to be taken care of, and especially the laborious maintenance of the CO_2.

They tried a bunch of different people to see who could take on the added responsibility along with their other jobs. One guy, Klondike Bill, who was the head of the ring crew, tried it and seemed to like it, but eventually, that didn't work out due to him having to take care of the ring as well. After Klondike, a few of the referees assumed the helmet handling here and there, but again it didn't work out either.

Eventually, we opted to just stop using the smoke, but still have me wear the mask. That eliminated having to goose chase down some Pepsi guy with Coke-bottle glasses who could figure out how to get the chemicals inside the gas canisters. I know it was not as spectacular a site without the high streams of white flying up into the air, but honestly at this point, I didn't want to deal with the helmet myself, so that was the end of it.

Later on, when my son Jesse was first getting into the business, we talked about him wearing the helmet but decided against it because it was just too logistically impractical. The U.S. helmet is still in its case in my basement and comes to life every so often at appearances.

HARD TO SAY NO

Even though I originally signed with World Championship Wrestling in 1990, I was only able to be used sparingly until around 1992. I was pretty much running around the world like a chicken with my head cut off. I was jumping back and forth to Japan where I was still working full time for that full first year in 1990. I was working some WCW televised events and also doing some shots in Germany for Otto Wanz.

During this time in 1990, I continued to also be booked against Stan Hansen from All Japan Pro Wrestling in a series of matches that made us a ton of money. This was when I also found myself finally working some for Giant Baba. Not only was it an inter-promotional dream match feud, but it was the very guy that knocked my eyeball out of my head. People paid good money for tickets in hopes to see if I was going to get my revenge or not.

I remember it all happened so fast. Otto Wanz knew I was a big deal in Japan being the IWGP champ and getting a lot of press with the Hansen feud and he wanted a taste over in Austria. He was a great guy so I couldn't just say, "no."

In return, he decided to put the belt on me there. I literally had just finished a match in Japan and immediately showered up to jump a plane to Germany. The very next day, I found myself back in Europe for a two week run.

There in the CWA, I found myself wrestling a guy named Rambo in the tournament finals to reclaim the vacant CWA World Heavyweight Championship. That made me a three-time CWA World Heavyweight Champion in the process and really upped my game even more. This meant more magazine coverage and subsequently more international credibility. The more I looked like a global dominator, the more promoters around the globe would want to book me to come and dominate their promotion.

Come January 1991, I was back in Japan again, but now carrying a different belt with me - the CWA Championship title. Knowing I was a hot commodity, they had me defeat Tatsumi Fujinami to earn another third heavyweight title reign with the IWGP strap. This title reign may not have been as long as before but it was a cool idea holding the CWA and the NJPW belts at the same time.

Soon after losing it back to Fujinami in NJPW on March 4, 1991, Rambo would then also claim revenge against me too and recapture the CWA World Heavyweight Championship. It would have been great to really have a longer run with both of those titles, but honestly, flying back and forth all over the place didn't make sense. No matter if I was wearing gold or not, my bookings in Japan and Germany from 1990-1992 only furthered WCW's interest in me.

With some weird crossover booking, I eventually defeated New Japan's Fujinami for the CWA Intercontinental Championship in Germany.

Boy, I'll tell you, this schedule was impossible and tough to keep track of. I was all over the world working for different promoters and it was becoming very hard to manage. I also had absolutely no down time at all, and no life at all.

I also wasn't around much at home and that was beginning to take its toll. I had a family that I would barely see, and that wasn't good.

What people don't often realize is that wrestlers give up everything for their lives on the road. They give up their birthdays, they give up special holidays, and they pretty much even give up their families to make dates happen.

WCW & NJPW WORKING AGREEMENT

Because of all my running around, WCW had kept in pretty good constant contact with the officials in NJPW, in order to see when they could snatch me up for an appearance. Since they were talking to each other anyhow, WCW and NJPW reached some kind of tentative working agreement amongst themselves! A door was opened to create a relationship that allowed for talent swapping that would mutually benefit both companies.

What was happening before the agreement was I was making a splash all over the magazines, internationally. In turn, I was better becoming recognized in America, especially with the occasional WCW exposure. However, I was still only moderately known by the "smart fans" and not so much with the American mainstream WCW audience. My infrequent appearances before the inter-promotional agreement did not allow the American audience to see me very often to get me established.

"Big Van Vader, oh yeah, I think I've heard of him," a casual fan would say. I wanted no question in their minds. I wanted to be unforgettable at first glance.

It was a catch-22. Things were taking off for me overseas because even limited WCW exposure was huge. However, more WCW would mean growth, but it wasn't possible because I was being spread out to thin with all the travel back and forth. The new agreement between WCW and New Japan made my schedule coordination become so much easier, with a bigger block in New Japan and then another bigger block in WCW. This helped alleviate my difficulty in gaining recognition in WCW, as all of my previous WCW matches (which incidentally were spread vastly apart) did not allow the audience to see me very often. This lack of exposure was not good.

The bigger blocks of sequential dates helped establish my character in the States. This cut out some travel time and made me more available. It also alleviated all my difficulty in gaining momentum in WCW from lack of consistent exposure in America.

PILLOW FIGHT WITH THE GREAT MUTA

Another one of the classic matches I was ever involved in was at the Sumo Hall in Tokyo, Japan against Keiji Mutoh, aka the Great Muta. This was a key match in the first ever G1 Climax tournament and it was also the only singles match between Keiji Mutoh and myself ever at the time.

The newly created NJPW G1 Climax tournament had two blocks of four wrestlers competing in round-robin rules. Each wrestler had to face all the competitors in their block, and the wrestler with the most points would reach the finals to crown the G1 winner. The wrestlers in my series, Block A, were Keiji Mutoh, Tatsumi Fujinami, and Scott Norton. (For those of you wondering, Block B included Bam Bam Bigelow, Riki Chōshū, Masahiro Chono, and Shinya Hashimoto.)

Much like the big sumo tournaments, the G1Climax event happened over the course of four days, with three days of tournament matches with an undercard and the final fourth headlining the big main event.

Mutoh had to beat two gaijin monsters and the reigning champion of New Japan to win his block. First was Fujinami, the reigning IWGP Heavyweight Champion. Then myself, a three time champion who Mutoh had never faced before in a singles match. And finally would be Scott Norton, who already had a recent victory over Mutoh in a singles match right there at Sumo Hall.

Mutoh may have been perceived by some as a long shot, but he was definitely the crowd favorite.

You see, NJPW was going through a passing-of-the-torch phase at this time. The top names of the 80s like Antonio Inoki, Riki Chōshū, and Tatsumi Fujinami were starting to step aside to make way for the new stars like Masahiro Chono, Shinya Hashimoto, and Keiji Mutoh. Mutoh had returned to New Japan in 1990 after a huge career-making run in WCW as the "Great Muta" that immediately elevated him to the top of the card status back in his home country.

Keji Mutoh never admitted in public that he was, in fact, the Great Muta. In fact, if the topic was ever brought up, he always dismissed the idea and pretended that Muta was a different person, altogether. This didn't matter, however. Everyone in Japan knew. Either way, his matches both as himself and Great Muta always captivated every crowd and everyone predicted his tournament matches in the G1 Climax would not disappoint.

They were right. By the time our match came, Mutoh had already upset the champion Fujinami on August 9th, 1991, and I had beat Scott Norton in a huge battle of the two gaijins. I was believed by fans to be one of the most feared gaijins ever to set foot in New Japan. I was still hot with massive wins over Antonio Inoki, Shinya Hashimoto, Riki Chōshū, and Tatsumi Fujinami. Booking me against Mutoh was perfect. It jumped fan response to new heights and they were hotter than ever to see the finals of the first ever G1 Climax.

The match itself was one of my favorites of all time. It told an awesome story and it was my pleasure to help push Mutoh in the end with a victory. The fans were ecstatic and so was I. Working with someone as truly gifted and great as Mutoh was made for an instant classic. It was a magical match that Japanese fans still talk about to this very day. The end of the match was even more memorable for me.

I stood up and looked around. The crowd was on its feet. Everyone was so happy that the fan-favorite underdog had beaten the giant.

Pftt...

As I was about to exit the ring, I felt something hit me in the shoulder.

Pftt... Pftt...

Then all of a sudden, I found myself under a rainstorm of pillows.

Pftt... Pftt... Pftt... Pftt...

This was quite different than when the fans lit their seats on fire, trying to burn me alive for beating Inoki in my debut. It was like the fans were using their seats as confetti in celebration.

Pillows continued to rain down from the crowd as Mutoh was recovering on the mat. He was supposed to be beaten and exhausted, but he was trying hard not to laugh at what was happening. He couldn't believe the response from the fans.

"We actually made them throw the pillows!" he would say later on.

I stomped around the ring like Godzilla dodging the pillow gesture as Mutoh finally gained his composure. Before I could leave the ring, it was totally covered in cushions. I side-stepped about a dozen of them and faced the also celebrating Mutoh. Then, I looked around and gave the fans back something special for their appreciation of the special thing they had just witnessed.

Mutoh didn't know what I was going to do and looked skeptical. He improvised anyhow, and pumped his arm into the air, as his character should have. Then just as fans wondered if I would attempt to hit him, I offered him my hand and shook it. I broke character for just one second and raised Mutoh's hand.

Then I pouted a little to get back into character and stormed off with Mutoh's music playing loudly and the crowd up on their feet.

Back in the locker room, the boys rushed me. They congratulated me for a great fight. Then they told me that we were the first wrestlers ever to get the "pillows of appreciation" for a wrestling match. Before this, it really had only happened before in a high profile sumo match here or there, but never professional wrestling.

It was a super rare thing and that moment was awesome. Even though Chono would go on to win, that match helped Mutoh and myself tremendously and we really did steal the show. Everyone loves a pillow fight.

This is one of the matches that I am most proud of in my whole career. It is available on the internet if you do some digging. If you haven't seen it, I highly suggest checking it out.

BAM BAM BIGELOW

During a period of time blocked off for New Japan, Bam Bam Bigelow and I were put together as a monster tag team. He was an awesome talent and we looked great together as a tag team.

I can't lie, however. There was always a little bit of professional jealousy. Bam Bam and I were both super heavyweights and typically you would want to protect your spot a little bit if you saw someone else come along who could take it. However, the little bit of professional jealousy that we had was actually good for us as a team. It made us bring out the best in both of us and we worked even harder, perhaps at first, to outshine the other.

Once the initial territorial pissings ended, however, that left us with a great tag team arsenal and us working hard together as the norm, as a unit. Because of this, we were called "Big, Bad and Dangerous," and I think it fit.

We may have had a little rivalry at first resulting in an urge to out-do each other, but we soon started to click and become a formidable tag team. We both knew the Japanese style very well. We both experienced working with guys like Hase who wanted to choreograph 20-minute spots with us, but found common ground in teaching guys like him that they didn't need to. We knew how to better turn on the Japanese crowd with the improv chops that we had learned in America.

Because Japan had different ring psychology, our matches were still really special. This led us to win the IWGP Tag Team Championship from Hiroshi Hase and Keiji Mutoh.

Around May of 1992, I started working matches with The Great Muta. During the intensity of these matches, I suffered a legitimate bad knee injury. This unsuspected obstacle created a problem because we were still the IWGP Tag Team Champions. For a short time, I worked some on a bad wheel, depending on Bam Bam to carry our matches. I would come in and do a few punches, but I couldn't really move much at all. We both knew that one-sided approach wasn't going to work very long.

Eventually, it only made sense to drop the tag belts, after about a four-month reign. To salvage the gaijins-with-the-belts storyline, New Japan used that talent swap agreement and brought in the WCW Tag Team Champions, the Steiner Brothers.

After dropping the titles, I immediately left Japan to get my leg looked at by my own American doctor. As I was leaving, I couldn't help but notice that despite the fact that I was injured, New Japan had already started advertising me for an upcoming major match against one of their main attractions, Fujinami.

HOMEBOUND

I technically left Japan right around the time that my block with them was up, anyhow, so I was contractually okay for the time being. I really didn't want to cut things off a bit early as I did, but I had suffered another injury and wasn't exactly sure how bad it really was. Back in the States, I learned that I had torn some cartilage in my leg. It was just before a big tag-team tournament I was supposed to return for in New Japan.

Now, with this type of injury, sometimes if the cartilage hadn't flipped, you could maybe shoot it up with a little cortisone and maybe be good for a couple of matches, so New Japan asked me to see if that was a possibility. I went to my doctor and did some further tests to figure out if Cortisone injections or something would have been an option.

I got to the point, where I had really injured my left knee. I went to my doctor about two weeks before the tournament and he said, "A chunk of the cartilage has flipped. It has wedged itself in there pretty good and you will need to take a little time off."

"Awe, Doc, this was really bad news," I said. "Is there any way I can work on it for at least a short time?

See, Inoki really wanted me to do one tournament, in particular. He was planning on having me win the tournament overall against Fujinami and that would have led to more gold and even more money. After that, there was to be a return tournament and then finally a tag tournament which we were going to team up and win, as well. I hated the idea of having to sever that tie again because I had the best of both worlds working for both New Japan and WCW at the same time.

"Are you sure?"

The doctor frowned and shook his head. "You can wrap it up or tape it, but you're just going to destroy your knee in the end. You really need to get this fixed."

I hated to hear it, but I knew he was right. I couldn't put any weight on my leg. I was taking some pain pills just to walk around, and I could feel a popping snap whenever I bent it a certain way. There was a piece of twisted cartilage that really needed to come out of there.

My contract was up, so I elected to have that operation while I wasn't officially contracted to be anywhere. I had to skip the next set of WCW dates, which wasn't as big of a deal as skipping out on New Japan's next set of dates.

You never really want to turn down a big NJPW tournament like I had to. It was a big deal to them, and they were really counting on me.

I am still good with Inoki. He was totally cool with me having to make that decision. I have also talked to Fujinami since then. He totally understands why I had to cancel, and there was no heat, whatsoever. They are both good guys. Inoki also didn't hold any ill will for me choosing not to return to NJPW for some time – it was simply the circumstances I found myself in.

I nursed up the injury and then decided to slow things down a little. It only made good business sense to work less dates for more money to prevent further injury.

WCW was the best answer at the time personally and professionally. That is when I decided to sign a full-time WCW contract in 1992. The first thing I did before I left NJPW for WCW was to have my lawyer write a letter to Antonio Inoki. In it, I gave my notice and also thanked him legally in writing for the helmet he gave me to use in other promotions and also for allowing me to have the name, "Big Van Vader." This way I at least had something to document and protect our verbal agreement about using the gimmick on American TV without legal recourse.

I am forever grateful to Antonio Inoki.

CHAPTER 10 - STING & HARLEY

For my approaching full-time run with WCW, I really wanted to make an impact so I decided to update my gear. The original Big Van Vader look was black tights with red lightning bolts and a matching Lucha spandex mask.

Even though I didn't wear any mask in my debut NJPW match, Inoki wanted me to appear more mysterious and soon had me add it. Coming from the famous town of Parts Unknown, wearing a mask only made sense. I loved the idea of a mask when Inoki requested it – but it got old real quick.

I ended up hating to have to wear those masks. They were uncomfortable. They impaired my vision. They would also get really hot and I would sweat like crazy in it. Sweat would run down into my eyes. When I would take the mask off, the material was always totally saturated. It was disgusting. I had to bring like three or four of them with me for a tour because, after one use, they would stink to high heaven.

Not wanting to bring the stink with me from the original black mask I wore in the ring every night, I actually came up with the idea of the leather strap mask for WCW. It allowed for more breathing, more eyesight, and less Vader-juice absorption.

When I showed my new prototype to the boys in the locker room for the first time, they popped. People loved it. It had a unique shape and look, and nobody else had anything like it at that time. I was pretty proud of it. I created the mask myself, custom building it for me. If you look at it closely, you will see that it's basically a series of V's all connected together. It was also designed so that you can see the double Mohawk.

Years later, I would guess my good friend Mick Foley ran with the idea and created something similar for his Mankind character's mask. (But mine is still better, Mick!)

Not only did I decide to update my look, but I also knew I needed to update my style. Before I began working for WCW full time, I was still working a really snug Japanese style. I had acquired some of the stiff inspiration instilled upon me from my early AWA rookie days with Brody & Hansen and the Japan matches didn't help much either.

Before I started officially fulltime with WCW, Dusty Rhodes had returned and was doing some booking. This part-time period with WCW was the first of what would be a great relationship with Dusty and myself. He too was a big man in wrestling and knew exactly how to book a super heavyweight in a way that made sense and would make money. In some ways, maybe I was an extension of himself.

Dusty was great.

"Listen, big man," he said in that filthy southern-drawl that made him famous, "You've been around the world and done it all, but to really succeed in America wrestling, you needed to adapt a little the American wrestling style."

He was super cool about it. He sat me down and didn't slam me at all. He knew the deal. He knew I was used to Japan and got over the message to me in the kindest, most understanding, yet effective way that he could.

Dusty asked me to work out "a balancing act." He wanted me to figure out how to keep the smash-mouth style that brought me to the table but to also develop some more of the lighter American style of wrestling that most of the WCW wrestlers were all accustomed to.

Dusty explained that bumps were finite. "You only have so many bumps on your bump card until you have to retire," he said. He also explained to me that, "as a worker, you have to wrestle smart so that you can be in it for the long haul, and continue to provide for your family for a long time."

The light bulb went off. The American Dream was right. He may have looked and sounded like a common man redneck at times on TV, but he was truly wise beyond his years.

He asked if I minded having a few mentors that could help me adapt and I, of course, agreed. It was then that he strategically paired with two people that could better Americanize my in-ring persona.

Dusty chose to put me with Sting, who was a great in-ring competitor, to help me with the American wrestling style. He also gave me a really smart manager that I could learn from on the road outside of the ring, a grizzled ring veteran named Harley Race.

STING

After being in Japan for so long, I knew I had to lighten up. This wasn't Japan, this wasn't Europe. This wasn't Mexico. It was America where they worked differently, and I knew I was going to have to tone it down. I guess I'm talking about stiffness, or how hard you lay in the moves and how hard you pull the punches, so to speak.

After working in Japan and having so many brutal matches with Bruiser Brody, I began to realize that I had to retrain myself a little. I learned in Germany that the style I was accustomed to working in was not the norm everywhere and I needed to tone it down a little. Over there, I threw some money to a decent referee that Otto had and a few other guys to help polish me up. After my initial training days with AWA, the boys in Germany showed me how to do little things to make my game better. They showed me how to climb up the ropes better and also how to wrestle smarter in the ring.

By the time I made it to WCW, the thing is, I had already decided to lighten up, in my mind. I had cut things down to half the aggression and physicality that I was used to working in Japan, and I really thought that would be good enough. I mean, I literally was moving at half the intensity that I did working in Japan, but evidently, that was not good enough. My watered-down Japanese style was still too rough for American wrestling.

I was working in a style that Americans weren't used to seeing, and maybe that was what brought me to the table in the first place. The problem was, I was still working too hard in some areas where the American audience couldn't tell the difference.

Sting was smart. He knew what was up right away. Sting is one of the greatest wrestlers of all time, bar none, and looked at wrestling from all avenues. He knew I was working with too many foreign styles bleeding in for WCW. He sat me down after a match for a chat.

"Leon," he said, "I know what you are used to and we had good chemistry out there together. The crowd liked it. But basically, you don't have to do a lot of what you are doing to make it work here."

I knew it wasn't the right style that they were looking for. I admitted it.

"You don't have to knock a guy out, or do this or that like in Japan," he would say. "You don't have to. I'm going to be there for you. I will make it look like you did."

Sting didn't just talk. He took the time to show me what I needed to be successful in WCW and what it took to lengthen my career.

I owe a lot of my success to Steve. He was patient with me. He showed me how to slow down and made me realize that I could do a lot less and get a lot more out of it. Every now and then I would hit him pretty stiff, and he would look at it as a work in progress with me.

He would tell me after the match, "You hit me pretty good with that one shot, but that's okay, the rest of the match was good, and we'll get there."

That is pretty much how Sting rolled.

HARLEY RACE

The other guy I have to thank for success in moving to WCW is Harley Race. He was actually still wrestling at the time I was called in to do my first WCW shot, but winding down his career a bit. During this time, he was making the transition over from in-ring competition to manager.

By the time I was fulltime with WCW, Harley had just finished his first successful run acting as the manager of Lex Luger. Luger had made the jump to WWE, and Harley needed someone else to manage. Dusty Rhodes decided that I was the perfect fit for the puzzle. I would get an excellent mouth piece and also get some insight that could really help me succeed in WCW.

Harley Race was a great guy to learn from. He was a grizzled ring veteran that had done just about everything you could think of in the sport. He wrestled around the world for every major promotion and held most of the major titles at some point. With that many accomplishments under your belt, however, you get a little set in your ways. Harley pretty much lived by the code of "It's my way or the highway."

Just as a side note, Harley liked to make a little cash on the side whenever he could. Harley was a hustler. One way we would do this is by shooting pool. Harley was a really good pool player. I was okay, but the more I drank, the better I got. Sometimes on the road, Harley and I would hustle guys in a bar, and take them for all they had. What we would do is have Harley job out to me when some of the locals were around watching. Then, he would make bets with a guy who would think he could beat Harley easy – who would then be in for a real costly surprise.

Today if you ask him, Harley will tell you that he wasn't paired with me to help mentor me and help me transition out of a different style of wrestling. Today, he will tell you that he was paid at that time to "babysit Big Van Vader." That's reinventing history. Let me set the record straight right away, when he says that, he is just trying to put himself over. That line is total bullshit, because half of the time, *I was looking after him just as much as he was looking after me.*

I'm not sure why he looks back at our time together as babysitting me. We never had a real dispute about wrestling. We

never had any heat. He is only saying this now, trying to make himself look better, "as the only man who could control the monster." I don't know. What I do know is when he talked, I always listened 100 percent. It wasn't like he wanted to coach me and give me information that I didn't want to hear, either. He only gave me advice when I asked for it.

"Hey Harley, how was my match tonight?" I would ask, looking for feedback.

"It was good," he would say like usual, offering no mentor-like insight.

It was always the same old thing. Every ride I went on, I had a walking encyclopedia of wrestling in my car, right in my lap, but I always had a hard time flipping through his pages to get to any good, useful information.

"Okay, well, if you were me, how would you make it better?"

Eventually, after this same question a number of times, I could work a gem out of him that I really could use. He would then tell me where I could have slowed something down in this one spot in the match, or maybe changed the flow of things. Those fine-tweaking moments are what I was looking for and when I got them, they really did help me improve how to call a match. His grasp of psychology was second to none. Harley wasn't really super gifted with athleticism, but he had one of the best experienced minds in the business.

One thing I think that bothered him was I was sometimes selective in using his advice. I often came from the athlete mindset and would put the "Vader touch" on his advice to keep my character's personality in the match. The problem was, it was all or nothing with Harley.

"I saw you added the one spot and then stopped and turned around to the crowd tonight to slow it down," he would say.

"Yes sir," I would say. "Thank you for that."

"Well, that isn't exactly what I said." Then he would proceed to bitch me out in the car the whole ride because I only used 80 percent of his idea and didn't do EXACTLY what he said I should do.

I knew, however, never to mess with his manager spot.

Some wrestlers don't know how to use a manager. They do a match and often don't bother to use the guy that is out there to help them at all. I always tried to work Harley into our matches for a manager spot. Maybe Harley's spot would be a feed for punches behind the ref's back or even his trademark headbutt off the ropes. He really helped with heat. However because of his OCD, it got to a point where I would listen to whatever he suggested, and then I would plan everything else around it so his spot would happen. That was the priority. If it wasn't, I would hear about it for miles on the road. I learned that you really had to pick your battles when you were working with Harley.

Another point of disagreement we had was related to his drinking habits. He always had to drink beer every single night. Harley had post-match driving rituals that by today's standards are scary. Now don't get me wrong, in the golden days, there was a whole lot of liberal drinking and driving going on, but when it came to booze behind the wheel, *Harley really was The King.*

Before every show, we had to stop at a convenience center somewhere to make sure everything was in line for the ride out. Harley had a special cooler that fit perfectly in his trunk. He had his name written on it in marker, "HARLEY RACE" and it had to be lined with a hefty bag and filled with of ice and a particular kind of beer – whatever Harley was drinking.

When we left a show, without words, I knew Harley was driving. He would be okay for the first hour or so, but the King of the Road would start driving really fast with 8 or 9 beers in him. The horrible part about this whole thing is, if you were sitting shotgun, you had to be an enabler. He had everyone who rode with him well trained. If you were sitting by his side, it was your job to monitor his drinking and know exactly when he had polished off that can of beer. When it was gone, your job was to put a fresh can in his hand, open and ready to drink. You also had to make sure that the hole was at the six o'clock position, so he could lift the can straight up to his mouth without having to look down at it and adjust it accordingly. Talk about being "the King!?"

Now if the drinking wasn't bad enough, and if the fact that he was endangering my life and the lives of others by being boozed up behind the wheel wasn't bad enough, he would also smoke the whole trip. We would really butt heads about this. I hated that.

Now, I am not sure if you know this or not, but most people don't know that most cars (especially rentals) have a built in "speed governor." The governor would kick in once the car got up to about 120mph and drop down to 60 again. It is a safety precaution designed to– keep people safe. The thing was, Harley knew how to bust it.

Harley would get up to about 120 miles an hour. I would tell him to slow down, and he would ignore me like I just didn't exist. He would then slow down a tiny bit and then drive slam the pedal down to break the governor. I don't know how he did it, but he knew how to make it not work. He would adjust his speed a little bit then rev it up, and then boom! No more governor.

Harley was used to being in charge and having everything his way; the wrestling ring, the driving, which hotel to stay in, and what to do while we were in the hotel. The "Harley Way" meant room service in the morning every day at about 8 AM (after coming in at 4 AM,) because he wanted eggs. So we would get the eggs then go back to sleep until noon, and get some more room service and then get some more sleep. Then we would go into tapings around 5 PM. Forget about whatever gym time I wanted. "Catching up on rest was the most important thing," he would say, despite the late arrival, the early breakfast and the lunch break between catnaps.

I remember one morning, I wasn't moving at the "Harley Way" speed. I needed to take a shower in order for us to leave the hotel when Harley wanted, but I was running out of time. I was in mid-conversation about the match from the night before when Harley cut me off.

"Goddamn it, Leon! Shut up, and get in the shower," Harley snapped.

"Yeah, yeah, Harley," came my reply. I knew his OCD was kicking in and I decided to mess with him and have a little fun. I stood up, took all my clothes off, and then jumped back into bed. "I will in a few. But again, about the match last night..."

Harley frowned and yelled even louder, "Get in the GODDAMN SHOWER!"

I didn't move. We were both stubborn. "Great match though, right?"

Harley got off the bed and threw the remote at the wall. He reached into his suitcase and pulled out a 50,000 watt taser gun and zapped me right on the thigh.

After that morning, things changed. Whenever I woke up and saw that Harley was in the other bed next to me, I got right in the shower so quick, he didn't even have time to say hello.

Harley was a character though, I'll tell you. My WCW contract covered the rental car and the hotel, so Harley didn't have to pay much of anything. However, he had an odd way of keeping records for himself, and also kept track of others. He kept a journal of his expenses right down to the penny, but he also wanted copies of MY hotel receipts and car receipts. He was both creative, and old school thrifty.

As my mentor, Race was often critical my style, but he wasn't very diplomatic about areas he wanted to critique. "Leon, lighten up or you're not going to have anyone to work with," he would say.

Normally, I would just listen to Race's advice, and say, "ah-ha" or "okay." But sometimes I would hit back with.

"Hell with it, if they can't take it, they can get out of the business."

After a few beers in a North Carolina hotel, I think I said something similar to that effect to Race when something knocked me off the bed. Sure enough, it was a Harley Race clothesline. We were rolling around the floor in a brawl that was half serious and half fun.

Together, our fat asses were about 700 pounds of flesh rolling around in the living room area of the hotel. I kicked a hole in the drywall. Harley knocked over a table and broke the leg on it. Chairs and everything else in the way were getting steamrolled in the process.

Did we worry about the hotel manager banging on our door? No.

We forgot about the guy who brought us the beer to begin with. The hotel manager was already in our room drinking with us. Watching us destroy his room before his very eyes, he's the one who finally broke us apart.

The next day we were all on good terms again, but he billed us for the damage six hundred each. The winner of that match wasn't me and it wasn't Harley, it was the hotel manager at $1,200!

CHEMISTRY

One unique thing that Sting and I could do was talk very little before the match and put together something great and believable. If you know how to improvise well, you can improvise a match in such a way that creates passion in every move.

Today's wrestling really comes off scripted at times. Because today's wrestler doesn't know how to improvise the way we used to back in the day. If someone misses a spot, everything goes right to hell. When your match is scripted to a point where you are scripting all the little things and calling spots like, "duck, block, duck, duck, block" then you are scripting way too much. The match looks and feels fake. You lose what this sport used to be about which was entertaining by suspending disbelief.

It is like trying to play the piano without feeling, just hitting every note on the sheet exactly how it is written. It doesn't sound real. There is no emotion, no feeling, no humanity in it.

This, of course, never happened with Sting. Sting and I didn't have to call much of anything, even in a gimmick match as difficult to make interesting as the strap match. For something like that, Sting knew there were certain things I just would or wouldn't do. Both of us would come to the table with an understanding on a short beginning of the match, then obviously we would talk about that major spot I call the "switch spot" where the tide turns and you start telling a different story. That story either changes slowly or quickly depending on what type of story you want to tell. Then we would figure out a finish for the match. Everything else in between, we created in the ring on the fly and I got used to working that way. A good worker could do that. Sting and I were even better than this because we also had chemistry, meaning he could predict what I would do and feed into it even more to make the match that much better.

Fast forward a few years, and the ability to improvise and tell a story from the new guys on the scene is gone. It is officially a lost art form. I took a few years off and now, it is all different. Now, someone like a director hands you a piece of paper and says, "Here, memorize this." Memorization is not the way I did it. That's not the way Harley Race did it, that's not the way they did it before him. I think you can really physically see and feel the difference. There is no character, no negotiation of strong and weak points, nothing being taken into consideration.

A lot of times, I called a big portion of my matches with Sting, but Sting contributed quite a bit. Sting trusted me because he liked the way I told a story. Heck, even Inoki did. My second week in Tokyo I was calling Inoki's matches. I thought that was quite an honor.

WHITE CASTLE OF FEAR

The January 30th, 1993 edition of WCW Saturday Night really pushed the envelope of entertainment. It wasn't just a wrestling program they put together that night, it was more like a mini-movie. What they decided to do was add some drama in an action film-type sequence to hype up my World Heavyweight Championship strap match against Sting at *SuperBrawl III*.

This splendid piece of cinematography was a massive piece of work called "The White Castle of Fear."

The segment opened with our hero, Sting, receiving an invitation to the game at my White Castle of Fear somewhere in the Rocky Mountains. For fans who may remember this madness, the segment immediately felt like a dream sequence. It was trippy, crazy, and weird. Nonetheless, Sting accepted and the challenge was on.

In dramatic fashion, Sting took to the sky in a private helicopter and headed out for an epic adventure.

The aircraft eventually brought Stinger to our secret exotic location. My dark dungeon was chock-filled with sinful pleasures. The White Castle indeed had piles of scrumptious foods everywhere, but sadly, no White Castle burgers were anywhere to be found. For the viewers' carnal pleasures, however, it did have a boat-load of bootylicious women in bodysuits and a wonderful one-eyed minion midget wrestler.

Cheatum, not unlike most one-eyed dwarfs, had an agenda. His role was to repeatedly scream, "Play the game, play the game!" almost ad nauseam.

The game at hand was revealed to be a classic; Tug of War. Sting and I were immediately tied together at the wrist with a thick leather strap. We were then positioned over a raging S'mores fire that violently erupted in spurts. The heat was tremendous. We could have died, for real.

Towards the end of the stunning segment, I pulled Sting closer and closer to the flames, and the screen faded to black. Finally, the words "TO BE CONTINUED" appeared to promote our PPV.

Nothing short of epic, I know.

I'm not sure who produced this segment, but I didn't really care at the time. It was arguably very un-wrestling-like and very un-Bill Watts-like. It probably was an idea that came from the network producers themselves. There is no way it could have been Bill Watts' idea.

Looking back on it now today, one thing I can say is that people remember it. They still come up to me and mention it, so yes, now I think it was a good idea, though it took a lot of flak back in the day.

You can't deny that was an effective memorable promo to get the news out about our match. I even remember it having an impact on my own son, Jesse. He came up to me after seeing the airing of the promo on television, as a young kid. He looked hurt. When I asked him what was wrong, we didn't understand why he had never been inside "my other home" – *the castle.*

"We are just getting it ready for you," I told him. "In fact, you even have your own room there!"

At the time we filmed the *White Castle of Fear*, I really didn't care about it either way. I wasn't for or against the promo. I just did what they said. It was of secondary importance to me compared to the actual strap match that it was promoting.

On February 21, 1993, at *SuperBrawl III* in Asheville, NC, the WCW World Champion Big Van Vader was scheduled to face Sting in a non-title Leather Strap Match at the Asheville Civic Center.

First of all, as far as strap matches go, they are very hard to do well. They usually die a very slow death with the fans, because the idea looks great on paper but usually doesn't deliver the excitement you would think it should. Since the wrestlers are strapped together, you would think this would make for some exciting spots, but it rather just becomes a boring tug-o-war where you have to touch each corner of the ring to win. This typically becomes less interesting than the actual excitement created from a good wrestling match.

Our match didn't follow the footsteps and stereotypes of older strap matches. We not only had a good match, but it was probably one of the best gimmick matches that I have ever been in.

One interesting point to mention, and I don't even know if this has ever been mentioned, but there was a blade accident in this bout. Sting had a razor taped to his wrist and he was using it to cut himself to bleed during the match. However, by the end of the match, he forgot it was there.

At the end of that match, after I had already won, we continued to brawl. I took a number of shots to the head to let Sting shine and look good to the fans after my victory so he could save face. Sting fed me to the corner and started to unload with punches. While this was going on, the protective flap of tape came undone on his blade finger.

I didn't feel anything at first, but all of the sudden, I tasted blood. One of the punches connected pretty good and the blade grabbed skin. It started slicing up the side of my face and didn't even know it!

When you punch as a wrestler, you keep your hand loose and let it glide off the surface. This made it even worse because it was like running a small box-cutter up and down my cheek. He accidentally sliced up my ear real good and then one shot really connected. His finger dug into my ear and ruptured my eardrum. The cut was so bad that blood was pouring out of my head.

Sting stopped. The little slices on my faces started to open up and he realized what had happened. I really didn't feel the injury but I started to see red. Then, all of the sudden, I felt light-headed, and my knees became wobbly. I was sitting on the edge of the mat.

"What the?"

Sting was concerned, but the show had to go on. He raised his hands to the crowd and headed off to the locker room, but that isn't what he wanted to do at all.

To the victor go the spoils. My legs were made of rubber. I didn't pass out, or anything. I was conscious, but I literally couldn't stay on my feet. I needed help walking back to the locker room.

After the cameras cut, the WCW medic rushed the ring with security and helped me out.

"Leon," the medic said. "Are you okay?"

I nodded. It wasn't a stinger. I had felt that before in my football days, but this was different. It was almost like being drunk without the burping, farting and waking up the next morning next to a hideous mustached woman I would regret.

They checked my vitals and patted my head down to stop the bleeding. I was then lifted onto a stretcher to head off to the ambulance.

Once I was wheeled passed the entrance way, Sting caught up to me and rushed to my side. "Oh, man!" he said. "I'm so sorry, man."

I knew it was an accident.

He followed me the whole way to the ambulance. I tried to stand again but to no avail. Sting helped me up. He was always a good guy with me. He was a consummate professional and always a gentleman. The medical staff pushed a new towel on the side of my face, as I wiggled into the back of the ambulance.

"It was the blade," he said.

"I know you didn't mean to," I replied. I didn't care about that. "Was the match good?" I asked.

Sting laughed. "It was awesome, man," he said. "Probably the best strap match ever, if that means anything in the end."

It really was a good strap match and one of my most proud moments on TV. Strap matches are typically really hard to do, and we really nailed it. Many historians have since said it is one of the best strap matches out there. What we did was wrap the strap up and really focus on having a good match, only using the strap sparingly as to not be constrained by it.

On the way over to the hospital to get checked out, I started to feel dizzier and was breaking out in a sweat. What had happened was my inner ear had suffered an injury that messed up my equilibrium so bad I couldn't walk. It only lasted a few hours, but it was very strange, to say the least.

Steve Austin, Leon White, & Rick Rude

INFAMOUS HARLEY BARBECUES

Harley Race, one of the very few people in the world to ever slam André the Giant, was a legitimate tough guy. There was no doubt about that in my eyes. I'm not sure what the reason was, but Harley always tried to be cordial and win over wrestlers who may have feared him in his later years.

Kansas City bookings quickly became the favorite among many of the boys, but not because of the arena. It became about what would happen after the booking and the next day. The wrestlers had a great place to visit with an open door policy, thanks to the hospitality of former NWA World Champion Harley

Race and the good home cooking of his late wife, BJ. Harley's place was a "home away from home" for barbecues, fishing, card games and games of pool.

I remember when my wife and son would go with me to these barbecues and sometimes stay at Harley's house when we went on the road. My wife would help cook. My son would run around and play-wrestle with some of the boys. I remember him throwing a football with Stunning Steve Austin.

When the other wrestlers would show up, they always seemed happy to be there, but nobody really wanted to shake Harley's hand. He probably had some of the strongest hands ever known to man. He could break your hand with one handshake. All the boys were always careful to make sure they only gripped the fingers and not the whole hand, or else it would be like crunching your bones in a vice grip.

One time, we ran out of ice and I took a solid fresh bag out of a cooler full of water. It was frozen solid, and there was no way we were going to be able to use it in our drinks.

"Harley, you got something like a hammer?" I asked.

"Gimmie that," he snapped.

Harley looked at it for a second. The bag was a solid cinder block ice. Harley grabbed that bag and held it in one of his bear paws, then he punched it one time with the other. The blow smashed the whole block of ice with one little punch. I swear to God that was solid.

Though Harley wouldn't be all that talkative, sometimes we would all go out on the lake. We would drink and fish and all have a great time.

Though I didn't bring it up all that much in our rides together, some of the guys would ask Harley about various urban legends in wrestling, throughout the years. Though he didn't often say a whole lot, I remember one time someone asking him about attacking Hulk Hogan.

While he didn't tell the story, he did fill in a lot of the blanks.

HARLEY ON HULK HOGAN

In the mid-'80s, the WWF started booming. When it went into syndication across the country Vince McMahon started threatening the status quo of the wrestling world. Until then, there were different territories with numerous promotions all across the country. They operated like franchises, paying in to use and compete under the banner of the NWA. WCW was even one of these for a time.

One morning, Harley flipped on the TV. He was eating his eggs and his jaw dropped into his newspaper. Wrestling was on the screen in his house and in his town, but it wasn't NWA.

Harley said that when WWF shows started airing out of his hometown station, Kansas City, this was like running a show and invading your territory.

"This means war," he said.

You see, Vince had a global vision. That was something most promoters did not and could not have due to the way that the territorial system operated back then. Vince began touring his group into cities everywhere, ignoring the traditional promoting rules. Harley knew about this, and the old guard was none too happy. It wasn't until Vince toured into the NWA territory of Kansas City that Harley decided to take action.

Since Harley was known to be a wrestler in Kansas City, he had no problem walking right into the arena that was hosting the WWF that night.

Harley walked down the familiar halls and found Hulk Hogan in the dressing room. Harley stormed in.

Hogan supposedly said something like, "Wrong building tonight, brother," and that's all Harley needed to hear. Race walked right up to a seated Hogan and smacked him with his sledgehammer hand directly in the face.

Hogan fell off of his chair and went down to the floor.

"Geesh, dude," Hogan said, knowing damned well why he got hit. "I'm surprised you just didn't come in here with a gun."

Race reached into this jacket and flashed a .38 revolver. The locker room cleared.

When Hogan's camp tells this story today, they claim Harley took a gas can that the hall used for their lawn mower and tried to burn down the WWF ring.

"That's untrue," Race said to some Hogan supporters at one of the barbecues. "There was no gas can."

The rest of the story was fair game.

Like most other territorial promoters, Race lost a lot of money after Vince took over. At one point, Harley even ended up having to go work for Vince. He figured that it was the only way to still work in the wrestling industry at that point. "If you can't beat them, join them," he said.

A couple of years after the gun incident, Harley knew he was going to be doing some spots for Vince and asked Vince not to tell Hogan. His first show with them was going to be in Kansas

City, so Harley started to float some rumors to make Hulk Hogan brown his yellow tights.

The rumor was that Harley Race was going to show up with a shotgun when the WWF came back to town. Just as before, he was still pissed that the Missouri territory was his, and he was not going to give it up without a fight.

Everyone in the locker room was nervous about the booking that night, especially the WWF front man, Hulk Hogan.

The night came and just as before, Harley simply walked right into the dressing room like he owned the place. The only thing different this time was he peeked his head in first to make sure he could strike at precisely the right moment.

A bunch of the wrestlers were moving about. Harley snuck in when Hogan had his back to the door. A couple of the wrestlers looked up, and Harley held his finger up to his lips. He signaled for everyone to be quiet and he snuck up behind Hogan.

When Hogan was least expecting it, Harley put him in a chokehold from behind. Before anything could happen, he slapped him as hard as he could on the ribs and released the hold.

Hogan turned around and winced. He turned as white as a ghost. Harley smirked and extended his hand in friendship. Hogan rightfully breathed a sigh of relief.

HARLEY vs. OWEN HART

Later on in the WWF days, the infamous Harley barbecues would continue. Bret's younger brother, Owen Hart, was invited to one. Harley had helped out Bret early on in his career and was on really good terms with the Hart family. Harley didn't know Owen all that much. All he knew was Owen was really known to be a joker.

I guess at one point during the party, Harley let his guard down. Little did he know that having Owen at one of the famous Harley Race barbecues was probably a bad combination, as they were often known for shenanigans. Owen had already planned to pull off a barbecue rib, no pun intended.

What happened was Owen ribbed Harley by pulling "the old switcheroo" with one of his bottles of BBQ with one he had doctored up himself. I guess before dinner, Owen went into Harley's kitchen when nobody was around, poured out the bottle's contents into a bowl, and replaced the sauce with a bottle of the hottest of hot sauce he could find.

Owen kept the bottle in his jacket and just at the right moment, he made the switch as Harley said, "Please pass the

BBQ sauce." Harley took one bite and Owen laughed his ass off, as we all saw the steam come out of Harley's ears.

A few days later, Harley decided to get his revenge. Just before Owen was to go out to wrestle one of his matches, Harley came over to say goodbye as his match was done and he was about to leave. He stuck out his hand to shake Owen's hand and Owen did the same.

Revenge. Harley was about to give Owen his receipt with his own "old switcheroo." This rib was obviously meant to be one of those classic handshake pranks where the prankster then had a buzzer concealed in his palm. The buzzer would then give its victim an unsuspecting small shock.

However, just like whenever Harley did something in life, he always did it big. This was to be no exception.

Instead of a dollar store hand-buzzer, Harley pulled his trusty taser out of his jacket and zapped Owen good. To defend Harley, he really didn't think it would have had the effect it did, however. Owen immediately dropped to the floor, pissed his pants and was out cold!

CHAPTER 11 - RON SIMMONS

My first shot at Sting's World Heavyweight Championship was on April 12, 1992. Sting wanted our match to look as real as possible to keep the heat on me. Sting won by disqualification after I clotheslined the referee; during the bout, Sting cracked two ribs and bruised his spleen which led to an impromptu finish (Sting's last match for more than a month).

That idea that Sting was not ready to return after that match due to real injuries suffered at the hands of Vader was leaked to the newsletters. Nikita Koloff filled in for Sting while he recuperated.

Sting didn't make it back into action until Wrestlewar '92, about a month later. I received a rematch with Sting on July 12, 1992, at The Great American Bash, which I finally won to become the new WCW World Heavyweight Champion.

Little did I know at the time, however, that my first WCW World Heavyweight Championship reign was to be short-lived, with me losing the title only three weeks later.

RON SIMMONS

Throughout history, things just seem to happen in threes. Ever hear of the rule of thirds, how our brain likes to section out what we see? Or how people talk about how when a celebrity passes away, two more follow him immediately? The number three seemed to surround me in titles.

I held the CWA Heavyweight Championship in Germany three times, the IWGP Championship in Japan three times and also the WCW Heavyweight Championship here in America three times.

Ron Simmons was instrumental in my title runs.

Ron is not a good guy, he's a great guy. Most often, guys don't enjoy the fact that they had to drop a title to someone, but I am real proud of the fact that Ron Simmons beat me for the WCW Heavyweight championship. Ron Simmons became the first African-American in a major promotion to ever win the heavyweight championship of the world.

So one day before a show, I was minding my own business and Ron comes by and taps me on the shoulder. "Man. Listen," he said in his deep timbered voice.

"What's going on, Ron?" I said shaking his hand.

"Listen, out of nowhere, they are talking about putting the belt on me, man."

I tilted my head. I hadn't heard anything and usually when a big move like that was going to be made, the main promoter would always first give you the heads up. Nobody had invited me into any planning meeting or anything.

"I just wanted to tell you that I was not lobbying for your belt or anything," he said honestly. "I was actually pretty surprised when they said you didn't even know yet."

"Well, Ron, if it happens, it couldn't happen to a better person," I said. I shook his hand. "You're right, though. It would have been nice if someone told me first."

"I agree," Ron said.

"No heat at all with you," I said and I meant it. "No heat at all, but I do have a problem with Watts. I may have to have some fun with it and make him sweat it out though. "

A week went by and I had still heard nothing. I got to questioning myself if I really should drop the belt so early without building it up. I had already made up my mind to do it, but it really seemed like a waste, though. Too rushed. It was a good idea, but we could have totally drawn it out and made even more money with it.

I mean, Harley could have put on a southern racist attitude and we could have really played it up. As the champion, it was kind of my right to have a little say in it, and I think we could have doubled or maybe tripled the buy-rate if we waited a month and really had time to build it. We were both football players; Ron was an All-American from Florida State. We could have played his speed versus my power and also worked in a shoot, push the racism card a little. Harley could have called him "a boy" or something on TV. We wouldn't have dropped the N-word, but I think something like that could have really made money.

I had a little talk with Harley before the day of the show.

"You really should just go right in there and tell them you know what they are wanting to do and demand to be a part of the meeting," he said.

"Well, I think that is really what I'm mad at, is that I wasn't invited in. I should have heard it from them first, not Ron," I said.

"What are you going to do?" Harley asked.

"If they were to ask me right now, I would say that a month from now I would totally do it. I'm just hesitant because I thought we could double the buy-rate and we could make even more money together," I said.

So anyhow, the end of the week came, and I arrived at the arena not sure how it was going to pan out. I was surprised when

Dusty Rhodes approached me as I was stretching in the ring hours before the match. He wasn't really who should have been dropping me the news.

"You got a second?" Dusty asked.

"Sure, Dusty," I said, pretending not to know.

"Listen, my man. You just keep stretching and all, but I wanted you to know that Bill Watts and I have been talking," Dusty said. "Tonight, we want to make history. Bill has an idea to create the first ever black heavyweight champion here in WCW and we think it could be really big. We would eventually get the belt back over to you, but we think it would be a good idea. What do you think?"

I paused for an uncomfortable amount of time, and I know Dusty didn't like the wait.

"I know big man, you are on fire right now. But we will do you right. You will still look good, and we will get your heat back for you, right away. You have my word," Dusty said.

While I had already made my mind up I was going to do it, there were elements of this last-minute "negotiation" I really didn't like. The first thing was, I didn't have Bill Watt's word, and he was really the guy I should have been talking to. If I was really mad, I had the ability at that time where I could have made a move to the WWF pretty quickly. Physically, I was at the top of my game and certainly could have also gone back to Japan and maybe set a few more records in a cash-money type thing. There were stories about what André, Stan and what Bruiser had made on a weekly basis, and I knew from a few recent offers, the Japanese would have topped that.

Truthfully, I can't say that I wanted to lose the title, because nobody wants that. But I have got to say, it was awesome to be a part of history, and I thought this was going to be a great move for both of us. One thing that bothered me, though, was that Bill Watts wouldn't come to me to tell me himself. It was almost as if he was trying to force me to do it by having Dusty ask because he was a guy I really respected.

Being a former professional wrestler himself, Bill Watts came to WCW as a no-nonsense promoter from the Mid-South area of the United States (which he would later call the UWF.) As a promoter, he was one of the first ones to really push African-American wrestlers as main stars. In Mid-South Wrestling, he gave great opportunities to the Junkyard Dog and "Big Cat" Ernie Ladd and really helped create their careers. So Watts as the WCW chief decided to use the same successful formula that he developed in Mid-South Wrestling, to make Ron Simmons one of the first African-American pro wrestlers to hold the World Heavyweight Championship in a major national promotion.

A real wrestling genius, Mick Foley, explained in an interview Watts' booking formula as being a success by, "creating a black babyface and building the company around him." This formula of giving a black man a push in order to increase the African-American fan base was a win-win for everybody. It really opened some doors for many wrestlers, changed the way that promoters think, and also opened the minds of wrestling fans everywhere.

But Bill Watts was still kind of a bastard to deal with as a wrestler working underneath him. I mean, I understand he's a born-again Christian now and I'm real happy for him, but he was kind of a power-hungry jerk back then and that's putting it mildly.

I took another calculated moment to make it look good before giving my answer. "Dusty, it is a decent idea, but I want you to know with all due respect, I know what's going on here, and Bill better include me in future decisions, or I just won't do it at all."

"Leon, he's not out to get you. Not at all."

"Then why isn't he here?" Then I raised my voice and tried to make my face red. "Why doesn't he ask me about it himself and make promises to me in person? Why did he send you?!" Dusty looked down. "Look Dusty, Ron and I are friends and all I have to do is just look Ron in the eye and say, 'Hey man, my time isn't up yet. I would do it for you, but right now, I'm not going to do it.' He's a good guy. He would get it." I shook my head and nodded over at Harley in the corner. "It's nothing about Ron man. He's perfect. Bill was just playing dirty sending you in last minute like this, so my answer is no."

Dusty swallowed hard. He nodded and disappeared. I headed back to the locker room and went and found Ron.

I told Ron that I was giving them a hard time, but I was totally in to give him the strap. He was relieved, as if he was maybe wondering himself, but I did think it was a really good idea. I just didn't appreciate how they were not keeping me in the loop. If it had been Sting or any other champion, they would have been the first to know.

Ron let me call the whole match in the back and when we got the end, I said, "...and then hit me with your powerslam."

"Oh, really man?" Ron was in awe. His face lit up.

"Well, if we are going to do it, we have to do it right," I winked at Ron. We finally got it all figured out.

The moment Bill heard about my stubborn reaction, I heard his stubborn cowboy boots clicking in the hallway. He was there in an instant.

"What, what, what?!"

Bill looked like he had seen a ghost. He was at a loss for words. I'm sure everything was already set in production and all. The whole show was probably already set, and here I was saying it wasn't going to happen only an hour or so before the event. He wanted to play a power trip in the locker room and tell me like it is, but that wasn't going to happen.

I looked up from lacing my boots and shook my head no. "I'm not doing it. You didn't bother to include me, you didn't ask me. I should've been the first one to know," I said. I went back to my bootlaces. I looked over to the corner and winked at Ron.

I had already talked to Ron for an hour, and the match was set. He was in on the work. It was great. I had everyone scared. I loved messing with Bill and keeping him in check. We scared the hell out of all of them, man.

So on August 2, 1992, history was to be made. There was a scheduled title match between Sting and myself, but it was canceled after Jake Roberts injured Sting in the storyline. WCW President Bill Watts responded by holding a raffle to determine the number one contender. The hometown hero, Ron Simmons, won the raffle and beat the odds. Then he beat me with his powerslam to win the championship.

When I called for Ron to do his finisher on me, he couldn't believe it. But as I told him before, "we were going to do it right." By the reaction of the crowd, it was the right thing to do.

In the end, Ron caught me and rotated it into his trademark powerslam. By defeating me, Ron became the first recognized African American WCW World Heavyweight Champion.

I had one of my best matches ever, which says a lot because I've had a lot of matches. It is one that I'm most proud of. That "pop" when Ron finally pinned me and took the belt was unbelievable. We changed the face of wrestling, and our match (along with the careers of guys like the JYD and Bobo Brazil) gave a lot of good black men a lot of better opportunities. I was just happy to be part of it.

REMATCH WITH RON

Around the turn of the year on December 30th, 1992, they finally made good on their promise to put the belt back on me. It was a great way for me to start the New Year, regaining the title from Ron Simmons. Nine days after that in Little Rock at The Barton Coliseum, fans saw WCW World Champion Big Van Vader defeat Ron Simmons again. In booking terms, seeing this second victory on the planning sheet made me happy. The second victory signified that the feud was over and the belt would stay with me.

At this time, I would argue the WCW World Title was the number one title in America, and I was happy to get it back and keep it. I wanted that title like no other title out there. Obviously, there were some other strong world titles like WWF, New Japan, and the AJPW Triple Crown, but I thought WCWs championship still really meant you were considered the best actual wrestler in the world. I took it seriously. It was an honor to hold it, but that's just my opinion. With Sting and Ron Simmons in the picture, we were three pretty strong representative athletes vying for the title. I was in great company. It was a win-win for all of us.

Being the WCW Champion was great. As far as travel was concerned, any additional engagements (like signings and appearances) really didn't change my schedule. They still sent me around to do stuff, but no more than usual.

Being the world champion in Japan always involved way more promotional time than here in the states. My responsibility to the press in Japan was a whole different animal over there. I couldn't ride with any of the boys in Japan to the shows, because my work day was always longer, start to finish. The champ had to do a hell of a lot of media-related things that the rest of the roster just didn't have to do.

In looking back at what life was like as WCW champion, however, many often ask me what it was like working with Ron Simmons, specifically in matches for the world title. Ron, in a word, was very explosive. Strength is one thing, but being strong in professional wrestling is not really that important without having speed. Your ability to basically extend your elbow and lift a bunch of weight doesn't matter. Ron Simmons was down-right "powerful."

There have been a lot of strong guys like Scott Norton, who was extremely strong, holding something like a 700-plus-pound bench press. There were other guys like Mark Henry who I think still holds world records for the biggest squats and deadlifts. But, in my opinion, as big and powerful as Mark Henry is, Mike Tyson is even more powerful than Mark because he could deliver and move and deliver again. So to answer the earlier question, Ron Simmons was well-rounded and more powerful than most wrestlers because of his ability to move from point A to point B and deliver blows that were explosive.

RON TODAY

A few years back, I was booked for a wrestling fan fest in Charlotte, NC. I figured, like usual, I would be doing the appearance alone. When I showed up, however, there, sharing a seat at my table, was a very familiar old face. You guessed it.

"Damn!" I said shaking his hand.

"I get that a lot, now," he said, referencing the newer-at-the-time catch phrase that didn't exist in our WCW days together.

The photo op that our promoter offered with us together was a sellout. We had them lined up out of the building. It was the 22nd anniversary to the day, 22 years after Ron took the belt from me. We signed a lot of autographs together, we posed in funny poses with the fans and we just had a ball. We both made a lot of money, too. That kind of made it even better!

At the end of this fan fest, he put his hand on my shoulder and in that deep, powerful, Shaft-like voice of his, he said, "Leon, I've had so much fun today reliving this moment and you changed my life and we changed the face of professional wrestling, forever.

"You didn't have to do the job because you were so over. And what about the powerslam finish? You didn't have to do that either," he said. "I want to thank you from the bottom of my heart."

It was quite a moment.

CHAPTER 12 - WCW POLITICS

For being a promotion run by all kinds of different people just in my short span with them, WCW was very political, to say the least. The term "mismanaged" may not be the correct term, but it is the first one that comes to mind. I almost could use the terms "over-managed" or "under-managed" in certain situations - maybe even "micromanaged."

What I do know is that the constant power-struggle behind the scenes made WCW a difficult place to work that often cost people their jobs along the way. Eventually, the politics behind WCW would claim my spot just as it did many others.

HANDICAP MATCH

I was asked to really light up a couple of the enhancement talents on October 27, 1992, at a WCW Worldwide TV taping. They booked me in a handicap match with a guy named TA McCoy and another one named Joe Thurman. Who knew that the term "handicap match" was about to take on a potentially different ironic meaning?

Everything was going fine in the match against TA McCoy, in the Augusta Civic Center. He took some snug shots and sold pretty well to boot. Then he tagged in his partner Joe Thurman and before you know it, it was over. I hit Thurman with the powerbomb, a move I had used many times before. This time, however, the finisher broke Thurman's back.

Many have heard of an infamous squash match where I broke somebody's back off a powerbomb at a TV taping. If there was one thing I could take back, one thing in my life I could change, it would be this match.

Watching this match today is very uncomfortable for me to say the least. It rattles me to see this match, and it is something I usually avoid. Really, underneath the leather mask and the bad guy image, I am more of a sensitive guy than most would think.

After I hit the power bomb, the ref said that something was wrong.

Joe told the referee that he couldn't move.

You can see that something was wrong at the end of the match, around the 2 minute and 10 second mark. I leaned over him for the pin, but I didn't even really cover him. I didn't want to risk doing any more damage.

The ref counted three for the finish and I headed to the dressing room, sucking back a sob the entire way.

I hid for a few minutes and cried like a baby. I was embarrassed and sorry that something I did in the ring could have totally changed that guy's life forever. I wiped the tears from my face with a towel and shook my head.

I feel horrible. I really want to see him and tell him I'm sorry, but not like this. This will only make him feel worse.

Mick Foley ducked his head in to console me after this incident, but I was dismissive. I didn't want anyone to see me crying. I really was in my own world and upset, to say the least.

Thinking I had paralyzed this young kid named Joe Thurman was horrible. It just about killed me. By the time I had gotten my composure back together, he was gone.

They pulled him right out of there before I could check up on him. I had no time to say, "I'm sorry," and no closure. Because WCW still needed me at the taping, I couldn't chase after the ambulance, either. Paranoia immediately set in.

I pictured Joe laying out on a cot in the hospital thinking, "I'm never going to wrestle again, and I'm never going to be able to walk. Where is the guy who did this to me?"

I figured beyond injuring him, he now also hated me even more for "not caring enough to show up" after something as important as that had happened. That wasn't the case at all. I was a wreck and worrying the worst had happened and it was my fault. By the time the show was finished, hours had passed.

He is not going to even want to see you now, you asshole.

I didn't go to the hospital that night. I got drunk and cried myself to sleep. The next morning, I contemplated going to see Joe, but it got back to me that he recovered feeling below his waist. There was a sigh of relief, and I used that glimmer of hope as an excuse not to go see a man that I figured now hated me.

For years after that, I never did hear if he was able to walk, or if there was any long-term damage or anything. That worry stuck with me in the back of my head forever, and I was too embarrassed to hunt him down.

A few years back, however, I did learn that Joe Thurman had no long-term repercussions from that bout. Though he never wrestled again, I heard he had a family and was doing well; a police officer now in Georgia apparently all is okay. I was very happy to learn that he was not paralyzed, living a normal life.

Huge regrets. I'm sorry I hurt him, and I'm also still sorry I was too embarrassed to face him. Joe, if you read this, I'm sorry for everything that happened and hope that you can forgive me.

THE CAREER ENDER

One thing that typically goes against the politics of any business would be injuring one of their employees. In wrestling, this unwritten rule is probably a bit more lax, but maybe not so much in the case of paralysis. Now, here is where the political side of things comes in. Let's for a moment set aside the horrible idea that a wrestler could no longer provide for his family at the hands of someone who was careless.

If you are looked at as being careless by the powers-that-be, you could be looked at as someone who could cost the promotion money. If one of my bosses at the time wanted to, they could have set up an argument that I was sloppy and should subsequently be let go. An argument could have been made that if I were to cripple one of the top stars whom the company has invested time and money into, it could cost the company thousands, if not millions of dollars.

Fortunately for me, I had someone on my side for the first part of my WCW career. Rather than to be buried by a bad reputation from this, Dusty Rhodes came up with an idea to use the incident to make more money with me. He decided to leak information that would make me look even more like a monster to the dirt sheets that were talking about the incident to further make me look unstoppable.

Dusty Rhodes was a genius.

After the accident with Joe Thurman, headlines got out there that maybe I was "too stiff in the ring for my own good." Dusty decided that we should run with that idea and make it seem like I actually was *a career killer.* He buried the idea that Joe was not paralyzed for a few hours and led the writers on to believe Joe was worse than he actually was. Many considered the Observer and The Torch to be gospel. These fans went on to believe that Joe was still in a wheelchair today.

Dusty then continued with the career-ender idea and booked me to work Nikita Koloff on November 7th, 1992. That date was already set to be Nikita's retirement match, but instead, Dusty made it out like I had injured him. It was then reported that Nikita suffered a real career-ending neck injury, a numb left arm, and a hernia after a Vader clothesline to the back of the head.

The career-ending storyline made perfect sense. I had recently been the cause of Sting taking time off for a cracked rib injury, the whole Joe Thurman incident, and now Nikita Koloff's retirement. These three incidents made me look even more like a monster.

For Nikita, the career-ending angle was also a blessing, as part of it was his idea to begin with. Dusty and Nikita got together and planned a match that would "retire" him, specifically with me in mind as the cause.

I found out later that Nikita Koloff wanted to take time off for some nagging injuries and wanted to make a claim on his Lloyds of London insurance policy to live off of. He was a great worker and pretty banged up, but to the best of my knowledge, there wasn't a specific spinal injury or anything that allowed him to leave and make a claim. He needed a match that could encapsulate "a need to quit" in the eyes of his insurance company. Having a brutal match with me helped to make Nikita's claim more convincing.

Dusty put the pieces of the puzzle together. He took Nikita's need and matched it perfectly with the boost my character needed.

It was great to have Dusty on my side early on in WCW when I was still establishing my character on American television. Anyone else could have gone the other way with the unfortunate Thurman accident that happened and really used it against me.

PAUL E. DANGEROUSLY

Not everyone had someone like Dusty looking out for them, however. Somewhere in the timeframe of early 1993 or so, I came into an arena early to work a show and saw a very angry Paul E. Dangerously, aka Paul Heyman. He was rambling on about a piece of paper that was going to change his life. He was holding a wrinkled-up piece of paper and calling his boss a coward.

"What in the hell is he thinking?!" he said to a handful of agents. "He's not man enough to face me? He's really going to do this *like this*?" Yes. Paul Heyman was actually getting fired from WCW by Bill Watts via fax machine!

"What a giant pussy! He can't come and say it to my face?" Paul said, fuming mad.

This type of weird management seemed to become pretty stereotypical of WCW.

The fax machine firing was based on the claim that Paul "faked expense reports from April through July 1992." I don't know Paul that well. I really don't. I have no clue if it was a means to get rid of a loud-spoken voice that didn't mesh well with the also loud Bill Watts, or if there had been some kind of "creative math" playing with numbers or not. I do know Paul was well liked in his tenure with WCW by the guys.

When Paul left WCW, he dropped me a line from time to time on the phone. He kept the door open for Vader coming into ECW and always had me intrigued. He is a good salesman and obviously a very talented individual. I don't know if you like him or not, but the bottom line is I think he is good for professional wrestling and is very talented at what he does.

BILL WATTS - WORKOUT PARTNER

Maybe Bill Watts as the boss and Paul Heyman as talent were just a bad mix at the time. Two kings but only one throne. Bill is a big man, about 6'4" legit. He had a company of his own that he ran, Mid-South Wrestling. Mid-South was a huge promotion and did great business under his leadership. A very good friend of mine, Dr. Death Steve Williams, worked for him for a long time and said Bill was a genius promoter, but you had to do things his way. (I guess the travel where they would just drive for hours from show to show was brutal. I'm glad I got to miss out on that.)

When Watts came into WCW, there was all kinds of buzz in the locker room. Some people liked the idea, other people hated it saying he would rule with an iron fist. However, like the idea or not, most people were afraid of him. To me, I didn't care who was coming in to run the show. They were taking over during my peak and nothing was going to stop me.

One day shortly after Bill's take over, I remember I was in a lame hotel gym somewhere. At this point during my first year run as the WCW champion, I was 427lbs and I could bench press 640 lbs. There weren't a whole lot of free weights kicking around in the facility, but I still really wanted to keep my pump on and get my workout in, so I had to be creative. I went around and collected all kinds of aerobic weights and anything heavy I could find. It may have looked like Fred Sanford's junk shop, but I strapped all that crap together and was making my workout happen.

I was right in the middle of my trademark "365 pounds behind the neck jump press" when Bill came in.

"Hey Vader, I need to talk to you," he said, kind of getting in my face.

I looked over and made him wait for an answer. "Yeah? Well, you're going to wait a minute until I finish this set."

Bill seemed irritated for a moment, but went over by the opposite wall and waited.

I did fifteen jump presses with all the strapped weights and then rested, but I did not head over to chat with my new boss. I watched him out of the corner of my eye through a mirror on the wall, as I continued to work out, lifting what looked more like the truck in the opening credits of the Beverly Hillbillies than it did exercise gear. I think the visual of that set must have really got him. He went from first having an annoyed, determined look, into one of amusement.

Bill paused a second and then started my way to approach me again. Before he could even speak, I turned around and acted like I didn't see him. I decided to show him I wasn't like the others and I wasn't going to be afraid of him.

"Alright, Vader," he said.

"Listen, Bill, I know you are the new boss, but we can talk later. I don't like my workout being interrupted anyway." At that, I went right back into another set of jump presses.

Bill smiled. He laughed and walked away.

After that, I think I set a good mood. I impressed him by standing up to him. Eventually a few days later, he met up with me about what he wanted at the gym. He had wanted me to come down to live in the area where WCW was probably to save on airfare. I told him, "I would like to Bill, but I have a nice big home in Colorado and I won't be doing that."

I never had a problem with him. You know, I think being the boss in his company kind of carried over with him and created an impression that he fed off of. I never fed into the "it's going to be his way," and he was okay with it from me.

GREEN GUYS

Bill Watts wasn't exactly loved by the boys in the locker room. I remember them setting up to shoot for the WCW Worldwide show back on January 16, 1992. They had a nice little set and got it ready to air the first "WCW Magazine" segment, hosted by Eric Bischoff.

A few of the boys gathered around a monitor and saw them showing footage of Bill Apter presenting PWI's 1992 Rookie of the Year award to Erik Watts, Bill's son.

The boys groaned.

They weren't at all groaning about Bill Apter. Bill has been a staple of the wrestling business as a whole. He has always been one of its most valuable resources. He's a very nice man; always polite, an intelligent gentleman. I don't think he's been given his due. He provided a lot of inside knowledge and the ability to keep that serious fan involved above and beyond the average fan. In this case, however, it was a simple case of nepotism. Out of everyone in the whole locker room that you could push, Bill was putting over his own son, Erik Watts.

Now don't get me wrong. The way Erik treated me was always very respectful. He was pretty much a gentleman, too, and I think his dad brought him up right. I felt sorry for him because he was a big, strong kid. He was really tall like his father, a legitimate 6'5". However, the fact that he was the son of the booker and a very dominant booker at that, made him an easy target – especially because he didn't have the "It Factor."

I think he could have been a great "middle-of-the-card" guy, but his daddy was pushing him without merit. I didn't see "It" and neither did most of the locker room. You can identify the It factor when looking at a Sting and say, "Wow, there's talent there," or a Muta, or a Shawn Michaels for sure. Those are some pretty extreme examples of talent obviously, but you can look and see them do certain things that other people don't do.

Take a look at another booker's son who did have the "It Factor" and you can see what I mean. The Dustin Rhodes push was legitimate in my opinion. *Dustin is talented.* Being the son of Dusty Rhodes didn't hurt, but he really was skilled and creative. Later on, his Goldust character was pretty much conceived by him. One of the first matches I had with Dustin was as a young cowboy coming in. I could tell right away he could wrestle, and it didn't matter whose son he was. That had nothing to do with it. You just either have that certain edge or you don't. Dustin had it; Erik sadly did not.

A few others in the locker room were new around this time and somehow made it into the big leagues being rather green, to say the least. These were Van Hammer and Johnny B. Badd, aka Marc Mero. They were getting pretty good pushes because of who they knew, not because of their in-ring ability. A lot of guys in the locker room really didn't like this and for good reason.

CALLING A MATCH WITHOUT OFFENDING ANYONE

I can't lie. Back then, it was tough for a new guy coming in. He had to get his ass kicked, compete with all kinds of good talent for a spot and he also had to be a politician.

Shortly after filming the *White Castle of Fear*, I vaguely remember meeting a new guy in the locker room, named "The Tazmaniac." He had just come in for a few tryouts and they had him upset Joey Maggs.

The wrestler who would later be known as "Taz" was perhaps a little on the short side, but he was still very powerful and had some real explosiveness to him. While he may not have been all that big in stature, in other ways he was very gifted.

Around this time is when I started to really recognize the inner-workings of WCW politics. It didn't matter how gifted Taz was in the ring because Bill Watts didn't even watch his match. Bill watched him call his match with Maggs beforehand and had already made up his mind before he even got in the ring.

Taz lost his WCW opportunity because of the way he negotiated his match. His in-ring skills had nothing to do with it. Taz didn't get a job with WCW that day, or with WWF when he tried out there a few months later. It would be some time before he would learn the politics behind the scenes, catch a break in ECW, and really have to fight hard to work his way up the ladder.

There was a lot more to getting looked at than just a guy getting a tryout with WCW. This was before the WCW Power Plant training camp could evaluate you effectively to see if you really had what it took to be a wrestler for WCW. At this time, if you were getting a tryout, Bill Watts was the judge, jury and the executioner.

The ability to negotiate the match before the match starts was huge to Bill. He felt a wrestling match was really created in the locker room, and if you didn't compete during that process, it was over. You needed to be competitive in the creation of the match, or else you would never amount to anything. For example, if the guy you are working with is a veteran and he says, "We're going to do this and you're going to do that," and you just sit there and go "Okay, that sounds good," then Bill would want nothing to do with you. He wanted you to stand up for yourself and make the match the best it could be.

Now I know there is a huge thing in wrestling called "respect." Many think that a new guy should never say no to the experienced guy. Well, this isn't exactly the case. If you want to make a living from this business, you have to find a way to change the match in your favor without pissing off the veteran. It's a juggling act with respect in one hand and your own interest in the other.

Believe me, this is hard. Coming up, I had to deal with a couple of guys who really were set in their ways. If you were a young Leon White about to wrestle Bruiser Brody, a 6'7" version of Charles Manson, you would find yourself examining your words before speaking them.

So how do you do that? To answer my own question today, I guess I would just have to say, "Very carefully."

I eventually got pretty good about thinking about both sides of the ring when trying to negotiate the match. This became my strong point so much so that, quite often, most of the guys I worked with would have me call a huge portion of every match we had.

OLE ANDERSON

In a meeting with WCW executives, Bill Watts was eventually reduced in his decision-making role in the company. Come the beginning of February 1993, Bill Watts was Vice President of Wrestling Operations for WCW and Eric Bischoff was announced as Executive Producer for WCW.

Watts didn't like his new role at all and resigned.

Ole Anderson was named the new Vice President of Wrestling Operations. At first, I didn't care all that much who was going to be VP. Ole was just as particular as Watts was, but maybe a little more forward and confrontational than his predecessor.

For example, one day, I was practicing a bit in the ring before the taping. For the last couple of weeks, I was perfecting some moves off the top rope that I figured would really shake the audience. Never had such a big guy ever come off the ropes and nailed such a risky move before. I knew that it would make fans crazy. Not only was it risky for a person my size to flip their body in the air like that, but the perception of that much weight to come crashing down on an opponent in the fan's eyes would be incredible.

Ole watched me in the ring warming up, and I imagined it looked incredible in his eyes, as well.

"Leon, can we talk a second?"

"What about?" I asked, thinking he was about to give me some ideas about how we would use the move.

"Well, I think a man your size should never come off the top."

"Coming off the top?" I asked. "The top rope?"

Ole nodded. He scratched his chin and waited an uncomfortable amount of time for my response.

"Altogether? So, what you are saying is, you don't want me to climb the ropes?"

"That's right," he said.

I shook my head. "Wait a minute, so you don't want me to do something in the ring? You're questioning what I want to do in the ring?" I was like, "Wow, I've never been approached like that." It made no sense to me that he would want me to wrestle differently when that is why I was where I was. My being able to wrestle quicker, stronger and faster as a big man was what led me to being used as their champion in the first place. "What if I want to do a moonsault?"

"Yeah, you're 400 pounds," he laughed. "You don't need to be flying around like Peter Pan."

Being the individual I was at that time, Ole only left me with a choice couple of words that I could say, so I said them and I left.

Ole and I didn't get along anyhow, but this was the icing on the cake. I didn't understand his pointless micromanaging input. Why wouldn't you want a "400-pound Peter Pan" as part of your show? That is what made me special in the fan's eyes. I had proven to be able to do some moves that a man my size normally could not do. That special arsenal of attack should have translated to ratings.

Now, one could say in Ole's defense that maybe he thought I was going to injure a wrestler, or maybe myself during a moonsault. Or, maybe someone from the network had come down on him about it and didn't want someone getting hurt, or what-have-you. However, this was not the case.

I happened to pass by Ole again later that night. "Hey Ole, I'm just wondering," I said. "Is not doing the moonsault because of a ring-psychology concern or a safety concern? I'll bet you I can do it just fine."

"It has absolutely nothing to do with your being able to execute the move at all, Leon," Ole said. He was busy fumbling through some papers on a clipboard. "It's not about safety, or insurance, or pulling it off. It just isn't believable."

Looking back now, it was just generational wrestling gap. It was a difference of opinion, because of how wrestling has changed.

You have to make things relevant in the ring and not just do stuff because you can. Ole was old school. He was coaching me to entertain his fans from the 1970s and 1980s. However, my argument was to make it part of the match and turn that special moment into something special for my fans of the 90s.

Fast-forward to today.

I recently had a little "Twitter war" with a younger guy in the UK named William Ospreay. I started openly criticizing him, based on his crazy moves with no context to the match; gymnastic moves for the sake of gymnastic moves. It was all about me being old school and criticizing the new school. After a few exchanges, he direct messaged me. I explained while there was some truth to what I was saying, I was really working it and looking to turn it into a booking for both of us.

Eventually, that is exactly what happened. A promoter picked up on the Twitter stuff and booked us both for a good payday.

I came to realize that his style of wrestling is what wrestling is today. That is where the sport has gone. He wasn't wrong for his audience. It was the generational wrestling gap. Will Ospreay and others like him are, changing the way a whole new generation of wrestlers are wrestling. Respect, that's the ultimate form of flattery.

It's funny. Looking back at this now, everything came full circle. I found myself in the Ole Anderson role. I was trying to teach my 90s reality to the new world of wrestling.

The student had become the teacher. Time marches on and things change.

WCW WELLNESS POLICY

Around this time, Davey Boy Smith made his WCW debut pinning Bill Irwin after just being fired from the WWF. It was discovered by the WWF that he was receiving shipments of human growth hormone from a pharmacy in England. Davey was fired for violating the wellness policy, yet he came to WCW right away.

Some may wonder if his offense was something that he was better able to hide from WCW. Others in the know wondered if WCW was less tested, and more enhancement-drug friendly than the atmosphere in the WWF. WWF had the spotlight on it at one time as accusations were out there that Vince McMahon himself was distributing steroids. Therefore, they needed to really step up their game in the early '90s to show that there was no problem in the company.

The actual rules that we had in WCW around this time and the rules that were in the WWF were pretty much precisely the same because they were both based on federal law. The big difference was that for most people in WCW, you had a few days' notice before someone was coming to check your pee, whereas I think there were on-the-spot tests given in the WWF.

I can't give a better answer on this topic because I had less of a problem at that time in that area. During my WCW days, everything I put in my body was legal, from protein powder to double cheeseburgers so I never really had a problem. My doctor gave me a few prescriptions legally, but there was nothing shady going on. He wasn't some small town doctor or a shady physician that needed money, he was a family doctor; my son's doctor and my wife's doctor, as well as mine.

THE MASTERS OF THE POWERBOMB

Before this, I had been working a brutal program with Mick Foley, who was, in turn, out on injury. So Davey Boy came in as Mick's replacement and I wrestled at *Slamboree 1993* for the WCW Heavyweight Title. In order to make both of us look good, I lost by disqualification when I hit Davey Boy Smith with a chair, but I still retained the title.

After that PPV, on house shows they needed my matches with Davey Boy to go on even longer. Sid and Sting were both in a program, and Mick Foley continued to wait for medical clearance to get back into the ring. So the Davey Boy feud kept on and we had some really good matches together. Eventually, we decided to work the two feuds in together.

It was then that we staged some kind of press conference with our respective managers, Col. Rob Parker, and Harley Race. They announced my new union with Sid under the uber-creative name, "The Masters of the Power Bomb."

It was awesome working with Sid though because of his height. I'm 6'4" and he's a legit 6'7"…6'8" with a boot on! I was a lot taller than most of the WCW guys, but compared to Sid, I was nothing. Sid towered over me, and it made for some interesting double-team spots inside the ring.

It was pretty cool being teamed up with Sid, but if I were to do it over again today, there is one thing I would probably have changed. I would have had us both slow down a little in promos. We both, I think, were trying to "out monster" each other. One of us needed to calm down and actually talk a little bit. At times, our interviews had just too much testosterone flinging.

Working with Sting was always great, but then adding Davey Boy was the icing on the cake. Davey Boy was a little shorter than me and a lot shorter than Sid, but he wasn't just strong, he was super strong! He could get me for a vertical suplex and just hold me up in the air forever.

This combination led to what would be a very memorable event on pay-per-view for me and one that would further my career to a level considered by magazines as being "one of the greats."

WCW's Beach Blast 93 was a major pay-per-view event that place on July 18, 1993, at the Mississippi Coast Coliseum in Biloxi. It was the second year that WCW had used the name "Beach Blast" for one of our big shows and we were hoping to use the gimmick more in the future. That is why WCW executives had no problem spending a little money on promotion for what was hoped to be a new franchise in PPVs.

The main event for this one was The Superpowers versus The Masters of the Powerbomb. Sting and Davey Boy Smith took on the name "Superpowers" playing off America teaming with England. Their name made total sense. "The Masters of the Powerbomb" had a little less thought behind it, however. Our team's name was based on the fact that both wrestlers in the team used a powerbomb as a finishing move. Oh well. They can't all be winners.

I think the main event was one of Eric Bischoff's better ideas. The thing I liked about this particular PPV was you had an extremely strong card underneath it. The matches that took place before the actual main event were as good as it got in the industry.

This main event was a great idea for a draw, though, as we had all been taking each other on in some way or form as part of a longer running rivalry between both sides.

As part of promotional efforts to get fans to buy the PPV, WCW produced another one of their splendid mini-movies, not unlike "The White Castle of Fear" for which I humbly admit that I deserved an Oscar.

This time, this excellent piece of WCW cinematography had all four participants in tow on, you guessed it, a beach. Sting and Davey Boy Smith were hanging out on a tropical island with a bunch of kids. As they were playing with the kids, Harley Race and Col. Robert Parker approached them, offering them a bribe to not wrestle at Beach Blast. The Superpowers, of course, turned the bribe down, which led the villainous duo of Sid Vicious and myself to do the only thing that makes sense; *hire a midget to kill our opponents.*

The midget doesn't have a gun, however. He rather chose to tail Sting and Davey Boy for a while on their boat. Then, when the time was right, he swam out to their boat with a fake shark fin on his back and planted a bomb!

Just when all hope looked lost, at the very last moment, Davey Boy Smith saved Sting from being blown up by the powerful Midget Bomb. After a heart-warming Superpower moment, the two decided to seek revenge on the Powerbombs at Beach Blast.

If I were a fan sitting at home drinking Kool Aid on the couch, I would have bought that shit.

THE FIRST BIG-MAN MOONSAULT

Before the show, Sting, Sid, Davey Boy and I were sitting at a table with one of my favorite people in the business, Ole Anderson. As we were getting ready to plan out some of what would happen in the main event of the PPV, Ole asked us what ideas we had that could really make the match special to try and further the success of the newer *Beach Blast* brand.

Seeing how a midget in a shark fin almost bombed the heroes in the commercial, we knew we had to produce something very special to live up to the hype. A few ideas were tossed around, but nobody imagined the bomb that I was about to drop until I did it.

"Well, you know I've been trying to add something different to my character," I said. "2 Cold Scorpio and I were training a little, and I've pretty much got a moonsault down pat."

"What the fuck?!" Ole said.

That's right. I offered to do the first super-heavyweight moonsault in wrestling history.

(Now, before this night, what nobody knew was that I had been doing my homework. I dug a huge hole in my backyard and put a trampoline in it so that I didn't have to keep climbing up to practice my flipping. Then, I had 2 Cold Scorpio come over to give me some lessons. It was probably a funny sight for my wife to see, out the kitchen window. After 2 Cold would leave, both me and Jesse would jump around like crazy for hours, trying to learn the moonsault. But eventually, I got it, and Jesse did too.)

Just before that meeting with Ole, 2 Cold Scorpio met up with me in the ring so I could apply what I had learned there. He was an excellent high jumper and he worked with me for about a half hour and coached me through the moonsault for the PPV. The first time I did it, I actually landed on my feet with even more rotation than I needed. The second time I did it, it was perfect.

The boys' eyes opened wide at the possibility of me doing a move like that when they heard about it first at the table, even though they hadn't seen it yet. It seemed for a moment though that it wasn't going to matter because Ole was shooting it down.

"Now, listen Leon. No disrespect, but we have talked about this before. It just doesn't make sense for a huge guy like you to do something like the little guys. In fact, it makes NO sense at all!"

Ole was booking and acting as an agent for our match so what he thought did have merit. But I didn't really care whether we had a conversation about this months ago, or not. It was going to happen.

"Look, Ole," I said. "Whether it happens tonight or a few weeks from tonight, I'm going to eventually be doing it, so tonight is as good as any."

"Leon, are we going to go after this again?" Ole asked, looking around the table for support.

"When you see me do a moonsault and all the fans pop, I mean, I guess you can fire me."

"Well, wait a second, Ole," Sting said. "I would think you would want Leon to try it. It could really mean money with a big guy like him doing it."

Ole shook his head.

"Yeah," Davey said. "If he thinks he can do it, I'm down." From what I learned later, Davey really didn't want to take the move, but just wouldn't say it. Sting didn't want Ole to wreck the match with his bullshit input so we all agreed to have each other's backs before we even went into the meeting.

Either way, with Sting's endorsement, there wasn't really much Ole could say or do to keep it from happening. After Ole left and the finish was confirmed, we decided to fill in the blanks on our own.

Sting knew ahead of time that I wasn't getting along with Ole and made sure we would all have each other's backs. That is why he immediately helped usher the moonsault idea into the match. We called out the most important spots, and when the moonsault made sense, it was Davey Boy who looked like he was going to have to take it.

We all laughed. I just thought it was funny that Sting who was calling out that part of the match volunteered his partner, the new guy Davey Boy, to take the move rather than himself.

"Leon, I think you are amazing if you can do so much for a big guy," Davey Boy said in his English accent. "But, I have to say, I want to see it first before I take it."

I can appreciate Davey Boy being a little skeptical. A moonsault is a pretty sick move to take, period.

You are lying there and you watch as a guy climbs up high above you, then flips over blind at you. You could get hit with a knee in the face, or in the balls or anywhere, and you are pretty much dead meat. Now, add to the fact that this one would be a moonsault that weighs 450 plus pounds – a moonsault from a big ass like mine falling out of the sky and possibly hitting you in the face? Can you imagine how scary it is seeing a big ass like mine coming down straight at you?

So we all marched out to the ring in the still empty Mississippi Coast Coliseum.

"Was today the first time you have ever tried doing one?" Davey asked cautiously, as we stepped into the ring.

"No, no. Actually, I attempted one in Japan about six months ago."

"How did that turn out?" he asked.

"Honestly, not too good," I said looking over at Sting as I started climbing the ropes. "I landed on his head."

We all laughed again.

I remember thinking to myself, *I better not botch this one up, or it's out.* But then I hit it perfectly and landed on my feet. Sid started clapping and the rest followed.

Davey Boy exhaled hard and was impressed. "Well, I guess it's on then."

Hours later, the match came off great, as expected and "The Vadersault" was born. Davey Boy and Sting were victorious, but I went for the moonsault twice in the match and nailed it the second time, much to the amazement of Jesse Ventura and Tony Schiavone. They had no clue it was coming. You could hear the unbelieving tone in their voices.

The birth of my new move was a huge success that night in the ring and in many rings to come.

OFTEN IMITATED, NEVER DUPLICATED

After my moonsault made wrestling magazine headlines around the world, my former tag partner Bam Bam Bigelow did one a few months later on *Monday Night Raw.* This was probably a catch-up move to save face by our competition at the time, but most people still gave me props for being the first and the best. Fans and, more importantly, magazine editors alike have always been really good to me about giving me credit. They argued that the second "big-man moonsault" by Bigelow wasn't even a real "moonsault" as he kind of turned a little bit off to one side almost like a cartwheel.

The magazines have actually always been pretty kind in ranking me one of the absolute best wrestlers as far as "super heavyweights" are concerned, and I'm forever grateful. I figure this is a great place for me to thank them publicly.

First off, let's not be confused who I am talking about when I say "Super Heavyweights." It isn't just how much a guy weighs. The "Giant" weight class/category includes really big and tall guys like, André the Giant (ABOVE), Kevin Nash and the Big Show. The Super heavyweight class, however, traditionally includes a bunch of regular heighted "big men" who typically couldn't move around much because of how heavy they were.

The classic, legendary super heavyweights include guys who weighed in at around 400 pounds. These non-giants included wrestlers like Bam Bam Bigelow, Yokozuna, King Kong Bundy and myself. Then, there were also a bunch of sideshow attractions, dudes like Haystacks Calhoun, "Plowboy" Uncle Elmer, and a bunch of almost super heavyweights like Mantaur, Man Mountain Rock, and other lesser known guys who eat better at the buffet than they can wrestle.

Though I never held the WWE title, I've always been pretty proud to be considered among the top elite super-heavies by the top name magazines and the general consensus at WWE themselves. I take pride that in the fact that many have considered me to be one of the best super heavyweights ever and that's just the deal. In the past, people have argued for me to top this list in looking at my move set including the dropkicks and the moonsault again, and I'm forever thankful and humbled to be in this conversation.

Bam Bam Bigelow himself often ranked me, his partner, above himself. He was certainly physically gifted, may he rest in peace, but he would often openly admit it he couldn't go out there and put in twenty five minutes like I could with a Japanese guy of 225 pounds. I don't know, but Bam Bam was still fantastic and extremely talented, and that's what I'm talking about here. He was a perfect example of a super heavyweight having athleticism. He could moonsault and dropkick; he could do it all.

It's too bad the Bammer is gone. However, if he were still here with us today, I would rib him, call him a "copycat" and say, "I did it first!"

I miss the Bammer. He was a great talent.

JIM ROSS

In the early part of spring, Jim Ross resigned from WCW. Someone at WCW decided to remove one of the best commentators ever from TV and re-assign him as a syndicated television salesman for the company. Why did they do this? Probably because they felt threatened by how good he was on the mic, and also behind the scenes. Jim knew this was a misuse of his all of his abilities and soon after, he signed with the WWF, making his debut at *WrestleMania IX*.

To me, this was a huge loss for WCW. On a selfish level, as well, Jim was a friend and a big supporter of mine. When you listened to a Jim Ross commentated Vader match, you could hear the horror in his voice. He really understood how to tell the story in order to bring out the monster side of my character.

The announcer has a lot to do with the match that you see on TV than the average wrestling fan would recognize. I remember watching some matches after Jim left and thinking to myself that something felt lame. I thought, "What's missing?" I eventually realized it had nothing to do with what I was missing in the ring; it was Jim Ross that was missing. It was his way of telling the match that was missing.

It was something that no other announcer could really capture.

Jim Ross' demotion came, maybe not so coincidentally. He found himself having to bail at a time when there was a political change in power.

Ole replaced Bill, and Eric was rising in the ranks. Am I wrong to guess that someone was forcing him out?

STEVE AUSTIN

Another guy that didn't really get his just due in WCW was a guy who would arguably become one of the biggest names in wrestling later on due to his firing, Stone Cold Steve Austin.

In my prime and in Steve's prime with WCW, we were teamed up together on one occasion, and it was for a match I will never forget. We wrestled Ric Flair & Arn Anderson for about 27 minutes on TV, yet it felt like a massive PPV.

Now opponents play a big part in the overall scheme of things in a tag team match, but Steve and I as a tag team? Wow! We had perfect timing. Our styles complimented each other very well. We had a big man brawler and one of the best technicians of his time. We had instant chemistry. Along with the very talented showman, Ric Flair, and the storyteller master, Arn Anderson, the four of us together just tore the house down.

At the end of the match, the audience erupted like they do at the biggest events of the year, yet it was just a little unimportant filler match for a television angle that was going nowhere. Steve was excited and came up to me in the locker room. Steve said to me, "Did you ever feel anything like that? Did you ever gel with a new partner like that?"

"I know exactly where you are coming from," I said. I agreed. I had been in a number of oddly paired tag teams before and none really worked out like this one did. It really was perfect.

"We need to do something about this," he said.

We both tried and it didn't happen. We both really didn't have the stroke we needed in order to make us a permanent tag team, because neither of us was any good in the game of politics.

If this were today and Steve Austin was asking to tag team with someone, you can bet your life that the backstage would listen. We just weren't there yet politically – either one of us, however, and maybe we missed a pretty good opportunity. I don't know.

We would not have been the first visibly gifted tag team that Ric went out of his way to put the kibosh on in the locker room behind the scenes. I have been told that Ric didn't like good tag teams because he didn't want the possibility of anyone outshining any rendition of the Horseman that Ric had going on.

Incidentally, soon after this, Austin was irritated with his booking and would start to butt heads with Eric Bischoff. After suffering a shoulder injury, Eric found just enough reason to get rid of him. He fired him over the phone, not predicting that he would soon become one of the biggest names in WWF history.

BEING THE BEST YOU CAN BE

As the saying goes, "It takes two to tango." I can honestly say that it wasn't always the other guy's fault. One time I remember where this case was true was in Columbus, Georgia on the WCW Worldwide show. That night I probably didn't give my very best performance for the other guy to work with. This wasn't in the ring, however, it was for the debut of Ric Flair's talk show.

Flair triumphantly returned from WWE as a hero in February 1993. Because Vince McMahon was a master of contracts, Ric Flair could work for WCW, but he couldn't wrestle right away. As the result of a "non-compete" where Flair was unable to wrestle, they decided to have him host a short-lived talk show during WCW programming called *A Flair for the Gold.*

This new interview segment was to borrow a page from the popular *Piper's Pit* on the other channel but, of course, it had Ric Flair as the host. Rather than to have a bodyguard like Cowboy Bob Orton in the background, Ric Flair chose to go more sexy; Fifi, a model named Wendy Barlow in a French maid costume. (Incidentally, she was so sexy, she's now Ric's actual wife.)

On this new segment's debut, WCW advertised Ric Flair to interview "Big Van Vader and his manager Harley Race." This looked great on paper. Ric was always very good at improvising and saying some pretty interesting things, and it seemed like an interview with us after his absence should have been great. As far as this interview segment was concerned, the sexy maid Fifi certainly shouldn't have hurt either.

Looking back at it today, I'll be the first to admit that, out of everyone on the set, it was me who didn't deliver because of my own agenda.

At this point, I had decided that I was a monster. I was pretty set in my ways that my character needed to be a growling, grunting, caveman-type guy and I just wouldn't budge. Some of that "madman persona" should have been toned down a little bit in some interviews. In doing so, I probably could have got more depth out of the Vader character outside of the ring with this approach, and it certainly would have helped in Flair's interview that night with me. In retrospect, I probably should have given a little more coherency to my character to allow Ric to have something to work with.

I remember standing on the set and saying to myself, "if Ric puts the microphone in my face, I'm just going to go nuts." I remember thinking Harley was my mouthpiece, so I wasn't going to give anything to Ric. And just as I figured, Ric tried to get a word out of me and I gave him nothing but violent ogre gruntings. I don't know if it was to protect my character, or if I subconsciously wanted to see his interview segment fail. I just remember being uncooperative for no real reason.

I'll agree, it's pretty hard to interview the grunt and the growl. If I had slowed that down a little bit and just given him a little room to work with, the segment would have been more memorable and something that could have drawn better money.

Sometimes, guys would intentionally "stink up" an interview or "stink up" a match for political reasons. They would do this to see the other person fail and cause problems behind the scenes for them. But I wasn't thinking politically yet in my career. I just wanted to be a monster, so it was more selfish than it was malicious.

Speaking of *A Flair for the Gold*, a few weeks after my train wreck of an interview, the Four Horsemen were set to appear on the same interview segment. It was advertised for weeks as a reunion of the original Horsemen, but when the day finally came, Tully Blanchard no-showed due to behind-the-scenes politics. His replacement was Paul Roma.

Flair was pissed.

Tully was first set to return with Arn Anderson after their WWF Brain Busters stint back in 1990. Back then, it is said that Flair had heat with Tully and pulled some strings to keep him from returning to WCW. However, they had since patched things up and were excited to get to work with each other again.

Before Flair's reunion interview, the locker room was also abuzz, excited to see Tully, but it just wasn't in the cards. Tully was replaced last minute. I don't know who had politicked against Flair's wishes on this occasion. I wasn't privy to a lot of information from his clique. It's just another fine example of all the political crap you had to sift through.

Rumor has it that Tully was offered a spot in the reformed Horsemen, but turned it down when they only offered him $500 a night, a strategic lowball number to keep him out and keep Flair's support group down in numbers. That is when they replaced Tully with Paul Roma, last minute. The last thing Flair wanted was Paul Roma as a Horseman, so I guess he didn't get everything he wanted and there was still a power struggle going on.

All I knew was at this point, the Flair camp was slowly taking over. They would soon be pretty much running the company, due to Flair's ability to politic.

MASS SHOOTINGS

On July 7th, 1993, there was a mass shooting, and it was probably the biggest in wrestling history. When I say "mass shootings," I don't mean Sid went psycho on some of the boys in the locker room in some kind of "postal worker" moment or something. That would come later. What I mean is that a huge set of syndicated WCW TV tapings were shot all at once.

WCW held its first set of TV tapings at the Disney/MGM Studios in Orlando where they taped six months of WCW Worldwide television episodes over only four days.

An executive playing politics decided that they could be a savior and save loads of money for the company by shooting everything all at once, at a point in history where WCW was afraid of bankruptcy. What they did was fly everyone down to center stage in Florida, all in one group, one time to shoot a ton of programming. It came down to being all about the dollar in that they would save so much time and save so much money.

You see, *Clash of The Champions* XXIII should have been a huge event, but it wasn't despite all evidence that it should have been. It was the return of Ric Flair wrestling in WCW in Norfolk, VA. His no-compete contract was up with the WWF and he was cleared to team with Four Horseman member, Arn Anderson, against the hottest tag team, Hollywood Blondes. This anticipated broadcast only drew a 2.6 rating, which was horrible. Therefore, WCW executives felt their "mass shooting idea" was well worth doing.

Now, of course, mass shootings wouldn't work today. Every "smart mark" in the audience would go running instantly to report the results on Twitter from their iPhones. People would know what happened and not bother to tune into the show, as a result. This would really kill ratings. However, back then there were no smart phones or internet wrestling community.

Because we were shooting so much, so many months in advance before it would air on TV, title changes were being revealed to the live audience way before it would be seen on television. Quite obviously, WCW felt possible spoilers were worth the risk due to the current state of their bank account.

Another problem I was very vocal about at the time was that the crowd at Disney (where it was being filmed) were not wrestling fans. I think that's something WCW failed to recognize. When you wrestle in front of a crowd that isn't really a wrestling-fan-based crowd, you have to wrestle differently to get the reactions that come inherently with traditional fans.

What we needed to do to get that reaction would have been to change our format a little and entertain for that non-wrestling fan crowd. More good versus evil, more playing up to the audience, as that would have gone a long way. All the complicated wrestling angles and this and that needed to ease up. We basically needed to simplify all that, get the crowd cheering, booing, making noise and then move on in the shows.

We didn't do it, and the vibe made for some pretty lame television, which further contributed to a dropping off in the ratings.

Come that August at *Clash of the Champions XXIV* in Daytona Beach, FL, we drew a 3.8 rating and was viewed in 2.32 million homes for me and Davey Boy in the main event for the WCW title.

Back then in '93, I was aware of the importance of ratings, but maybe not enough. We were aware of buy rates, TV ratings and who was doing what, but I didn't really think of it as an important negotiating factor with the promoters. My learning curve as a politically-savvy, intelligent wrestler was really slow-coming back at that time, although it was something I really needed to know. I think it was a real negative move not to play that game enough. I should have kept my eyes open to a number of things on the marketing end and not focus solely on the wrestling.

THE BIG GOLD BELT

By the beginning of September in 1993, WCW pulled the ultimate in backstage politics. They lost their relationship with the National Wrestling Alliance by making decisions without asking them about their own title.

At this point, we had two major heavyweight singles titles; the WCW World Championship (mine) and the NWA World Title (Ric Flair's.) My title belt was fairly modern and had a globe in the center. Ric Flair's was the famous big gold belt that a lot of people equate with WCW still today.

Before Flair even lost his NWA title, WCW went ahead and taped some segments at Disney Studios with Rick Rude as the new NWA champion. The problem was, they never asked permission. WCW just assumed that since they were now the bigger promotion, they could do whatever they wanted. The NWA got word of the bold move and was pissed. Like any other promotion under the NWA banner, WCW was supposed to seek their approval before they ever changed the title holder, and it was obvious they did not. So the NWA publically withdrew the recognition of WCW's big gold belt as their title a week before Flair could even lose it to Rude on TV (before the episode had actually aired.)

The heat between WCW and the NWA Board reached a boiling point that ended their relationship. WCW didn't scrap the belt, however. They stopped calling it the NWA title on television, but since they owned the actual belt, they just kept on using it. For a while, they called it the "Big Gold Belt" and Rude would defend it without any company affiliation until it was renamed the "WCW International World Heavyweight Championship."

So here I am, the WCW World Heavyweight Champion, and now we have someone else being called the "WCW International World Heavyweight Champion." My title seemed to indicate I was the best in the promotion, but the other title seemed to indicate that someone was the best in all of the nations in the world.

It was redundant and one of the most confusing things ever.

The story on TV was that a fictional committee within the company called "WCW International" declared the big gold belt to be their world championship title. It didn't make sense to a lot of people, even the commentators. During matches, the broadcasters would often call it the "bogus championship" because it was on Rick Rude and helped him get cheap heat.

I didn't care much at the time what the belts were really called. I had the confidence that if I didn't like whatever WCW was throwing my way at any moment, I could just pack my bags and go. I had established my name enough so that I had the ability to just go to Japan and perhaps make even more money. I was in a good position.

To look back on that time and to see who was running what and what was being done is certainly interesting. Why didn't this happen, and why didn't that happen? It's just so obvious now, years later, after more experience in the game. It was all ego and politics. Keeping the belt on TV was a power play against the NWA.

My belt was the real belt they chose to focus on, however.

Here's how you know in the long run which belt actually meant something... On the same show where Flair beat me for the WCW World Heavyweight belt in the main event, Rude defended the International World belt against "The Boss." At the next PPV, Rude lost the belt to Sting in the middle of the card, while Flair defended against Steamboat in the main event. At SuperBrawl, when Flair defended against me in the cage, and Rude didn't even get a WCW International World title defense.

At the *Clash of the Champions 27* in June '94, Flair finally beat Sting and unified the two titles. That is when they chose to scrap the modern belt that I had always held to go with the sexier big gold belt that was more "photogenic for a champion."

The funny thing is, the way my reign fell, I never held that iconic version of the NWA/WCW big gold belt. Though my championship was the more important one, I never held that big gold belt.

Can you imagine me with the big jewel-encrusted golden title as the WCW World Heavyweight champion? That may have been too much sexiness for any one man to grasp.

BUSINESS DROPPING OFF

Let me jump back a second. Come October '93 or so, there was a really poor turnout at The Omni in Atlanta. The show only drew 700-800 paid fans when we were used to drawing thousands. We had about an $8,000 gate which was believed to be the smallest crowd in WCW in nearly 20 years since the Omni had housed professional wrestling.

As a result, WCW management canceled the traditional WCW Thanksgiving and Christmas night shows. Morale started to change in the locker room for guys who got some kind of percentage in their paychecks. They were counting on that booking. I was okay because I had a real good guarantee-based contract, period. What I made at house shows stayed the same. My pay-per-view money stayed the same. I didn't have to worry about things like the others did. The loss of those shows for a huge portion of the roster meant a pretty lousy Christmas financially for a bunch of the boys and their families.

Business started to slow down around this point in America as a whole. Some guys thought about leaving and others figured it was just a slow point in the cycle and would hunker in and wait it out.

See, we used to have clear cycles when it came to wrestling. Cycles had their ups and down, but at least guys still had options and other places to work. Now let's face it. That has definitely changed. The territories are all gone. There's only one real major company now worldwide and just one guy that runs the show.

The thing that saddens me most about professional wrestling today is the drop off of business in Japan. At one point, New Japan, All Japan, and NOAH on any one given night of the week had 15,000 plus people watching wrestling. To see where Japanese wrestling is now, it's just not the same. I always loved the Japanese fans. They treated professional wrestling with respect and didn't look at it like it was a comedy.

There is a glimmer of hope, however. Recently, NJPW is at an all-time high in attendance and business is booming. Hopefully, the machine that put Vader on the map can regain all the success it once had.

AN OFF NIGHT

Battlebowl was a WCW PPV where we were supposed to be randomly paired in weird Lethal Lottery tag-team matches where they literally just drew names out of a hat to create the pairings. Whichever team won would then have its members pitted against each other to compete for a Super-Bowl-like ring.

The idea was to pair people up with unlikely partners to see some interesting combinations, but it really just led us to bad booking situations, working with people we didn't know.

For my match, Mean Gene Okerlund did the honors with the lotto-drawing and it turned out to be Cactus Jack tagging with me. I guess they figured the audience wouldn't guess it was rigged that I had to tag with my own archenemy.

Next, a possibly drunk Mean Gene Okerlund was supposed to call out Harlem Heat's Stevie Ray (who was called "Kane" at this time.) But since nothing was written on the paper and Mean Gene had to go from memory, he called out "Kole" which was Booker T's original name in Harlem Heat at this point in time. Gene either did this because he couldn't remember who was who, or honestly because he really couldn't tell them apart – I don't know. I wish it was Booker T who was actually booked for this match, but that just wasn't the case. Stevie Ray came out anyhow like he was supposed to, and the commentators just went along with what Gene said and called Stevie "Kole" for the hell of it.

So next, Gene finally drew Kole's partner. To an audience of crickets, the big reveal was this really, really welfare Tatanka knock-off guy come out to ringside. His name was Charlie Norris. Now, it was not Chuck Norris, by any means. If you are not familiar with Charlie Norris, take Tatanka's head off and put it on a body made of Silly Putty, Play-Doh, and rope. That is pretty much what Charlie Norris looked like.

To start, everyone just beat the crap out of Cactus including myself as his partner, because we were still feuding at the time on TV. It was an interesting dynamic with Cactus and myself teaming up, but after our in-fighting, I eventually ended up in the ring with the stickman.

The moment I locked up with Norris, I knew had to give up the "beating-on-Cactus" game plan entirely, because he was just so horrible. He was freezing up at the wrong moments and his timing was the worst. I tried to get something good out of him, but it wasn't happening. He was the worst piece of crap going.

Charlie Norris was beyond bad, so I decided to go into total destroy-mode on him to try and get the audience behind him as an underdog. But that just wasn't happening, either. The crowd wasn't stupid. They got even more behind us - the Cactus/Vader team, probably because we weren't trash like Charlie Norris was.

After I had had enough of throwing Norris around like a ragdoll, I told him to go over and tag in Stevie Ray. Now, don't get me wrong. I love Stevie Ray, but he was still fairly new at this point. He wasn't as green as Norris, who was greener than baby poop after cream of asparagus for supper. In his defense, Booker T and Stevie Ray had both worked in GCW for quite a while by this point. However, when Stevie hit the ring trying to save a shitty match without the know-how to do so, he too showcased just how bad a wrestler like Norris could be.

"Oh man! I give up," I said retreating. I tagged in Cactus, hoping maybe he had an idea on how to get something good going.

Cactus happily sold all of Stevie's crappy offense including bumping from his big boot right out of the ring. I thought this was funny. I was standing outside on the apron watching all that garbage and figured it couldn't get any worse and then it did. I watched in horror as "Kole" tagged back in Charlie "Welfare Tatanka" Norris.

Norris comes back in a house of fire, or maybe should I say, a brown paper bag of dog shit on fire, I don't know. Either way, he came back in stinking up the place with his vast array of offense; big boots, jumping chops and chin locks from hell to try and get a pop beating on Cactus.

"Ugh!" I said.

Sick of seeing all that lameness, I got back in just to smack Norris upside his head. I immediately started no-selling Norris's lame karate chop offense. I was in no mood to take shit from anyone. That scrub team sucked something fierce. Though we had another minute or two to go, I made an executive decision to save the audience of the torture early. I called a powerbomb for the finish, but Norris jumped like he was trying for a leapfrog. I don't know what he was thinking but I fell into the ropes. It looked sloppy as hell, but I covered him anyhow to put him out of his misery.

That botched powerbomb twisted my back (which caused me to miss a few dates.) I would once again brave out injury and go on to win the 16-man Battle Royal in the main event. In the end, I eliminated Sting to become the 1993 WCW Battlebowl Champion.

Maybe I'm being trivial coming from a football background, but at the end of the night, I was upset. Sting received an awesome Battlebowl ring from winning the year before, but Eric didn't bother to buy me one. I'm serious! Sting's was a really nice ring, like a Super Bowl ring, and I wanted one! Maybe I wasn't the best at politics, I don't know. I guess Charlie Norris wasn't the only person who was on the losing end that night.

RIC FLAIR

After Flair finished his contract up with WWF, Ric Flair came back over to WCW. Months later, Dusty Rhodes was the booker then and came up to me in the locker room to discuss his concerns.

I was supposed to be facing Sid Vicious for the title at Starrcade '93 on December 27, 1993, from the Independence Arena in Charlotte, North Carolina. However, something super crazy happened with Sid and they decided to replace him. (Fear not. Rather than to breeze through what happened with Sid that got him replaced, I decided to dedicate the entire next chapter to the topic.) Ric Flair was being considered as the replacement.

"Leon, look. We still need to build Flair's stock back up after the jump so he could be a major player once again," he said in his smooth southern pimp voice. "I'm hoping that you will help us out with this. We think Flair coming from Charlotte and all would be the best option to take the title now, instead of Sid."

Back when Flair left WWF, he gave an advance notice to leave on good terms. Therefore, Vince just had him "do the honors" for the younger talent in WWF on house shows to get their guys over in his final days with the company. WWF knew he would end up back with WCW, so it didn't make sense to still put him over on TV. But it also didn't make sense that I needed to job for him in WCW, because he only really lost to Curt Hennig once in his final WWF appearance and they didn't really bury him.

Flair was already back. When Flair initially came back to WCW, he already got himself over with his *Flair for the Gold* segments. Those interviews were like giant Ric Flair commercials. After he was cleared to wrestle from his WWF non-compete clause, Flair immediately beat Barry Windham for the NWA championship. His one loss to Hennig on RAW before he left WWF had now been repaired. Eventually, he dropped the NWA title to Rick Rude. I understand the importance of being a team player to move storylines forward, but dropping my title to Flair (who just lost to Rude) wasn't about trying to save Flair's career from the minimal hurt that WWF did to him on the way out.

About the "not wanting to job" thing - it's not an ego thing at all, but if you lose to someone who just lost a high-profile match, then your character looks weak. The fans don't buy you as being a good competitor and then the bookers eventually end up using you less on TV. Jobbing out (in some cases) is, therefore, a bad idea as it is a negative investment in your future that can actually hurt you financially. It is important to look out for your best interests.

Flair just lost the big gold belt to Rick Rude.

"I don't know, Dusty."

"Listen, we won't make you look bad," he said. "What we will do is we will have you drop the title to Flair in his hometown Charlotte, to really get him over. And then afterwards, we will build you back up to get revenge and win the title back in the steel cage on pay-per-view."

That plan sounded great. I figured that a big steel cage match would really make me look good, beating someone like Ric Flair on PPV.

"Promise? I have your word?"

I nodded. Dusty shook my hand. He took care of me before with Ron and made good with his word, so of course, I agreed.

What happened in the meantime, Dusty Rhodes got an offer he couldn't refuse and left for the WWF, just before Starrcade. Ric Flair then lobbied behind the scenes to take over the book at WCW.

Ric Flair became the new booker.

DROPPING THE TITLE

Flair is one of the very, very best ever. What brought him to become one of the most successful wrestlers of all time was his entertainment value and his ability to tell a story. There will never be another person like him. However, at this point in his career, he pretty much had what I like to call a "cookie-cutter Flair match" that frankly to me was boring, not because it wasn't good, but because I had seen it hundreds of thousands of times.

Flair was a good wrestler, *but an even better entertainer.* He had worked out a routine that made him famous in every arena around the world. Because of this, many Flair matches at this stage of his life started to look similar. As a fan at this time, you could predict a lot of what he was going to do in the ring and it was arguably more exciting to see Flair's entrance or hear him talk than to actually see him in the ring anymore.

I felt that being beaten in the same boring way would make me look like all the rest – *nothing special.* You see, I really didn't want to have a crappy match and then also lose, because everyone would only then remember the pinfall. I wanted to have an awesome match so people would remember the wrestling, not the finish.

To try and diminish hurting my brand from a loss in a cookie-cutter Flair match, I decided to get advice from yet another one of the biggest names ever, my manager, Harley Race.

A little before the PPV, we were staying up on a high floor in some kind of dive hotel. Harley just got out of the shower as part of his morning rituals and cracked open a warm beer.

There was a little bit of a balcony there, and Harley was taking advantage of it. Harley had a bit of OCD or some kind of control issue and he had to sleep by the window in most of our hotels. This also meant he claimed territory on possible decks if there was one leading outside. He walked over with his drink and cigarette in hand, then sat on a white plastic lawn chair, and deeply inhaled the pleasant carbon monoxide from the fresh highway air.

"Hey, Harley," I said, interrupting his morning Zen.

"Eh," he said, as a man of many words.

"Harley, I've been thinking. I don't want the fans to remember only the loss. If I'm going to lose the match to Flair, I want the match to be memorable," I said to another former NWA Champion. "I want to get a real fight out of Flair so people remember the wrestling, the match itself, not just the finish. How can I make this happen?"

Harley took a long drag on a cigarette and then pulled on his beer. "With Flair, today? I don't see that happening," he said.

"That's what I mean. It's bad enough I have to put him over when it is my turn to save face, but because of the cookie-cutter match he will want to have, it is even worse."

"Hmm," Harley said rubbing his chin. "You're right, but maybe it doesn't have to be cookie-cutter." There was a long pause. After a minute of figuring, a light bulb went off underneath Harley's sweet Tom Jones hairdo. "Well, maybe it could work."

"What could?"

"It very well could work," he said wearing nothing but a towel, looking out over the lovely hotel parking lot. Harley Race, a wise former NWA Champion, got up and grabbed his beer and then went back out on the little patio. He sat back down on the chair and opened his towel to air dry his nutsack.

He lifted his leg and farted hard.

"Godammit, Harley!" I said. "The breeze is blowing right in here." Sick bastard. I had my mouth open and everything.

Harley no-sold the flatulence. "I got a plan."

After the fart wafted away, he explained that I should plan to do the job to Flair, but first beat the bejesus out of him for 35 minutes and get him really riled up. He figured if I really gave it to Flair, he would have to fight back for real. That would get the fight we wanted out of him, to make us both look good even with him going over.

Harley was a genius.

Knowing that I couldn't get my revenge match to keep my character looking strong, I had to throw some hard potatoes around in hopes to get some back.

So during the match, just as Harley and I had planned, I would hit Flair pretty hard. Then, Harley would wince and shout something to Flair like, "That wasn't right!" or "Geesh, are you going to just let him hit you like that?"

Eventually, it worked. Harley convinced Flair to start throwing some potatoes back, and that's when the match got good. Even though it took some time to get the real fight to come out of The Nature Boy, eventually it worked.

Ric started throwing some hard shots and the match really came together. It wasn't the lame stereotypical cookie-cutter Flair fight! Dragging it out of the aging Flair was tough because being the man for so long meant he could do mostly anything that he wanted. He had become set in his ways, but not on this night. Our match stole the show.

If you can find this match on YouTube or the WWE network, you will see that Flair was all black and blue and purple at the end of the match.

In a post interview, one of the announcers came up to Flair and said, "You really took it to Vader then right?" and Flair said, "No. Vader really took it to me."

THE THUNDERCAGE

I continued to feud with Ric Flair wondering if he would make good with Dusty's promise. Things looked good, at first. I was still booked for the PPV rematch at *SuperBrawl IV*, and it seemed like we were on track for our big match in the Thundercage.

WCW's Thundercage was a fierce looking thing clearly based on the fighting pit from the movie *Mad Max: Beyond Thunderdome*. Ric Flair and I would be facing each other in this weird steel cage that bent upwards to form a dome. While the cage didn't have a closed in top, the sides curved in to prevent escape. The one thing that really made this cage different sometimes was the top of the cage was supposed to be "electrified."

Before my agreed upon rematch with Flair, the boys were already telling me that certain people didn't want me in the heavyweight title mix anymore. The problem was, the person I shook hands with on with the winning-the-title-back deal was no longer the man-in-charge. My opponent in that match was.

Losing Dusty was a big deal. Dusty had always had my best interest at heart. My whole career in WCW, the people above Dusty kept changing, but they were Executive Vice Presidents who sometimes acted as bookers, but none of them were officially bookers. They included guys like Jim Heard, Bill Watts, Ken Frye, Ole Anderson and eventually Eric Bischoff. Dusty was always the constant, however. I had my three world titles with Dusty on the book and the one time US Champion with Dusty, as well.

Well, all good things come to an end, and as always, new obstacles were coming.

Ric Flair came up to me the first time acting like my new boss. As the new official booker, he was talking about taking some time off from being in the ring to heal some nagging injuries (and our match in Charlotte) and really concentrate his efforts backstage in his booking role.

"Leon, I'm probably soon going to be taking some time off, but I need to look pretty good in the Thundercage," Flair said. "I can't leave a loser."

I knew exactly where he was going and didn't say a word.

Flair continued to explain in very political terms that since he was thinking about leaving in-ring competition in a few weeks or a few months in an attempt to fill Dusty's big shoes.

I shook my head and tried my best not to show how pissed I really was. *I can't believe the massive plate of bullshit that Ric is trying to spoon-feed me here.*

"I'm sorry, but we are going to have to change things."

His excuse for not wanting to honor the plans we had made originally was because if he was going to go into a semi-retirement from in-ring activity, he should give the fans a proper "goodbye moment" down the road.

His goodbye moment didn't mean anything to me. I wasn't born yesterday. I knew that nobody ever really leaves. Hell, Terry Funk has made a whole career out of retiring. Wrestlers have a history of making up fake retirements to make more money, and I could smell this one a mile away. What he really meant was, despite the fact that he got his turn to shine at the beginning of our deal with Dusty, he was not going return the favor.

"I really appreciate what you did for me a few weeks back, and I'd really like you to send me out for my last few matches with another win like that."

"But what about what Dusty said? And winning the title back in the cage?"

"It will happen," he said, "just not with me, right now. It's just bad timing. You'll shine again, big man." Flair made it perfectly clear not in so many words that, "you are not going to get the belt or the revenge victory that Dusty Rhodes had promised to you."

I was bummed, but I didn't bother to argue with a guy that was now considered one of my bosses. There was no point.

The match took place on February 20, 1994, at the Gray Civic Center in Albany, Georgia. This event was the only SuperBrawl never released on home video. Don't worry. Your collection isn't missing anything much, and you can now see it on the WWE Network.

Trying to probably save face for me, Flair had all kinds of run-ins to keep me looking strong. Arn Anderson ran out there, Ricky Steamboat ran out there, and a clearly biased "The Boss" Ray Traylor was the referee. (Bobby Heenan incidentally said in the open of the show that BOSS stood for "Big Old Southern Sow.")

In the end, Flair got me in the figure four. I never clearly gave up, but the partial Boss motioned to ring the bell. At the end of the show, Bobby Heenan and Tony Schiavone even admitted that he never heard me quit, but it didn't matter.

Ric Flair was still the WCW World Heavyweight champion.

After beating Sting to become the unified and undisputed WCW champion, Flair feuded with a newcomer to WCW in June 1994. It culminated at *Bash at the Beach* in July and Ric Flair lost the WCW World Championship to the new guy, an even better locker room politician, Hulk Hogan.

Ric finally got his time off, but it was only really for a few months as I recall.

I never got my title back.

Nobody made good on Dusty's promise, the bastards. From what I heard, there was some talk and scheming on how to reduce my infringement on Hogan's potential TV time.

When Ric Flair started wrestling again, apparently the politicians wanted me gone from the main event scene so there would be less spotlight to share and more money for them in the end. It was kind of like the same mentality as Pepsi and Coke. The two mega companies dominate the entire scene so only they can own it all. You only get one or the other and no other companies even make a dent in the share, like A&W or RC Cola.

I've also been told that the whole Paul Orndorff incident was a bit of a setup, as someone was looking for a reason to put me in the doghouse and keep Flair and Hogan happy. I don't know but will discuss this shortly.

KNOCKED DOWN A STEP

After the Thundercage, executives took me out of the main event scene. I knew it was coming, and it bugged me. I knew not to say anything, but I figured maybe I could make my actions speak louder than words in the ring and force them to keep me in the mix.

My first mid-card feud was with Ray Traylor who many may remember as "Big Boss Man" in WWF. He had just come in pretty hot off of his stint with Vince. In WCW, they just called him "The Boss" at this point, but would later call him the Guardian for legal reasons. Ray was excellent and worked really snug. Our matches were better than they had hoped, and for some reason, they attributed this to me and my storytelling. Therefore, they decided not to just kill off my stock just yet. They had me defeat him at Spring Stampede and tried to figure out what to do with me next.

Next, they put me with another person sitting out from the Flair/Hogan main event spotlight, and that was Sting. We did a whole build up for *Slamboree 94*, chasing the vacant WCW International World Heavyweight Championship. What had happened was Rick Rude got injured over in Japan and was never able to wrestle again. They decided to put Sting in this category and were just going to put the belt on him out of default. However, behind the scenes, Sting actually requested that a match happen with me, rather than to just be awarded the title. Sting was smart. This was good for both of us. You gotta love Sting for that. He looked out for others, as well as himself.

Sting and I had a great match as always, and I think this impressed the execs. This was a great way for him to earn the championship. Still not knowing exactly what to do with a super-heavyweight with my abilities when there was no room in the main event, they decided to put a secondary belt on me. So at *Clash of the Champions XXIX*, they had me beat Dustin Rhodes to earn the opportunity to face the United States Heavyweight Champion, Hacksaw Jim Duggan. (As a side note, not a lot of people know this, but I am the godfather to Dustin's daughter, Dakota, as well.)

In the Starrcade title match, they put me over Duggan to win the United States Heavyweight Title. It was kind of cool having this title, as it gave me back some recognition from the fans, but just when things started to show a little hope for me, I was forced to end my on-screen alliance with Harley Race.

THE END OF THE RACE

In January of 1995, Harley was in a pretty bad car accident and forced to leave WCW to recover. Harley's drinking had caught up with him. He retired from wrestling around 1991, and I'm pretty sure that took a toll on him. Without the rigors of the job, he worked out less and ballooned up to more than 300 pounds. I knew gaining the weight pissed him off. Leaving the spotlight also depressed him, so I think he took to the bottle even more. Without the physical side of the business anymore to neutralize his avid alcohol consumption, Harley just drank whatever he wanted. There was no match the next day he needed to worry about.

I think Harley realized he was only going to play second fiddle, from now on. The fact that he was out there in front of those people performing in the ring, may have made him feel old, and Harley was a proud man. He was revered as being one of the toughest guys in the industry and probably didn't like this change.

After sticking around the business for a few years as a manager, promoting stars such as Lex Luger, Steve Austin, and myself, it all wound down to a horrible finish.

After one night of drinking his sorrow away in January 1995, he crashed his car into a concrete barrier near Kansas City. The impact fractured his forearm and crushed his hip.

Harley Race hasn't set foot in a big-league wrestling ring since, except for a few minor cameos.

The news of this unfortunate accident crushed me as well. I felt horrible that this was the end for him. Not only was I emotionally hurt for him, but selfishly I knew my career would suffer as well. It was then that I realized that he had played a big role in keeping me going behind the scenes. I also felt bad for his family, whom I had grown close to for many years.

It turns out that Harley fought battles for me that I didn't know even existed. He squashed heat I may have received for being too stiff. He squashed heat for me saying something I didn't mean from having a short fuse. He kept my brand alive in WCW and well in the spotlight. He was such an advocate for me that when he was gone, I could tell right away that his absence was the beginning of the end for me.

Harley was the political guy in our team and with him gone, I was left to float alone in a sea of politics where I, unfortunately, didn't know how to swim.

Looking back, I have to give Harley all the thanks in the world. He really was a mentor and looked out for me when nobody else would. Thanks Harley!

CHAPTER 13 - SID & ARN

Back before Harley's accident during my third run with the WCW World Heavyweight title, there was an "accident" even far worse.

Now, before I place judgment on either Sid or Arn on what has gone down in history as one of the scariest behind-the-scenes wrestling fights ever, you have to put all this together in terms of "wear and tear." Before any sort of altercation between them happened on that one horrible European tour, the road was getting the best of all of us. If I was asked to go on the stand and testify today, I would have to put the blame entirely on the company. WCW beat the living hell out of us so bad, it felt like they were trying to kill us.

We had already been on the road for ten days straight with no breaks so we were exhausted. To top it off, we finished a daytime shot in Florida and then had to hurry off to our next gig in England. We showered quickly, got dressed up, darted off to the airport, turned in our rental, and got ready to board.

Everyone was dressed up nice, you know, with nice clothing and leather coats on because that's what WCW expected of us for international flights in case we were spotted by any fans along the way. This was no big deal, but it means we were also not in our most comfortable attire for travel. Before boarding, they set up in this lounge with a bunch of cocktails. We all got to drinking and getting a primer on for the flight, adding alcohol to the mix.

Guys were swapping pain pills and getting pretty messed up. We weren't even on the plane yet and I remember one guy got up and put his headband on, then fell face-first right back into his seat. That is how bad things were getting.

Once boarding time hit, we divvied out the seats. It was me, 2 Cold Scorpio, the Nasty Boys, Flair, Davey Boy, Steamboat, some agents, just a bunch of us. We had the correct number of tickets in our envelope, but as usual, WCW only had a couple of first class seats in the mix so we couldn't all ride first class. This added to the bad formula for the trip for us big guys who had to sit in the tiny seats in the back. (Fortunately for me because of how I negotiated my contract and because I had one of the biggest butts on the tour, I was not sitting in coach.)

WCW pretty much dominated the flight to London, acting like a bunch of assholes, for sure. We fly all the way over there, got off the plane, and got right onto a bus to travel four more hours on one of the bumpiest roads the United Kingdom had to offer. Nobody got any sleep because of the time change. The sun had already come up, and it was only afternoon there.

We did another daytime show. Yes, we had just wrestled one and traveled all that way without any sleep. Then we rushed out of there to catch a bus for another eight hour trip to the next town.

I was physically exhausted. I was bitching to anyone who would listen about all the running around we were doing, saying, "Now wait a minute, man, this is just crazy."

The bus ride was brutal. It was tight and uncomfortable and by no means could you sleep on such a vehicle. The boys made the best of it. We had run out of food at some point, and everyone just started drinking beer on an empty stomach; yet another formula for disaster.

We drove way up in the Highlands or some damned place in the middle of nowhere on what was probably the second bumpiest road in all of England. I mean, to look back at it now, all I can say is "Wow." I couldn't have done this today. Somewhere along the ride, I would just have had a heart attack and died. It was just too much to ask of us, and it's no wonder Sid and Arn were easily at arms.

I don't even know where the hell they took me, but we ended up in front of a nice hotel. We finished the trip frazzled and worn, then finally headed into our hotel. It was getting late and everybody wanted to just rush up to their rooms and crash. However, we were all starving with nothing but beer in our bellies.

One of the boys, I don't remember who it was, insisted they open the bar up for us so we could get some food and all. It was the middle of the night, but we didn't give a shit, right? I can only imagine the manager was pissed at us already.

We all sat down at the tables around a pretty nice looking bar and ordered some food. We were all anxious and wanted the food served as fast as they could. The boys were beat. You could see it on their faces.

"Man, this trip really sucks so far," 2 Cold Scorpio said.

"I'll second that," I said.

The boys kicked into a full-fledged bitch session about the company that eventually turned into how they were getting screwed with money. They started comparing notes and talking about paydays. About that time Sid said something like, "One of the problems is you got an old man named Ric Flair, who needs to get the hell out of the way."

The room got silent. He said something that most of us were thinking. It wasn't what he said that was shocking; it was who he said it in front of.

Sid continued. "You all know it. Ric Flair is the one that is taking all our money, and that's why we are bitching right now. He really needs to step aside and let some of us get some."

Everyone looked across the table. That is something you don't say in front of Flair's long-time partner and Four Horseman stable mate, Arn Anderson.

Arn stood up and started arguing with Sid. It got so heated that Arn threw a beer in his face. They went at each other but before anything really could happen, there was a big pull apart. A hotel manager came over and demanded that we all go to our rooms.

Some of us hadn't even found our rooms yet and were waiting for food with our luggage. We all just said, "Forget this," and headed out of there.

While still looking for my room, I saw Scorpio come around the corner. "Man, I really wanted to grab something to eat," I said.

"Shit, I'm just going up to have some hash in my room. Shit, big hash!" The thing is, Scorpio wasn't talking about food. (I'm not outing my man, either. Scorpio admits this in interviews today. He doesn't give a shit.)

I laughed. I wandered around a bit looking for my room.

Later on, I found out that out Sid and Arn got into it again on the way to their rooms. They were only about four or five doors away from each other and as they started to bring their stuff in, they saw each other. Sid says at this point, Arn broke a beer bottle and threatened to cut Sid with it right there in the hallway.

On my way to my room, I wandered back into the bar. It had been pretty much filtered out after the beer throwing incident, and where we had completely taken it over at one point, now it was just a nice big bar with nobody in it. Nobody, that is, except one person: *Stunning Steve Austin, aka Stone Cold.*

"Hey Steve," I said.

"Hey, Leon. Didn't even make it to my room yet."

"I hear you there," I said. "Don't blame you with all this running around."

"You going to pull up and have a cold one? I'm buying," Steve said.

Not to be one to turn down free beer, I replied, "Thanks man, maybe I'll drop my bags off to my room and take you up on that."

"I'll be here," he said, nursing a bottle.

He was just having a few beers to unwind, you know, after that long ride of torture. So I brought my bags up to my room and quickly changed into some night clothes. Now, I was beat. I think I laid down for a minute and probably passed out. I'm not sure how long I was asleep, but it probably didn't last long. Maybe I figured Steve was waiting for me with a few drinks and that would help me sleep better.

The next thing I know, I snap to it and Steve and I are sitting there at the bar alone having a beer. I didn't remember really leaving the room or walking back to the bar. I was just in a daze from sleep deprivation but somehow made it to the stool with Steve for a nightcap to end the mother of all road trips.

Now, the way that Steve tells this story, I wandered down the hall in nothing but my underwear. "No shirt, no shoes, NO SHORTS, no problem." He claims he looked over at me as I sat down, and couldn't believe his eyes.

Steve says, "There we were in a four-star hotel in England, and out of nowhere comes a 420-pound man in nothing but his tighty-whiteys." He says he looked me over for only a few seconds and just said, "Hmm," and then he shrugged it off.

"Hey man, what's going on?" Steve said.

"I don't know, I couldn't sleep," I replied.

"You want a beer?"

The thing is, Steve was out of it. Not only did he have to endure the same exact trip that I had, but he already had a few beers in him on top of that. His judgement had to be off on the whole underwear thing. I may have been a little punch-drunk from jetlag, but I was not walking around the hotel in the middle of the night in some sweet Fruit of the Loom!

Seriously! They were white shorts. You know, like those trunks you'd go to the gym with, right? You don't really think that for one second, that Big Van Vader would go parading around a public place in a big city in nothing but his skivvies, do you?!

Or maybe I was? It was a long flight. Either way…

Steve and I just sat there talking and started drinking more beer like it's nobody's business. We started by talking about the bum deal WCW gave us on this tour. Then we talked a little about some matches and then all of the sudden, all hell broke loose.

There was banging. There was a loud crash. There was glass breaking. Coming from my background in Compton, I thought there was some kind of robbery going on.

Neither one of us could really see what had happened, but we both jumped off the stools and headed for the noise. It wasn't clear exactly where the sound was coming from but one thing was certain, somebody was in a violent fight and it was still going on.

I walked further in that direction and the next thing I know, man, Sid comes walking right up next to me.

"Sid!" I said. "What the hell was that noise?"

Sid didn't say anything.

If memory serves me well, I didn't realize that he was hurt until I looked down. Either just to the left of his belly button, or just to the right, Sid had a dark nasty hole in him the size of a penny and a black trickle started to spill out onto the floor.

He was doing the Frankenstein walk and couldn't hear me. I shook him and looked him in the eye.

"Sid. Sid! Look at me." I said grabbing both his shoulders. "What happened?!"

He stopped moving around and tried to focus on me. He swallowed hard and found difficulty in talking at first. Then he focused again and just said, "Leon."

Sid lifted his palms and looked down at his stomach. He put his hand on it again and immediately turned red. Sid tried to pull away from me, but I held him there.

"Sid. Sid. Stay still."

I looked at the hole and it was getting worse. A nickel sized stream of dark gooey blood squirted out every time his heart pumped and dumped onto the floor. It launched out of his body about four inches before it fell down. It wasn't trickling down his stomach, it was projectile, squirting outwards.

Sid's mouth opened, but there were no words. More syrup-like blood spurted out about two to three inches and dropped again to the splatter pile collecting on the floor.

He's not going to last long like this. He'll bleed to death.

"Sid, trust me," I said. I grabbed one of the chairs off the floor and pulled it up to Sid's paling body. I got eye level with the deep laceration and I sat down. I said, "Sid, you have to trust me. Okay? Don't move, or you're gonna die."

Sid looked like he saw a ghost. He didn't speak but watched me measure each of my fingertips up to the open spout on his stomach. Once I realized that I needed my thickest finger to do the job, I stuck out my thumb like Little Jack Horner and pushed.

It was more like "The Legend of Hanz Brinker." You know, the story of the little Dutch boy who saves his country from a flood by sticking his finger in a leaking dike. The boy stays there all night, in spite of the cold, until the adults of the village find him and make the necessary repairs. In the end, he was a hero and saved the village from a broken dam. The only difference in this case was, this hole was a little more gross, and a lot more red.

I slowly eased my thumb into that hole. Blood oozed out down my wrist and I paid it no mind. I pushed my digit higher up into the gaping slit.

"You're hurting me," he said, with his knees beginning to buckle under him.

"You gotta take it, Sid. You gotta take it. Now, hold on."

I wriggled it around and one real thick glob hung off my wrist like a roasted red pepper. I finally got it in there a little bit more and the hole conformed around my knuckle. It slowed the bleeding enough and we waited.

Steve Austin came up to the scene. It must have looked like the darnedest thing with me staring at my penetrated thumb in Sid's gut and blood trickling out all over the place. He turned his head away from the horror show and gagged.

"God damn!" he said. "Ugh. I'll go get help."

I waited there for what seemed like an eternity. Neither of us talked. I could feel the warm wet goo rolling off my wrist, and it was the worst thing I ever had to endure. I remember looking down and seeing some of the thick-like-syrup droplets on the floor.

Finally, we heard some commotion of people rushing down the hall. I am happy to say that my thumb kept him alive until the ambulance came.

WCW should have taken some of the blame for this, for driving us bat-shit crazy like they did with the schedule. But, of course, they didn't.

The next day, I got some more of the story. Sid and Arn Anderson got into a major fight after we left the dining hall. The fight was initially broken up by some of the WCW wrestlers, but the fight started up again around the time that Steve and I were having a drink at the bar. The second time around, someone ended up with a pair of scissors. The result was Arn Anderson ended up with 20 or so superficial lacerations, while Sid took some very deep puncture shots to his body.

Both men spent the night in the hospital and were deported the next day, as the UK wanted nothing more to do with our fucked up, American wrestling bullshit.

They canceled a bunch of the dates from the tour. Some might have thought that we, as a whole, would have been reprimanded for all the drinking, but that wasn't the case. Actually, this is one of the few times I was singled out by the administration and praised.

"Good job, Leon," they said. "You kept your cool and saved a man's life."

Finally, I wasn't the bad guy.

No matter who was right or wrong, neither Sid nor Arn have thanked me yet. You would have thought that at some point Arn would have come up to me and said, "Hey man, I want to thank you for sticking your thumb in Sid." If I hadn't, Arn would have been in a heck of a lot more trouble than he was. He could have been up for murder charges had Sid died.

Both men should have been fired, but WCW officials felt that Sid had started it. So instead, they fired Sid and only suspended Arn Anderson. You can bet that Flair politics probably had something to do with this decision.

This fallout messed everything up on TV. Some of you may recall that I was originally advertised to defend the title against Sid Vicious at Starrcade, but that never happened. The backstage dismissal of Sid forced WCW to find a quick replacement.

Executive producer Eric Bischoff ironically decided to put Ric Flair in the match, instead of Sid. It made sense, I guess, because the PPV was scheduled to take place in Flair's hometown of Charlotte. For the new replacement storyline, Flair challenged me, but I didn't take his title challenge seriously until he agreed to put his career on the line.

For that career vs. title bout, I pretty much dominated with most of the offense, but Flair capitalizing on a failed interference attempt by Harley Race. After the miscue, Flair won the match with a chop block rollup to end my third World Heavyweight Championship reign.

Sid was supposed to beat me at Starrcade for the title anyhow, so it didn't really matter to me at the time. The funny thing was though that a full month's worth of television tapings with Sid as the WCW champion were already in the can. During some mass shootings at Disney Studios that were planned to air after the PPV, Sid was filmed defending a title he never won. Those matches, of course, never aired.

In the end, it was Ric Flair, the same guy that Sid was pissed about sparking the scissors fight with Arn in the first place, who took Sid's spot.

He then became the new WCW World Champion.

CHAPTER 14 - UWFI IN JAPAN

On May 6, 1993, while still under contract with WCW, I would find myself in a familiar place. I walked into Budokan Hall of Tokyo, Japan, my old stomping grounds. There was music playing, but it was different. I was walking down the familiar aisle towards a familiar ring, but everything was under a different banner.

開始早々、中野のローキックをもらった
ベイダーは、すかさず張り手で反撃。ド
迫力とは、このことをいうのだろう

My opponent for the bout wasn't Sting, or Cactus, or Davey Boy, or Inoki. My opponent was a Japanese fighter named Tatsuo Nakano. It also wasn't expected to be a normal, predetermined wrestling match.

The fighting part was real – a shoot.

In late February 1993, I signed an eight-date agreement with the Union of Wrestling Force International (UWFi) in Japan, the same country where I got my gimmick and the same country Vader was born.

Even though Japanese wrestling seems very different than the wrestling American audiences are used to, it has been a huge influence over here. One of the things that Japanese wrestling has arguably brought to the table is to make people look at wrestling as being more real, like a sport. The UWFi was one of the first Japanese promotions to take this idea to a new level.

Back when they were still trying to get everything together for their debut show, a few of their representatives doing the legwork for an American tour gave me a call. They offered X amount of dollars for something like 8 matches at first, and it was good money so I was in.

Politically, my signing with UWFi may not have been the best thing I could have done to stay in good graces with the office at WCW. From statements I have heard from Eric Bischoff today, apparently WCW management would have liked to stop me from taking high-profile bookings outside the company, but they couldn't.

There was a danger in letting the WCW Heavyweight Champion compete somewhere else. For one, I would be making money for another promotion off of WCW's investment. Week after week, if WCW was spending money and time pushing me on their TV program, the other promotion would benefit from this. However, this wasn't the only thing WCW was worried about.

Not only was I helping to promote another promotion on WCW's dime, but I was also set to appear in a shoot fight. This was worse in the minds of WCW, due to the possibility that an injury that could occur to one of their top stars and mess up stories on TV.

Many people have often wondered why I was able to do this as a contracted wrestler in WCW when many wrestlers were not able to wrestle outside of the promotion. Wrestling since day one has been very territorial, and promoters were often territorial over where their wrestlers could work. I myself have found this to be a little hypocritical, because at the same time we were all considered to be sub-contractors and not employees for the major promotions, but I digress.

The answer is simple; WCW didn't have a choice. The additional overseas booking option was part of my contract.

I had negotiated with Bischoff five years with WCW for X amount of dollars and the ability to go to Japan X amount of times. Going to Japan was my contractual right, and I was exercising it with UWFi.

It was tough balancing my image in Japan and also doing what people in WCW wanted me to do. In an interview from Kayfabe Commentaries with Greg Oliver, regarding my UWFi tour on August 18, 1994, Eric Bischoff discussed why he had an issue with me.

"I couldn't care less what people in Japan thought of Vader when I was paying Vader half a million dollars a year. That's just the way my brain works. I never did then (and nor could I probably now) understand that balancing act."

Eric explained that wrestlers wanting to work in other places was a big conflict with not just me but others, like the issues he had with the Luchadores from Mexico.

Eric said, "It would be great if someone were to say 'Look, you don't have to pay me a full-time salary; forget that half a million dollar guarantee and give me $250,000 so I can pick up some money in Japan.' Then, I would easily have that conversation with you. But don't ask for a top contract and then ask me to treat you like a part-time employee with hours."

However, these terms were in the contract that WCW gave me. If he didn't like it, he shouldn't have allowed it to be on the table during negotiations.

The ability to perform outside of WCW was a great deal for me, particularly at this time in my career. Being the WCW World Heavyweight Champion, I could negotiate a pretty good rate anywhere in the world going back over to Japan for whoever wanted to pay the price; Inoki, or even Baba.

As a professional wrestler, I wanted as much longevity as possible. I had to be careful about a lot of things. I protected my health and all, but I didn't feel that competing in what essentially was an early form of MMA was going to cut my WCW run short, due to the risk of injury. As a wrestler, you have to pick your spots and be worried about that all the time.

I didn't really want to fight in a hard-hitting, mostly real match, but fear had nothing to do with it. I was pretty confident in my abilities and strength. It's not like a shoot fight championship was a personal goal of mine. I wasn't like Brock Lesnar, looking to add a UFC championship to my resume. It was all about the pay day. You see, I was building a shopping center at the time, and the bill was pretty hefty. Just the development of the blueprint plans themselves for construction was $4,000! I figured this high-paying opportunity was a great way to supplement income and pay those bills.

On paper, Salman Hashimikov was only one guy in the UWFi that kind of scared me, if any. He was a two-time legit badass gold medalist from Russia at 6'1" and 340 pounds. I was really in the best shape of my career; 6'4" and trimmed down to 415 pounds and stronger than ever, but this guy possessed a different kind of strength than mine. My power was all about push. I could push a door over by exploding outwards and pushing it in. However, Salman could yank it off the hinges. He had that other kind of strength, where he could pull you in for the kill. So he scared me.

But should he have scared me? Was it real, or was it predetermined?

WHAT IS REAL?

To describe how the UWFi worked, it's probably best to first explain what shoot-style really was in professional wrestling in a time that predated UFC. "Shoot wrestling" became a genre of professional wrestling that incorporated realistic moves and finishes to matches to make them look as real as possible. Therefore, it was important for a shoot-style promoter to make sure their product was always seen by the fans to be a shoot; a real MMA fight in a wrestling ring with real strikes and real submissions, as exciting as any competitive, real fighting sport.

Most of the time in a shoot promotion, the only thing that was predetermined was the finish of the match. Depending on the way that the shoot-style promotion operated behind the scenes, there was often no actual interaction between the opposing wrestlers as far as a meeting before the fight to discuss what should happen. This would make it feel even more real for the audience. The moves and strikes were also encouraged to be pretty much full force.

I don't want to insult anybody's intelligence here, because it was a "worked shoot," but the strikes and the kicks were totally full force. It was totally a different thing for me in the ring because a lot of the action is blocking kicks and punches so they didn't connect, but when they did, you were in a world of hurt the next day. I would sometimes have trouble just walking around. One of the strategies I would do is, when they would go for a kick to my leg, I would often take a step forward with the one foot and drill them with a punch while they were in full momentum so they couldn't block it. In other words, if you were going to get a piece of me with a kick, you were going to have to pay at the same time. This often eliminated some of the kicks that people were trying to throw.

Pro wrestling had been exposed, and fans wanted something like the mega-promotion UFC that didn't exist yet. A number of these shoot type of promotions popped up around the world in the mid-90s as an alternative to some of the less-than-hard-hitting wrestling products that were being viewed on television. UWFi was one of the answers to this need. They borrowed talent from many different fighting sports. Fans would be excited to see their favorite fighters in a new style. Because of this concept, they drew really well.

The UWFi had a unique scoring system to create the allure of being real. It gave each wrestler to start 15 points for singles matches and 21 points total for tag teams. A wrestler would lose a match if they submitted, if they were down for a 10-count, or if they lost all their points. A wrestler/team lost 1 point for using the ropes to break submission, 1 point for a suplex takedown and 3 points for a knockdown.

In 1991, UWFi promoted hard and produced about one big show a month. They used Americans like Gary Albright and Bob Backlund to become top threats to their champion, Takada. Japanese fighters like Masahito Kakihara, Kazuo Yamazaki and ex-sumo Koji Kitao were also real big draws.

To further the appeal in diversity and among the old school fans, Nick Bockwinkel, Billy Robinson and Lou Thesz were also brought in as "American Classics" to give the promotion even more street credit.

Then, to create controversy that would equate to more buys, the UWFi had Lou Thesz issue a challenge to all the world champions of all other wrestling promotions throughout the world to come take a chance at "the new measuring stick."

This open challenge idea was similar to what Masa Chono, then NWA Heavyweight Champion, was doing at that time in New Japan for promos, but in the UWFi it made even more sense. This challenge in this form really meant something to the Japanese fan. UWFi was perceived to a melting pot of fighters, and it was also perceived to be real. If someone were to take this challenge from a major promotion, it was believed that they would be dropping everything and going to show what they could do in a real fight. It was the ultimate display of toughness.

Only one outer-promotion world champion would step up and accept Lou Thesz's UWFi challenge. That champion was me.

THE NAME GAME

By 1993, I was a three-time CWA Champion, a three-time IWGP Champion, and also a three-time WCW World Heavyweight Champion, as well a one-time in UWA Mexico. The magazines typically put me over as being a legit badass tough man with a worldwide reputation to back that up. My accepting this challenge only continued to build on that global reputation.

However, I received word that I could not compete as "Big Van Vader," because the rights to the name were soon to be contested in court. So I started my UWFi days competing as "Super Vader."

New Japan never had a real problem with me wearing the big helmet in the States. We only stopped using it some because it was a royal pain in the ass and it did somewhat hold me back, but NJPW absolutely did not want me to wear the helmet in the UWFi and did not want me to even use the word "Vader" in my billing.

People at that time figured that working in Japan for the UWFi and not for New Japan drummed up a legal battle over the name. People speculated that working for a possible competitor ticked off Antonio Inoki, the creator of the gimmick.

It is true that Inoki had come up with the whole thing. He made the mask, the helmet, the look, the name, the persona – everything. So, understandably so, it would make sense that maybe Inoki did not like the fact that I had returned to use the gimmick in his country with one of his competitors and not with him. However, sour grapes from Inoki was not the case. He told me I could use the gimmick anywhere I wanted and even gave me my own big helmet to make that happen!

Inoki and I are still good friends, to this very day.

NJPW TITLE COMMITTEE

The legal concern actually came from the people who took over NJPW from Inoki. They didn't want me using the Vader gimmick. New Japan had a legit title committee with stakes in the game that did not like the fact that I was using a name that was "birthed under their banner" in a different Japanese ring. They felt I was using something that was theirs against them. This name dispute bred lawyers to try and sort everything out.

While this was happening in Japan, at another court hearing in the States, WCW was being forced to change my name from "Big Van Vader" to just "Vader" after New Japan's lawyers claimed that my costuming paired with the name was a copyright infringement to their intellectual property. This was yet another reason for Eric Bischoff to hate me.

I will say this about the Japanese court system: They don't play around. It was just one judge and one lawyer for each side, in the courtroom. They ask you to leave the room, and each story is simply told to the judge. He listened to both sides and made his decision quickly. In America, this legal idea would never fly. A case like this in the USA would have been drawn out forever with all kinds of additional people putting their hands in the mix eating up money and tax dollars. My case in Japan was just so much more efficient than others like it I had seen before.

The judge ruled that NJPW title committee couldn't cease and desist the word "Vader," because they didn't and couldn't even legally ever own the name "Vader" alone. "Vader" was trademarked by movie producer George Lucas, and it was also a mythological character like "Hercules" and "Zeus," so it was common ground and fair game. I was to stop using "Big Van Vader," but I was able to at least salvage the surname. That's all I needed.

The dispute was mostly a bruised-ego thing and probably had to do with me not playing politics very well. The NJPW Title Committee was just upset because I left New Japan for WCW, ran with the gimmick, got even bigger without them, and didn't give them a taste of the proceeds.

Inoki is still a good friend of mine, and I know he had nothing to do with the lawsuit. We had each other's backs and still do today. That's the way you did business over there. If you were friends, you looked out for each other. I think the people who took over for Inoki when he left felt betrayed that I was working with a competitor. I'm sorry they looked at it that way. But as far as Antonio Inoki, we are still good.

Inoki always had my best interest in mind - maybe more than anyone else he had ever done business with. Right away, he started paying me a great deal of money on a weekly basis, which he never did for anyone prior. He gave me my gimmick and the ability to feed my family. He had me destroy him in my debut and end his undefeated streak. He made me the first gaijin IWGP champion (3x), and needless to say, we really did good business together.

SUPER VADER DEBUT

I beat Tatsuo Nakano for my debut fight on May 6, 1993, in less than 4 minutes. My quick victory was the beginning of a series of UWFi matches that would even further secure the legend surrounding the legitimacy of my fighting abilities. The master plan story was to keep building me up to a big finish; a massive bout with their top man Takada by the end of the year.

UWFi's United States programming debut was in the summer of 1993. The UWFi set up a number of PPV broadcasts described to the fans as being "real professional wrestling."

One of my early bouts before any of the PPV exposure I would get was on August 13, 1993. It was billed as "WCW World Champion Super Vader vs. Kazuo Yamazaki."

The undercard was phenomenal, and my main event match was a great way to end another great UWFi show at Budokan. I didn't want only shoot-fighting fans to enjoy this match, so I decided to try to actually force emphasis on psychology and entertainment, without Yamazaki really even knowing what was going on.

Before the match, I even went down to his dressing room and contemplated telling him of my plan to work the match a little for entertainment reasons. Kazuo Yamazaki was much smaller and rather than to just job him out, I figured the underdog story would be great for him in his match with me. But then I got second thoughts and walked away. I knew Yamazaki wouldn't want to go against the promotion's rule of predetermining some spots of the action. The UWFi wanted it to look sloppy so it would look real. That was their gimmick. I figured that Yamazaki wasn't a big name and would never have gone for breaking that rule for risk of losing his spot.

The match was on.

As I planned, I tried to make a good show for the fans. I hit Yamazaki with some crazy hard strikes to put me over as the monster, dominating early. I got him really good and probably could have knocked him out. Then, I let my guard down intentionally. I actually gave myself to Yamazaki to take over. I decided it was the underdog's turn to come firing back and get the crowd going.

Being as all of this was real, Yamazaki saw the opening and rushed in to give me a pretty good test, not knowing I was letting him have his turn for storytelling reasons. Yamazaki went nuts. He started whaling on me with as many shoot kicks as he could to the knees, shoulder, back, and head.

WHAP! WHAP! WHAP!

I grimaced. A ninja kick made a veritable dent in the back of my head. *This is what I get for trying to make things look good.*

I didn't want to just take over and make Yamazaki look like a complete pushover, but those fucking kicks started to hurt like hell! I got myself into a sticky situation and knew I was going to soon have to get myself out.

I was eating some stiff kicks, even though it was worth it. The crowd was really going crazy for it all, eating up the underdog story I was trying to tell.

I hit the ropes for some air. No luck. Good old Kazuo kept on coming with his fucking kicks. Now, I was still selling them big to make the show look good, but a good portion of that was not a work. They were really starting to hurt.

Finally, the ref got between us, knowing there was still supposed to be a worked finish, even though the strikes and all were real. I told the ref to get the word over to Yamazaki that we needed to start to transition into the end. However, the ref wasn't listening, I think he was enjoying the fight. He didn't get the message to Yamazaki that I wanted, so I tried a different communication technique.

I legit punched the ref right in his face.

Maybe there was a language barrier. Maybe the ref might not have spoken English very well, but he at least knew that language. The ref then finally got word to Kazuo Yamazaki to move into the ending sequence of the match, because I had taken enough of his bullshit kicks.

After that, we went into a great planned lead-in for the finish. We both went over the top rope, which is very rare for a shoot-style match and got a great crowd reaction. Soon after, we got back into the ring and I put Yamazaki away with a chokeslam.

I can't lie, man, those shots hurt but mission accomplished. I looked like a million bucks and Yamazaki didn't come off looking like a complete pushover, either. That made me even bigger. The match totally served the purpose we wanted, and that was to create more momentum leading me up to what we were hoping to be a big payoff in a title match against Takada.

UWFi ON PPV

October 4th, 1993 was our first PPV taping to air in American households for the next night. Even though I competed on the show, they didn't air my match on the 5th. However, they hyped the heck out of me to try and present a "legitimate product" in the boxing-like way that American audiences were accustomed to. The PPV was a success! It drew a 0.5 rate which was considered an awesome number for a foreign promotion. Because there was no American TV pushing the PPV whatsoever, it impressed a number of cable providers.

Keeping me off that initial PPV programming worked. It was just the tease needed to make the American fans want more and go even crazier for the next one.

NOBUHIKO TAKADA

UWFi treated the promotion like the biggest names ever were competing in a high-stakes heavyweight boxing match. And when it finally came, it felt like the Olympics.

It was standing room only. There were 46,000 fans at Tokyo's Jingu Stadium, crazed out of their minds for the final buildup of *Super Vader vs. Takada*. Everything in UWFi felt much different than any promotion in America, especially on this particular night. The feeling was more regal, more official and high class by construct. Lou Thesz and other legendary dignitaries were on hand for pre-match speeches. They brought the air of credibility.

When I finally walked to the ring, I looked around the huge body of people who were all waiting on my every step. Then they played my national anthem. Even thought we had just talked about what was going to happen, *even I felt like it was real.*

Takada is a great guy and quite a competitor. We did talk some before the bout and decided that since everything was riding on us, we had to pull out all the stops. We hit hard. We threw bombs the whole fight and didn't pull one even one bit.

It was a straight shoot the whole way until the last thirty seconds. If one of those kicks knocked you out, it was over. For anybody who has ever viewed the match, you can clearly see Takada legit kicking me. There is no way he could've kicked me any harder. In fact, Takada's kicks felt more powerful than a blow from a baseball bat, which I had taken a few shots from back in punk days growing up in Compton. Those kicks were the absolute worst ever.

I defended myself with legit blows, as well. After three or four of my own big roundhouse rights, he thought twice about getting in close again.

Takada had a legit shooting background, with previous matches ending prematurely against the likes of Trevor Berbick and Bob Backlund.

In the end, Takada was victorious. He had to be, in order to initially prove the superiority "real" pro wrestling. He defeated the WCW champion to retain the UWFi title.

The UWFi leaked rumors that I was injured during our match to further push the envelope of realism. Those rumors weren't so far from the truth, however. I legitimately left the ring with my arm in a sling, and I was so sore after that match that I could barely walk for the following two or three days.

Vader vs. Takada created even more excitement around the UWFi, bringing them their most success ever. After this high-profile PPV, Japanese wrestling, in general, reached new heights of popularity. New Japan, All Japan, and FMW, all saw huge number increases. Massive numbers of fans were thirsting for more, and many saw the increase as being a rubbing-off effect from the UWFi's rise to the top of the wrestling world.

UWFi decided to continue the challenge idea that did so well for them. This time it was issued to champions everywhere, daring them to participate in a "real wrestling" tournament that really would decide "who the best pro wrestler was on the planet."

The final bracket of this highly-publicized tournament came on August 18, 1994. Inevitably, it just coincidentally happened to end up being a rematch between Nobuhiko Takada and me.

THE REMATCH

In front of another sold-out crowd in Budokan Hall, Takada and I stared at each other from separate sides of the ring, moments before we went at it again like two bulls in a China shop. We pounded the piss out of each other and, at one point, I felt like I was back in the ring with Bruiser Brody. Even though we were inside, I was seeing stars.

It was my turn, this time. Takada did the honors and helped me tell the story of a comeback kid. Kind of like Rocky, I lost the first match but learned from my mistakes to win the next with hard work along the way. The whole journey thing led me to becoming victorious and becoming UWFi's second champion.

UWFi again sold out Budokan Hall for a show on January 16, 1995, with me defending the UWFi title against another big man like me, Gary Albright.

From what I understand, the fans didn't like my match with Gary very much. It wasn't just like two slower big men going at it. The real problem was the booking itself wasn't great. Putting two fighters together with no contrast in styles created a situation where we basically just canceled out each other's strengths.

After this "not-so-great" booking, more similar not-so-smart promoting occurrences happened outside the ring. The effect was a drop in numbers. Non-sellouts continued into the summer of 1995, leading up to the third match between Nobuhiko Takada and myself. For this bout, you could see that UWFi was losing its allure. The promotion drew 8100 fans (6000 paid) after drawing 46,000 fans for the same match only two years before.

Disputes over money had soured me on UWFi, and I ended my tenure there with another excellent match against Takada, losing the UWFi title in a little over 15 minutes.

The booking mistakes of UWFi continued and eventually things fell apart. New Japan bought them out and Riki Chōshū continued to book a less-successful version of the promotion featuring their own stars, much like when WWF ran ECW.

Death Valley Driver Video Review writer Dean Rasmussen referred to that final era as "Chōshū masturbating over the decaying corpse of UWFi."

CHAPTER 15 - MICK FOLEY

One of the smartest minds in professional wrestling storytelling ever was Mick Foley. During my championship run in early 1993, I was fortunate enough to be able to work with him and it was great to be instrumental in Mick Foley's first big babyface turn as Cactus Jack.

At The Civic Center in Montgomery, AL, Mick was in a match with Paul Orndorff when I attacked him. The psychology on who was heel or face at this time didn't matter to us, but it really was heel-on-heel. The character of Cactus Jack that Mick had painted was much more complex than anyone had seen on American television at this time.

With him, wrestling as a babyface or a heel didn't really matter, because he was something new, something ahead of his time that didn't really exist yet in the early 90s.

In some aspects of style, Cactus Jack was very much like my character, Big Van Vader. As far as actual move selection and mannerisms in the ring, we both wrestled exactly the same as a babyface or heel. Mick was one of the only other people in the WCW locker room who didn't change their style and adapt what they did in the ring whether they were supposed to be a "good guy" or a "bad guy." We were the only ones who fit into a "what you see is what you get" category at this time.

Working with Mick Foley was pretty awesome. Our matches were brutal and told quite a different story in the ring than fans were used to seeing.

Mick's biggest ring attribute was his ability to endure pain. He may not have ever been in the best shape he should have been. He wasn't the fastest by any means, but boy, he could take pain. Crazy levels. I enjoyed working with him.

On a creative level, Mick was smart and knew what the audience wanted before they even asked for it. In my opinion, Mick was a wrestling savant, though people didn't know it back then. They thought he was crazy, but what they didn't know was it was a smart, calculated crazy that really brought him to the game. While his character portrayed someone who enjoyed pain, in all reality, he didn't.

Ninety-nine percent of the time, he really was the smartest guy in the ring, if not the whole building as well. Obviously now, one can totally see that he's an intelligent man. People have since figured this out by reading his books and also seeing how he has reinvented himself after his wrestling career.

What Mick lacked by not being the biggest, the strongest, or the quickest guy in the ring, he made up for in creativity. He was always able to see the big picture and figure out how to work with it. He had the courage to speak up and make others see value in his ideas. And in the end, he had the ability to make sure his vision was carried out. Like when Taz initially failed his tryout because he didn't put a match well together backstage, Mick was a political genius and also one of the best at putting matches together.

HE'S HARDCORE

In April of 1993, I wrestled with Cactus Jack on WCW Saturday Night in Atlanta, GA. Many people after this match and many years later even today have asked me if I "took liberties." Some people have even gone so far to ask if I had a problem with Mick and things turned into a shoot and got real. This was absolutely not the case.

Mick was an innovator. He was the first guy I know that pushed for "hardcore wrestling" before it even existed.

For those of you who haven't seen this match and really like horror flicks with lots and lots of blood, this may be a match worth looking up. The match was so violent that it had to be edited for TV. Reports say he suffered a concussion, 2 black eyes, a broken nose, and 27 stitches. (That's bullshit, though. After the match, Mick only needed 24 stitches to stop the bleeding. He needed 17 above his eye and 7 stitches below it.)

In my defense, I would like to first credit myself for not being a sadistic bastard. Whether or not we should give Mick that label is entirely up to you.

Before the match, Mick came up to Harley. He had already figured out who he wanted his character to be out of his mind and was advocating strengthening this vision from the outcome of our match. He had been pushing for the idea of bringing "extreme wrestling" or "hardcore wrestling" to the United States, and he really wanted to be the statesman to usher it in.

"Hardcore wrestling" today means disqualifications, count-outs, and most of the different sportsmanlike rules do not apply. Today this means using ladders, tables, chairs, thumbtacks, staple guns, barbed wire, florescent light tubes, cheese graters, shovels, baseball bats, golf clubs, sledge hammers, axes, chains, crowbars, wrenches, salad tongs, live chickens, and any other improvised object as a legalized weapon. However, the style of wrestling that Mick wanted Cactus Jack to be known for was still in an infancy stage.

Mick's vision of what Cactus Jack should look like was only really taking place overseas around this time and only in small amounts. This hardcore style of wrestling possibly showed up first in Japan with promotions such as Frontier Martial-Arts Wrestling and W*ING. It eventually came to America with ECW and later in the WWF with its "Hardcore Championship."

"Harley," Foley said, "I know this may sound a little out there."

"Uh oh, here we go," Harley said.

"I have an idea that can really do us both some good," he said with a devilish grin.

"Ok, let's hear it," I said.

"Leon, I don't want you to wear your gloves. Just put some tape around your wrists and when you hit me, twist it and cut me on both sides."

"Hard way?" I asked. ("Hard way" in wrestling means when someone ends up bleeding by physical means and not by using a razor, which was more prevalent at this time.)

"As much as you can, Leon. I can take it. Puff up my nose, cut my forehead up and make as much color as possible. If we don't get it right away, I want Harley in on it, too."

I shook my head and laughed.

"So at some point, I want you to lead me over to Harley so he can do the same thing."

As we said before, Harley Race had pretty much has a steel-grip hand. Literally. He's got these big, big giant fingers and these big knuckles that really would hurt when he hit you with them. Mick asking to be hit by Harley to make him bleed was pretty much suicide.

"Then when I'm totally bloody, I want you to powerbomb me on the floor, outside the ring," Mick said.

The match that you see is exactly what Mick wanted! He knew what direction his career was going in and wanted this to happen. In hindsight looking back, it worked. He changed the entire face of the sport and was a pioneer of hardcore wrestling on American television.

After the horrific bout, there was an instant concern about how to edit the footage for television because of the blood and the violence. To the best of my knowledge, this was the only match that I'm aware of where WCW had to remove massive amounts of footage off of television, due to the excessive blood spill during the match.

A week later, we were set to wrestle again. Mick came up to me and thanked me for kicking his ass hard the week before.

"So, now I have an idea on how we can top last week. I want you to powerbomb me again on the outside as hard as possible, but to move the pads this time and do it on the concrete floor."

Well, I did just as he asked and this spot resulted in Mick suffering a concussion and temporary loss of feeling in his left hand and leg. I honestly believed I had sent Mick into retirement, but, I'll tell you, that Cactus Jack is one tough son of a bitch. I can honestly say Mick Foley is one of the toughest people to ever step foot in the ring.

Not too much later, he was back on TV working his injury into the storyline. He appeared in a series of skits involving his powerbomb-inflicted amnesia and a search for his past.

While Mick was healing up, I needed someone else to work with. The WWF had just dropped a big name wrestler due to political reasons, so WCW grabbed him right up. Not planning on Mick being down and not having anyone for me to work with, I began to feud with a great substitute for Cactus Jack; the newest arrival to WCW, *"The British Bulldog" Davey Boy Smith.*

Following the whole first moonsault episode that I covered earlier, my Cactus Jack feud restarted as Jack was cleared to return for Halloween Havoc in a Texas Death match. Once again, Jack stood up to a series of the most brutal, devastating moves ever. Near the end of the match, Harley Race even stunned Jack with a real cattle prod that kept him down for a ten count.

LENDING AN EAR

Of course, this book would not be complete without discussing how Cactus Jack lost a piece of his body in a match with me.

The legend surrounding this match furthered my reputation for being the greatest monster in the business. On paper, I guess it looked crazy to begin with. My stiff style with Mick's self-punishing style left those in the know that our pairing could be bad news from the start.

It was March 16, 1994, in Munich, Germany, during the same tour where Sid and Arn had their alteration. I was sitting by my bag in "The Sporthalle" just like I did any night in America getting my gear laid out for the event. I had just come back from stretching a bit in the ring. I was about to lace up my boots when Mick came in. He had read the night's card posted on a wall somewhere and came into my dressing room looking somewhat excited.

"What are you smiling about?" I asked, knowing damn well that the sick, sadistic, crazy bastard that Mick was, he was happy to be working with me, again. I shook his hand and laughed. Because of our history, I knew he expected a pretty rough match when he saw his name opposite mine.

"We are going to tear the house down, again, right?"

"Awe come on, Mick. Not tonight," I said.

Now, I didn't say this because I was worried about Mick taking it to me because he was a professional. I was more worried because I really didn't want to have to kick his ass like that again. It was a strange thing working with a guy who got over by having you practically kill him in the ring. Our responses seemed like they were reversed with him wanting to be killed and me not wanting to do it. I had messed up my arm pretty good too by this point, and I really didn't want to further injure it from hitting him too hard in the head.

"Why, what's up?"

"Well, I think I injured my shoulder good the other night, and I think I made it worse in the gym."

"Hey, don't worry about it, then," he said. "I can do most of the work tonight and take all the heat."

We called a few spots and it seemed easy enough. I wasn't going to have to beat the hell out of him really, and that would save my arm some. It seemed like it would be an easy night. The show started, so I went out to the curtain to watch my buddy, 2 Cold Scorpio.

A lot of people don't know this, but 2 Cold was one of my favorite guys in the business. I've always treated him like a brother. In fact, he was pretty much my "Clint Howard." For those of you who don't know what I am talking about, famous director Ron Howard is famous for getting his brother booked for every movie he makes. Whenever he gets a movie deal, he always seems to be able to work his brother into the deal using his own star power to make it happen. I did the same for 2 Cold for quite a long time, forcing a number of promoters to use him just so I would have someone I like to hang out with on the road. I was also the godfather to his children.

After 2 Cold Scorpio finished his match, I decided to bust his balls about the finish. His moonsault looked a little sloppy for him, and I knew it wasn't his fault. It was obvious that the ropes didn't have a whole lot of spring to them.

"How did it go?" I asked, laughing. "Looked like you almost fell on your head."

"Leon, the ropes are way too loose," he said. "Don't hit them too hard. You'll fall right out on your ass."

Hearing that one of the agents (I don't remember who) went right to work on getting some hands together to tighten things up for the rest of the night. WCW was pretty good like that. They didn't play around. A few guards grabbed some wrenches and ran out to the ring before the second match to set the turnbuckles straight.

I later learned that those guys cranked those ropes to the max, which would be instrumental later on.

Later that night, it was Vader vs. Cactus Jack again, but the Germany translation. Jack started out the match and did just what he promised. He took all the heat and was bumping left and right even more than normal because he knew my shoulder was a mess.

I went for my Vader bomb and missed. Mick hit me with his "Cactus clothesline" where he would clothesline me outside the ring by throwing himself over the top rope. As I stumbled back into the ring, Mick went to charge me and I stepped out of the way of a second Cactus Clothesline.

I figured Mick was going to just fly out of the ring and I would follow after him to take it to him out on the floor. However, that isn't what he did. Mick, the showman that he was, flipped his whole body right into a "Hangman," a spot he called often.

Mick caught his head and neck between the second and third ropes. In this move, you use your body's own momentum to twist the middle rope up over the top rope with your head in between.

I looked at the two ropes crossed squeezing Mick's neck right in the center.

"Here we go again," I said under the mask.

Mick was up to his old self again. The Hangman is something you have to actually try hard to make happen. It isn't something that ever really happens by mistake, but you don't see it much because most wrestlers don't like it. That shit REALLY hurts. I wasn't expecting to see him play this card so it threw me off a little to see Mick hanging there.

This is one of those moves where you don't know what to do when you see it. You actually want to go over and help the other guy get out of it because it is very difficult for him to get out of it himself. However, it wouldn't make sense to help your opponent out as a villain, so you have to pretty much just stand there and watch it and hope the ref steps in if there is a problem.

It looked pretty insane, and Mick wasn't getting out of it.

I shook my head. There was no doubt about it, Mick seemed very committed to making me look good, but I don't think he even knew to what extent.

Then it hit me, the stagehand had tightened the hell out of those ropes! The extra tort was making this Hangman's dangle even worse than usual, and even more difficult to get out of!

Overseas, you never know what you are going to get. A lot of wrestling promotions use rings with real rope, which is softer and preferred. If Mick were strung up in a real rope ring, it may have not been so bad. However, some of the older WCW ropes used cable. In this case, underneath the brightly colored tape were elevator cables covered with a hard rubber hose – not rope. With these particular "cable ropes" tightened to the max, they were almost impossible to pull apart and had absolutely no give.

Mick couldn't get out.

I watched Mick's head quickly turn red and then turn purple. He was, in fact, choking for real and in a vice-like steel sleeper hold. Instead of the normal pain that he had signed on for by selecting this maneuver, the ropes were totally stopping the flow of blood to his brain. Mick knew that if the cables continued to stop the blood flow on his carotid arteries, he could experience brain damage and could even die.

There was no question he was in danger. Then, I heard Mick scream for help.

It all happened so fast. Again, I know I wasn't supposed to do anything, but the ref wasn't helping. Maybe he thought it was just Mick selling and didn't really help him get out. After a moment or so of that, he realized that something was wrong. The ref wasn't really working it anymore, he was shooting. He had his foot on the rope and literally was struggling to actually get that rope open.

Only a few seconds later into the Hangman, I decided I was probably going to have to break kayfabe and pull him free. As I stepped forward, Mick beat me to it.

Mick said that "it felt like an eternity" in that compromising position, though it was probably less than five seconds. He knew he had to act fast before causing permanent damage. So before I could break character and help him out, he did what he "likened as a fox does by chewing off its paw to escape from a trap."

Mick ripped his head out of the rope's clutches. In doing so, he fell out of the ring, *but left his ear behind.*

I looked down over the ropes and saw Mick sprawled out. There was a pool of dark red forming under his head. When he got to all fours, it looked like an open Kool-aid faucet on the side of his head. The blue mats underneath him turned purple, mixing with the red mess falling out of his face.

That didn't stop Mick Foley.

"Nice juice?" Mick said.

At this point, I didn't know that his ear was only dangling from a thin strip of Cactus meat underneath his hair. I just figured he had cut himself open the hard way. We continued to duke it out and neither of us knew how bad it really was. I threw a few forearms at him. Then he returned the favor.

I saw the blood and figured this is a perfect time to "go home." I figured I would hit him a few times and get some heat and get out of here. But a few times didn't happen as planned. After one more shot, I watched something fly off of Mick's head in horror. His bludgeoned ear had flown clean off his face and was lying on the mat.

From what I understand, the referee was a French substitute. To add to the chaos of it all, he spoke absolutely no English. The official we were supposed to have had been injured the night before and would have been perfectly able to tell us that we better stop because he had Mick's ear in his pocket, but that didn't happen.

Not sure what to do, the French ref ran the ear over to the corner and handed it to the ring announcer, Gary Michael Cappetta. Once the ring announcer saw what was handed to him, I am sure he wanted to puke. From how Gary tells the story today, he says that he put the bloody mound of flesh on one of his index cards and scurried it back to the dressing room.

"Ric?" Gary shouted in the entrance way. "RIC?!" Ric Flair was the booker for the show. Sting came running to Gary's call sensing something was not right.

"What's up?!" he asked.

"Look!"

Sting looked down on the gruesome paper card. Gary says that Sting looked at it puzzled for a moment and squinted. Do you know that face you make when you get behind someone at the airport that smells like body odor and fish piss? Sting was making that same face.

"What in Christ's name is that?" Ric asked, coming over to Sting's side.

"It's Cactus Jack's ear!" Gary said. "What should we do with it?"

Because eBay wasn't invented yet, there was still a small chance that Mick would be able to wear sunglasses again, one day.

Fortunately, Ric was smart. Wondering if it could be sewn back onto Mick's head like you would do with a freshly-sawed-off finger, he quickly rinsed out a plastic cup and put the ear in it with some ice.

Back in the ring, the newly-crowned one-eared-wonder Mick Foley and I didn't go very long after that. I wasn't exactly sure what to do, but I knew there was a lot of thick nasty blood and I knew a piece of Mick's head was missing - so I made an executive decision.

"Let's go home man," I said. "Your ear just fell off."

Whether Foley believed me or not, after that, we rushed through the finish and got the hell out of there.

After the match, I about lost it. I was bawling my eyes out walking in the back like a baby. After being informed that it was true, Mick's shadow now looked like a Mr. Potato-Head with a missing piece, I ran to find Mick.

In the doorway to his dressing room, I saw a number of bodies circling around Mick. I quick dried my eyes and sucked back my sob. Inside, I saw that medics had gathered and were patting him down, getting ready to put him on the ambulance.

I felt responsible for not making it over to the ropes more quickly to help Mick out. I remember thinking, "because of me, a man is missing a part of his body now."

"Mick," I said about to apologize.

Mick nodded no. He shook my hand, before leaving to let me know he didn't blame me. Then he was off to another battle, a four-hour operation to save his ear cartilage.

Today, Mick says he knew I was really upset and finds humor in the fact that one of the "toughest wrestlers ever looked like he was going to cry."

Mick losing his ear was something I took heat for over many years. After this bout, many wrestlers heard different exaggerated versions of this story and did not want to work with me. The snowball story grew and grew until legend had me savagely tearing the appendage off of the side of his head with my teeth in an attempt to eat the damned thing!

One of the urban legends I heard later on from the fans was that I had bit off his ear and air mailed it to Ric Flair to actually intimidate him.

I've also been told that a lot of enhancement talent would actually leave the arena after seeing their name on the board opposite mine. Many were actually afraid to face me because of that match - not willing to "lend an ear" to the cause themselves.

It's funny how bad injuries can help get wrestlers over. I had to pop an eye out to get LOOKED at by WCW, and when Mick lost an ear, people everywhere HEARD about it. His injury along with his body of work eventually led him to really become the "Vincent van Gogh" of wrestling. If you don't get the artist joke, Google it. It sucks to have to explain a punchline! (After you are done, look at the cover of this book to find Mick's ear.)

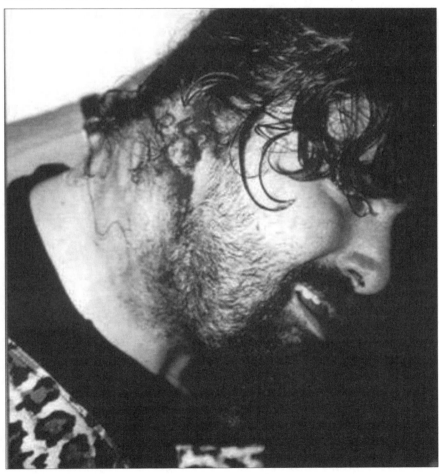

CHAPTER 16 – NOT SO WONDERFUL

Paul Orndorff beat cancer, but then got sick with a brain disorder. I've since made peace regarding the differences we have had. I've prayed for him to find strength and for him to find patience with the horrible condition he is facing. I truly wish him well and hope the very best for him. Now, I wouldn't even put this next story about Paul in my book, if I didn't have to. But the editor said there would be heat if I left this out, and the readers would bury me online. So this story has nothing to do with the 13 world titles I've earned, it has nothing to do with my athletic ability, and it has nothing to do with how I feel about Paul now.

Like Mick's ear, this little anecdote has also become an urban legend that has snowballed out of control over time. One of my most famous fights in the minds of many was not a wrestling match at all. It was actually just a couple of quick punches with "Mr. Wonderful" Paul Orndorff, backstage.

So one morning before a big show at Center Stage in Florida, I was hanging in my hotel room and heard the phone ring. It hurt to move. I didn't even feel like reaching for the receiver. I was still healing from a completely separated-chest injury and a torn rotator cuff from a sloppy match with the Hulkster. Now, I was just about to head out the door to grab a bite to eat before heading over to the event, but I picked it up anyhow. In hindsight, I shouldn't have and wonder what would have been if I hadn't.

"Hello?"

"Leon, it's Eric," he said. "What are you doing, sleeping?"

"Morning, Eric." I answered, "No, I was just about to grab some breakfast."

"Leon. I've been having problems with the boys not doing promotional work, and we can't have this anymore. Now, I need you to get your ass up, head over to the studio and get your photographs done for 2 o'clock."

Eric knew full well that there was a TV taping that night. This meant that you had to get there early for interviews and other spots for preproduction. "But what about Center Stage? It's almost an hour from there, and I will kind of be late."

Bischoff waited an uncomfortable amount of time. "I'll let them know over at the show. If you're not at the photo shoot though, Leon, I'm going to have to fine you. I have to start making an example somewhere for everyone else."

I got ready quickly. I grabbed my best Vader gear and headed out to the studio for the photo shoot. It lasted about two hours, and then I had another hour or so commute to the show. There was just enough time to go over my match and wrestle.

Now, Paul Orndorff was one of the ring agents at this point. To his credit, he had no knowledge I was directed to be late for the shoot. And likewise, I had no knowledge I had to do a taped promo before the show over at Center Stage. I walked into the locker room and saw a familiar face come around the corner. It was Meng, aka Haku.

"Hey Leon," Meng asked, patting me on the shoulder. "Where have you been? Paul's looking for you for some interviews with Gene Okerlund." Just as he gave me the heads up, Paul came around the corner like a bat out of hell.

"Where the hell you been?!" Orndorff cut me off before I could answer. "Doesn't even matter. You're two hours late."

I got up and walked over to the sink. Orndorff followed. "Look, man," I said. "Bischoff knows where I was."

Technically, Eric was my boss and all who really mattered in the end. To me, even though I had a lot of respect for him, Orndorff was more like an assistant. If he had given me the opportunity to tell him why I was late, I would have. I think Orndorff lost his temper because I wasn't treating him like a boss.

"Goddamn you, you fat ass."

"Paul, go fuck yourself," I said, agitated at the fact that the right hand didn't know what the left one was doing.

At this point, another agent, Terry Taylor walked in and tried to diffuse the situation. "What's the problem?" he asked.

"Leon can't get his fat ass to work on time to do interviews, that's the problem," Paul chimed in.

"Terry, Eric said I had to do a photo shoot before the show, and that he would tell you."

"Paul, I think Leon's right," Terry said. "I did hear about Leon's shoot. Either way, it's still okay. There's still time for the interview," Terry nodded at me. "It's cool."

"Look, let's go do it. Just wait a second, and I'll get changed." I took my shirt off and put my mask on to get ready to film the promos with Mean Gene.

(EDITOR'S NOTE: Terry Taylor in an interview recently said, "Paul Orndorff, the guy Paxil was invented for, went right on talking shit to Vader. Vader ignored him, and then Paul walked away. But then something happened and Vader ended up in Paul's face.")

What happened was, I was getting ready and Orndorff sat right down next to my locker waiting for me, cursing under his breath. I made eye contact. "Paul, I said I will do the promo! What else do you want? Just give me a second."

"Okay," Orndorff shook his head. "But, if you're ever late again, I'll knock you on your fat ass."

He wasn't a threat, but it sounded like he wanted to go. I had had enough of his garbage. He didn't have to ask me twice to take that shot, so I took it, in front of a number of the boys in the locker room.

WHAM! I knocked Orndorff down with one open-hand slap.

I immediately felt horrible. I know that in today's society, you can't just run around putting your hands on somebody. I was probably about 400 pounds at this point, bench pressing over 550. Orndorff, on the other hand, was around 220 and one of his arms was *completely crippled.* It looked like my wrist all the way up and he could barely lift 50 pounds with it. He was absolutely no threat. I should've shoved him, or let him hit me first, but I shouldn't have done that. I didn't want to hurt him.

Paul Orndorff wasn't really "Wonderful" anymore. He was semi-retired. He was an older guy, an agent, kept around as a figure head to help organize things in the locker room. Therefore, he went down hard, but wonderfully.

"Paul, are you alright?" I asked, squatting over him. I immediately rushed to check on him. It looked like his head may have hit a metal cabinet on the way down. I didn't want to hurt the guy. If he had hit that tool box just right, who knows what could have happened? Orndorff shoved my hand away. Now, I never even thought about finishing him off. There was no point. It would have been too easy to knock out a crippled guy half my weight. Instead, I just shrugged and went over to stand against the opposite wall.

Regardless of being right or wrong, I just hit an agent.

I was the only one to get a hit in. That meant I would be looked at as being completely in the wrong. It would be described as being a cheap-shot on my behalf, instead of a fight. I didn't want to get fined, and I didn't want to get fired. Rather than to take all the heat, I decided to strategically provoke him into hitting me back and let him get a shot in. That way we could call it even and that way I probably wouldn't lose my job.

Before Paul got up, I looked over at some of the boys and put both hands behind my back. I'm pretty sure they knew what I was doing. They knew I was giving Orndorff his revenge. In my mind, it was also Paul's turn to save some face in front of his peers.

"Are you ok, Paul?" I asked, leaving myself intentionally open for a receipt. I got the exact response I was looking for.

Pop! Pop!

Orndorff hit me twice. I didn't block the shots at all so he could get his vengeance to make us even. As I had predicted, blows from a man with a dead crippled arm didn't even hurt. Not at all wanting to hurt him, I didn't touch him again. After I took those two shots, I blocked his attempt at a third one.

"Ok, Paul," I said. "You got yours." After he missed the fourth and a fifth, I realized Paul wasn't letting up. "Ok, Paul. We are even now!" Paul continued to throw haymakers that I wouldn't let connect. A few more boys gathered around to enjoy the show. It was like the olden days. They were letting us fight it out and settle our differences in our own way, and nobody was really stepping in to stop it.

For me at this point, it was kind of like blocking punches from a girl. You want to hit back, but you know you can't. So I hooked him in a front face lock to calm him down. It didn't work. His arms were flailing. He was embarrassed so he just kept on swinging. Orndorff threw his arms around in the air and kicked his feet. I held him still in the headlock. "Enough, Paul!" I said.

Eventually, he knocked a drink off the bench. We both went down. We rolled around, and that was about it. I put him in a choke hold, and he gave up. I let him out of the hold and figured it was over, but I was wrong. Then, Orndorff pulled a chicken shit move. He kicked me in the face twice, after I was nice enough to break the hold and let him free.

Right after that, Orndorff ran to the executive's room, which was a coach's office. Bischoff wasn't there yet, Tony Schiavone was and so were some of the other officials. He went in there as fast as he could, just to talk smack about me, so I followed him. There was no way I was going to let him just say whatever he wanted without me there to defend myself. The moment I stepped in the doorway, he tried to pop me right in front of the executives!

"Jesus Christ, Paul!" I grabbed his arm in one hand and his neck in the other and slammed him hard against the wall and held him there. Tony Schiavone and the executives had no idea what was going on. Just like the other boys, they were in shock, but nobody stepped in to stop it.

"Paul, I'll tell you what, I've not thrown a punch yet and yet you've hit me three times," I growled. "Now you come running in here to try and make it worse like a bitch?"

"Fuck you," he said, with me mashing his face against the cement wall. I looked around. The suits and ties loved it! The guys in the office had stopped what they were doing and were ready to watch us fight.

"Okay!" I said, letting him out of a bear-hug against the wall. "Let's go outside and finish this. Now, I want to fight!"

The audience was growing. We marched out into the hall with the executives and some of the boys from the locker room following in tow.

Just as I was ready to kill him, Meng came around the corner of the hallway holding a hotdog. He pulled the two of us apart and immediately forced us to get away from each other. It's a good thing he did too. After being separated for the final time, Bischoff finally showed up and sent me home. Orndorff worked the TV taping with a black eye clearly visible, defeating a jobber named Barry Houston.

(EDITOR'S NOTE: Dave Meltzer reported that Orndorff came out of the fight like "a John Wayne type hero" in the front office behind the scenes. Since I was the bigger guy, he really could do no wrong. I was reported to Bischoff as being the villain in the fight and Orndorff was the hero for his bravery of trying to take on a giant. Meltzer said that both of us should have been reprimanded. "A supervisor shouldn't be telling a guy "to make your move," particularly with other wrestlers watching thus the macho image would be hurt if either backed down.)

Paul Orndorff's initial version of this unfortunate story was one-sided. He said in interviews, "I hurt my foot from kicking him so many times in the head! It literally hurt my foot, because I only had flip-flops on."

But again, this was just a bad situation. I should have never slapped him. He shouldn't have been so hot-headed. Paul really is a great guy, and I'm very sorry things turned out as they did, that day, as well as where he stands today health-wise. Even though there was a time I wasn't too happy with him, he really struggles. I was happy to recently offer an olive branch, and I think all is cool now. Later in life, you learn that holding on to anger is no good for anyone. I wish I had taken my own advice that I had once given to Steve Austin early on in his WCW career; always let a cooler head prevail.

My bad reaction to a bad situation eventually ended up costing me dearly for the rest of my life.

CHAPTER 17 – BISCHOFF & "HIS BEST FRIEND"

Ever hear of the "Vader Invader Kill" tour?

Months before our business relationship ended, one good idea Eric actually had to put a little steam on me was pretty funny. Eric decided it would be cool to have me just show up at any non-WCW promotion that wanted me. The stipulation was, however, I would only appear for one reason and one reason alone, *and that was to kill jobbers.*

Towards the final days in WCW, Eric sent me into a bunch of territories to put a buzz back on me in a very different way. I think the idea was that he wanted to get me back over after losing the run with Hogan and figured this was an interesting way to get people talking about me, again. We especially figured that the smart wrestling fans, ones who particularly always sided with me, would really make some noise about me taking these bookings. The idea that people would actually get to see Vader wrestle under banners they never expected would also get some press in the newsletters which was always good.

The most memorable booking we accepted for the Vader Invader Kill Tour was on June 26, 1995. It was at the USWA, the official training territory of the WWF!

There was a bit of controversy surrounding this booking in that I was one of the top dogs in WCW and WWE's mainstay the Undertaker was also on the card. This never happened. Both promotions would never allow such a thing as the implications of two worlds colliding was one that most fans couldn't wrap their brains around. The other reason was that something could possibly happen that could make one promotion get over on the other and neither WCW nor WWF would be there to control it with other promoters in charge.

Going in there to the USWA that night was very different than most would think. Many must have thought it would be stressful for me because I still get asked about this one-shot even today. It would be great for me to say I instantly jumped on the WWF's number-one star swinging to make a statement that "WCW was the best promotion in the world, baby!" But, the thing about it is, it wasn't like that at all.

It was all very quick. I just walked in with Terry Taylor and all of the sudden there was Paul Bearer with the Undertaker! I said, "Hello," and we smiled. I immediately shook their hands and there was mutual respect. It was just another show.

I had never met Taker before and thought it was pretty cool. Little did I know at the time, but I would be working with him in the future and he would actually be instrumental in saving my ass overseas. See? This is exactly why you would not do something stupid to defend your promotion's flag. You never know when you would be working with them in the future.

I didn't get to watch him work or anything that night. He was in a weird tag match for the main event. He was tagging with USWA's Bill Dundee against another Memphis staple, Doug Gilbert. Gilbert's partner was another guy you probably have heard of, and another I had never met, either. He was another pretty agile super heavyweight, Kamala.

Kamala was a super nice guy, very friendly and a total gentleman, but this was the only time our paths ever crossed. I was about to leave WCW and go to the WWF. Kamala left WWF a few days before this and was just coming into WCW.

Come intermission they had me fire up my getaway car. Terry Taylor sat in it behind the wheel, literally ready to drive me out of there the very moment I was done. We did the same thing everywhere to really give any unsuspecting fans on the sidelines the appearance that we were totally invading a promotion.

The bell rang. Two sweet jobbers, Mr. World Class and TD Steele, were in the ring battling it out like ham-and-eggers do with some pretty piss-poor exaggerated stomps and punches.

I came in out of nowhere and everyone was in shock.

"Vader? VADER?!"

"Is this real?"

I attacked both men in the true spirit of "The Vader Invader Kill Tour." I powerbombed both of them to hell and got the hell out of there like I just committed a crime.

It was a pretty cool idea of Eric's and did get me a lot of press. I did find out, however, that the tour was a way to keep me working but also just kind of kick me off to the side while I was not wanted in the spotlight. After the fact, I learned that guys like Flair and Hogan wanted me out of the dynamic of the main event for a time, so this was created to "keep me busy."

Whatever the reason, the dirt sheets said it was historic in the U.S. because never before had a WCW guy been on a card with a WWF guy while both were on top of the world and both were under contract. (However, little did I know, my contract was about to be broken.)

ERIC BISCHOFF
At first, Eric Bischoff didn't know much about the business. He couldn't find his ass with both hands as far as wrestling was concerned back then. The thing that Eric had going for him was that he was smart.

Eric was intelligent and well-spoken and a good looking guy on the camera. I mean that's what he was hired for because he looked like a mannequin. Before he became the Executive Producer of Television for WCW, he may not have known much about running a major wrestling promotion, but you can bet he had a plan on how he was going to learn it. That plan involved listening to only one person.

Hulk Hogan.

Investing your time and energies to learn from one of the highest-earning wrestlers of all time only made sense. Hey, Hogan Knows Best, right?

The problem was, however, by shifting gears and becoming a full-time Hulk-a-maniac himself and turning your back on everyone else, he forgot about who had got him to the dance at all. The main reason why he was considered to become the top man, was all the hard work of Cactus Jack, Sting, Ric Flair, Ron Simmons, Rick Rude, and Sid Vicious - the whole WCW group before the Hulk Hogan era.

Some people behind the scenes today say that if you look at the ratings during the time before Hulk Hogan, the nWo, The Monday Night Wars and all that, WCW was more profitable because they obviously had a lot less money in salaries going out, know what I mean?

HULK HOGAN
When Hulk first got to WCW, he seemed great. He was real nice and polite. He was cool with all the boys and seemed to be sincere. Little did we know that he was obviously really working on winning over one person behind the scenes, the only one needed who could really get him over by winning – Eric Bischoff. Once he got in with Eric, real quick, everything changed.

When Hogan first came in, it was perceived as a positive and people believed it was what would be good for business. However, he lobbied to go over clean on Ric Flair. That booking certainly didn't help Flair.

After Hogan destroyed him four times in a row, which made absolutely no sense to do so early, Eric let him then hand-select his next opponent.

More politics. To get his buddy some main event PPV money, Hogan chose "The Butcher" aka Brutus Beefcake. This match drew horrible money at a PPV, and the fans booed Hogan the whole match. After that fiasco, they decided to call me in to save the day.

Harley was hurt, so Flair was sort of acting as my manager in a storyline twist. To end their program, Flair lost a retirement match to Hogan in October 1994. He came back a few months later to just sit in the crowd and interfere in matches. Then to keep him in the top heel scene with me, for about two months, he started managing me. It made very little sense to me at the time, because we technically should have hated each other still on TV. Other than the idea that the enemy of my enemy is my friend, I couldn't think of anything else to justify the logic, and I was part of the storyline.

I saw what Hogan got away with working with Flair. I knew it was bad, so I told anyone who would listen to me exactly just what I thought. People knew I wasn't happy about what I was seeing with Hogan falling back into the undefeatable pattern he enjoyed in the WWF. I had no problem with letting word get out about what I thought.

Back then, there was no internet to post behind-the-scenes wrestling gossip and all, there were weekly newsletters that smart fans subscribed to, however, to get the dirt. A bunch of these dirt sheets like *The Torch* and *The Observer* were saying that I was going to, in essence, shoot on Hogan and hurt him to get him out of the picture because I had enough of how I was being booked, but that just wasn't the case.

I am a professional and never went into a match with the intention of hurting someone. Sure, I hurt some people by accident and was also hurt by accident, but I wasn't going in to actually hurt Hogan.

Ric double-crossed me for the title at Starrcade. He took Dusty's job two days before the PPV, scrapped all of our plans, and never made good with it. Therefore, my first reaction to being asked to work with Hogan was, "No."

I told Eric I would not cooperate or work with Hogan at all with whatever they want to throw at me unless they agreed to make good with old promises. I refused to work with him unless it meant getting my title back.

Eric didn't like that and really wanted me to work with Hogan, so I got called into a second meeting with Eric. At this one, I tried my hand at politics.

"Flair screwed me on what Dusty and I had agreed and you still owe me for that," I said. "Not only that, but you should pull the belt off Hogan because we don't want to hurt WCW with a long stale championship like they booked Hogan in WWF."

Eric promised change, but he wasn't budging yet.

"Eric, if you don't want to go with my idea and do this for me, you should do it to save Hogan's stock and to do it for the company," I said.

At this point, Hogan was totally getting booed, and it was obvious that they would soon have to turn him heel. I was getting cheered so hard as a heel, because of how much our fans did not like the old idea of the immortal storyline. The "can't-be-beat" Hogan coming into our promotion to just tell the old boring story again was a waste of everyone's time.

Also, Hogan was seen as an invading northerner coming into a southern territory. The old fans of good 'ole boy southern rasslin' weren't having it. They hated his Yankee ass.

It soon became more and more evident that Hogan would either need to quit or *become a heel.*

Eric agreed. We both knew by now the audience was not buying it and that eventually, something was going to have to change.

I didn't want to feed into the "Invincible Hulk Hogan" booking route. What I proposed was that with Flair acting like my new advisor, I didn't care how they took the belt from Hogan - Flair could shoot him in the back with a bazooka - just so as long as it did happen. But Eric didn't go for it.

He did, however, throw more money around and agreed to me not having to job out, or do any sort of clean finish for Hogan which would hurt my character's image and lower my stock.

Before our first match at *SuperBrawl V*, I attacked Hogan in an angle to promote our upcoming series of matches. Before the run-in, he said, "Brother, you do your finisher to me. I'm just going to lay there. Get you over as a monster."

So he was supposed to take my finisher and lay there, out cold. But then you want to talk about a swerve? Hogan got up off of my finisher to make himself look strong, even before our series of matches.

Nice. That set an awesome tone.

I hit him with the Vader Bomb and I look over and Hogan gets right up like it was nothing. "You sonofabitch," I said. That was my first experience with him. I was like, *Jesus, this is how these guys get over? They lie and backstab you?*

At SuperBrawl, we had an okay rematch, as good as you can with a guy like Hogan. But, I'll tell you, I made good and sure to kick out of Hogan's trademark leg drop after a one-count, as a receipt for that nonsense he pulled on me earlier.

The referee was knocked out before I hit the Vader Bomb on Hogan. Then, Ric Flair ran to the ring, made the three count, and attacked Hogan, resulting in my disqualification in the match.

On the first WCW Uncensored PPV, I wrestled Hogan, again, this time in a strap match. Flair once again was booked to intervene (this time in drag which still baffles me to this day) costing me the match. After this, it was obvious that Flair was being booked into all my finishes. This became a way to meet the promise I had with Eric of not having to job to Hogan.

To Flair's credit, it has come to my attention that he has since mentioned he hated this and wanting nothing to do with it.

I would have preferred beating Hogan senseless and then being disqualified over Flair running in and costing me the match and making me look stupid all the time.

It's funny because Eric Bischoff was the one who begged me to work with Hogan and talked about future programs, but a return series with a possible title exchange never happened. Today in interviews, however, like a recent one with Greg Oliver, Eric says, "Vader was known for being a bit unpredictable and unprofessional and, as a result, Hogan didn't really want to work with him (again)." I find this ironic coming from the same person who would say one thing backstage, then do a different thing in the ring i.e. no-sell the Vader-bomb. Now, who is the unpredictable and professional one?

To this day, I don't know if Eric decided to keep me away from Hogan, or if it was a request from Hogan himself.

Politics. There was no incident, nothing stiff or anything in any of our first series of matches. I took good care of Hogan in all of our bouts. He always thanked me after and said how "Everything was great," and "It was a pleasure." Clearly, he was telling Eric something else behind the scenes to keep me out of the spotlight and keep himself on top. If it wasn't Hogan himself, then maybe Eric was trying to bury me and keep me out of the main event. I don't know.

After that, I was booked into another feud with Flair, based on my frustration at Flair's constant interference in my title matches and Flair's annoyance at "my inability to defeat Hogan." This frustration angle booking was probably a rib on me because it was also what was going on behind the scenes. They were frustrating the hell out of me.

The weird thing that I cannot explain is that before the very end, it seemed as if I started to gain Hogan's respect. Maybe Hogan was impressed that I was hanging in there. I don't know. But Hogan started coming around more and seeking me out.

He seemingly grew interested in working with me some more. One day, he surprisingly asked me to help develop his feud with the Dungeon of Doom. He said he wanted me to join him, Randy Savage and Sting for the main event at WCW War Games.

We got together, went over some spots and came up with some really good ideas, but the storyline never developed.

It is possible, however, that Hogan was just practicing politics with me to keep me at bay. Maybe the whole War Games thing was a ploy to cover up his true feelings of not wanting to share the spotlight with me in future main events. Who knows? Somebody was working somebody.

BISCHOFF'S RISE

You have to give it to him. Eric Bischoff's rise from being a B-team announcer to the head of WCW television was impressive. Now, it didn't just happen overnight. Nobody in the WCW locker room just woke up the next morning saying, "Wait, who's this new guy in charge?" Eric politicked for a long time to sit in the throne, and people predicted that it was going to happen.

I have to be correct in how I say this; *Eric Bischoff became a very good promoter.* He was the one who made WCW really give WWE a run for its money. Early on, he was just a pretty-boy announcer that got promoted because Bill Watts got fired and this other guy got fired, then another guy got fired. However, Eric learned. He stayed quiet and watched everyone make their mistakes and when he saw the right opportunity, he knew exactly what to do and struck like a snake.

There is no doubt Eric's a smart guy. He looked good, he had the jet black hair and the Ken Doll smile that all the Barbie Dolls loved. Initially, he didn't know a lot about wrestling, but he rapidly evolved and to do what he did with the nWo and "the new WCW" was very exceptional for a long time.

For that, I do take my hat off to him. Eric did what no one's ever has done, he gave the WWE a run for their money, despite the fact that he got his ass whipped and ultimately sent home in the end. That didn't matter. His impact was tremendous.

CRAZY MONEY

Right around the time Eric took over, I was making good money. Sting was making good money. Rude was making good money. Everyone was making good money, but it wasn't the "crazy money" yet, that was soon to come. Then, Eric played the Hogan card and all of a sudden, he's paying out crazy money, hiring everyone in sight.

The thing that didn't make sense, however, was that even though the ratings were still about the same, money was being thrown around like crazy. It didn't make sense. Where was it coming from? We went up a little in business, but not enough to justify the new revenue stream of blank checks. All I can guess is that Eric must have worked Ted Turner into giving him all the money he needed to "beat WWE."

With all of the new signed talent and the price tags involved with Hogan taking the main spots up for him and his friends, all this must have cost substantial amounts of crazy money. Since I didn't always see eye to eye with Eric and was often stubborn in protecting my character, I guess I no longer fit into his plans. Couple this with the fact that since I wasn't in the Hogan clique, I think Eric eventually decided to figure out a way to sideline me and keep some of my payouts for his new pals.

DEPARTURE

One day before a show, Eric randomly called me into his office. Hogan had taken some time off and I was filling in more dates for him and I was expecting a surprise thank you for taking on the added responsibility.

Eric had a different surprise in mind.

"Leon," he said abruptly. "You know, I know I haven't had a chance to talk with you about this, but we still have to suspend you for the backstage fight with Paul Orndorff."

I was surprised because this incident happened some time ago, and it felt like the statute of limitation for this crime had long since passed.

"I can't have my guys thinking it is okay to run around doing whatever they want," he laughed patronizing me, "so the suspension will be for six months without pay."

I shook my head. I knew Orndorff wasn't being reprimanded, even after I let him kick my ass. "So much for that plan," I thought. I waited an uncomfortable amount of time before responding, as to not lose my cool.

"Six months?" I said.

"You can go to Japan if you like," he suggested.

I was pissed. I knew Eric probably just overdrew his Turner checking account and was looking for some trivial ways to save a couple of bucks. Why else would he wait that long to come after me to pay for an old sin?

"Eric, you know I'm a company man, now. I have been doing whatever they ask, working for two months on a shoulder that needs surgery. I've been doing that all for you," I said. "Do you know how many pain pills I have been taking just to work some nights?"

"And I appreciate that," he said, tilting his head in that Eric Bischoff manner.

After the cage and the match with Hogan, my shoulder got really bad. I worked two months after that and there was no question that I needed surgery. I was in a lot of pain. I really was doing that for the company, you know. The company called on me to fill Hogan's absence, so I didn't want to let them down for the opportunity.

"I've endured working on my shoulder, taking on a heavier schedule because Hogan wanted some time off. And he wasn't even hurt," I said. "But I didn't bitch. I just said, Ok, that's my role, I gotta do it. But, now he's back and now it seems like you just want me to step aside?"

Eric shook his head.

At this time, I was, in fact, taking pain pills just to make it through the day, let alone work a match. I did and said some things that I probably shouldn't have said, but I was under a lot of pain and I was "pilled up," working under the influence of pain pills. However, I never said anything to Eric to get under his skin.

I'll be the first to admit, I was taking way too many of them to get in the ring, but if I didn't take them, I couldn't have worked and I would have lost my spot. It was horrible what it became.

I had to take them to get into the ring, to get out of the ring, and then to just get into bed and get out of bed the next morning. The vicious cycle would start up the next day and you do it again all over.

"I think it should be with pay."

I explained to him that my shoulder injury was, in fact, diagnosed as being a very serious injury. I had seen a doctor about it and he told me it would be like an eight or ten month recovery period, away from work. I figured I had a long-term contract and could take time off to take care of the injury, but I also should be getting paid during recovery since it was suffered in the ring. He said I could go over to Japan, but really I couldn't work to earn money if I were to use the time off wisely and get the operation.

"You know, what you are proposing is over $300,000 – *for a slap.*"

I mean, I know I did slap Paul first, but he did much more damage with me letting him get his turn with my hands to my side. I take full responsibility, but I was on some mood-altering pills to keep up with their schedule. I couldn't help but think that if Sting was that injured, he would have been given time off. If Flair or Hogan were that injured, they would have been also been given time off. However, in my case, they specifically asked me to suck it up and keep on working no matter how bad it was.

I decided we were both half at fault, me for the slap and him for the injury.

"Seeing how I'm injured and can't work, how about half that?"

"For what you did, you can take six months off, without pay, and come back and all will be forgotten," Eric said. "I promise."

I snapped. Eric wouldn't budge and see me half way.

"No," I said without even taking a second to think about it. "You can shove it. You can take your six months and shove it up your ass." I got up and pushed the chair back hard. "Suspend me, you know, fire me. Do what you have to do. I'll get my shoulder fixed and go back to Japan, or go somewhere."

I left the room. *I slammed the door and WCW behind me.*

Looking back, I'm glad I moved on, but I don't know what really could have been if I had stayed around. I could have taken that time off and got the surgery then returned. Who knows, but my pride was hurt and I wasn't going to put up with their shit anymore.

It probably wasn't that bad an offer. I had a long term contract that would have put me through until 1999 and could have done some really good things in WCW. But honestly, my pride wouldn't let me.

He did give me an opportunity to not just throw my career away. My behavior that night was bad and my behavior a month before that was bad as well. I understand now that he did also want to send some kind of message out to the rest of the locker room that you can't just hit people.

WHAT GOES AROUND?

Now, this isn't just karma, this is how I straight up believe God works. I believe that God has a whole rewards program here on earth. If you do good things, good things come back to you. If you are bad, however, then you do not get off free. Bad things eventually catch up with you and you get punished for them.

If I am right, we really can see existential punishment, "Hell on Earth' now, with some of the things wrestlers have done over the courses of their careers. To become "The Man" in this business, many find they often have to step on a whole lot of people on their way to the top. But at what cost later on?

Hulk Hogan was on top of the world and was loved by everyone everywhere, then a huge scandal happened and Hulkamania "came crashing down" for a time.

Ric Flair boasted his riches and having the lifestyle of a playboy, and now there are rumors that he pissed it all away and knows what it is like to be almost dead broke.

Karma. For the top performers in the game who are still with us, the bad stuff they did is now catching up with them. It is almost like that movie, *Bedazzled*, based on the idea of selling your soul to the devil. You have all the riches you want now, but in the end, you will pay for it. That Karma, she really is a bitch.

Now, I am not complaining or whining about anything. Part of my exit from WCW was admittedly my own fault. But I do feel that I was set up to fail as a result of others' greed.

I'm no angel by any means and I will be the first to admit it. This concept of being punished for doing wrong applied to even me. I know there was a point in my life where I was being punished by God for all of the bad stuff I had done. The darkness and the demons I fell into after semi-retirement was because of some bad things that I did earlier in my career. For a time, my punishment was that I could not even use my body, the one thing I relied on to make money with by athletic means – but I will speak more about that in a later chapter.

SNOWBALL EFFECT & STRIP MALL DEAL

When I left WCW, the differences in my professional life were like night and day. Everything was going very well for me, but then instantly it quickly turned into a snowball downhill.

I was making almost $700,000 in WCW a year. Being forced to go to WWF and start over again from scratch would immediately cut my salary in half, but the WWF deal wasn't even on the table yet. The timing of this leave also hurt a real estate investment that I had been working on for some time. I was really counting on that for my retirement.

No WCW contract at that particular point in time meant no regular income and that ultimately meant I could no longer secure a loan by myself anymore. I didn't realize that not having a regular WCW paycheck would have affected my credit as it did. I had already begun to purchase a huge strip mall but learned I could no longer do it alone. I had to partner up with a plastic surgeon and another investor in order to make the deal go through.

That strip mall purchase still proved to be a good one, as we eventually flipped it and it sold for $18.5 million, a hefty profit for us all. However, without the WCW contract as collateral for my own loan, I didn't make nearly as much money off of the sale as I would have if the whole deal was mine. The cosigners ended up getting a much bigger piece of the pie than me, the person who set the entire deal up.

Leaving WCW ended up being a costly thing to do. I often wonder what would have happened if I'd had just taken that six-months-without-pay deal, but at the time, I think they would have just buried me either way for some other reason. The writing certainly felt like it was already on the wall.

In hindsight, I learned a valuable lesson, albeit a little too late. I never did my fighting outside the ring, but I should have. I should have realized that politics were important when Flair and Hogan were coming into WCW because they were both being political geniuses. I guess I should have handled myself differently backstage. I should have upped my political game, but I didn't.

I still can't cry and have to look at the positive side of things. Despite the setbacks at that time, I still had my name, my health, the potential to earn a massive amount of money in Japan, and I had far more money in the bank than anyone I knew growing up. Despite getting screwed behind the scenes in WCW and making a bad decision to leave when I did, *I was still a success.*

That mall was and still is a real prime piece of property. We fixed it up and made it into a real success, as well. It's right off Highway 36 & McCaslin Boulevard in the South East corner of Superior, Colorado. That's the mall that Vader built, in case anyone is wondering. I'm pretty proud of it.

CHAPTER 18 - INOKI

After leaving WCW, my theory was right; Japan was happy to have me. It only took one call to say I was available, and they immediately had something for me. Just like a bad Richard Marx ballad, Inoki was "right there waiting for me."

"Wrestling World" was the name of New Japan's big annual show that traditionally takes place in early January at the Tokyo Dome. (It is now called *Wrestle Kingdom*.) This event is NJPW's version of WrestleMania.

On January 4th, 1996, Wresting World % had a storyline behind it that was perfect for me. It was the final faceoff between two different promotions, and I had competed for both.

The rivalry between NJPW and UWFi finally was coming to head. The show consisted of 10 matches with three inter-promotional bouts that would pit one NJPW wrestler against one UWFi fighter. The rest of the matches were also nothing to scoff at. They really booked a real "who's who" of Japanese wrestling.

The undercard had Jushin Thunder Liger defeating Koji Kanemoto to win the IWGP Junior Heavyweight Championship. It also featured a high-profile bout with Hiroshi Hase winning his retirement match against his former tag team partner, Kensuke Sasaki. (Ignore the fact that Hase was out of retirement one year later and wrestling for All Japan.) And the main event had The IWGP Heavyweight Champion, Keiji Mutoh aka The Great Muta losing the belt to UWFi representative, Nobuhiko Takada.

For me at Wrestling World, I was having my first post-WCW match facing the man whose four-year winning streak I had ended over eight years ago, Antonio Inoki.

Inoki came up to me before the event and was very happy to see me. He shook my hand professionally, hesitated, and then hugged me like a lot of the American wrestlers would do. Then we had a conversation the best we could in broken Japanese English.

"I just wanted you to know, lawsuit," he said, "that not me."

"No, no, no! I know!" I said. "The committee, I know." I knew Inoki wasn't behind the court case, but it was cool of Inoki to immediately point out the elephant in the room. I thanked him for the booking. Clearing the air proved what I already believed. We shook hands like brothers.

"I wouldn't have had it any other way," he said. "For my last match in the ring here, I only wanted you."

I owed him a lot.

Short of only maybe Rikidozan, you would be hard pressed to find any wrestler in Japan more legendary than Antonio Inoki, and the audience knew it. This was for Inoki's Final Countdown Retirement Tour ending his 35-year career, one of his last matches ever in Japan.

Despite his age, the match we were planning was intense and fantastic, which was a real testament to who Inoki is. The story we decided on was Inoki dealing with the size and ferocity of "Big Van Vader," the evil monster he created. Just as he did before back when we first introduced Vader to the Japanese wrestling world, Antonio Inoki encouraged me to hit him as hard as I could for his last match ever in that arena.

"I would much rather be hit solid than to have the match come off sloppy and weak," he said, planning out our last match.

"I'll give you my all," I said to the 53-year-old, fearless man.

BEATING UP MONSTERS

Antonio Inoki then told me a story about another "Antonio" wrestler he faced long ago. This Antonio, however, was very different than Inoki. He was a total disgrace and the perfect example of coming off both "sloppy and weak" in the ring.

Antonio "The Great" was a monster gaijin like me, only from Canada. He was 6-foot-4 and weighed in around the 450-pound mark. His suits were a size 90 and his shoes, a size 28. Unlike me, however, he was illiterate, dumb and pretty much a pussy. Stories about the Great Antonio, however, included myths of his strongman feats that were not unlike those of Big Otto Wanz and André the Giant.

The insane urban legends surrounding Great Antonio were ridiculous, and most of them birthed from a lot of his bragging and boasting. For one, Great Antonio claimed to be part extraterrestrial. He pulled a 400-ton locomotive 20 meters. He could eat 25 chickens in a sitting, or 15 steaks. He pulled four buses connected to each other in one shot. He hijacked a bus full of passengers trying to prove he could pull it. One stated he lifted an enormous tree trunk with 13 people hanging off of it.

Just like many wrestlers without a lot of in-ring ability, the Great Antonio couldn't get over early in his career. He wasn't really successful until he started promoting his own shows. By doing this, he would often showcase himself in main events and battle royals, as nobody else figured he was worth investing a push in. He kept putting himself over until other promoters around the country eventually started to notice. Eventually, big-name promoters like Stu Hart in Canadian Stampede started booking him in their main events simply because of the buzz he had created around his name.

After some fairly impressive exposure, the Great Antonio began to find an interest outside of the country, in particular with Japanese promotions. In Japan, they would pay a big premium on great gaijin giants. They liked to follow the booking template of their Japanese underdog taking on the likes of monster, Godzilla-type wrestler of a different race. This is why big, non-Japanese guys like André, Abdullah the Butcher, Bob Sapp, Bam Bam Bigelow, Terry Gordy, Bruiser Broder, and Stan Hansen did so well in "The Land of the Rising Sun." Time and time again, Japanese wrestling fans paid top dollar to see this type of exotic booking unfold in the ring. When promoters would bring in a huge super heavyweight to pit against their babyface local hero, the fans would just eat it up. This is the very reason both Inoki and I saw a lot of success and money with the Big Van Vader gimmick.

Just like me, the Great Antonio fit the Japanese gaijin monster bill perfectly. The only difference, however, was he was a pretty terrible wrestler. In North America, the importance on entertaining gimmicks and showmanship could often outweigh wrestling ability, but in Japan, that wasn't the case. When Inoki booked Great Antonio for a match back in on December 8, 1977, at Tokyo's Sumo Hall, he had no idea that "The Great Antonio" was all just a great hype. In the ring, he was a great pile of steaming, drizzling shit.

There were around 10,000 fans all in attendance, ready to see their hero take on the likes of a monster. However, they had no idea that the legends surrounding the Great Antonio were pretty much myths that were about to be debunked.

In one corner stood Antonio Inoki, in the black trunks. He was "the real deal" himself; a student of Rikidozan, an excellent shooter, the founder of New Japan Pro Wrestling, and one of the creators of "strong style wrestling" which arguably created the need for modern MMA. In the other corner stood the Great Antonio; a French Canadian strongman and legit crazy person, sporting banana yellow pants and Captain Cavemen hairdo.

This booking was interesting in that you were putting a highly-respected man with legit shooting skills in the ring against a legit, real deal nut job. Add to the mix that there was a language barrier and you just knew something bad was going to happen.

Inoki explains that things were just fine at the start. There was a stare down and some showmanship at the start and that was all fine. Soon after that, the Great Antonio went into his lame big man routine which looked like a fat 10-year old trying to impersonate Godzilla walking.

A few minutes in, Inoki hit a dropkick that he didn't even bother to no-sell.

Instead of showing his big guns and shrugging off the dropkick, he just stood there like it never happened. This was the beginning of a diarrhea squirt offense move set that was about to really piss off Inoki.

The commentary then had to basically go into apology mode to defend Antonio's lack of in-ring splendor.

"Great Antonio's gut looks loose and fat, but punching his body is just like punching a big piece of raw rubber wall!" one commentator said. "He barely feels anything."

"Great Antonio seems to be head-locking Inoki without effort, but his grip is much stronger than you would think."

After some prodding from Inoki for Antonio to initiate some kind of credible offense, Antonio began to forearm-club Inoki in the back. This is where things got REALLY sloppy.

Antonio's great forearm shots missed and were more elbow than forearm. His strike work was sloppy and rather than finding their target on Inoki's back, Inoki then found he was taking elbows to the neck. That was the last draw. This was exactly what would throw an old school wrestler into shoot mode. Inoki became offended by Antonio's poor technique and considered it borderline dangerous.

Inoki jumped up and started pummeling Antonio in the face. Antonio immediately put his guard up and covered his face up like a school girl. Inoki sensing even more unprofessionalism took him to the mat with a perfect Gotch-style, single-leg takedown. Then, Inoki kicked him as hard as he could and as many times as he could until his own feet bruised. The announcers played along just like it was a normal match but you could sense they knew he was shooting. They finally woke up to a flurry of kicks.

BIFF! BIFF! BIFF!

"Inoki is kicking Great Antonio's face and doing great damage to the Great Antonio!"

POW!

"The right kick hit Great Antonio's chin, but the left kick just hit the great bones around his great stomach!"

THUD!

"Great Antonio's mouth is ripped, and he is bleeding greatly!"

CRACK!

"Inoki's stomping just broke Antonio's ear!"

"Great Antonio cannot wake up! He has no energy left! Inoki's upper kick to Antonio's chin seemed to be the final blow! His face is now covered with his blood."

By the end of the match, the Great Antonio was knocked out cold. When he came to, he was covered in a mask of his own blood. His manager came storming in to protest the attack to the referee, but that was not really the case. He really jumped in to tell Antonio to stay on the mat and allow the match to end so that he didn't further anger Inoki.

The bell rang and Inoki raised his special trophy in the air. Another monster gaijin had perished at his hands and the fans loved it. Antonio Inoki had saved the match and quite possibly saved himself from injury at the hands of Antonio "The Great Piece of Shit."

After telling me that other monster fighting story, Inoki said to me that, "...it was good to be great, but being great could also get you kicked in the face, greatly."

As a side note, I learned that the Great Antonio went home to Montreal after that fight and didn't dare step in a ring ever again. He never wrestled another match. In his old age, people said that the Great Antonio got even weirder. He could sometimes be seen selling his pictures to commuters in the subway station or a city park. Other sightings would often include hanging out in a Dunkin' Donuts he liked to frequent.

In 2003, Antonio Barichievich, aka the Great Antonio, died at age 77 while shopping in a grocery store.

INOKI'S FINAL MATCH

After calling the match, it was time.

The building was so hot for Inoki. As I came to the ring, you could tell that it was a special moment leading to the end of his legendary run with New Japan Pro Wrestling. What a huge pop for the entrance of Inoki. It was one of the loudest entrances I've ever heard, and it was almost scary to see the response. I was so overwhelmed at the response that I actually lost my sense of awareness for a moment taking it all in. Then like a klutz, I tripped and fell to the ground, while allowing Inoki to enter the ring. (Hopefully nobody saw!)

Just as planned, we took out all of the stops. As an insult to get the audience even more behind him, I applied one of Inoki's own trademark slaps on him. Then he had me just take over.

I played up the monster; I took off my mask and gave him a ridiculous German suplex. Inoki had the most awesome death sell of a suplex, ever, so bad I thought I killed him myself. He literally did not move for almost a whole minute.

After that, we made the tide turn, and Inoki got some offense in. We went outside of the ring and Inoki walloped me in the head with a chair and busted me open. When I recovered, Inoki said to me, "Make me bleed!" I returned the favor the hard way and he got busted open too. In the end, it was like a horror movie. It became a brutal slugfest with stiff punches, kicks, and headbutts that sprayed blood droplets and sweat into the crowd with every shot. There were probably some tears in the mix, too.

To really put Inoki over, we had him recover from everything. I hit him with a Vader bomb and also a huge Vadersault. Inoki kicked out of everything. To end the story and his career, Inoki finally found the power to bodyslam the big monster he created. The crowd went nuts. Then he put me in a Jugi Gatame cross arm-breaker for the win.

Antonio Inoki was 53 years old but still so very impressive! The match lasted almost 15 minutes, and it was my pleasure to do the honors for the man who handed me the biggest gimmick ever and helped me make my career.

Antonio Inoki handed me the Big Van Vader gimmick which allowed me to feed and provide for my family for many years to come. For this, I will always be grateful.

CHAPTER 19 - THE WWF

After returning home from New Japan's Pro Wrestling World and working in the Antonio Inoki retirement match, I got a big call from Vince McMahon.

I've worked for so many great promoters such as Misawa, Inoki, and Baba who were very topnotch at what they did. However, as far as Vince McMahon and the WWF were concerned, I knew that Vince was the best.

At one time, Inoki was bringing in money hand over fist in Japan. Giant Baba also sold out houses years upon years as did Misawa when he started Pro Wrestling NOAH. Before the Attitude Era, NJPW was killing WWF at the box office during the back-to-back runs of Mutoh and Hashimoto. But after the WWF created stars like Stone Cold and The Rock, you could no longer even compare them and the money that they made to Vince McMahon. Vince's product was as big as theirs in his own country, but it also transcended everywhere to a global audience – something the others in Japan could never quite do.

Another thing about Vince is that he is pretty much a self-made man. He didn't start out with all this money. Though his father did sell him the initial legs of a decent territorial business, Vince created all that you see on TV today. He's done wonders for what has become an international company.

Everything Vince wanted to do with the WWF, he has done and done it to a level of success that has been unmatched by anyone. WWE is now the largest pro wrestling/sports entertainment company in the world and has been for a long time. I don't see this changing anytime soon, if ever.

So when Vince called me upon leaving WCW when I did not exactly know where my next paycheck was going to come from, there was new hope. Things were looking up.

NEGOTIATION

Vince was a class act. He offered a great opportunity, global exposure, and really good money. To return the favor, I was upfront with Vince right from the start.

I told him about the shoulder injury I was working on in WCW and let him know that I really needed shoulder surgery.

One of the big problems for me initially was that shoulder injury. I was hesitant to sign on with the WWF because I felt I couldn't deliver "The Monster Vader" that I wanted to. I could barely lift my shoulder up over my head, let alone bodyslam someone.

Vince didn't care. He didn't want WCW to change their mind and call me back. He also didn't want another promotion coming along and scooping me up.

"Do you think you can heal up in a reasonable amount of time, say, within a year?" he asked.

"Yes, sir," I said. "I've had this issue before. I just need the operation."

"Good, then it's settled."

He didn't care about the injury and brought me in anyhow.

After signing, we decided I would work some with the injury and get some interest in my character, before taking some time off for the surgery. There were a number of weeks leading up to the WWF Royal Rumble. Vince decided that he would announce my debut for the PPV to boost sales and hype it up like crazy on television. But before they could promote my coming in, they had to first figure out what they were going to call me.

THE NAME

There was some discussion at first behind the scenes as to what Vince wanted to call me, right after I debuted. Since Vince likes to own your name, he wanted to change my gimmick into something he was going to call "The Mastodon," which was like a giant, prehistoric Wooly Mammoth.

Jim Cornette, one of wrestling's top managers of all time, stepped up and went to bat for me. He was a fan of my work and approached Vince McMahon.

"He's fucking Vader!" Jim said, "He's already one of the biggest names ever in WCW, Japan, and around the world, and you want to change his name and call him the Mastodon?!"

Cornette was convincing. Rather than having to dress up in some elephant costume or perhaps something worse, I was able to keep my name for the most part as, "The Man They Call Vader."

I've often wondered, what if we had gone with the Mastodon gimmick, all in? Vince wanted to change the name to Mastodon to create a whole new character, with a whole new look to make money with. You know what? Not having the business sense that I do today, I probably should have done it.

Vince was a creative genius. He said to me, "You've been Vader, you'll always be known as Vader, but I want to change your name here in the WWF officially to Mastodon."

That was a big change. Rather than to make a quick decision, I asked to think about it.

I knew he would own the name and he would market it because it was his, but I would have still gotten a good piece of it. He would have made money with it and maybe even more than with the Vader gimmick. Who knows? There would have been new Mastodon shirts, new Mastodon action figures, and just all kinds of new gimmick stuff that Vader fans could buy who already owned Vader merchandise.

I'm not sure why, but I didn't do it.

There were a bunch of action figures made when I was Vader with the WWF, probably a dozen of them, but they all portrayed me as I had always looked. But when Vince creates a character, it becomes his baby. He loves it more. I might have had the royalties to thirty or forty action figures coming in had I let him change my name and look. In hindsight, I probably should have. That was a mistake. That was just stupid on my part.

Maybe I should have said, "Yes sir, The Mastodon sounds just fine. Please. In my contract, however, I want to see at least five action figures on the market, every year." And he probably would have said, "You got it," for getting behind his idea.

Mick took the "Mankind" character and look where he went. He did what they asked to start and then became one of Vince's favorites. Steve Austin did, too. He played some character called, "The Ringmaster" and then also went on to what he is today.

This, again, was my lack of understanding politics. Not taking on "The Mastodon" gimmick may have alienated Vince and hurt my future in his company to some degree before I even started with the promotion.

Live and learn.

WWF DEBUT

My very first World Wrestling Federation appearance was as a participant in the Rumble match. I entered at number 13, an unlucky number for everyone in attendance. I eliminated Jake Roberts, Doug Gilbert, one member of the Headshrinkers I think, and Savio Vega. I was then eliminated by Shawn Michaels, but then to come off as a real monster, I reentered the ring and kicked everyone's ass that I could, including 'ole HBK.

I have to admit it, when I went back into the ring after being eliminated, I was so mean! I took some pain medication to get through the pain of my shoulder injury, and I didn't care who I steamrolled over. I was still four hundred pounds, and I made good and sure that everyone knew just who I was.

My shoulder should have been on fire the whole time, but the pills blocked it. I feared that I was going to do further damage, but I couldn't feel it. I knew I wasn't going to be around long, however, so I gave it my all. Vince McMahon was totally cool, too, how he let me go on TV. They had me written off in the best way to make me continue to look bad and strong. I was written off by "suspension."

Rather than an injury angle coming in that would have made me look weak, they had me defeat Savio Vega on the following Monday Night Raw. Then, unable to calm me down, WWF officials became my next victims, as I plowed through whoever got in my path like an angry bull. Eventually, WWF President Gorilla Monsoon stepped in. He demanded that I stopped my attack, and he too received a fresh Vader Bomb for his peacekeeping efforts.

As a result, Vader was suspended in the story, while in real life; Leon White was off to get a much needed shoulder surgery.

It all happened so fast. The very next day after the Gorilla Monsoon angle, I was off to the hospital. My agent agreed for me to come back in ninety days, when in reality, I probably needed more like ten months to recover! Even though that was what was in my contract, it didn't happen. When I came out of surgery, I couldn't bench press a hundred pounds. I couldn't do a pushup. I can't raise my hand over my head, yet I'm in the ring with the WWF? It was just too early. The whole first year with the WWF, they had a monster of a guy who could usually bench press 600 pounds who had to fake it.

If I had had the ten months recovery time like we had talked about, it may have been a different story. I may not have had that fan come up to me at an appearance, saying he was disappointed on how they used me in the WWF. If all of a sudden, I came back to the WWF after ten months a healthy Vader, at four hundred pounds, things may have been different. But instead of 400 pounds with lots of muscle and power, I was 370 pounds of fat. At a fat 370, I wasn't as big where I was supposed to be big, so it was a bad time physically in my career.

My agent went against my wishes and agreed for my return way to soon. After the surgery and the ninety days were up, I continued to have to fight the office over my contractual return that the agent agreed to. I remember telling Vince, "I can't even do a pushup," yet I was scheduled to do a match with Yokozuna, someone who weighed even more than I did.

"You don't understand, I can't physically do it."

"You'll do fine," Vince said. He just wasn't hearing me.

Someone who would really hear me was my agent because he was the guy who put me in this position to start with. He finally heard me when I said, "I'm done with you," and fired him over the whole situation.

During the recovery time, Jim Cornette had acted as a great mouthpiece for me in my absence. While I wasn't there, Cornette kept my name alive on television and campaigned for my "reinstatement."

Come February 18, 1996, at *In Your House 6,* I returned in a surprise. Yokozuna, who had recently left Camp Cornette, was about to pin Bulldog when I attacked him. I handcuffed him and beat his ass with my strong arm.

This led up to my first big PPV with WWF at *WrestleMania XII.* It was a six-man tag match with me teaming with Owen Hart & the British Bulldog against Yokozuna, Ahmed Johnson, and Jake "The Snake" Roberts. The stipulation was that if Yoko's team won, he would get five minutes alone with Jim Cornette in the ring.

The tease never paid out for the fans because our team won with me pinning Roberts.

JIM CORNETTE

One thing I thought I would mention is that while Jim Cornette was an excellent speaker, sometimes his love for wrestling was almost too much. I respect Cornette. I knew he always had my best interests at heart, but sometimes he just got too passionate with his visions of what should happen.

Cornette was so good in many aspects of wrestling that he sometimes felt he should be able to dictate the actual moves that should happen in the ring. This bothered me and some of the guys because he was never actually a wrestler.

One time I remember of this instance was when Jim Cornette tried to choreograph our six-man tag-team match at WrestleMania.

Now, this match was supposed to be just me versus Yoko, but when Yoko really started to pack on the pounds, they decided that the original plan was not going to fly. Yoko was an excellent worker, a hall of famer, and one of the best super heavyweights of all time. However, with the extra weight, he may not have been so effective with a singles match at the level expected for

WrestleMania. That is why they worked in Owen and Davey Boy into the match.

Cornette decided that he was going to salvage what could have been a cluster from adding all the other people to the match. He really had good intentions. However, when he started calling the moves that we should do in the ring, I felt like I had to object.

Jim wanted Yoko and me to start in the tag match at WrestleMania. Immediately, I looked over at my old friend from WCW days, Davey Boy Smith, and he wrinkled up his nose, too. I knew Davey Boy wasn't going to say anything so I spoke up.

"Jim, no that's not what's going to happen. It won't work."

"What do you mean? Why not?"

"Yoko is 600 plus pounds and I am 400. If you put us into start, where can the match go from there? I just think it sucks. This is WrestleMania and we want things to be right."

"What do you mean that sucks?"

"Starting with both of us big guys has no build up. It wouldn't mean anything to the fans," I said. "We need to build up to that. Neither of us should get in the ring for like the first 6 minutes."

"No, no, no," Jim said. "We need to start out strong."

"Starting with the two biggest wrestlers would blow it too early," I argued. "Why don't we start off with the other guys and tease the tag with us until it finally happens. I was thinking to have him no-sell a bunch of clotheslines and then have him Samoan Drop me on the run. The fans will go nuts."

Jim waited for a second and tried to make it look like he was processing what I told him. But really what I think he was doing was figuring out a way to denounce my idea and save face for offering poor advice to begin with.

I laughed. "Jim, I could call that match drunk and hung over better than that."

"Well, Leon, it's just that Vince doesn't want it that way," he said.

If I could have a nickel for every time someone said that line in the WWF, I would be a billionaire. People would say that whenever they felt their idea was right, and then just pass it off as if Vince was the one that had come to them with some kind of fine detail that totally didn't make sense. The problem was, I was still so fresh in the company and if there was a possibility that Jim was telling the truth, I didn't want to piss Vince off.

In the end, just as I had suggested, we had nowhere to go after Yoko and I started.

I will say this, I had always been told by people that Vince knew wrestling. I didn't like the way our match had turned out, because it felt like a cluster-fuck. So out of curiosity, I asked Vince why we had to start it that way.

"I never said that. No. Jim doesn't have the right to call your match. You wrestle, and we can leave the managing to him."

I got to hand it to Jim, though. As much as his passion for the sport may have got on my nerves when the writers and management didn't know what to do with me, Jim was the only one backstage going to bat for me, besides the other "Jim," my good friend Jim Ross.

CHAPTER 20 - SHAWN, ROCKY, & KUWAIT

At one appearance, a fan came up to my table. I signed an action figure for him and also took a picture with him. He was a happy camper. Before walking away, he praised my whole career, but then said the only thing he didn't like was my WWF run.

"It was a huge disappointment to me, he said. "They finally had someone with legit tough guy cred, and then they put you with Shawn Michaels and messed it up."

It's weird. I hear this a lot, but the WWE has treated me well.

Many fans absolutely love Shawn Michaels' work and they absolutely should. He was by far one of the very best in the ring. He was one of the most exciting performers out there to watch, bar none. So when some Vader fans comment on me not finishing on top with my program against the Heartbreak Kid, sometimes they overly passionate. However, I was just doing my job at the time and to have some really great matches with Michaels, in the long run, was worth it.

If you look at my house show results online for 1996, some Vader fans say it's clear that someone wasn't really sure how to use a hard-hitting wrestler with my reputation. While I did okay on some TV and PPV shows, I'll admit, I had my share of losses that year.

Sometimes, fans mention that my 1996 WWF win/loss records for house shows sucked. I lost to the Ultimate Warrior in less than 30 seconds. I lost to Sid every night with a chokeslam. Oh, and I even lost clean to Ahmed Johnson! (Okay, I'll admit it. That one hurt.)

The smart-marks say it is like they literally brought me in, "…just to job to everyone on the roster to give them a win over a former WCW champion."

Here's what I think happened.

When they paired me up with Shawn, I was excited. I certainly knew his great work would complement my style. It was going to be the big brawler verses the technician. Our pairing would create all kinds of potential for a good match. So when Shawn Michaels started that program with me, we were immediately drawing good money and I had high hopes for our program.

Leading up to our big *SummerSlam 96* match, it was supposed to be us splitting wins 50/50 every night or so, but that is not exactly what happened. Shawn Michaels went over clean with the superkick a lot.

Don't get me wrong, Shawn was an excellent worker! I didn't mind doing the job here and there, to him. We had some really great matches. In fact, some of them were among the best in my life. Shawn Michaels, after all, was one of the absolute greatest workers ever and still is. I do, however, think that having the heel lose before the PPV maybe wasn't the best way to promote a major upcoming match.

On house shows, if you gave away the happy-ending and gave the fans a clean victory over the villain, why would fans want to pay more to see it again on TV? It's not rocket science. Maybe that was why PPV sales were down and no one thought I could beat Shawn at SummerSlam.

I also didn't have Harley around anymore to help fight my political battles. Now, remember, I had just fallen victim to the whole Flair/Hogan/Bischoff regime.

Before our program, I was told that one of the original plans for *SummerSlam 96* was to have me to win the WWF Championship. Then, I would continue to go on a mad tear destroying all the competition until Vince decided to build someone up to "slay the beast." Another one of the plans had me scheduled to beat Shawn at SummerSlam for the belt, then lose it to Bret, regain the belt from Bret then lose it to Shawn.

This seemed to make sense, but something happened and unfortunately, none of those plans ever happened. I can't lie; I would have loved to have held the WWF Heavyweight Championship at least once. It was and still is one of the most coveted titles in the world.

WWF SHAWN MICHAELS

It is no secret that Shawn Michaels was the man in WWF at that time. He was one of the most popular and hated wrestlers of all time. However, boy was he difficult to work with. By the time I made it to the WWF, Shawn already had Vince's ear. He had good ideas, and Vince rolled with quite a few of them. At this point, Shawn had built a reputation from being the measuring stick in the ring.

Leading into SummerSlam, it certainly seemed as if they were getting me ready for a title run by the way they booked us on television. They had me attack the then WWF Champion Shawn Michaels after one of his matches. Then they had me opposite him in a six-man tag-team match with me pinning Michaels to win the match for our team.

There were a number of times back in the early days of the AWA that me and the boys had to come to his rescue in bar fights after he did something not so smart. He was always getting into trouble. I wanted to believe that after saving him so much in the past, maybe he was going to return the favor and just give me the nod in return.

SUMMERSLAM

I cannot stress enough; Shawn was difficult to work with. Before my first SummerSlam match, I finally got the call. A day or so before the PPV, I was informed that I would not be taking the title from Shawn Michaels.

I wasn't happy, but I figured I would stay positive. *Maybe they are still testing me, or getting me ready for it at the next PPV,* I thought. Figuring I needed to make the match look as good as I could for a future opportunity, I decided to meet with my opponent extra early to talk about some ideas.

I pulled into the crowded Marriott Hotel across from the Gund Arena. There were fans around wearing wrestling T-shirts, so I waited for the right moment to sneak in for my secret meeting with Shawn Michaels about the match.

Once we were up in his room, we started to throw some ideas at each other. Very quickly, I noticed that he was planning a lot of spots. It seemed way more than what would be needed for a 15 or 20 minute match, and I didn't understand how we could fit all that stuff in.

"Wait a minute, Shawn. How long is this match supposed to be?" I asked

"Probably somewhere in the area of 40 or 45, is what they want," he replied.

I wasn't wearing my mask, of course, and I'm sure Shawn saw my face turn red. I was pissed. I don't know what happened. I really missed the boat on that one. Maybe it was my fault. Maybe it was a communication error. I don't know.

I'm sure he already had been training like mad to be on his game for an abnormally long match. I should have been pushing a ton of cardio into my workout to get my wind up to par, too. I would have been on the bike every day for an hour. I would have done loads of "jog back and run to the wall" type exercises to get ready and I would have been just fine.

Because of my football background, I was one of the very few big men that could go 45 minutes easily without blowing up, no problem, with a little notice. Other big super heavyweights, like King Kong Bundy, or Yokozuna, were often hard pressed to go 10 or 15. Back in the day, I had some really long matches with Flair, Brody, Hansen, and many others without even skipping a beat.

But I wasn't ready.

Come match time, we headed out to the ring, and I hoped for the best.

I was not conditioned and I knew it.

I hammed it up, as I always did for my entrance, all the while knowing it wasn't going to be a great match if I got winded. I was jaw-jacking all the way down the aisle to the ring about how great I am, thinking the whole way, *I better not blow up. I better not blow up.*

I was worried I was going to run out of air.

All things considered, I did really well for about 20 minutes. Somewhere around the 25 minute mark, I started losing my breath chasing that little bastard around. I blew up just as I had feared, and that was something I almost never did.

The lack of oxygen got to me. I will admit it. Huffing and puffing made me forget some of what we had planned. That led to Shawn getting frustrated.

People expected his matches to be the very best. Shawn was a perfectionist with high expectations. So when things didn't exactly follow his vision out in the ring, I knew he wasn't happy.

I knew I had to immediately fix that sequence I had forgotten, so I called a new fixer-spot.

Calling spots was the traditional role of the heel in any match anyhow, and figured I could just go off the script get everything back in line, but Shawn didn't want me taking over after I just messed up. Shawn got pissed.

"What the fuck?!"

"Relax," I told Shawn.

Michaels turned up the volume and started working even faster. I couldn't keep up at that pace and I'll admit it - I really hated my performance in this match.

To make matters worse, the finish had three different endings in one and lasted forever. I would first win by count-out, but Cornette realized the title couldn't change hands that way and got the match restarted. Shawn would next hit me with Cornette's tennis racket and get disqualified and Cornette would get it restarted again. Then, Shawn would finally pull something out of his hat and win by pinfall.

By the very final finish, I didn't have the title, and I also didn't have any air in my lungs at all.

Backstage in the hallway after the match, I headed off to the showers knowing that I was going to have to deal with a bitchy Shawn soon, who would just yell at me about the match. I knew I had messed up that one spot, but he also knew going in that nobody mentioned how long the match was scheduled to be.

Just as I was rushing off to avoid any conflict, there he was.

"Get over here," he said, waiting for me by a separate hall to the showers.

I ignored him. I was in no mood and needed time to diffuse. Even though I messed up, I felt he could have worked with me to make it better. So I continued to make my way to the dressing room and wouldn't show him the time of day.

"Get over here, right now!"

"Yeah, when I get done," came the reply.

"No, I said right now!"

"Go fuck yourself, RIGHT NOW," I said. I bit my lip without saying anything more. If I said anything else, I knew it was going to be a heated exchange and I was going to end up knocking his teeth right down his throat. I too had a reputation for having a temper and he was pushing it.

Rather than the showers, I slammed the door behind me in my dressing room. That was like taking a deep breath for me and counting to ten. We both needed to cool down. I'm telling you, if I hadn't bounced to my dressing room, Shawn would have been bouncing off the floor.

Sometimes, good wrestlers take a mistake in the ring so passionately that they could let a fake fight turn into a real one. That night was one of my big regrets.

We were both disappointed and I clearly was fuming!

I remember sitting on the bench just waiting, hoping, praying that Shawn was running off to Vince for a sit-down meeting. If he had, I had already planned out exactly what I was going to do.

If he calls me into a meeting with Vince, I'm going to walk in acting very calm, cool and collected. Then, I'm going to break Shawn's nose right in front of Vince and say, "Okay, I'm fired," and walk out.

Fortunately for the both of us, Vince was never called, and we never let our tempers get the best of us.

Before SummerSlam, Vince promised me a two-title run. After SummerSlam, nothing happened. Vince decided to change his mind. My guess is that match was probably a factor in the change of plans.

In my mind, being misinformed about the length of our match messed everything up for me and began a downward spiral. I imagine Vince watched the match and wrinkled up his face like he just sniffed a shit and said, "He's blowing up."

For whatever reason, Vince ended up taking my potential title run away and gave it to Sid. And I hate to say it, but Sid blows up faster than anyone else in history! After that match, I think Vince figured I just couldn't run with his top guys. I know Vince didn't hate me; he just stopped seeing me as a top contender. Vince is a stubborn guy, and once he gets something in his head, it's hard to make him see differently.

But I wasn't going to just give up. I was sure going to try and change his mind about me. I had had other obstacles before and this was just one of the many I needed to overcome.

TRAINING THE ROOKIE

After the missed opportunity, there was no point in harvesting sour grapes. Sid took that run, but I was offered a great opportunity, though I didn't know it at the time.

To try and make up for my shortcomings from that match with Michaels, I decided to put on my very best performances every night of the week. Word got back to Vince that I was telling excellent stories in the ring, and the hard work was paying off. He sat me down one night after a show and offered me extra money to help coach a new guy coming in.

"I know we ended up going with Sid," Vince said, "but you're not just a good worker and storyteller. You're a great one. There's this guy coming in here soon, and we think he can really go far. I want you to take him under your wing for about three months and just beat the living hell out of him. Can you do that?"

"You want me to beat him up?" I asked.

"I want you to teach him how to sell better, but be really rough on him. Teach him the right way," Vince said. "I'll also make up for not getting that title."

He started talking my language.

"You go it," I said. That is when I signed on to coach a newcomer who would start under the name, "Rocky Maivia."

Dwayne Johnson and I had something in common; football. He was a college football player for the University of Miami, winning a national championship on the 1991 Miami Hurricanes football team. His football success led him to be a professional wrestler just like his grandfather, Peter Maivia, and also his father, Rocky Johnson.

The Rock is considered to be one of the biggest superstar in WWE history, as well as one of the top box office draws in wrestling history. Hulk Hogan calls The Rock "the biggest superstar in this business", John Cena describes him as being, "the biggest superstar in the history of WWE" and "the most successful WWE superstar ever."

I had the pleasure of being able to train him.

So right away, I got on the road with him and really rode him. Before he was "The Rock," for the next ninety days, it was going to be, "Yes, sir," and "No, sir."

Before the show, I would get in the ring and train with The Rock hard every night. While we did have a handful of matches in front of audiences, most of the time it was just agents, writers and some of the boys hanging before the show watching us train.

I hit The Rock pretty hard as Vince had asked, but I made him listen between punches. During most of my matches with him at first, it was mostly me saying, "Hit me harder," and "Do this now." Then after class, I would talk to him about this psychology and that psychology in the car. The lessons never stopped.

I told him about my AWA days. I told him about WCW and Japan. He was a very fast learner. He pretty much had the moves down pat, but he really didn't know what to do with them yet.

Next, we would talk some matches out and I would add a serious flaw, then I would ask him, "What would you do to change this?" This helped get him ready for anything, which in turn, would make him even more creative.

The Rock got better and better until we were having 15 min matches that he could call entirely on his own. The last night of my 90 days tour with him, we wrestled in front of a live audience and finally, I had him beat me. In the middle of the ring, we shook hands.

I hit him on the shoulder and said, "You are ready."

The Rock grabbed me backstage and thanked me for everything. He went on, and I think he did a pretty good job.

Vince thanked me too and told me I did a hell of a job with The Rock. He said when the time was right, he was "going to give me the intercontinental belt, as a reward." I left before he could make that happen, but that's okay.

Incidentally, years later, I saw The Rock at the 1000th show at RAW. He told me I was quite a coach and did a great job coaching him. He's the real deal and a real class act.

UNDERTAKER & KUWAIT

Following the Undertaker's feud with Michaels, I started a program with Taker around the buildup for the 1997 Royal Rumble. Taker was great to work with. For such a big guy, he was one of the lightest guys to work with in the business. He also had a great work ethic. We would always try to set up the very best fights that we could.

I do remember that when I would try and get more offense in, I would sometimes get the "Vince doesn't want that," response – the same passing the buck thing I mentioned about that one time with Jim Cornette. But Taker was cool. He would then try and work me more into the match and I appreciated that. He really tried to help when he could.

On one particular tour to Kuwait, a strange thing happened to me. It was Friday, April 11, 1997. I was on a promotional appearance for the WWF tour along with the, then WWF Champion, Undertaker. We were about to go on live for a show called "Good Morning Kuwait," one of the most watched morning news shows in the country.

Before the show, the show's producer asked to meet up with me for a pre-interview meeting. "Big man," he said. "I like wrestling very much and so does our host, Bassam Al-Othman. Can you rough him up? We want you to have fun and to really go after him. Wrestle with him."

"Ok so, you want me to actually rough him up a little?"

"Yes! Oh, thank you very much," he said shaking my hand and smiling, thinking about the ratings potential.

I knew what he wanted. He wanted a show where it looked like the big monster was almost going to kill their main guy, right there on TV. "No problem," I said.

I walked onto the set. Al-Othman was a skinny little worm of a guy. He was Kuwait's version of Matt Lauer. He wasn't there at my pre-taping meeting but, at the time, I assumed he at least had an idea of what was supposed to happen.

So first off, the Taker and I are brought out onto the show's set and have to practically sit right next to each other on the set. I remember Taker was pissed about that because we were supposed to be fighting each other that night and "here we are, getting comfy," he said.

We sat down far away from each other to keep kayfabe and ignored the pretty flowers all around us. There was some real lame elevator music playing full blast. It was hardcore, cheerful piano music jazz that made me want to sip a cup of tea and run barefoot across a field somewhere towards a little house on the prairie. It wasn't at all the right mood setter for an interview with two super-heavyweight professional wrestlers.

Al-Othman crossed his legs uncomfortably high. "I'm sure you heard this before, but in Kuwait, they say that this wrestling is not for real. Is it like you act, or what is it?" he asked.

Taker's body language said he was pissed.

Wrestlers hate this question on live TV. It puts us in a weird position and for the most part, it is an insulting thing to have to deal with. How are we supposed to answer that? "Um, yes it is totally fake. What we do is not real, so I am pretty much just bullshit and a con-artist." ...You can't say that!

Many of you probably heard of "Dr. D." David Schultz's encounter on December 28, 1984, with 20/20. What happened was reporter John Stossel was backstage at Madison Square Garden doing a story on pro wrestling and told Schultz that he thought it was fake.

Shultz lost his cool. "You think it's fake?" he asked, hitting him the first time on his right ear. Before the second smack, Schultz said, "What's that, is that fake? Huh? What the hell's wrong with you? Do you think it's fake? I'll fake you!" he said hitting him again as hard as he could and chasing him off the set.

Stossel filed a lawsuit against the WWF. It settled for about $500,000.

So back to Kuwait. The Undertaker is sitting next to me and I can see that he wants to handle the question. Now, I know I am supposed to attack the host at some point and was waiting for my lead, but Taker didn't want it to be at this moment. It probably would have come off too "John Stossel."

"What we do - is it acting?" the Taker asked, repeating the question. "What we do is take a normal man and break him in half (for asking such a bullshit question like this). You know, that's such an unoriginal question to ask. My fans, the creatures of the night, don't care what it is. Let me assure you, it is the most physical thing that you could ever do in your life," he said.

Taker is the man. He continued on and talked a bit about the athleticism surrounding pro-wrestling, and said everything calm and cool and matter of fact. I'm not sure I could have responded the same. If you can find this clip on YouTube, watch it and keep your eyes on the Taker's body language. Just picture the big bad Deadman sitting around in the flowers; it was is priceless.

Bassam Al-Othman nodded and then translated Taker's response to the Kuwaiti audience. He seemed like a smart enough guy, speaking two languages and all, but I had already had enough of the pansy interview. I decided to make that topic my cue to light up the place like a bull in a china shop. It was time to go home.

As Al-Othman began his next question addressing me, I cut him off. "Excuse me, excuse me. You gave him a chance to answer that last question, but I would like to respond to the same question," I said.

"Ok, please. Go ahead."

"My astute college, the WWF Heavyweight champion of the world, is a very diplomatic individual. I am perhaps not quite so diplomatic." Then, just like Vince McMahon did in an interview with Bob Costas, I leaned forward in my seat to push for the intimidation factor.

"In fact, I find your question and your remarks insulting to what I do. Physically, no man can do what I do in the ring. If they could, why wouldn't they be out there, making the kind of money we make? Enjoying the type of fame and lifestyle that we enjoy? So I find your remark and question insulting."

"It's not my question. It's somebody else's," he said.

At that, I jumped off the couch and flipped over the coffee table. The pretty flowers hit the floor and the vase broke. "Perfect," I thought. I grabbed his tie and turned my wrist to the side, as if ready to choke him out. "Does that feel fake, huh?! Does that feel fake?!" There was a pause as the interviewer looked off stage for help. "Does it?!"

"Hey. Oh no, no," he said, playing it off perfectly I thought. "Please just sit."

I continued to hold him by his neck, using his tie as a handle. Al-Othman sold it perfectly. He cowered back in his chair and held his hands up in defense. "Why don't you come down tonight? And before I kick his ass, I will kick your ass!"

I looked over at the Undertaker. He is an excellent worker, you know. The whole time, he didn't move. There was an overturned table, broken glass all around his legs and a fight about to break out before his eyes. The funny thing was, he didn't give a flip. He didn't move even for a second. He just sat there quietly, mocking the interviewer.

"Okay, okay. Just calm down," the announcer said to me looking off stage for help that was not coming.

"Hey. We're not here to be insulted," I said pointing my finger right in his face. "I'M NOT HERE TO BE INSULTED!" I released my grip, threw down his tie back down to his chest and sat back down.

It was a perfect way to end the interview, with only one question having been asked. Bassam Al-Othman had to interpret it first for the non-speaking audience but then did just that. He did so in a very frightened manner.

Immediately following the incident, the producer shook my hand and thanked me. Then we set up for another interview with another announcer and all went well with that one as well. After that shot, Taker and I went back to the hotel and didn't give it a second thought.

Little did I know that, in the meantime, Al-Othman was pressing charges against me.

There was a knock at my door and all of the sudden, I found myself in handcuffs. I was being dragged off to jail.

I knew why they were doing it, but argued the whole way. "Come on guys," I said. "It was part of the show. He was in on it."

It didn't matter. The Kuwaiti police took my belongings and brought me to jail to figure out what they were going to do with me. I wasn't their citizen, and they had to go through some international tape to figure out what was supposed to happen in a case like this.

One of the men mentioned my actions as being like David Schultz. That wasn't the case at all. If you watch the tape carefully, all I did was touch the man. I grabbed his tie, yanked it. He was not harmed in any way, shape or form. Mr. Schultz was out of control. He slapped Stossel as hard as he could and ruptured his eardrum, and *it wasn't a planned situation*. For the first few hours in the holding cell, I believed that Mr. Al-Othman was holding me responsible for the actions of his director and producer.

The Kuwaiti police didn't rush to get me out of there. I was in there about a full day. Thank God I wasn't in there overnight or anything long like a week or something, because if I had in hindsight, I think I would've been killed.

One guard came up to my cell at one point who seemed a little different than the rest. I don't know if he was a wrestling fan or not, but he showed interest in my stay there and my case. "Vader. The people here... They want you dead!"

I sat up to talk through the bars on the door's window to my cell. "It was part of the show. He was in on it," I repeated.

"Well, if this is true, nobody knows it. Not even Bassam Al-Othman," he said. "We are getting many, many phone calls on you. After what you did on Kuwait television, attacking their beloved morning guy, the public, in general, wants to kill you. There is also a rumor that you have been fired from your wrestling company."

I shook my head.

"I will try and calm them down," he said.

I never saw him again.

After being setup for a fall in WCW, it felt like the same thing was happening again. It was all out of my control. Not knowing that the director told me to act in this manner for better TV ratings, the WWF powers-that-be probably thought I had pulled another David Shultz deal on them.

Boy, I'll tell you, I didn't dare blink in that cell.

Other guards came by too who were not as understanding. This incident was happening during Ramadan, a holiday "to praise Allah." I was the big, evil foreigner who represented all the American stereotypes they hated. The guards and prisoners alike wanted a piece of me. Both went out of their way to stop at my door to pound on it and shout insults in at me. In their eyes, I was a big, bad, white devil in their country, going against one of their own people on a day of worship.

Eventually, one of the guards silently opened the door to my cell. I was escorted out of the jail and taken back to my hotel. I thought it was finally done, but it wasn't over. I was informed that I wasn't allowed to leave or have any visitors. The judge enacted "a travel ban" on me, detaining me in my Kuwaiti hotel room for nine days. My visa was frozen, and I couldn't leave the country.

After that, I spoke briefly to one of the WWF producers because they were about to leave. I had to get my bags off of our tour bus. Before that bus pulled away, a few of the boys shook their heads and came out to wish me luck.

Taker knew I was worried. "It will be over soon. Hang in there," he said. "They will learn the producers asked you to play it up, and you will be back home in no time."

Taker tried to downplay it to make me feel okay, but when that bus pulled away, I carried my bags up to my room and started crying like a baby.

The realization of being left alone in Kuwait finally hit me. I was scared.

After my hotel door closed, I immediately started getting what I would assume were death threats on my hotel room phone. I guess my good friends working the hotel desk were putting strangers right through to my line. I don't know what the callers were saying, but they did not sound happy. The calls kept coming so much that I yanked the cord out of the wall for a time.

People want to kill me.

I was stuck in a small room and becoming paranoid as hell. The first night was the worst. Random people would knock on my door, but I wouldn't answer. Worried about a break in, I pushed the end tables and two chairs up against the door. I made the same barricade every night for enough piece of mind to try and get some sleep.

Then, people started driving up to the hotel, trying to take pictures of me through the windows. To remedy that, I snuck out of my room at like 3:30 am in the morning and stole three extra blankets from housekeeping, a few doors away from mine. I wasn't worried about pictures, however. I blocked out the windows so nobody could see me and so they couldn't get a shot at me.

It was nothing less than traumatic.

A few days later, the hotel manager asked me if there was somewhere else I could go. He didn't want my business anymore because he felt "something terrible" was going to happen in his walls.

One good thing I learned was that the WWF was backing me. Taker had my back. He told Vince that I was asked to act as I did and that I didn't lose my cool; I was performing. The WWF left town without me, but they did leave me an envelope with a company credit card to handle any expenses I would have.

My imprisonment in the hotel caused me to miss the rest of the tour, as well as American dates. I missed the *In Your House* PPV on Sunday, April 20, 1997, as well as the following night's Monday Night Raw. I was losing money. And if found guilty, I was facing a pretty big sentence; up to one year in Kuwaiti prison.

After about a week of insanity, I had enough of people pounding on my door and calling me on the phone to yell at me in another language. I finally called my wife Debe and broke the news to her. She was freaked to say the very least, but she had an idea. She went over to call in a favor for us to a real important neighbor who lived a house down the road from us – but worked out of a more important one; the White House.

The next two nights were hell. I remember listening for any little thing outside the blanketed window. I couldn't see any evidence of a threat anytime I pulled it aside to look, but if I heard so much as a dog bark blocks away, I was worried that someone was coming to get me.

Paranoia really set in. After laying there for hours one night, analyzing every little sound I could hear for danger, I finally closed my eyes. I finally feel asleep.

CRRRACK!

I jumped out of my sheets and I almost shit the bed in the process.

"Oh my God!" I remember saying out loud. "Am I going to die?!"

I looked over to my right. The door had just been literally kicked open and the frame was broken. My make shift barricade was in shambles.

There was a guy in camo standing over me holding some kind of assault rifle. I tried to swallow, but it didn't work. I was afraid to speak. I was afraid that if I opened my mouth I was going to get it filled up with lead. I rubbed my eyes with a trembling hand, and then almost in disbelief, I saw the red, white and blue.

There was an American flag patch on his shoulder.

"You Vader?" he asked.

"Yes! Yes, sir."

"Come with me," he said.

He didn't have to tell me twice. I quickly pulled on some clothing and we grabbed my bags. As much as I enjoyed the room service every morning on Vince's company credit card, I had no problem checking out.

I found myself scurrying through the middle of a military takeover. Every hallway, every doorway, everywhere you could see, there were good guys looking to get me out of there. The Americans were there. They scared the shit out of me and then everybody else in the whole hotel. They did it as big as possible to make a statement.

It turns out that our neighbor was a big name in the Democratic Party. He knew the president. He actually worked for Bill Clinton. Boy, I sure was lucky to have that contact back home. He got right on it and made a couple of calls. The president himself got news that there was "an American captive on foreign soil who was thrown in jail for doing a fake pro wrestling skit."

There was no more nonsense after that.

It was very clear. They came to save me. I was one of them, an American, and we stand together.

Forty-eight hours after our neighbor made that call, and I was being protected. They ushered me right out of that awful hotel room. I ended up waiting at the American military base for my court case. There was no more craziness. They treated me like a king. After that, rather than angry people pounding on my door making threats, it was military officials knocking politely asking for autographs!

It seemed they all knew me from TV. So many of them were wrestling fans. It was nice. I was a hero to my heroes. The rest of my stay there was pretty much the same. It was just me working out with the soldiers and telling stories of my battles in the ring!

I learned at the base that my travel ban was the first in over a decade in Kuwait and it was also the first one with a dumb charge like mine. Someone was looking for money because of who I was and obviously who I worked for, the multi-million-dollar WWF.

I had threats on my life. I had 24-hour security, all because of one simple thing: extortion. After apologizing to him during the commercial, Al-Othman immediately filed charges on me at the police station, saying his integrity had been damaged. However, twenty-four hours after the incident he told me his "integrity" could have been repaired for $25,000. By the next morning, his face was all over the news saying his integrity was worth $400,000.

He was very adamant about me not leaving the country because the longer I stayed there, the more it put more pressure on me for a settlement. I was damned if he was going to make anything off of me or the Vader name.

The people at the base saw my TV appearance. They said after the alleged attack on Al-Othman, they saw me interviewed by other reporters from their station and then, they reran the whole thing again. That was surprising to me. If you saw the second half of the interview, it was obvious they knew it was planned. The first thing out of the second announcer's mouth was, "Ladies and gentlemen, what you saw was not a serious incident, please stop calling. This was a planned session."

After my public apology for bad language after the commercial, I talked about the benefits of education, staying in school and not trying to depend on your athletic endeavors to make a living. I explained I was a college graduate with a degree in business from the University of Colorado. It was very clear that I was level-headed, smart and only acting a few minutes before.

If you have a 400-pound man on your set trying to injure people, you wouldn't keep him around for another interview. You would immediately cut to a commercial, call the police, and have him thrown in jail. They didn't do that. They had another one of their announcers say, "This was all planned. Let's continue with the interview." Mr. Al-Othman was maybe upset because he wasn't involved in that planning session or just a scam artist who saw an opportunity. Their poor communication wasn't my fault; it was theirs.

In the end, nothing ever became of it and it was dismissed. It never even made it to court.

I would just like to point out that the young men and women of the Armed Services basically stand guard while we live our lives. They lay their lives on the line. After this incident, I grew a new found respect for them. When I was there, the soldiers of Camp Doha and the Marines at the American Embassy in Kuwait were extremely supportive and offered their help in trying to resolve the situation. As an American, when your liberty and freedom are stripped, you realize what these people do for you.

I would like to thank them again very much for all they did for me, and all they do for America.

CHAPTER 21 - YOKO, BOY MEETS WORLD, FMW & USA

Rodney Anoa'i was a super heavyweight and very good one, I might add. He was best known for his time with the WWF where he wrestled under the ring name Yokozuna. To me, not only was he a very good super heavyweight, but he was also a very good friend.

YOKOZUNA

The term "yokozuna" actually means the highest rank possible to achieve in another fighting sport, professional sumo wrestling. Although the Yokozuna character was portrayed as a champion sumo wrestler, Rodney never competed as an actual sumotori. He also wasn't Japanese.

In real life Rodney Anoa'i was Samoan. During his stint in the WWF, he was managed by the Japanese character Mr. Fuji, who would follow him to the ring with a wooden bucket of salt and waving a Japanese flag, but that's about it.

Rodney's career in professional wrestling was hereditary as it began growing up in a family full of wrestlers, the Anoa'i family. His uncles were The Wild Samoans, Afa and Sika. They trained him from an early age in the family business. He had been wrestling since he was in diapers and being in the Anoa'i wrestling family meant it was in his blood. Other family members include Roman Reigns, Rikishi, Samu, Rosey, Manu, Umaga, the Usos and somehow even, The Rock.

His first major exposure came in my old stomping grounds, the American Wrestling Association as Kokena Maximus. Rodney was much younger than me, like 18 years old. At this point in his career, he was weighing in at about 380 or so and when I first saw him move in the ring, I thought to myself,

"My god, what a talent!" Even at such a young age, he looked polished, and he wanted his matches to be great.

I remember when he came over to Japan for the first time. We had met before, but I really didn't know him until our time together working for Inoki. We were two giant Americans from the same setting; me growing up in an inner-city area like Compton and Rodney from somewhere nearby like it, like Carson. Pretty much everyone in Japan was Japanese, so it was nice to have someone from home there with me to talk to and relate to. We talked a lot about wrestling and music. Knowing I was from Compton, Rodney introduced me to his love of rap music and gave me my first real rap mix tape with Easy-E and The NWA, to work out to.

I liked it. I mean, I wasn't a huge rap guy, but it was something fresh and different and it was in my own language. Rather than to have to listen to Japanese radio on the tour bus that usually sounded like a drunken Laurence Welk to me, when Rodney showed up we started playing gangster rap on their cassette deck. We would bob our heads on the way to a show as long as we could until the other conservative Japanese guys just couldn't take it anymore - and would tell us to "shut that shit off." Boy, would we laugh!

We may have looked like an odd couple, but built a great friendship. What a fantastic human being. I mean, I really enjoyed being around him. We always tried to time our schedules so that we could both go to Japan together.

While we did have a lot in common, he didn't share my passion for lifting weights. I wish I could have helped him train a little, but he just wouldn't go to the gym with me. Being a big man, I knew how important it was to make sure you get some cardio and weights in to stay as healthy as a big man can. Rodney didn't seem to care, however.

I would say, "Come on, Rodney, just come to the gym with me."

"We will soon," he would say, but soon would never come. He had other priorities. His training was more like a sumo than a wrestler. *That boy loved to eat,* as did I.

We spent a lot of late nights together in NJPW. Quite often, we would walk back to our hotel late after a show. We couldn't just call a taxi so late, and even if we did, it would have been way too small for one of us, let alone both. So I started up our tradition, figuring that walking would do some good for him, as he really showed no interest in cardio.

Most nights, it was just me and Rodney, walking and watching the sun come up in "The Land of the Rising Sun." And believe me, Rodney and I saw that sun rise a lot of times. Our walks were good, but eventually, Rodney added to the tradition. I wanted cardio, but Rodney wanted food. So after the show, we would walk home and also look to make a pit stop to a late-night Yakitori House. Yakitori is a Japanese dish that is pretty much just meat on a stick, but it is not just meat on a stick. That meat is slathered in tasty teriyaki and other sauces, and that meat is scrumptious.

I will admit it. Rodney made me a convert – I started loving these little mom-and-pop meat shacks.

We became the "Kings of Yakitori." Every night before a show, we would do our homework. We would find a Yakitori House within walking distance and set up arrangements to force them to stay open late for us. They'd serve cold beer and chicken and rice, and boy, we'd keep them open. They didn't really like to be open that late, but they sure liked our money. More money always meant more chicken, more rice, and more importantly, more beer. I'll admit it. After a match, I could really be a pig, but Rodney could really put it away, brother. Know what I'm saying?

Now the Japanese, they do not eat very big portions. If you have ever been over there, you know that a soda machine serves these little cans of drink that you can swallow in one gulp or so. So can imagine what the restaurants were used to serving as a regular portion?

These little Japanese guys would open the door, see Big Van Vader and Kokena (aka Yokozuna) walk in, and just about dump their pants.

One night, we went into a place that was about the same as a bed and breakfast. It was this one guy's house essentially, and we kept him up for hours cooking and serving us beer. He was having a grand old time drinking with us and laughing himself until the fun suddenly stopped.

We ordered more Yakitori, and the old man said nothing. He just sat there and shook his head.

"What's wrong," Rodney asked.

"Yeah. ITADAKIMASU!" I said smiling, which meant something like, "LET'S EAT!"

The old man shook his head. "Yes, yes. I sorry, there just no more food," he said very embarrassedly. We had literally eaten all of his supply! He walked us over to his freezer and there was nothing in it. We had eaten him out of house and home.

We laughed our asses off but tipped the man well. His eyes lit up.

"Now, you just make sure and buy more food with that for next time," I said.

"We will be back tomorrow for more," Rodney said.

Yakitori (and even more so the rice) was taking its toll on old Rodney in Japan, however. We couldn't possibly walk to and from every show, so sometimes we had to take the NJPW bus.

While I was still IWGP Champion, I remember them always loading us all on that bus for away shows. Well, Rodney kept getting bigger and bigger, and I had not given it much thought before. He always sat next to me and in his little, small chair, and we talked for hours. During this period of time, I watched him grow and grow and grow. Boy, I'll tell you, he kept getting bigger and bigger before he finally debuted in WWE. It was like, he was 380, and then 400, and then 450, then 500. Yokozuna had to squeeze that big butt of his into that tiny chair, but he never said a word!

Being 500 pounds in Japan was comical; it really was. Nothing was built for a man that big. Nothing. Your average Japanese man was probably like a little over 5 feet tall and likely 150 pounds or less. Their furniture, their door fixtures, everything didn't work for me – let alone someone the size of Rodney.

You may have heard about the 7-foot-tall André the Giant and his stay in Japan. Nothing worked for a man the size of André, and he would get really pissed about it. He often couldn't fit in the little corner where the toilet was in the hotel bathroom, so he would just shit in the bathtub. Or sometimes if the bathroom was too small for André to even get in, he would just take a big dump on the bed and wipe with the sheets.

The architects who didn't design a cheap hotel bathroom big enough for a 7-foot man, they really pissed André off. If you were among the lucky staff and got the friendly giant at your hotel, André would maybe take the time to actually tie up the sheets and throw his shit-sheet wonton out into the hall for housekeeping. However, 99 percent of most maids were not that lucky.

Rodney, on the other hand, was not that angry about being a big man in a little world.

I was a big guy too, but I would see him sitting there in that little chair on the bus and it looked like trying to pour 20 gallons of feces poured into a five-gallon hat. One day, I finally just stood up and said, "Come over here, man, take my chair."

"No, champ," he said. "That's for you." Rodney refused, but I wasn't having it.

Not to make a scene, I told Rodney under my breath that there was going to be an even bigger scene if he didn't just quietly get up and switch places with me. Rodney smiled and we switched places. He leaned back and smiled. You could see the tortured look removed from his face.

All the other young boys and wrestlers on the bus couldn't believe it. Japanese people are always about tradition, and that chair was supposed to represent something as much as it was also supposed to bring the IWGP champion comfort. It was like the king sitting at the head of his table, but I didn't care. That was the way it was going to be. Being a big guy myself, I wouldn't have done that for anybody else because it was a comfortable chair, but that was friendship.

I really loved Rodney, he was just fantastic. He went on to represent his family and dynasty, just fantastic in WWE. He was one of the best of all time, just a beautiful human being. He always had a smile on his face. It was incredible. I was honored to call him a friend.

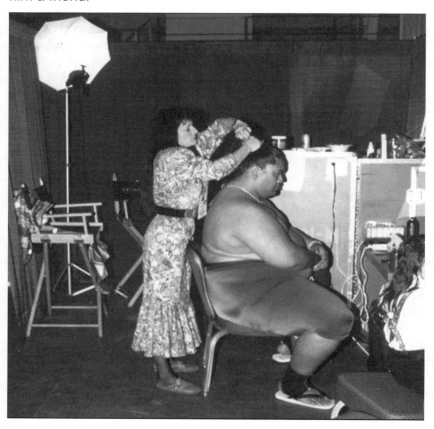

THE MILE HIGH BONSAI DROP

Another Yokozuna story that he told me worth mentioning had to do with his interaction with a real bad prankster, "Mister Perfect" Curt Hennig.

Curt and Yoko were both flying together, heading to a show on the outside of the country somewhere. Yoko had to sit in two seats as he did for most flights, but Curt was in the third. Curt came well prepared for the flight, as he was enjoying some kind of Wonka chocolate bar that he bought at the airport before the taking off.

"Mmm," Curt said, eating his delicious chocolate bar in his own little world with his headphones on.

Yoko looked over and saw the treat that Curt was enjoying and ignored it.

Curt was bobbing his head along to some song on his Sony Walkman and continued to eat up his tasty snack. He flipped through his fitness magazine. "Mmm," he said again.

Yoko's mouth began to water like a dog watching his master eat a steak dinner. If there was one weakness that Yoko had, it was food.

Curt continued to devour that chocolate like there was no tomorrow. He pretended to not notice as Yoko looking on and just kept reading his magazine, but Curt knew damn well what he was doing.

"Mmm," he said again.

That was it. The 500 pound Samoan couldn't handle it anymore.

"Mmm! Mmm! What's so good, Curt?" Yoko asked. "What do you got there?"

Curt shrugged and turned his shoulder away from the former WWF Heavyweight champion. He continued to eat his candy bar facing the aisle.

Yoko leaned over, almost directly in Curt's lap, finally taking the bait.

Curt smiled, "Ah, I was just messing with you, Rodney," he said. Curt reached into his pocket and pulled out another a large bar of chocolate.

"For me?"

"I knew you would want one, too, so I grabbed an extra one."

"Awe, thanks, brother!" Rodney said, quickly opening the wrapper

Now, why Yoko would even consider this gift is unknown. Curt's reputation was terrible when it came to practical joking, but Yoko's will power took over. He accepted that chocolate, nonetheless.

Of course, that chocolate bar was no ordinary treat. It was actually a generic Ex-Lax bar he picked up somewhere else earlier with the sole purpose of the purchase being "just to rib someone."

What Curt had done was cleverly measured the laxative up against another candy bar in the airport store and then switched the wrappers after he bought it.

Eating a very large dose of stool softener at the start of an international flight meant that the very large "sumo wrestler" would soon be needing to take a very large dump. The only problem with this situation for Yokozuna was that he wasn't going to be able to use the very small facilities on the plane.

Yoko's stomach started a churnin' and he started to sweat like a pig.

"Hey, Curt," he said. "Mind if we switch seats? I'm not feeling well and want to be away from the window."

"No problem," Curt said, knowing full well that Yoko was feeling nature call. Curt got up, Yoko moved into the aisle for a moment and then Curt took the window seat.

It was the same reason that André the Giant used to defecate in the bathtubs of many Japanese hotel rooms; physics. Just like everything else in an airplane, bathrooms are created small to save on real estate. Airplane toilet stalls are not designed for a 500 pound sumo wrestler to sit in one and therefore Yoko couldn't fit in one, either.

Yoko sat there in the aisle seat for a few minutes and then excused himself. "I'm going to go stretch my legs," he said. That was not it, however. Yoko was trying to figure out an escape plan for the laxative-induced dump that he was brewing deep from within.

Yoko walked up to the plane and sure enough, he was right. For the same reason Yoko always tried to use the facilities before getting on the plane, and the same reason why he barely ever drank or ate anything while flying, the bathroom was just too small. There was no way he was going to fit in there.

Curt watched from a distance with a devilish grin. The fruit of his labor was about to pay off. Yoko went up to one of the stewardesses and whispered something in her ear.

The young lady's face immediately turned pale white like she had just seen a ghost. Then, she took a deep breath and had a quick conversation with the head stewardess. They both nodded and she bravely decided there was only one way to manage this situation.

"Please, sir," the second stewardess said discretely. "Stay here with me for a moment and she will call for you."

The first stewardess walked to the very back of the plane with a scared and disgusted look on her face. Without alarm, she said quietly to the last couple of rows. "We have a few openings in first class if you would like them.

Like kids in a candy bar store, the last two rows of passengers quickly rushed to the front of the plane for their good fortune.

The stewardess then covered the floor with newspapers and motioned for Yoko. Yoko then did the walk of shame right passed Curt with the other woman in tow, right behind him. Curt was now red in the face with laughter.

After Yoko made it to the rear of the plane, the two ladies held up a large blanket to protect the huge Samoan's modesty.

Yokozuna then did his first ever mile high "bonsai drop."

When he was finished delivering the worst bowel movement in the history of American Airlines and perhaps Samoan culture, he cleaned up with a roll of paper towels. After that, he walked back to his seat and the whole plane started to smell like shit and coco puffs.

WWF YOKOZUNA

By the time I worked with Yokozuna in the WWF, he was weighing in at 660 pounds. We were both managed by Jim Cornette at first, but after much butting of heads, Yokozuna left our camp in the storyline to begin a short stint as a fan favorite. They had him change his character a bit. He smiled more. He spoke English to the fans and even had Mr. Fuji wave an American flag during his matches. However, our feud was to be cut short.

One day, Vince called Rodney into his office to tell him he needed to take time off to lose some weight. That night, they had me jump on Yokozuna's leg and "break it" to write him off of television. Instead of a stretcher, a real forklift was brought in to carry Yokozuna out on that edition of RAW. Rodney didn't like the idea of being carted off that way. He knew what the commentators would be saying on TV in order to get the storyline over, and he told me it embarrassed him. But he went along with it, nonetheless.

During his time off, Yokozuna was sent to Duke University's weight loss clinic by Vince McMahon. On the road, I remember that often Rodney wouldn't sleep in the bed because he was too big. He would just prop a bunch of pillows on the floor and maybe pull just the mattress off the box spring to make a wedge to lean upon. You see, he had to sleep sitting up because the weight on his upper torso made it impossible for him to breathe lying down.

The weight loss clinic was a great idea by Vince, but unfortunately, it didn't work. Rodney loved his food, despite the fact that at this point in his life it was killing him.

Rodney called me up one night and told me he was hungry as hell, at the hospital. He said that he would actually escape from the clinic during the night and find a McDonalds or a Burger King and binge eat whatever he could. I warned him again and told him that he really needed to start worrying about his health. I did this a number of times throughout his life, but it didn't work.

By October 1999, Rodney had long since given up on losing the weight. In fact, he decided to just go the other way. He was a reported 760 pounds and was actively trying to gain even more weight in order to become "the heaviest professional wrestler in history."

A year later, Yokozuna died. He was only 34 years old. Boy, what a sad story. He was a gifted member of the Anoa'i wrestling family, and it was a shame to see him go. Yokozuna let his love for food in excess consume him and his great wrestling career.

BOY MEETS VADER

Now, I need to go back in time just a little to explain something to you about something that happened that everyone asked me about during my days with the WWF.

Back in 1995, I was an unstoppable, super heavyweight monster with a hardcore fighting style. I brought many of my opponents' careers to an early end. I had my eye ripped out of its socket and continued to fight for 15 minutes. I was a feared champion holding three massive titles on three different continents at the same time. However, with all my accomplishments across the galaxy, there was only one place left I had to conquer while I was still with WCW, and that was the exotic set of *Boy Meets World*.

Some readers might not think that I would be what Hollywood producers would call ideal for a '90s kid's show. I was known for being pretty brutal, but *BMW* wasn't brutal. (Well, maybe some of the writing was.) There were no ribs getting cracked. There were no backs being broken. There was no violence. It was mostly a bunch of middle schoolers sitting around eating pizza. It was a wholesome, all-ages, silly, bubblegum sitcom on network television.

So just how did Big Van Vader find his way to ABC's star-studded roster back in 1995? Easy. Hollywood finally witnessed my superb performances in the starring roles of two WCW masterpieces, *The White Castle of Fear* and *Beach Blast*. You see, those sitcom producers saw those splendid pieces of WCW cinematography. They considered them quality and said, "Boy, can this guy act?! The world needs to see more of him on television and he needs to be compensated with good network money!" (Those producers were right, of course.)

When my agent called me with a *Boy Meets World* offer, we booked it immediately. There was no question on whether or not it was a good match for my monster reputation in the ring, or not. An international network appearance was the kind of opportunity that could really further a wrestler's career.

My three appearances for *BMW* on the set aren't all that memorable. They were filmed quickly, and I have no real stories to report. One of the things I do remember was that their catering was fantastic. I spent more time eating, honestly, than I did acting.

In a real stretch for me, I played a professional wrestler named Vader. I was also the father of a teenager named "Frankie Jr." who picked on the show's star Cory, played by Ben Savage. (You might recognize my TV son Ethan Suplee from *My Name is Earl*, *Mallrats*, *The Butterfly Effect* and *Remember the Titans*.) There was a big challenge to settle their differences in the wrestling ring. In the final big swerve, the principal of the school Mr. Feeny threatened to expose my real-life wimpy name, Leslie, in order to get me to back down from a fight. (Isn't that Brutus Beefcake's real name?)

I wasn't the only cameo for this star-studded episode called, "The Thrilla' in Phila," first airing on May 5th, 1995. This gave the world something else everyone really wanted to see; Robert Goulet and Vader in a wrestling ring. I could have taken him, too! The very smooth Goulet was hired by Griff to sing the national anthem rather than to face me, however. I think it would have been better writing if we got to sing "The Impossible Dream" together, but I guess it just wasn't in the cards. Robert Goulet, incidentally, was a real class act on the set, for the whole three minutes I actually spent with him.

My second episode had Cory befriending my son Frankie, while I pretty much just got paid to just be the Kool-Aid Man. They had me randomly break down the back door of Cory's kitchen like something out of a comic book to cut a promo in this cameo. The guys at Wrestlecrap so wisely said that breaking doors like the Kool-Aid Man with no repercussions was perfectly acceptable writing on ABC because it was the same network that allowed, "Steve Urkel to time travel and clone himself."

In my final episode called "Sixteen Candles and 400-Pound Men" which aired on November 15th, 1996, Frankie Jr. took up poetry. My character didn't like the idea of his son being like Lanny Poffo and figured Cory must have encouraged it. That made my character have some major heat with him. "I'm going to crush him like garlic and put him in my spaghetti!" I said in a truly moving performance that deserved an Emmy.

To remedy our heat, Cory coached Frankie on how to use some inside wrestling terms to get back over with me. That was all I needed. The idea moved me so much that I insisted they manage me at a show against Jake "The Snake" Roberts. However, there was a plot twist. Cory had to also attend his girlfriend Topanga's Sweet 16 birthday party at the same time. It then became the classic sitcom story where the main character hectically bounces back and forth between both locations, with nobody noticing he is gone.

During our match, Cory would sneak out to Topanga's party down the street and rushed back to the wrestling match many times. Things started to look bad for me, but then, out of nowhere, Frankie's words of love for his father inspired a second wind, leading me to victory in the end.

TAPING THE MATCH FOR THE BMW EPISODE

As you will note, I was originally the US Champion in WCW for my first two appearances on the sitcom in 1995, but I was with the WWF for the third shot in 1996.

I was a little nervous at first about approaching Vince about the offer to do more with ABC. In the past, Jesse Ventura was very vocal about the fact that Vince gave him a hard time for taking a part on *Predator*, and filmed it without his blessing. The same thing happened to Roddy Piper for his part in the movie *They Live*, and the same thing with Vince Sr. who didn't like that

Hulk Hogan took a part in *Rocky,* which made him famous. However, times had changed. And since the shooting of one sitcom episode didn't mean having to leave for a long period of time, Vince allowed participation under one condition: *he could promote the WWF within the episode.*

With this provision, the WWF got a free commercial on network television whenever and wherever it aired. It also worked out well for *BMW*, because they didn't have to build a huge wrestling set and pay hundreds of people to be extras. They just signed the paper and paid Vince an additional producer credit – which he really liked.

Before the actual taping of the match footage, I briefly saw Ben Savage (Cory) and my son Ethan Suplee (Frankie.) I just said "Hi," again, and shook their hands. Basically, we didn't interact for the shoot. They mostly just stood ringside some and were instructed not to do much until the finish of the match.

The specific show was at Anaheim, CA at The Arrowhead Pond on October 13, 1996. With around five thousand extras on hand courtesy of the WWF, fans watched Vader pin Jake Roberts with the Vader Bomb. However, there were some confusing points that went against normal WWF programming.

In my corner for the match, for one, were the actors acting as my managers. Vince also threw Brother Love (Bruce Pritchard) a bone by getting him some network money to play both the ring announcer and live commentator for the match.

There were additional *BMW* camera men filming the footage for the episode. They were coached by Vince's guys and were informed to catch everything in one take. Typically, sitcom directors would shoot a scene many times until they got it right, but Vince refused to break kayfabe and reshoot any parts of the match if anything wanted had been missed on camera. They did, however, take additional footage of just the audience, requesting that everyone cheer and also boo as loudly as possible, so that they could splice it in where needed in post-production.

If you watch the episode carefully, you may notice that the ring ropes were looser than shit. There was some kind of mishap in a tag match that they taped earlier for a *WWF Superstars* match with the Grimm Twins vs. the Smoking Gunns. Two of the ropes broke and they didn't have time to fix them, so we just worked the match around saggy ropes with no explanation.

The match itself was also the drizzling shits, intentionally. It had to be slow in order to get enough low-impact wrestling footage in the background, as to "not distract from the lines of the kids at ringside" per the director. The fans pretty much saw a boring contest loaded with rest holds, except for a sweet Vader bomb in the end and me celebrating with the kids.

At least I finally went over at a WWE house show.

BACK: Big Van Vader. FRONT (left to right): Rider Strong, Howard Busgang, Bruce Prichard, Ben Savage, Mark Blutman.

Boy Meets World put my face on international TV in front of an audience that was not exclusively WCW or WWF wrestling fans. The overall exposure was a great help for my brand. It also led to more offers and even got me a spot alongside one of the greatest actors and singers of all time, David Hasselhoff on *Baywatch*.

Baywatch wasn't my only other acting accolade. I was the big boss bad guy at the very end in an independent film called, "Fist of the North Start." I kick myself a little now too. They also offered me the role of Bane alongside Arnold Schwarzenegger as Mister Freeze in one of the Batman films, but I declined due to a scheduling conflict. Can you imagine if I had taken the part?

KEN SHAMROCK

In Ken Shamrock's WWF 1996 debut, he was set to go up against me in a "No Holds Barred" match. Ken Shamrock was coming from an MMA background with some experience in shoot-style worked matches. However, what many people didn't know was he was classically trained in pro wrestling. In 1988, Shamrock trained first to be a professional wrestler under Bob Sawyer, Buzz Sawyer, and Nelson Royal. Having him work with me after all of his mixed-martial arts success only made sense.

There's an urban myth attached to our match that Vince chose me to fight Shamrock as a means of punishment. Something about me not working well with Michaels or working too stiff against other members of his Kliq. I don't believe it. I think it was more like Vince knew that Vader-Shamrock would make for a classic slobber-knocker of a match, and it was.

Ken was as stiff as hell. The difference is, he didn't have a great guy like Sting there to talk him down. He didn't yet know how to work a WWF match. He hadn't done any professional wrestling in a long, long time and the ring rust was evident. He had forgotten how to throw a fake punch.

Irony hit once again. The tables had been turned. Maybe it was karma, maybe it was turnabout is fair play. I was now the older American wrestler looking for an easy match, facing a stiff Japanese shoot-style that I hadn't bargained for!

We got to working and I didn't expect the shots I was taking. It felt like Brody and Hansen all over again. If you watch the match closely, you can see me tell Shamrock to, "Ease up, ease up!" Eventually, I just said screw it. I gave up and bailed from the ring for a breather.

"I didn't realize how stiff I was in there with him. I wondered why Vader broke from the script at that point where he jumped out of the ring. I didn't know I actually hurt Vader and, as a result, Vader was PISSED!" Shamrock later said in an interview.

Before the end, I got my second wind. It didn't take long to realize I was the Baby Bull again and I needed to charge like my old AWA days.

Once I was finally fed up with Shamrock I snapped. I hit him with the hardest clothesline I ever threw in my whole career.

"It almost knocked me out," Shamrock said recalling it.

The clothesline was "a receipt" as they say for Ken's hard shots. Finally, Shamrock eased up for good and the match finished smoothly.

After the match, anyone could clearly see I was angry. But I was more angry for letting myself get hurt than actually being hurt. I should have returned the favor a few times earlier and I would have come out of there in better shape. It would have sent the message to lighten up better than saying it.

Shamrock broke my nose in four places, and I could barely walk the next day.

I worked with Shamrock again here and there in other WWF encounters and by then, things were getting better. He was adapting to the style needed by the WWF. One point worth mentioning after winning by count-out, I made fun of Shamrock's nickname by asking the camera "Who's the World's Most Dangerous Man now?" He would actually have to think about that answer even more so down the line, outside a WWF ring in Japan.

KEN SHAMROCK REMATCH IN FMW

Later on down the road, I would meet up with Ken Shamrock once again. Only this rematch would be for Frontier Martial-Arts Wrestling in Japan.

For those not familiar with the promotion, FMW is known for having some pretty hardcore matches. To get an idea of what I mean, their promotion's founder, Atsushi Onita, once wrestled Kintaro Kanemura in a "No Rope, Barbed Wire, Electrified, Dynamite, Landmine, Time-bomb, Double Hell Death Match."

We were still under WWF contract mind you, but we had a hall pass. You see, from time to time, Vince would actually allow some of the guys to grab some bookings over in Japan, but only if it made good sense. Despite what some people think, Vince would allow his wresters to work outside of his company to grab great paydays when it was also beneficial for his company in some way. This was one of those rare cases. He figured it would give us both some more tough man credibility, in a time when he was working on adding that aspect to his brand.

In order for FMW to get our rematch match, they also had to bring in Michaels for an excellent payday, as well. That is just how Vince rolled. So Michaels was the special ref for fake Hayabusa (Mr. Gannosuke) versus H (the real Hayabusa) on the same card.

For my rematch with Shamrock, Onita knew Vince expected it to make us out to look tough as hell, in the end. Therefore, Onita decided to book us again to go at it full force in a "No Ropes Cage Match," on September 28, 1997.

There was no WWF agent there to tell us what to do and not to do, so we decided we would shoot a little. We would go at it pretty hard and also throw in some entertainment value to tell help tell the story. We decided we would go right after each other from the start. And for this time, I had decided to lay in some real hard shots, way harder than in our first encounter.

Early in the match, one of my hooks took him right down. Shamrock then popped up and kicked me in the head, following up with his own strikes, thereafter. Eventually, I turned it around on him and powerbombed him. I was supposed to powerbomb three times, and on the third one, things were going to turn around back on me.

After the second powerbomb, I looked down. Shamrock was spitting up a mouthful of thick blood.

Wow, the blood! Nice touch. You don't see that much.

FMW was pretty close to the shoot-style wrestling like I had competed in with UWFi. It was a work, but as rough as it could get. So I thought the blood was planned by Shamrock. I thought he spit up some kind of blood capsule or something, but that was not the case.

"I already had a problem before I went in there," Shamrock said. "I had a tear in my lung, and I did not realize it at the time. I was coughing up blood a few days earlier but just passed it off as whatever, because it goes away. But then when I went to Japan, I got powerbombed twice, and I remember choking. I could not breathe, I was spitting up a lot of blood."

Shamrock started to pass out because he was drowning in his own blood. Before I could do anything else, the ref told me to wait. He checked with Shamrock. It was no work. The injury was serious and the referee had to actually stop the match, legit.

To dispel any rumor that the blood was fake, I can assure you, it was not. I was pretty shaken at first thinking about how much blood he was spitting up that I had caused it with a powerbomb. Flashbacks of Joe Thurman facing permanent injury worried me.

I caught up with Shamrock immediately backstage. He couldn't talk. They were considering oxygen and how to go about draining the fluid. The medics said he had torn open his lung. Soon after, I had learned that he was working on an injury and the lung tear was not entirely my fault.

You got to hand it to him. Ken Shamrock is a tough son of a bitch. He was already considered a massive name in Japan for being the first King of Pancrase (one of the first big MMA companies), but after enduring this match, he was a legend.

ALL-AMERICAN VADER

To give credit to WWF, even though some will argue that they didn't really know how to use me, they at least they kept me in the mix with all the big guys right until the end.

While my tough man credibility was huge, I still think my acting experience gave me an extra added value in the back of Vince's mind. Maybe it is this same mainstream value was the same kind of thing that has kept The Miz in the spotlight for many years, after his initial work with MTV.

Later on, I received an opportunity to work with the Undertaker, but this time in Canada at *In Your House 16: Canadian Stampede*. I didn't win the title, but we had a great match that set me up for an interesting babyface turn in the company out of patriotism. I was positioned to be an All-American again, but this time in the wrestling ring and not on the football field.

The next night on Raw after the PPV in Canada, I faced Dell Wilkes, aka "The Patriot," a guy who I always loved working with. The Patriot won our match. Upset after the loss, I attacked Patriot in typical Vader fashion. I brought him back into the ring and climbed up the ropes to go for my Vader Bomb. In the meantime, Bret Hart jumped into the ring.

He was working a territorial angle against the Patriot and came out to ringside earlier during our match. He saw me about to crush The Patriot and decided to add insult to injury. He draped his Canadian flag over The Patriot's body before I made impact.

Then using my best acting chops, I looked down at the flag. I got down off the ropes, picked up the Canadian flag and broke the stick. This patriotic movement turned me into a babyface and served to bring my character into the big USA vs. Canada feud that was to ignite at Survivor Series.

With Patriot out on injury, they made me the leader of "Team USA" with Goldust, Marc Mero, and Steve Blackman. We were set to take on "Team Canada" with The British Bulldog, Jim Neidhart, Doug Furnas, and Phil LaFon. In the end, Goldust walked out on us and we lost the match when The Bulldog pinned me after hitting me with the ring bell. I was happy to take the fall for my friend Davey Boy. I owed him one for being the first to take the monster moonsault back in our WCW days together.

Interestingly enough, something else happened at the 1997 Survivor Series that would change wrestling forever, and I was there to see it firsthand.

CHAPTER 22 - SCREWJOB

Everyone knew there was real heat between Bret and Shawn leading up to the 1997 Survivor Series. All the boys knew, and it was no secret. One thing that was a secret, however, was that Vince McMahon had planned on having Shawn beat Bret for the title, but he told Bret quite the opposite. Because of this secret, wrestling was about to change, forever.

The term "Screwjob" is where a wrestler is promised a particular ending to a match backstage to keep him happy, but then it is not carried out live in the ring on purpose. The Montreal Screwjob concept wasn't invented in Canada. It certainly wasn't a new idea. In the early days of pro wrestling, a promoter would often actually have to select his champion by how well he thought they could shoot in the ring (fight for real.) They wanted a company man they could trust who could handle a rogue wrestler who wanted to go against predetermined plans to make themselves look good.

The Montreal Screwjob is probably the most famous of all screwjobs because the platform where it was to take place, Survivor Series 97, was such a big event with a massive buy-rate. Many were tuning in for this particular Survivor Series because they thought something real could potentially happen. They were right; there was more "realness" here in what many people considered to be normal "fake" pro wrestling. Not including one of the opponents in on the actual finish would lead to very real actions.

There was a work within a work.

As far as the biggest screwjob ever, I was there for all of it. Weeks before it went down, I watched it unfold behind the scenes, and I also saw all of the fallout after it happened.

First off, months before the now infamous PPV, Vince had already given Bret some awesome deal like a 20-year contract. They were making good money at the time of the deal, so it only made sense. Vince planned to continue to push Bret, then eventually transition him into a behind-the-scenes guy after his retirement from the ring. Bret was very happy with the deal, and all the boys congratulated him when he signed it.

When business started to pick up at WCW, they started throwing crazy amounts of money around, stealing WWF talent to use against them. Vince began to worry more about money in general and specifically that generous Bret deal. So when Bret mentioned WCW offered him an obscene amount of money to jump ship, Vince jumped at the chance for renegotiation. Bret's deal was close to 2 million a year, probably double what Taker and Shawn were making along with the new guy, Stone Cold Steve Austin. McMahon knew wrestlers talked. If Hart was making that much, soon the other three would want the same.

Eventually, Bret took the even better deal with Ted Turner. He told Vince he really had no faith in WCW's management, but the money they were throwing around was too good to pass up. In hindsight, you can see he was right about management concerns. Many wonder if Vince knew WCW wouldn't be able to continue to pay money out like they were and expected he would soon get Bret back anyhow. I don't know.

Bret's move to WCW saved Vince a considerable amount of money, but it left him with a difficult decision because Bret was still the WWF Champion. Vince let a world champion sign a contract with a competitor before having him lose the championship.

THE CREATIVE CONTROL CLAUSE

Bret's contract stated that in the last 30 days of employment he had veto power. He had a creative control clause where decisions about his character had to be a collaboration, and both sides had to agree on everything. That's just how the business was in that era. I had the same type of thing written into my WCW contract. Sure, this type of agreement made it harder to book shows for promoters, but it kept your brand alive and kept you marketable for future promotions. Wrestlers had an easier time finding work with other companies because of this clause because they still looked strong when they left. You see, we could protect our image and stay valuable by controlling how fans viewed us on television, even when leaving a market.

People have said I sometimes had problems with finishes and not wanting to job out to certain people. For example, I never did a clean finish for Hulk Hogan in WCW because I didn't want to. I felt it lowered your stock. I didn't want to become just more fuel for his name and weaken my character's image in the process. Being conscious of this worked. I continued to get more work after our run because I exercised my contractual right to refuse certain things. Protecting yourself as a wrestler kept you hirable.

Because of a creative control and a collaboration-exit clause, neither Bret nor Vince could agree on what was going to happen. This left Vince's promotion at the mercy of someone who was about to leave it to work for the other side. If Bret won, WWE looked weak. If Bret lost, he looked weak to WCW.

A week before the PPV, Bret was dressing next to me in the locker room. He and Davey Boy Smith were talking about how the finish should go in his final match. Because of the clear lack of direction, I decided to chime in with my two cents, too. Bret knew I was pretty good at calling a match so we started to riff off of the possibilities and eventually Bret told me some of what Vince had suggested. Something smelled fishy.

It sounded all too familiar. It reminded me of a story Harley Race once told me about, which I will get to later.

"Listen, Bret. Some of what he is proposing leaves you vulnerable." I said, being a bit of a conspiracy theorist. "You really need to be careful and watch your back. Did they ever ask you to just do the job? Or was it DQ from the start?" I asked.

"Vince did want me to drop the title to Shawn at Survivor Series, but he seems cool with disqualification now."

"What were some of the early ideas?" I asked.

Bret told me that Vince initially wanted him to lose clean in Montreal to Michaels, but Bret said, "That was not going to happen." He didn't want the belt to be dropped in Canada, and he also didn't want to drop it to Michaels. Well within his contract to do so, Hart said he "offered some other fair scenarios."

He explained that he didn't refuse to leave without losing to someone. He offered to lose to Austin in America. He even said he agreed to lose the title to one of the biggest jobbers of all time, "The Brooklyn Brawler" Steve Lombardi in Madison Square Garden, but he just didn't want the loss to be in Canada and he didn't want it to be to Michaels, "due to the nature of their feud."

"You aren't worried about not having anything definite yet?" I asked.

"No. It doesn't really matter though," he said. "Everything will be fine."

"You really think so?" I asked. "I wouldn't be so sure."

"I think there will be some kind of DQ and I will just relinquish the belt on Raw for a tournament or something. Some heel promo thing before I go," Bret told me, lacing his boot up for a different match that night.

"So they wanted you to drop the title, but now they are going to let you leave as the champ. I don't know." I laughed. "No hint at the new finish yet?"

"Not yet," Bret said. "He knows I can just use my creative control clause in my contract and refuse anything I don't like last minute, so he doesn't care anymore."

"Oh, I'll bet he does care," Davey Boy said. "He's just too afraid to say it."

"I would have just done the job for Shawn, too, if he didn't go around running his mouth," he said to me. "Davey heard him bragging that he would never put me over - no matter what. That's why I told Vince "No," in the first place."

With all the professional jealousy going on between the both of them and with both often being considered "the best in the world," neither wanted to come out anything less than being on top at the end of that PPV.

"Listen, Bret," I said. "I hear you about Shawn running his mouth and that's one thing. Now, if you are going to go this route to make a statement or whatever, if it was me, I would be kicking out on the one count." Bret knew what I was insinuating. I was warning him that a swerve was a possibility.

"There is no way, Vader. The ref would never do that. It's Earl."

"I don't know," I said. "I would just watch over my shoulder and kick out of every pin at one. Also, don't let Shawn get you in any submission holds at all. I'm just saying."

Bret laughed.

"It could happen," Davey Boy said.

A lot of wrestlers always believe in conspiracy theories. They live a life that always has you pulling the wool over people's eyes in some capacity. It's all part of the business. So, Davey seeing the possibility of a screwjob as well was not unexpected.

"Maybe with someone else, but this match is with Earl Hebner," He said. All the boys knew that Earl was well respected and the top ref in the game. "He wouldn't do that to me after all we have been through. That's just crazy talk."

"Brother, this is business. I know you are Bret Hart and all, but there is no way Vince will let you go to WCW if you are still champion," I said. "Too much ego. It makes his competition have an edge."

It was just common sense to me. Now, I had never been on the receiving end of some kind of screwjob double-cross in the ring, but I had heard similar stories of things like this happing from Harley and Inoki and others in Japan.

"No way," Bret said. "I'm supposed to talk to Pat tonight and hear more of what they want, but that is the least of my concerns."

After my match, I made it a point to seek Bret out and see what the planned finish was and if there was a late-in-the-game submission or anything that could allow for foul play. He laughed again but said it was nothing to worry about. End of discussion.

I was a smart guy. I have a business degree and could see it was a possibility as clear as day. A double-cross made good sense for business; Vince's business. Bret's no dummy, I don't know why he wouldn't hear my warning. I don't know why Bret couldn't see it, at least as a possibility. Maybe his own ego blinded him thinking, "They could never do that to me – I am Bret Hart." Maybe he had an inflated vision of himself, I don't know, but it seemed that he wasn't concerned about the possibility and, in hindsight, may have let his guard down.

The main event came, and all of the boys were watching. Owen and Bulldog were watching out the curtain with Pat Patterson. Others were peeking around the entrance. I wanted to see what was going to happen too, so I headed over to a TV in the back. I made my way toward some of the other boys, huddled around the monitor ready to watch from their own front row seats in the locker room.

I hadn't showered or dressed yet. I was in full gear from my match, minus the mask, and I pulled up a chair next to Taker. The match was physical, mostly a brawl to start. It was good though, and both Bret and Shawn were being professional and right on point, as usual. It was a great story in the ring, and there was no sign of potatoes from either wrestler or anything foul play.

At the very end, we watched Bret climb to the top rope to hit Shawn. Shawn, in turn, pulled Earl Hebner in the way of the blow. The referee took the shot from Bret's double axe-handle and went down. We watched on the monitor to see Shawn look down at Vince McMahon, who was at ringside for no apparent reason.

I called it!

I pointed at the screen. I threw a red flag right there, as he was really not an onscreen personality at this point. I had told Taker my theory before the match, but he too didn't expect any foul play and dismissed my prediction as a crazy conspiracy theory.

"No. No..." Taker said in awe at what he was looking at on the screen.

Vince nodded and Shawn put Bret in the sharpshooter, just as both parties had planned.

Now, this is where the script that Bret was going by changed. In the infamous final seconds, another ref was ready to take over for Earl who was knocked out. He was likely written in for some kind of referee confusion finish that was planned, related to the DQ or something. His presence was probably related to whatever they promised Bret was to happen the next night on Raw. But whatever that storyline was, it would never happen.

Rather than a substitute referee making a bad call that was to be reversed, a supposedly injured Earl Hebner just got right up. He was miraculously healed. Bret had not motioned to submit, but Earl pointed at the time keeper anyhow. Neither the second unused referee nor the timekeeper had any clue what was going on. "Ring the bell! Ring the bell!" Earl yelled furiously at the timekeeper.

"Ring the fucking bell!" Vince elbowed the timekeeper.

The bell rang and it was all over.

"What the hell was that?!" Taker looked at the screen and his jaw dropped. He was red with anger. He stormed right out of the room.

The rest of the boys in the locker room were also furious.

What came next is as legendary as the sharpshooter screwjob finish itself.

Bret got up off the mat. Looking confused, he had a smirk of disbelief on his face and approached Vince. Before he could get away, Bret hocked up the biggest, frothiest, filthiest camel loogie he could, and spat it directly in Vince McMahon's face.

"OH SHIT!" we all yelled.

Bret was pissed and Vince got the hell out there. Bret was on a mission. He went crazy. He destroyed some WWF sound equipment and the commentator's monitors. Then he got into the ring and drew the letters "WCW" in the air to all four corners of the audience. It was clear that only a very few select people were in on the screwjob, because the cameramen kept on filming all the debauchery to the very end.

"Look," I said to the others in the locker room. "It's still rolling!"

The directors did not get the cue to stop, because they were in the dark that what was happening was not part of the show. Earl knew the finish, Vince knew and maybe one or two of the agents, if that. Earl knew for sure, however, because he did his job and split. He had a getaway car gassed and ready for his exit. He was probably already out of the building while they still were ringing the bell.

From there, I felt the urge to leave as well. I rushed back to my bag which was right next to Bret's. I had no intention whatsoever of hitting him with an "I-told-you-so" moment or anything. I actually wanted to get the hell out of there too before Bret showed up, as to not have any part of whatever kind of meltdown was going to happen.

I remember thinking that if Bret came back to get his gear and Vince showed up, it would be bad news. I pictured Bret saying something like, "I should have listened to Vader. He knew you would try something like this!" That would have further infuriated Vince and put me in the dog house after Bret was gone. I didn't want any shrapnel, whatsoever. I decided to move my bag to a different dressing room immediately, clean up, and then get the hell out of there.

I walked into our room and looked. The coast was clear.

There were a few agents there, obvious they wanted to talk to Bret. I ignored them and headed to my corner. Just as I was about to grab my bag, Bret came storming in with Davey Boy.

He was tense. His shoulders and arms were flexing. He was practically breathing fire. Before he could say anything, there was a noise.

Vince and his people rushed in right behind them. They ushered a few people out behind them and they locked the door.

Oh my God. I'm locked in here with this?!

I kept my head down. I went about my business. I tried to ignore the situation and get dressed. According to several reports, people say the Undertaker demanded that Vince McMahon needed to go and immediately apologize to Bret. Trying to act like I had no clue what was going on, I looked at Vince out of the corner of my eye. He didn't look angry, he looked like he felt bad and was attempting to do what the Taker allegedly asked.

Bret Hart had been filming a documentary about his final days in the WWF called Wrestling with Shadows. If you watch this video, you can see that Vince is shown entering our dressing room, but the cameras didn't get in. They did, however, get a shot of Bret asking Michaels if he had anything to do with that finish. Shawn denied it.

At this point, I was like a fly on the wall. Nobody even noticed I was there. That's exactly what I wanted, considering that I was locked in a room where I didn't want to be.

Vince went up to Bret and was very soft-spoken. It was difficult to hear what he said from my vantage point, but it was some kind of apology. Then he said something like, "I did what I had to do for the business."

Bret ignored him. He continued to get dressed and pretended that he wasn't even in the room.

Vince couldn't handle the cold shoulder treatment and continued to try and get Bret to look at him. Vince had often referred to Bret as being a "second son" to him, and he clearly was saddened at Bret's reaction to the double-cross and also perhaps at his own actions.

"Come on, Bret," he said. "You don't understand. I just couldn't take the chance."

Bret stopped ignoring him. "Listen, Vince. I understand perfectly well what you did out there. You are a snake and a liar. Now get out of here or I am going to have to hit you."

"What do you want to do, hit me? Would that make you feel better?" Vince did not leave.

Bret finished getting dressed and then there was nothing left he could really do. In order to leave the room, he was going to have to barge by Vince who was at this point forcing him to confront him about the situation.

Now, I'm not sure if Vince wanted Bret to hit him, but it sure seemed that way. It actually reminded me of wanting Orndorff to hit me so I wasn't the only one at fault. Maybe Vince was thinking the same way. I don't know. Maybe he felt a hit would get the anger out of Bret's system and then they would be even. Maybe he just wanted to let Bret save face for Bret's rep with the boys. I'm not sure, but Bret was going to have to walk by Vince in order to leave and a shot seemed inevitable.

Vince got what he wanted.

Bret walked up and drilled Vince as hard as he could.

It all happened so fast. Vince dropped. Vince's people weren't going to let it get much further than that. Shane McMahon jumped on Bret's back to hold him back. Davey Boy Smith pulled Shane off and hyper extended his knee in the process. Everybody jumped in, but I stayed calm and minded my business. I put on my sneakers. Finally, there was a big pull apart, then Bret headed for the door.

"Are you planning on screwing me on the money, too?"

"No," he replied. "Of course not." Since then, people say that Vince did make good with the $85,000 he owed Bret. It wasn't about the money.

After Bret left, everything fizzled. If you watch Bret's documentary, you can actually see footage of Vince stumble out of our dressing room, punch drunk.

I can kind of see Vince's side to all of this. It wouldn't have hurt Bret at all to job on his way out. That's pretty much what you always do when you left a territory anyhow. But from Bret's point of view, he just didn't want to lose to Shawn. I get that, too.

After they all left. It was quiet. I think I took off my sticky clean clothes that I was pretending to put on to stay out of that mess and then went and took a shower.

WAS THE SCREWJOB A WORK?

There have been people who have doubted that this was a real screwjob. Earl Hebner has even himself said that it is 50/50 possible Bret was in on the deal and staged everything in front of the boys. Kenny Casanova, the guy who helped me write this book, thinks Bret was in on it and that people like me were allowed to see the aftermath so that we would truly believe and pass it on - to push some "bigger plan," as the theory goes.

I don't know. It seemed very real to me, but who knows. Vince is a genius. It's possible.

There was no fallout. Everything worked out great for both Vince and Bret. Vince didn't run away from the booing fans, he gave them who they wanted. Mr. McMahon was born, one of the greatest heel characters wrestling history who would eventually pair up with Steve Austin and put WCW out of business.

Some people like Kenny "The Conspiracy Theorist" think Bret came to Vince with the huge WCW offer and they decided to have him take the money just to milk the competition, to inject a venomous cancer into their competition that would eventually take them down. Maybe they concocted the idea that Bret should go to sabotage WCW by taking the millions of dollars they were stupidly offering over the next couple of years, knowing the company wouldn't be able to afford it in the long run. Vince knew money and must have known that they couldn't continue to pay what they were paying at the rate they were going.

Others also think part of a possible Bret and Vince master plan was for Bret to do a lousy job in the ring. If Bret just did what they asked him to do without offering any extra help, or just allowed Hogan to play politics to bury him without stopping him, they would be paying big bucks for Bret, but reaping no benefits.

There were lots of signs that the screwjob was a written-out, insider storyline that Bret was in on. For one, a documentary was allowed to film backstage when this was unheard of. Also, Bret had a creative control clause, so Vince would have legally been in breach of contract to tell Bret he was in "X" angle but then do a "Y" angle. The cameras also continued to roll and show Bret "acting angry" and WWF left the footage on the PPV video tapes; if this were real, Vince surely would not want to include footage of being spit on. Then, there is also the fact that Owen remained working for Vince.

Some also argue against the fake screwjob idea and say that Bret would have come back earlier after WCW went out of business. However, Bret was collecting off of his Lloyds of London insurance after being injured from Goldberg. He actually couldn't get in a ring or he would lose his insurance money.

Bret and Vince are both old school kayfabe like me, so I can see why people could believe that it is possible that the screwjob was all a big work.

What do I think? I think it was real and Bret didn't know. It seemed very real to me, but Vince is a genius so who knows?

Maybe it was a work, within a work, within a work!

ANOTHER SCREW JOB

Screwjobs were around long before what happened to Bret in Montreal. Everybody thinks they're smart and knows what is going to happen. Even in a day and age when the internet exposes everything, many learn the hard way that you never really know what is going to happen.

Bret thought he was too good to be worked liked that, but look what happened to him.

So, you may ask, how did I get an inkling about Bret's situation? It reminded me of another screwjob story; one that Harley talked about during one of his famous barbecues. In this story, he talked about the time someone tried to steal the NWA World Championship from him down in Abilene, Texas.

"The Lawman" Don Slatton was the promoter for a card he was running in West Texas. He had Harley and himself booked in a match for the championship. Because Slatton was a legend in his area and also because of the special stipulations for the match, this main event for the World Heavyweight belt was preselling tickets left and right.

At the time, the National Wrestling Alliance was the most recognized promotion in the world. It maintained that status with a series of great title defenses by their one world champion who traveled literally everywhere.

The way it worked was the NWA champion had to travel from territory to territory to defend the belt in all of the different promotions that subscribed to the banner. That was one of the main lures to being an NWA affiliate. As a promoter, you would get a title defense against a major name. This would increase your promotion's credibility and also help sell tickets.

Before this big match in West Texas, Harley got a call in his hotel room from the NWA President Bob Geigel.

"Hello, Harley?" he asked.

"Yes, Bob. What's up?"

"Just checking in," he said. "Listen, I need to warn you about your match against Slatton, tonight."

"Why?"

"I don't know, but one of his boys in the locker room got word back to us that he is planning on doing something to force us to have to put the belt on him.

"Shoot?"

"I don't know, but rumor has it that you need to watch your back because he is looking to steal the title. Something shady."

"Don't you worry, Bob. If he tries anything other than what we have planned, that's the last time he ever will," Harley said.

You never knew what you were going to get when you went into a town to work a match as the NWA champion. Guys would often do all kinds of crazy things to try and put their name on the map and get their promotion some kind of attention. That kind of thing helped them to make money long after the touring champion was gone. It really was the "wild wild west" in those days, with an anything-goes mentality in some of the smaller territories. They would do anything to get noticed.

The night came, and the two went over the match in the locker room. Both men were to be chained together at the wrist by a ten-foot chain in a "Russian Chain Match." This bout was worked by the same set of rules as my own favorite stipulation gimmick, "The leather strap match."

There was no pinfall to be had in this match. The only way to win one of these types of fights was to beat your opponent so badly that you could drag him around the ring and touch all four corners in succession without him stopping you.

The thing about the chain match was it was "The Lawman's" specialty. Just like the Undertaker had his own "Casket Match" later on down the road, this match was Slatton's signature stipulation fight. He had wrestled in probably hundreds of them by this time and had never lost a single one of them!

On this particular night, it would have to be different. The NWA was not putting their strap on some local. There was too much money behind making a decision like this, and it wasn't something any one person had the power to do. So what Slatton had agreed to do was something where the NWA champ would just narrowly squeeze by.

The match was on, and everything seemed to be going as planned. When the time came for the finish to take place, Slatton was supposed to hit three of the corners then Harley was going to stop him and make his comeback to retain the title.

Slatton touched, one, then two, then three and then crawled towards the fourth and final buckle. In doing so, Harley pulled the chain hard as planned. Slatton was supposed to fall back but he tripped on the chain and fell forward.

Slatton "slipped."

His bad acting was horrible. It looked like something a clown would do in the circus and it was obviously not an accident. His slipping made it appear that he touched all four corners, therefore winning the match and the world title.

"Sorry Harley," Slatton said. He immediately took the chain off his wrist and rushed back to the dressing room.

Harley wasn't that stupid.

Harley went up to the ring announcer, grabbed the mic, and smashed it to the floor, so Slatton couldn't be announced the new champion. Then he went through the crowd of celebrating people and made his way to Slatton's dressing room. He literally kicked in the door and grabbed Don Slatton by his face.

"It was an accident!" he said, cowering.

Harley beat the dog out of Slatton with his rock-like fists. He knocked him out in record time. After that, Harley dragged Slatton's body back through the curtain to the arena.

None of the Texas fans had left. They were confused and waiting for the official decision. They thought it was possible they had a new hometown champion and were continuing to celebrate in the aisle when Harley came barreling through the masses. He was dragging an unconscious Slatton in tow behind him.

Harley literally hoisted Slatton's body under the bottom rope and rolled him back in the ring. He then wrapped the chain around his waist and legit touched all four corners.

After that, there was no doubt in anyone's mind who was the world champion.

Don Slatton tried to pull a fast one, but that noise was not going down – not on Harley's watch.

In my 1997 feud with the Undertaker, we faced off in a match where Paul Bearer betrayed the Taker and allowed me to get the win. After unsuccessfully winning the WWF title, however, they kept me with the Undertaker family and teamed me up with Mankind, aka Mick Foley.

Traditionally, WWF never talked about WCW. Part of what made this storyline fun was giving the smart fans, the ones who knew their wrestling, a little something back. We decided to fall back on our old WCW history without really saying it and not get along. This left for some interesting tag team matches where we would never agree on anything. We would always mess something up somewhere and that miscue would result in a brawl with each other that would cost us the match.

After the short-lived tag team with Mankind ended, the WWF writers didn't know exactly what to do with me. The idea was that my program with Foley would have been booked to lead up to a possible WrestleMania match, but that idea was eventually scrapped. The reason for this was probably because it was glorifying a historical moment in their past; Cactus Jack's ear falling off. However, this incident was one that happened on the competition's programing in WCW. I went on to have a lot of short term programs with other people like Goldust, the Hart Foundation, and eventually back over to the Undertaker with his little brother, Kane.

Kane kind of reminds me of Sid. If you watch Sid in the ring, the way he moves is stiff, like a robot, not really fluid, mostly because he is a really big dude. I noticed the same thing with Kane. Kane gets up to the top rope and he comes off and it's kind of difficult for him. It's kind of awkward. When the Undertaker walks up backward gracefully and comes off the top rope, there's just a noticeable difference in athletic ability. Don't get me wrong; Kane is a Hall of Famer and has had a heck of a run, but not only did he move "big man" stiff, but he sometimes hit pretty stiff, too! (But, then again, who am I to talk?! Haha!)

I began feuding with Kane for the first time at a PPV called *No Way Out of Texas*, under hardcore match rules.

Paul Heyman's ECW was really starting to take off, so WWF decided to jump on the "anything goes" bandwagon. These "hardcore matches" brought the birth of more tables, more trashcans, more steel chair shots and more use of unconventional weapons that ultimately led to more injuries.

Eventually, Kane and I moved the match to the outside of the ring. I remember I sprayed a fire extinguisher in Kane's face and then powerbombed him. Toward the end of the match, Kane took over with a chokeslam and a Tombstone Piledriver, and I was out. I lost, but it was not over. After the match, Kane wanted revenge for the fire extinguisher and showed up with a big massive wrench.

The wrench wasn't a real wrench; it was actually a movie prop. It was made of some heavy kind of rubber, but it was really dense. It probably would have been better for me if it actually was steel, because then maybe Kane wouldn't have felt it was okay to swing it so hard.

Bammm!

I saw purple. I saw black. I saw stars. Right in the noggin. Boy, he really belted me hard with that mother fucker.

He was supposed to hit me hard because the plan was I was to be taken away on a stretcher and kept off of TV for a while.

The funny thing about the stretcher idea was, after that hit, I think I needed that stretcher for real.

They wheeled me out of there to the backstage area. I got off the cart and could feel the heaviness already building in my shoulders and neck. I touched the hot spot lightly, and it stung even more. It was only a minute or so after that wrench connected, and there was already a massive lump on one side of my head.

Talk about a goose egg! It hurt tremendously on the outside and had to have bruised my brain on the inside.

I felt drunk as I made my way to the dressing room. A few people after the match came by to check on me in the locker room.

"Hey, Vader. Good match. That wrench looked brutal! Are you okay?"

"Sure, sure. It was just rubber, you know," I said. I always tried to play the tough guy, you know? There wasn't any way I was going to admit that a rubber wrench left me seeing stars. So when Kane came by and a number of others, I was pretty quiet and pretended that everything was fine.

"Nice match, brother," Kane said shaking my hand. "Thank you." We exchanged pleasantries. It is funny how, as a wrestler, you actually thank your opponent for kicking your ass, especially after shots that really leave a mark. I couldn't blame him at all.

The wrench was just rubber.

I stayed in that locker room for some time not knowing exactly what to do. I didn't feel like driving just yet, so I when I finally came out, I just tried to socialize a bit. I guess I was being macho. I felt the need to cover up the fact that I was in pain from getting walloped with something that shouldn't have hurt me.

"Hey man, could I get a cup of ice from that, er, door there."

While wandering around attempting to look okay, I realized that I was having a hard time thinking of words for a few common things. Like, I called an icebox cooler a "door," or something to one of the stagehands. I don't know if it was because I was in too much pain or what, but it was like a handful of words were missing from my vocabulary.

I went back to my locker and stayed in that dressing room icing my head for a long time that night in pain. I closed my eyes. I tried to take a 10 minute nap or something to get rid of the headache but quickly learned that wasn't going to happen in a chair. After maybe an hour or so of ridiculous pain, my whole head went numb and felt like Novocain at the dentist.

My skull felt dead.

I could hear them taking the chairs down in the arena. By the time the custodians started coming around, I knew I had to get the hell out of there. I got into the shower, and the warm water made the goose egg sting even more. I kept my head away from the water, then went back and got dressed.

I was driving alone, and it took everything I had to make it back to the hotel. Once I made it to my room, I took a few Percocets. Nothing seemed to happen. My head was still on fire, so I took a few more and climbed into bed.

After hours of not being able to sleep, I decided to get up. The back of my neck and the lower part of my head felt like it weighed a thousand pounds. Another Percocet. I managed to prop a cushion up on the bed and a half a bottle later, I think I got maybe a few hours of sleep.

The next morning it felt like I was hung over, and there was a new ringing in my ears to go along with the new bump on my head. Then the realization hit me that I was traveling alone. I didn't know how, but I was going to have to get out of bed, check out of the hotel, and drive.

It was days like this that I really missed Harley.

I really wanted to "call in" so to speak. If I was in WCW, I would have, but the heat with Shawn Michaels already had me walking on eggshells. I didn't want to take any time off at WWF and risk the potential loss of my spot. By this time, I was winning some matches and losing some matches. I was a true "mid-carder" pretty much jobbing to Kane every night when I wasn't going over on Goldust.

For the next few weeks, the pain only continued. It was really bad. I couldn't think straight. I couldn't sleep, but I continued on and just wrestled matches in a daze.

I really should have gone to the doctor and taken some time off, but you just don't do that as a big-time professional wrestler. You don't take off and risk losing your spot for something as simple as a shot to the head. If your arms and legs still worked, and your neck wasn't broken, you had to get back into that ring.

The aching, hot pain inside my skull was unbearable at times. I figured eventually, I would just overcome it, but it was taking much longer than I thought it would.

To tell the truth, the pain has dulled, but it has never fully left me. Ever since that wrench shot, I still get the same crazy headaches to this very day. I know now I shouldn't have wrestled while dealing with that head injury. I really should have taken some time off.

ADDING FUEL TO THE FIRE

A few weeks later, something probably made my working head injury worse. I was still working a program with Kane, and I was supposed to do a big run-in on TV, during one of his matches. The run-in was supposed to signal my return for vengeance in the storyline.

In order for this to happen best, they needed me to get to the ring precisely at the right moment. Rather than having me try to watch from my cue from a monitor and then run all the way down the whole entrance ramp, they sent me underneath the stage, where I could slip out to the ring more quickly.

When the match finally came that night, the lights were out. I was already under the stage before the entrances. I just waited there in the dark for some time, under the stage with nothing but a bunch of wires and all. I was getting ready to wait and watch for my cue when something big happened that somebody forgot to mention.

WOOOSSSHHH!

The flame thrower, or whatever the hell that thing was, went off. It was only a few inches next to where I was hiding. I thought I was leaning up against some grid iron supporting the ramp, but that wasn't the case at all. *I was actually leaning on a jet-engine pyrotechnic machine when it went off.*

Now, I don't know if you have ever been to a live show, but Kane's original stage pyro was impressive. It was really like a 747. You could feel the heat off of it, way up in the cheap seats. The blast that thing threw in the air literally knocked the wind right out of me. I can only imagine it was like the next closest thing being hit by the blast of a bomb.

The pyro was my cue to come out from the side of the stage and run along the ramp. I was supposed to then hop up on the middle of the ramp and then jump Kane in the ring. But feeling like I just got hit with a grenade, things didn't go quite as well as planned.

That blast was so strong, it seemed like it actually lifted my body up and pushed me up against a steel support beam under the stage. It was hot as hell, and it felt like I was having a heart attack. Mix that bullshit with me probably working on a "walking-concussion" and you guessed it, I saw stars.

I pulled my dizzy ass up on the ramp in the dark and maybe walked a few steps, but that was about all of the plan I could handle. I think I stumbled around a few seconds, and then I fell off the stage.

I guess I had enough sense in my scrambled-brain head to roll back under the ramp before I blacked out, but I don't remember anything else.

When I came to, I didn't know what had happened to me. The ringing you hear in war movies is real, except it doesn't immediately fade away like it does in the movies. It sounded like the emergency broadcast system was running a test in my head.

I have no idea how long I was out, but it seemed like an eternity. Pulling myself back out from under that stage seemed like an eternity too, because I couldn't feel my arms or hands and my legs were all rubbery.

I could hear people yelling, but I wasn't sure what they were saying so I figured there was still time to save the match. I just knew I had to get out there before I missed the spot.

When I got to my feet, I started running towards the ring. I almost made it to the front row barricade when I realized that it was a whole different match. Kane was gone and two other guys were in the ring.

I fucking missed my run-in spot!

I turned about face and ran just as fast as I could in the opposite direction to the locker room. While I was running, I felt more and more ill with every step. It almost felt like I had the flu.

I remember on my way out, a few kids spotted me and started pointing, yelling, "It's Vader! It's Vader!' But that's all the Vader Time they were going to get. I was nauseous and I knew I was going to puke.

As I made a mad dash for the dressing room, I passed one of the agents in the hallway. It was Blackjack Lanza. He wrinkled up his face and he was red with anger.

"Leon!" he said.

I didn't answer. I took off my mask and covered my mouth.

"Leon," he yelled following me. "Where the hell were you?"

I kept running.

"Stop ignoring me! You missed your spot," he said angrily chasing down the hall after me.

I ran into a random dressing room and slammed the door behind me to buy me some alone time, right in Blackjack's face. I looked quickly for a toilet to barf in, but there was only one stall and it was locked and in use. Perfect timing. Someone was taking a shit in it.

By the time Blackjack had caught up with me, I had found my only viable target – a trash can. Lanza cracked open the door, but he didn't run in at me. He just shook his head.

"Leon," he said, about to scold me for missing my cue, but hesitant to enter the room. "...Oh." He watched me a second and finally figured out that something was up.

I vomited a long rope out my nose into a garbage can with no liner.

After that first heave, I managed to force the rest of the puke through my mouth. If you have ever yakked through your nose, you know it smells like a deadly sharp cheese and burns like hell. That was something I didn't want to do again.

"Ewww!" I heard a women wrestler back in the stall sitting on the bowl yell, "Ewwwwww! Gross! Get out of here with that nasty shit!"

"Leon," Lanza said, tapping me on the shoulder. "This is the girl's room."

Nice, I thought. *I am puking up a cheeseburger sub in some girl's locker room.*

After shooting the remnants of regurgitation out of both nostrils into the can, I tore off a paper towel and wiped my face and mouth clean. Then we both stepped out of the room to let the diva finish taking her dainty dump in private. I imagine she was already engaged in mid-shit when a lost my lunch, and she was then imprisoned to inhale the fumes in her booth as the acrid stench wafted up from under its walls.

"Ewww! It really smells!" I heard her cry before the door slammed shut behind us.

Even though I was in horrible pain, we both kind of laughed.

As we walked down the hall, I told Blackjack Lanza what had happened. If it weren't for him actually seeing me puke, it is possible nobody would have believed me and I would have taken heat for missing that spot in the ring. *Thank God for the barfing, I guess.*

Anyhow, on top of my difficulty in sleeping and my pounding headaches from Kane's wrench, his pyro added new difficulties to the mix. My ears rang again, and then they randomly bled for a week or so afterwards.

I also started to randomly fall over, if standing still for any length of time.

PIECE OF SHIT

After missing that one key spot due to the pyro, they had me interfere in Kane's "Inferno match" with the Undertaker to rekindle our planned feud.

Kane and I were then booked for a rematch at "Over the Edge" in a Mask vs. Mask match. In this match, I attempted to use a wrench on Kane like the one used on me months before, but Kane managed to recover and beat me, costing me my mask in the process.

Losing my mask wasn't really what was remembered from this bout. The thing that everyone seemed to focus on was my post-match interview with Michael Cole at ringside.

I was supposed to save face for myself for not winning the rematch. I was supposed to say that I got my ass kicked because I trained all wrong. The general idea to be conveyed was that I trained for power and size and I just got too big. "I need to train differently and I'll be back." The idea was to drop some weight to be more agile to take on someone like Kane, not to be able to out muscle him.

You see, I had told Vince personally I was in the process of dropping weight, on my own. After shedding some pounds, Vince was going to have the writers show some kind of comeback storyline with me. However, that comeback was one that would never end up happening.

After the wrench and the pyro incident, I wasn't thinking well and didn't get the words out right. After that match, I tried to show my acting chops. I was under some pressure to really come off looking emotional, so much so that it made me forget my lines. Rather than the idea of training wrong, it pretty much just came out.

"I'm a fat piece of shit."

I improvised my forgotten lines and got some of the gist of it out, but, I'll admit, not at all in the best way that I could have.

"I made the biggest mistake of my life. Maybe Vader time is over. I'm a piece of shit. A big fat piece of shit."

So for the record, no writer actually asked me to say that. That was my own nonsense coming out of scrambled brains. To my credit, at least I didn't choke and say nothing at all when I forgot my lines, I suppose.

After that, they had a laugh in the back at my expense. Then, I had a series of losses that was supposed to eventually turn around into a comeback. For a time, I was reduced to the status of a jobber to the stars. Rather than to continue to see where they were going with me and my eventual comeback, I decided to ask for my release. Instead of letting my status with WWF send me into an early retirement that could have killed my brand internationally, I decided to negotiate my release so I could once again wrestle in Japan.

You have to hand it to Vince, he was an honest guy and always a gentleman to work with. He was smart and super creative, but we both knew my strong style wasn't really working there at that time. He let me go and we parted ways on good terms.

I still had a few obligations. At the end there, the fans would still chant "Vader time." Playing off the whole underdog/comeback storyline that would never be, I would get on the mic sarcastically and say, "Yeah it's time, it's time! Wait. Nah! It's not Vader time. It's time for you to all kiss my fat ass."

On September 27, 1998, my final WWF pay-per-view match was a loss to JBL at *Breakdown: In Your House*. Then, I lost to Edge on Sunday Night Heat the next week in my final televised WWF match.

My last real match in a WWF ring, however, was on October 25th, 1998, at a Madison Square Garden house show. It was in a Triple Threat Match with Mankind and Ken Shamrock, which I lost after he tapped out to Shamrock's ankle lock.

LEAVING ON GOOD TERMS

If I had really wanted to, I could totally bury some people not really being with the WWE, but it is kind of a sin to do something like that, so I will leave that alone. For the most part, people were okay with me. I never pulled too many of any shenanigans. I do look back at it as one of my favorable times. The WWE helped push even more global exposure to the Vader name and for that I am forever grateful.

Everyone was always treated the best in the world. The bosses treated everyone with respect. The staff was always helpful. The talent treated everyone great. It was one big family, with employees who are still there to this very day. That being said, there was only one unprofessional moment I can recall in my three years with that business.

You know what? Quite often when you leave a job, there can be some hard feelings. As far as WWE goes, I am not bitter at all. Even though our styles clashed, it still worked for me, in the end looking back.

I made a lot of money with the WWE, and that was a good thing. While some fans may argue that they may not have booked me right, they treated me right in the one area I needed it most. They took me in when I was having issues at WCW and I am forever grateful for that.

I drew money and when it was time to get out, again, I just asked Vince for my release and he gave it to me. We left on good terms. We parted friends. I think he respected my being upfront about trying to further my career in Japan. I've never said anything bad about him and, as far as I know, he's never said anything bad about me.

It is a tough move and takes a lot of courage to walk away from a regular check like that. Who wants to walk away from an ATM spitting out hundreds? But I did it. The day after I had my release, I made a few calls, looking to move on.

I was worried at first. *What if my losing streak in the WWF had hurt my stock?*

That wasn't the case at all. One of the first calls I made after leaving the WWF was to my old friend Stan Hansen. Before long, I was packing my bags and ready to go back to Japan. It really wasn't going to take me long at all to get back on top. I learned that Inoki had made me a valuable commodity years ago with New Japan, and I was still in demand.

Two weeks after leaving WWF, I already had a tour scheduled back in Japan. I was going to be a world champion once again, and life was good.

CHAPTER 24 - AJPW AND NOAH

With Inoki retired and NJPW under the rule of a title committee that I didn't get along with, I decided to look at what was once my competition. Having made so much money with Stan Hansen, it was a no brainer.

Giant Baba immediately made me an offer for All Japan Pro Wrestling.

Back in the early '90s, All Japan had already started to undergo a transformation. Their bigger stars, Jumbo Tsuruta and Giant Baba, himself, were getting older. They knew that they were going to have to transition new talent into the mix and create the stars of the future to take the veterans' places.

Baba decided to pass the torch then to Mitsuharu Misawa, Kenta Kobashi, Toshiaki Kawada, and Akira Taue. That was the locker room I was about to walk into. His wisdom was sage. They were arguably one of the greatest groups of wrestlers to ever wrestle in one promotion at the same time, and I was lucky to get to work with them.

Back when Big Van Vader was just being born, this group was putting on some of the most highly-praised matches in Japanese wrestling history, selling out the Budokan for every single show. They were the reason Inoki originally saw some decline and needed to stir things up with me in the first place. Back then, the group was referred to as "The Four Pillars of Heaven." Baba also brought in some great gaijins to work with them, some real bad asses like Steve Williams and Terry Gordy.

Even though I did work with Hansen a lot, it was because of an open door with an inter-promotional feud between New Japan and All Japan. I never technically worked for Baba up until this point, as I only really answered to Inoki. Eventually, I left New Japan Pro Wrestling to work full time at WCW. This left a hole in NJPW, and all the years in my absence AJPW continued to pick up the slack.

Once my run with WWF was over by 1998, the Four Pillars of Heaven were beginning to slow down a little in momentum. Their intense smash mouth "strong style wrestling" started to take its toll on them. Having hard, brutal matches every night was wearing their bodies out quickly, but fans were still coming out in the droves. Akiyama had been elevated to make it a big five. The Big 5 were fine and continuing to draw, but something was still missing.

They needed a new foreigner.

Baba believed that I was just what they needed to ignite things up again, but figured he would never see it happen as I was a New Japan guy. Gordy was so beat up he was a walking zombie, Hansen was on the verge of retirement, and Dr. Death wasn't really doing Japan anymore. What my presence added was a foreign monster, which they needed.

THE AJPW TRIPLE CROWN CHAMPIONSHIP

Just before I showed up to AJPW, in May of 1998, All Japan packed the Tokyo Dome for a massive Triple Crown title match event. They drew a huge attendance of over 50,000 people who were all waiting to see who would win the Triple Crown, ending a very long rivalry between Misawa and Kawada. (Kawada was victorious.)

Like New Japan's IWGP title, "The Triple Crown" is the name of the very top title in AJPW. The championship itself is actually a unification of the NWA United National, the Pacific Wrestling Federation Heavyweight, and the NWA International Championships. The belts were unified way back on April 18, 1989, when the NWA International champion Jumbo Tsuruta defeated the PWF and NWA UN champion, Stan Hansen.

Unlike most unified titles, the Triple Crown was for a long time represented by the champion still carrying all three individual belts, which I personally thought looked really cool. Seeing the champion with all that gold was always impressive to me, and I selfishly wanted to do it myself.

Following that huge card, I would get my chance. Baba said he had no idea how he was going to top the Misawa and Kawada match, but wanted to continue the success from Triple Crown 98, with a regular big title match event.

I was a free agent and he decided to snatch me up. He felt my name would be just what he needed for Triple Crown 99.

CLIMBING THE LADDER

Baba first brought me into All Japan as a competitor in the World's Strongest Tag Determination League, known by English-speaking fans as the "Real World Tag League." The name "Real World Tag League" was actually a mistranslation by Giant Baba. The actual Japanese word "saikyō" in Japanese means "strongest," not "real", but Baba used broken English for their early promotional material and it stuck. This tournament was, and still is, an annual event that AJPW has held since 1977.

The tag tournament is held under Round-Robin Rules. This means you get 2 points for a win, 1 for a draw and 0 for a loss.

For this event late in 1998, Baba planned a major twist. Baba teamed me up with my old nemesis, Stan Hansen. Fans couldn't believe the pairing and generated quite a buzz.

It was pretty cool to get to work with my old buddy Stan in the twilight of his career. Hansen was still the same old, violent gaijin who wanted to fight everybody, wearing the same old cowboy hat, leather vest and bull rope, spitting tobacco. Stan really is a legend. It was funny to see he was still giving his little pre-match speech in the locker room, even after all those years.

"Ok," Stan said to a Japanese opponent. "Now, I have to apologize right now before we get in there because I might be kind of stiff. Without these glasses, I can't see a fucking thing."

Many a night, I remember wishing Stan would have just invested in buying some contact lenses.

We made it to the finals, but we were eventually defeated by Kenta Kobashi and Jun Akiyama. (The next year, I would enter this tournament again, but with a different partner, Johnny Smith. Some of you may remember Johnny as being billed as Davey Boy Smith's brother, who occasionally tagged with the Dynamite Kid.)

THE PATH TO THE TRIPLE CROWN

Early in January of 1999, Baba started me on my path towards the Triple Crown. Following off the defeat in the tag tournament, I went after Kenta Kobashi in singles competition. What great matches we had. The feud ended with a big victory for me and it got massive press. Some of the writers said our program included some of All Japan's best matches ever.

After this, Baba called me in to see him. He wasn't doing very well, as he had been sick for some time with cancer. The treatments had been wearing him down some, so they stopped treating him. He thanked me for my good work and decided to show me the ultimate in respect.

"I am ready to give you the Triple Crown."

I was honored and thanked him like crazy.

On January 22, 1999, Baba was in pretty rough shape. Baba had been hospitalized since a bowel operation on January 8th, but somehow still made it to the show. Though he or nobody else would admit it, many thought he was just there to see his last wrestling match and to set up his final big storyline. That night Toshiaki Kawada defeated Mitsuharu Misawa for the Triple Crown Championship to lead up to an eventual match against me.

Nine days later, the Giant had fallen. It was announced that Shohei Baba had passed away.

A private funeral was held for Baba, then a public ceremony was thrown at Tokyo's Budokan Hall, the famous family site of many of Baba's biggest matches. Somewhere north of 15,000 fans attended to pay their respects and rightfully so. People of all ages were heartbroken at the loss of the fallen giant. The visual of this showing was moving and brought me to tears.

He was one of the biggest names in the wrestling business dating back to the '60s when he first debuted teaming with Antonio Inoki. Baba was a huge sports hero in Japan just like Michael Jordan is here in the United States. It was said that more than 100,000 letters from all over the world were sent to the All Japan office for Mrs. Baba offering their condolences.

The passing of Shohei Baba at the age of 61 sadly and truly marked the end of an era in Japanese professional wrestling. This was something that really hurt wrestling as a whole. It was a sad time for everyone and bittersweet for me to enjoy the idea of becoming the new face of AJPW, knowing he was gone.

Business continued as usual with Misawa helping out behind the scenes. The storyline progressed, and I won a big match to be declared the #1 contender to the Triple Crown by defeating Kenta Kobashi.

After that, on March 6, 1999, they went on to honor Baba's last bit of final booking wishes. I finally defeated Akira Taue to win the Triple Crown Heavyweight Championship. That victory meant the world to me. I am a very nostalgic guy. This title was a very big deal to me personally. Being able to hold the IWGP title in New Japan as well as the Triple Crown in All Japan was a dream come true. Getting that championship run was something I could cross off my "bucket list." I was happy I was able to thank Baba before making it happen in his final days.

To put the exclamation point on my accomplishment, I learned after winning the Triple Crown that Baba wasn't done thinking about me, not even on his death bed.

"Baba was very happy with what you have done for the company," Misawa said. "He was still raving about you, even at the very end."

"That's good to hear," I said. "I will do my best for him."

"He knew that," he said. "He was very happy that you decided to come to us and get things going again. That is why he also requested that after you won the Triple Crown, you would win another AJPW tournament, the Champion Carnival, as well."

I had no idea. Feeling a little choked up, I didn't know how to respond to another such great honor. I just sucked back a sob and nodded at Misawa.

The Champion Carnival, like the Strongest Tag, is another annual tournament that All Japan started way back in 1973, under round-robin rules. It is very much like WWE's Money-In-The-Bank in that the winner of the Champion Carnival gets a guaranteed title match against the Triple Crown holder.

We moved on with Baba's final plans. The 1999 Champion Carnival was a 10-man tournament and it was held from March 26 to April 16. I became the first man ever to win it in my first ever time in the tournament, beating Kenta Kobashi.

After that match, I got even more choked up. Boy, I'll tell you, I can be pretty sentimental at times. When Jim Ross says that I am nothing more than a big teddy bear behind the scenes, this is a good example of just that. After winning the Carnival, I cried like a baby in that ring. I sobbed like a real bitch. It was a bunch of things I guess that got to me.

I thought about my days in the WWE when I was looked at as a failure. Honestly, I didn't know how Japan was going to receive me upon my return. After quickly winning another Japanese wrestling accolade, I finally knew. As appreciated as it was, there was totally no real reason to win the Carnival, unless they were trying to tell me, "Thank you for coming home."

I thought about how guys like Inoki and Baba really saw something in that little chubby boy trying to play football with the older kids. I thought about Inoki giving up his streak to me. I also thought about Baba. He went out of his way on his death bed to help me get my career back, and that he did.

Tears of joy streamed down my face in front of 16,000 fans AT Budokan Hall when they gave me the giant Carnival trophy.

And that wasn't it for gold! They also teamed me up with Steve Williams and we won the AJPW tag team titles. All that success in such a short time was awesome. Big Van Vader was back on the map. My name had been completely repaired.

The tag team run didn't last as long as it should have, though. Another obstacle came about in the spring of 1999: another arm injury. I worked on it for a little bit, but it was inevitable that it needed some healing, and I was going to have to take time off while I was still super-hot.

Rather than to just have me lose the Triple Crown title cold and disappear, we did some belt trading to keep me looking strong. I dropped the Triple Crown to Misawa in a massive match at the Tokyo Dome. I regained it back from him again and then dropped it again to Kenta Kobashi.

At this point, my arm was getting pretty bad. I couldn't work anymore without risking making it worse. So seemingly right after winning them, I had to reluctantly suck it up in the name of health and vacate the tag titles. Being benched for a few months gave me some time to get healthy, but during that time I watched the company fall apart from the sidelines.

Political issues within All Japan started to run amok. With the death of Baba at the start of the year, Mitsuharu Misawa immediately inherited the position of company president, but much of the promotion was actually being run by Baba's wife, Motoko Baba. Both of them were very nice to me, but they didn't agree on anything else. She had a very different vision for the promotion than many of the wrestlers who were trying to keep it afloat.

Due to disagreements with Mrs. Baba, Misawa found himself at wit's end. They finally had it out. In late May of 2000, it was announced that Misawa was no longer AJPW president. Mrs. Baba claimed Misawa was "abandoning his duty," but that wasn't really the case. The removal from the presidency was actually a power play and ultimately led to Misawa quitting All Japan, just what Mrs. Baba wanted.

However, in my opinion, disagreeing with Misawa was something Mrs. Baba should have never done.

YAKUZA

Yakuza in Japanese loosely means, "Mafia."

Ever since this sport began, we can trace back a relationship between organized crime and wrestlers. In the states, there was a time when Bruno Sammartino was being "protected" by a couple of Italian brothers that he could not shake, and that he didn't want around. Rumor has it that he paid them a hefty sum for this protection. Another notable mention is Dino Bravo smuggling cigarettes across the Canadian border that left him with 17 bullets in the back of his head.

The Yakuza is the organized crime circle responsible for all kinds of chaos in Japan. There are many accounts of the mafia in Japan, aka the Yakuza, having their hands in everything from prostitution, to the forced selling of stolen/shoddy goods, to gambling, and to even forcing land owners to sell their land cheap so that they could flip it for a profit.

The Yakuza is no joke.

GIVING YOU THE FINGER

Yubitsume is a pretty sick form of Yakuza loyalty through dismemberment. It is a symbol of apology after one makes a mistake or acts in a way that is upsetting to his leader. Upon a first offense, the offender cuts off the tip of his left little finger and gives the severed portion to his boss as a peace offering.

Penance continues at the cost of a new finger segment for each shortcoming. Just as one might expect, yubitsume starts with the tip of the left pinky, then down to the knuckle, then down to the palm. The cutting moves to the ring finger, and so on and so forth, working backwards towards the thumb.

Since Yakuza stems back to the seventeenth century, this ritual's origin stems from having to hold a Japanese sword. The bottom three fingers of each hand are used to grip the sword tightly, with the thumb and index fingers slightly loose. The removal of digits, starting with the little finger and moving up the hand, progressively weakens your grip on a sword. The idea was created so that a weak sword grip would force a Yakuza member to rely more on the group for protection—reducing misbehavior within the sect.

Many Yakuza members wish to appear tough to intimidate the weak. Some of the more important members have something known as "irezumi" in Japan. They are painfully hand-poked full-body tattoos created by inserting ink beneath the skin using hand-made tools with needles of sharpened bamboo or steel. And yes, from what I hear, these full body tattoos include genitalia. Guys, imagine hand poking your nutsack with bamboo for hours.

The Yakuza has been tied to shenanigans that often led to the forced success of wrestling promotions. Just like Bruno not being able to shake his unwanted bodyguards, sumo and wrestling promoters alike have often found new investors that they wanted no part in – but had no choice. One story that people often hear about is getting pulled over by bad police, who would actually force people to buy tickets to a wrestling show that Yakuza had some kind of investment stake in.

BUDDY LANDELL

The late Buddy Landell once told a story about his experience with Yakuza. Many of the Yakuza would often offer to take an American wrestler out to eat to fancy restaurants, because, after all, they were wrestling fans - which was why they were connected to wrestling in the first place. In fact, on a number of occasions, I let the Yakuza buy me dinners and answered their questions and posed in pictures with them simply because the dinners they offered were always top notch.

So on one particular evening, Buddy noticed a few of the employees at a fancy Yakuza-run restaurant had missing fingers. They placed a bowl of noodles in front of him and it was very clear that something was missing.

"How did that happen?" Buddy asked. "Was it a Ginzu accident chopping noodles back in the kitchen?"

One of the Yakuza then explained the Yubitsume finger offering ritual for serious offenses against the big boss.

Later on that night, Buddy got out of the car and was greeted by one of the promoters for his big match. He ran up to Buddy, clearly excited, so Buddy grabbed his hand and shook it. While doing so, again, Buddy noticed that something was clearly missing.

The promoter was Yakuza. He only had three fingers on his hand.

"Goddamn!" he said, letting go of his grip. "Ain't gonna be no high-fives here tonight. Who the hell did you piss off?"

ONITA AND YAKUZA

The Yakuza was everywhere in Japan in every facet of business. No promotion was safe.

Frontier Martial-Arts was no exception. It was a Japanese professional wrestling promotion founded on July 28, 1989, by

Atsushi Onita. It was different than NJPW and AJPW in that it specialized in hardcore wrestling. Most of its death matches involved weapons such as barbed wire and fire, much like '90s ECW.

I worked again for FMW in the Ken Shamrock cage match that I talked about previously.

The FMW booker Onita was a real character. He was smart and, like Inoki, he later became a politician in the Japanese Diet. His exit from politics was a bit different, however. It was forced out of a sex scandal. He allegedly used government funds and accommodations to host a threesome with a porn star and a female employee of the Japanese Infrastructure and Transportation Department. He claimed to have broken Wilt Chamberlain's record of sleeping with 20,000 women!

One of the first memories I have of Onita was when I just started with WCW part-time and was still working in New Japan. I remember Onita coming to one of our NJPW shows and he was there to ask Inoki for a favor. He wanted his promotion, FMW, to run their anniversary show at the Sumo Hall, New Japan's home base.

He got Inoki's blessing, but Onita would end up making one of the worst decisions ever on the concept of selling this show to the public; a vengeance match on the killer of Brody.

Yakuza had their name written all over this one. They knew that their share of the tickets would be incredible.

After securing the location from Inoki around August of 1990, Onita flew to San Juan for a talent exchange meeting with Puerto Rico's WWC promotion, hoping to drum up interest for his FMW card in Tokyo. A wrestler named Mr. Pogo worked for both promotions and helped to initiate the talks with Jose Gonzalez, aka Invader #1.

Gonzalez is not famous because he was a great heel in the ring. He is the man that murdered my friend, Bruiser Brody, stabbing him to death in a shower after a show.

Brody was a huge legend in Japan. By booking a match with his killer, Onita and Yakuza felt that some people would pay any price to see this revenge. Others, however, believe Onita was actually trying to set up Gonzalez.

During the WWC meeting in Puerto Rico, Onita pitched and sold a storyline for a WWC and FMW feud. He would release pictures to Puerto Rican wrestling magazines of him being attacked by Mr. Pogo, El Gran Mendoza, Victor Quinones, El Professo and Jose Gonzalez, taken from a photo shoot by his photographers. Though Gonzalez didn't know it, Onita planned on only using a few key pictures to tell a totally different story in Japanese wrestling magazines.

The Japanese storyline was Gonzalez stabbed Onita alone, with no mention of the others in the group, very much like he did to Brody. This would set things up for a huge main event. Onita knew that Gonzalez would never have agreed to participate in the "Vengeance for Brody" storyline he was going to sell to the fans in Japan, so he kayfabed him on the alternative story.

Before the photo shoot, Onita stabbed himself in the stomach, sparingly. There wasn't enough blood so he cut his forehead and smeared the blood all around. Onita also wanted pictures of being stitched up, vowing revenge on Jose Gonzalez, but he couldn't find a hospital in Puerto Rico to stitch up his tiny wound. Eventually, Onita paid a random doctor to give Onita two little stitches, before returning home with pictures.

After Onita ran the pictures in Japanese magazines, the storyline had the exact opposite reaction Onita had hoped for. Instead of fans rushing out to buy tickets, they were appalled. There was a huge backlash from the angle. People were outraged at Onita for attempting to work with the same man who killed Brody, only two short years ago.

Tokyo Sumo Hall pulled Onita's reservation. FMW agreed and didn't look for a replacement venue. They felt that if Gonzalez were to come to Japan, the backlash would possibly kill FMW's fan base. What they didn't know, however, was the word "killing" was possibly an even more ironic word than they had thought.

Rumor has it that there was something else possibly in the works; a screwjob by Yakuza that would have been far more severe than anything that would later transpire in Montreal.

Many say that if Invader #1 did make it to wrestle a show in Japan, there was a strong possibility that he never would have made it back home alive. They say Onita was trying to lure Gonzalez to Japan so *Yakuza could actually kill him for what he did to Brody.* Onita now admits in interviews that the whole thing was Yakuza's idea. They wanted the money from ticket sales as much as they wanted Invader #1's ass.

As the story goes, Yakuza was going to wait until after the match happened to stab Gonzalez in the showers themselves.

There would have been a lot of money at stake, however, it is not too far-fetched to think that Invader #1 might have come up missing after the event and Japanese police not caring. It actually would have been great karma to mirror the Gonzalez injustice in

Puerto Rico. The Japanese would have "botched" the investigation just as the Puerto Rican court system did. The dirty police were just as prevalent in Japan as they were in the Island because Yakuza members, too, infiltrated the Japanese police force.

I can picture the Japanese police would have just said, "The Gonzalez/Onita thing was all just an angle and he will show up soon. Who knows where the guy is? He probably disappeared as part of a storyline."

Don't kid yourself. It's not too hard to make someone disappear, especially when you are involved in organized crime.

MISAWA & MAFIA CONNECTIONS

Misawa was 6'1 and 220 pounds, but in my opinion, he was heads and tails better than Ric Flair in the ring and a better worker than Shawn Michaels. His work ethic was ridiculous. He was always on the go, and even though he was laid back in his approach, he was one of the most productive guys I ever met.

He would get up and start working at six in the morning. He would work all day in the office setting up shows, selling advertising, and then head over to the dojo at 5 pm. He would train students and also work out himself.

Misawa was a hardcore chain smoker, sometimes smoking two packs a day. He was also quite the drinker. He could drink whiskey after whiskey before a match and he could still go.

As far as Misawa leaving AJPW, the damage would be far worse than just losing a great talent in and out of the ring. Misawa was linked to Yakuza, and Yakuza was a group you did not want as an enemy.

On June 16, 2000, Misawa held a huge press conference where more than 100 reporters and photographers attended. There, he announced that he was leaving the promotion and taking 24 of the 26 contracted AJPW wrestlers with him. He took every single All Japan native wrestler except Masanobu Fuchi and Toshiaki Kawada, who were on the board.

How did this happen? Well for one, many of the wrestlers sided with Misawa on an unjust removal from presidency. And two, it's not a good move to side with the enemy of the Japanese mafia.

A day or so later, Misawa announced his new promotion, *Pro Wrestling Noah.*

The name of his new promotion was, in fact, taken from the Bible. Misawa said the Biblical story was one where, "…Noah put two of all kinds of beasts on his sheltered arc before God was to destroy the world."

Misawa then went on to destroy All Japan.

On June 19, 2000, a press conference at All Japan's dojo was held by board members Fuchi and Kawada. They announced that the NTV Network decided to discontinue broadcasting All Japan Pro Wrestling after 27 years on the air but would not let them out of their contract to look elsewhere.

Misawa pulled some strings. NTV decision makers were Yakuza-influenced. When they were asked to sell their stock back to Motoko Baba, they declined and kept their 15 percent stock in AJPW. Being a part owner of the AJPW promotion, NTV had say in all decisions and also wouldn't allow the promotion to jump to another network.

On June 20, 2000, twelve AJPW office employees also resigned from their positions to follow Misawa to NOAH. On the same day, NTV also announced two new weekly NOAH programs replacing All Japan's timeslot on Sundays. A week after that, Misawa announced two more space-stealing shows set to air in Ariake.

NOAH NEGOTIATIONS

By the time I was ready to return from my hiatus from elbow surgery and recovery, All Japan was all but in ruins. Giant Baba was gone and Inoki was retired, so Misawa's new promotion seemed like my best option. However, before I decided to just do that, I figured I would first see what Mrs. Baba had to offer from All Japan.

A very tired looking Mrs. Baba asked me to sign with her company. With so many wrestlers leaving the promotion, she said she would offer good money if I went with her. The plan was to rebuild the whole promotion around me. She offered me a long-term contract with an okay amount of money that could increase over time. I told her that I appreciated the offer and would certainly let her know after I checked all my options.

That same night, Misawa invited me to talk with him at NOAH's dojo facility. When I got there, the sun had just set.

The door creaked. I walked into a warehouse, not unlike what you would see in a Rocky movie. It had a couple of beat up rings, some overused weights and a few kick bags. The dank air hit me in the face. It wasn't at all as clean and modern as the places New Japan and All Japan used for training. This place was pretty grim looking and lonely. The empty place was also poorly lit. It had nothing but a naked light bulb hanging above the ring.

"Come on in, Vader," I heard a familiar voice say.

I walked over to the ring where the voice came from and saw Misawa. He was sprawled out in the center, just lying there. He sat up and shook my hand. He gave me a pretty warm welcome, but once the formalities were done, he went right back to lying down on his back.

"You mind?" I asked, sitting down at a weight machine to do a couple of reps.

"No, no. Be my guest, he said.

That was how Misawa rolled. I knew the vibe he wanted. We were just two guys, two wrestlers, just going to talk it out.

"I apologize. I am very tired. Very rough few weeks," he said, making reference to the jumping to a new promotion and all the harsh politics surrounding the move.

"No problem, I heard," I said. "I know how that feels."

I was outside the ring doing the full rack on a leg machine. I remember thinking about how very different this was from all my other Japanese contract negotiations. Usually, contract negotiations with Inoki or Baba had a number of lawyers around taking notes inside some kind of office setting. Everybody was usually wearing their finest suits and trying their hardest to look as professional as possible. This meeting of the minds, however, was super low key. It was a very casual setting. Misawa was wearing a pair of cheap track pants and a dirty sweatshirt that looked like he just blew his nose on it.

I don't remember exactly what he said, but Misawa explained the whole falling out with Mrs. Baba and got me up to date on his leaving the promotion. Then, in so many words, Misawa admitted that he was not alone in his adventure to start his own promotion.

"There are some 'new partners' involved in the deal with NOAH," he said. Yes, the term he used was "partners," however, these were not your normal investors.

It was then I realized that Noah was not funded by the same type of stockholders or businessmen that you would see at some promotions. There was something very different going on behind the scenes. Misawa meant Yakuza. Misawa had to ironically "sell his soul to the devil" to make the new Biblically-named promotion.

"I even had to 'become friends' with Yakuza," he said, "in order to make it happen."

"I understand," I said.

He then went on to explain that the new "partners" were prepared to offer me a lot of money up front, for a short term contract. "But don't decide, now," he said. "I will give you the night to think about it."

With All Japan, I would make decent money for a long-term contract. With NOAH, I would make a whole lot more money faster, but for a shorter amount of guaranteed time.

When I left the dojo, I pretty much already had my mind made up to join the new Japanese promotion, Pro Wrestling NOAH.

Maybe I acted too quickly. I know Misawa would have brought me in, no matter what, even if I had chosen one more run with Mrs. Baba first. In hindsight, I probably should have gone with All Japan and took the long-term money with the longer-term contract and then signed up with NOAH after that. That plan would have stretched my run out in Japan even longer. But I'll admit, I was being a little shortsighted and decided to go for the quick money.

For making the "right decision," Misawa told me I could run with their new tag team championship with any partner of my choosing. I brought in my old friend, Clint Howard's favorite wrestler, 2 Cold Scorpio.

My stay in Noah lasted from 2000 until late 2001, and for much of it, I was teaming with my good friend Scorpio. Our run was really great and finally came to a head on October 1, 2001. At the Noah Tug of War 2001 in Yokohama, Japan we were crowned on day 10 of a tournament to become the first ever Global Honored Crown (GHC) Tag Team Champions. Misawa put us over on Jun Akiyama & Akitoshi Saito to be the first ever to hold the championship. It was a real honor.

Two months later, Misawa really started to like the direction I was going in and wanted me to start up on some singles matches. The singles bouts were a precursor to what would have been a massive main event. Misawa began running promos on my quest to win the GHC Heavyweight Championship. If I were to have won this match, I would have become the only wrestler at that time to hold all three major Japanese championships. However, that match never happened.

CUTTING UP THE DANCE FLOOR

Late one night after a great turn out for a live NOAH show, Misawa was feeling pretty good. He had made a lot of money and wanted to thank me, above and beyond the bonus I found in my envelope at the end of the night.

Misawa came up to me in the locker room as I was getting dressed. I was a big name, and I was invited as a VIP to a nearby bar/nightclub in Tokyo where Misawa had "connections." He was on a first name basis with Yakuza guys, and he told me to ask for one of them by name when I got there.

The Yakuza-run place was very modern. There were a lot of crazy dance lights everywhere, and they were playing J-pop loud over the speakers. It was difficult to make my way up to the bar because there were so many people. A few people were really nice and went out of their way to help me through the swarm of people. They were all patting my shoulder and calling me, "the champion," in broken Japanese English.

It was a lot of little 5'2" Japanese guys dancing, most of them poorly. As I finally bellied up to the bar, I noticed that a lot of the people there looked like normal civilians, but there were Yakuza members here and there, identifiable by their full sleeve tattoos.

Once I had the attention of the bartender, I mentioned the name that Misawa mentioned. Then everything changed.

"Oh, big wrestler!" he said. "We waiting for you!"

He yelled something to the people sitting around the bar and everyone clapped.

He immediately pushed free drinks at me and called for someone in the back. Then, he gave me my own pretty girl to wait on just me.

"I've got my own private waitress?" I asked.

"Oh, yes, Mister Vader."

Now just a heads up for all you perverts out there; as a gaijin, you didn't look to have sexual relations with girls in Tokyo, Japan. The Yakuza would have killed you. I don't know what I can liken their attitude to, maybe like an old school view of interracial couples. If I had made a move on one of their women, it would have meant big problems, especially in a Yakuza nightclub. The private waitress was just that; someone there to keep the free food and drinks coming just for me.

The girl was a beautiful little thing. She led me over to a booth in the corner and disappeared for a minute. Then, she returned with a huge tray of appetizers, all on the house.

This getaway seemed perfect. Misawa did me a solid. I was tired and wanted to get away from other wrestlers. I was hungry and the food was endless. Everything seemed great until a certain someone showed up.

I didn't know the guy, but I knew his type. I could spot him a mile away.

This tall, flamingo-looking asshole had all the tell-tale signs of a red flag in the making. He had his collar popped, he had the gold chain, he had the full body tattoo and he even had a toothpick in his mouth. He looked like a cross between "Chozen" the villain from *Karate Kid 2* and The Miz. This guy was pretty large for Yakuza, and it was clear he wanted even more attention.

As soon as who we will now just call "Chozen" appeared, I knew there was going to be trouble. He had a posse with him of about seven hanger-ons, and they were laughing at everything he said. He knew I was the biggest guy in the club and in typical narcissist fashion, I knew he was going to mess with me to show off for his buddies. When we made eye contact, Chozen headed right for me.

"This is going to be interesting," I said under my breath, taking another drink.

At wrestling shows, Yakuza were treated like the elite. They sat in their own section and did not want to be messed with. You did not look them in the eye, walk through their area, or even come near them. They were top-of-the-line royalty, like Julius Caesar watching a gladiator. The Japanese wrestlers knew not to interact with them, and even more so, the gaijin wrestlers.

Chozen came up to my table and immediately helped himself to one of my free appetizers. I didn't say anything, but rather laughed it off.

"You are big wrestler?" he said.

I nodded.

"You big enough to beat me up?" he asked. He elbowed his buddies who laughed at his dumb joke. Then shoved me at the table.

I did what you are exactly supposed to do in this case, nothing. I bit my lip, laughed, and continued to drink.

The flamingo walked away with his group right beside him. My private waitress shook her head. She came up to me and cupped her hands up to my ear and whispered to me.

"That is Chozen," she said, looking around first to make sure the coast was clear. "He is very, very bad man. Please be careful."

"Oh, I know about his kind," I said. "Thank you though, dear."

The waitress left and brought me another drink, and then another. I started to feel a little bit dizzy. They were serving me the best top shelf sake in the house - none of that cheap crap.

As I continued to get buzzed and eat my fill, I watched Chozen out of the corner of my eye. Everywhere he walked, he looked as if he was trying to emulate Rodney Dangerfield making an entrance in *Caddyshack*.

"Can I get you something else, Mister Vader?" my waitress asked.

"Ok, you talked me into it," I replied. "Just one more." I decided after the next drink, I was out of there. I really liked the female attention, but Chozen smelled like trouble.

I drank my beverage and found my way to the restroom. I made my way back to the table through the jumble of gyrating Japanese.

I left my server a great tip and put my jacket back on to head out. That is when Chozen decided he wanted to party.

"Wait, wait," he said. "You no go. You must dance."

I shook my head and started to make my way out. Then he put his hands on me, again, and shoved.

"You don't understand, gaijin. We want you to dance with us," he said to his buddies, who all laughed. "You not too good to dance with us?"

Chozen punched at me again, kind of like you would do to taunt a boxer, but then hit harder to try and get a rise from his cohorts. Being a part of the Yakuza, he knew he had some kind of power and was abusing it. He really was getting a charge out of being able to push around someone 200 pounds bigger than he was.

"Dance, NOW!" he said over the bad J-pop dance music. He pushed me in the direction of the dance floor with all the dance lights. The fog machine was going.

"Please," I said in the most timid voice I could muster. "I have had too much to drink, and I really need to get back to my room."

"Oh. Big wrestler too good for us?" he said. After that, he said some other words that I didn't recognize. He laughed and then grabbed me by my jacket like he was going to hit me.

"Please, I don't want any trouble," I said. Over his shoulder, I could see my waitress pointing my way at what was going on to the bartender. They both shook their heads. The bartender motioned that I should try and leave by tilting his head a number of times towards the door.

Chozen finally let go of me. I bowed a little and headed for my exit. He rushed in front of me again and punched me in the arm. I brushed it off, again and stepped around him.

He said something in Japanese to his friends. I didn't quite understand it all, but it was something like I thought I could kick his ass if I really wanted, too, but I wasn't really that tough.

He physically put his hands on me again.

I was six or seven drinks in deep and the rulebook was getting blurry. I started to forget the Yakuza rules.

Chozen pushed me again and laughed, but this time I shoved back a little - admittedly which was wrong, etiquette-wise. Chozen swung at me and I blocked it.

Then, he was all over me.

"Fuck this," I said.

Vader time.

I punched him once in the face so hard he fell about twenty feet back. I probably broke his nose. Blood trickled down his upper lip and into his mouth. You could see it collect over his teeth.

I saw him wipe his mouth and nose on his forearm, and the all-over tattoo sleeve peeked through his shirt cuff. Then through all the sake, I remembered he was Yakuza.

His face turned red with rage, I embarrassed him. It didn't matter if I had remembered or not, he wasn't going to let me forget. Before I could apologize or anything, the eight of them dragged me out of the bar and across the dance floor. It was like an attack from the Lilliputians of *Gulliver Travels*.

"Should have just danced, gaijin," the short stooge said.

They picked me up and my feet drug over decorative stone. Out in the back of the lot, I knew I was in the wrong place at the wrong time.

They pulled me way out back beyond the light by a commercial dumpster. I knew if I fought back, they were going to have to kill me. I figured I was just going to have to endure a couple of hits. I figured wrong.

Chozen punched me as hard as he could in the head. His shot wasn't all that impressive and I bet he did more damage to his hand than he did to my face.

The Lollipop Guild knew this and decided that it was disrespectful that I didn't sell the shot. To help their master Chozen save face, they tripped me up and I fell down to the cement, hard. I landed on my back. Before I knew what was happening, the Guild had pulled out their knives and started hacking away at my legs.

"Nooo! Stop!" I shouted.

They kept cutting and laughing.

In mere moments, there were little slices all over my lower body. They could have killed me if they had wanted to, but they were first trying to leave a message.

Misawa's friend the bartender was watching all this. Before things spiraled out of control even further, he showed up yelling that they needed to "look out." Fortunately for me, he ran over to the scene just in time and made up a story that there were police in the bar. His quick thinking may have saved my life.

Chozen and his Oompa Loompas pocketed their knives and ran to the streets. They scattered out of sight. "We not finished, Mister Vader!" one yelled as they faded into the darkness.

I stayed down for a few moments on the blood-soaked ground. Once the coast was clear, I tried to stand. I was light headed and toppled right over. The bartender helped me up.

I opened my pants and looked down at my legs. From my thighs to my shoes, I was covered in thick blood. I also had rough lacerations on my arms and stomach that cut through my clothing.

"Oh my God, I said," fearing I was losing a lot of blood. "Help me," I cried.

All of the cutting and the alcohol from the sake started catching up with me. I was drunk. The cuts didn't really hurt at all, but the sight of it scared me. The bartender was a real saint, however. He didn't skip a beat. He rushed me right over to his car, and we zipped out of there.

The bartender didn't bring me straight to the hospital, however. He got me back to the hotel first, basically bleeding to death. In a frantic, he looked for Misawa to find out what to do, but he wasn't anywhere to be found. The bartender made his way to one of the new boy wrestler's rooms. He helped me gather some fresh clothing together as the bartender made some calls. When I left his room only a few moments later, there was another car waiting for us.

I was off to the hospital.

Boy, that was something else, I tell you. The ride was rough in the back of that little Japanese car, bleeding like a stuck pig. I tried to stretch out my legs the best I could to reduce the bleeding, but the blood kept dripping down and pooling into the crotch of my shorts. There was so much blood everywhere. It looked like fucking Hellraiser.

Finally, at the hospital, two different doctors who knew Misawa took me in and went right to work on me. They cleaned me up the best they could and gathered together the sutures. Then they started stitching. They stitched until the sun came up. Some 200 stitches later, the bleeding was contained.

I somehow finally found my way back to the hotel. I pounded on Misawa's door at something like 4 or 5 in the morning, feeling like Frankenstein's monster below the waist. The door creaked open.

"Vader?" he said, not happy to be awoken from his sleep. I didn't speak. I pushed my way into his room.

"What's wrong?"

"What's wrong? What's wrong you ask?!" I took my pants off and showed Misawa.

My legs were a mangled mess. My skin was zigzagged in ugly knife wounds. Patches of crusty blood poked everywhere from the prickly barbwire-like sutures. I looked like the victim of a mad scientist.

"What do I do?" I asked, pulling my pants back carefully over my bandaged thighs.

He asked what happened, so I told him.

"You took all the beating and didn't fight back?"

"Yes, sir."

"Good man," he said rubbing his chin in thought, trying to choose his next words carefully. "Very smart. For someone like you, that must have been tough," he said. Misawa thanked me for not fighting back. I think he was surprised that I didn't at least kill one of the little attackers. He shook his head. "This could still be very sensitive," he said, "I'll try and get this settled."

"Try? What happens if they don't go for it?"

"If I can't, maybe you will have to just leave the country."

Misawa made a few calls. It got back to Misawa that I did what I was supposed to and that Chozen was "really out of line." The bartender seemed to tell Misawa everything he needed to hear, except for one little detail. I did land that one punch in defense that probably rearranged Chozen's face. Misawa knew that Chozen was going to make some noise, and that fact wasn't going to settle well with the partners.

I remember almost passing out in the lazy boy chair in Misawa's hotel room, as he continued to talk with the partners about the incident. The buzz of Misawa talking about the future of my career in Japan was startling, but I had been through so much that night, I could hardly keep my eyes open. Eventually, the conversations stopped. Misawa was standing by my side and nudged me awake in the chair. He put his hand on my shoulder.

"Vader, again, thank you for not fighting back. But for now, I need you to just leave me for some time to pass, for things to calm down," he said.

That meant someone in the Yakuza was still not happy.

"I understand," I said.

"You can still work in Japan," Misawa continued, "but just stay out of this area when you are on this side of town."

"I understand," I said.

So just as odd as it had started, it was over. I was gone from Noah after that, with various rumors circulating on why I had left. None of them had it quite right, but I had my mind set up. I wasn't leaving Tokyo just yet.

DRIBS AND DRABS IN JAPAN

After the run-in with Chozen and his midget knife wielders, I started popping up in pretty much any promotion that could pay the price I was asking.

I was a free agent in Japan.

Diehard Japanese wrestling fans often ask which promotions I have worked for and are sometimes surprised to hear that I even worked for some of the more obscure, smaller promotions. These bookings mostly took place right after the NOAH / Yakuza fiasco, and most of them are too uneventful to even remember.

After leaving NOAH, I stuck around in Japan for another two years. I worked for Riki Chōshū's new promotion at the time called "Fighting World of Japan Pro Wrestling" which was supposed to become something really big. However, I only worked one tour with World Japan though and saw limited success. My biggest matches for Riki was over a guy named Dan Bobish. World Japan folded soon after that fight.

I bounced around in a bunch of different independent promotions after that and on January 4th, 2004, I wrestled Shinya Hashimoto in a high profile match for HUSTLE.

After that, I was back for a few dates with Mrs. Baba in All Japan. On December 5th, 2004, All Japan had me play a major part of Kohei Suwama's "Trial series."

I also worked for DDT Wrestling in the summer of 2006 and for the WRESTLELAND event in the fall of that same year.

After entering my early 50s and suffering from so many knee surgeries, I was forced to slow bookings down some in

Japan. Honestly, it was just becoming so hard to keep up with that style for me physically. Without a doubt, I had achieved what I wanted to, and that was to become one of the greatest wrestlers in Japanese wrestling history.

CHAPTER 25 - CAMEOS

On February 19, 2003, I was the big surprise for an angle a promotion was doing, pitting two classic bookers against each other; Vince Russo of the WWF and Dusty Rhodes of WCW. Appearing for my first time in Total Nonstop Action Wrestling (TNA), I helped to defend the honor of Dusty Rhodes my former booker, against Vince Russo and his tag team, the Harris Brothers. The next week, Dusty and I beat the Harris Brothers via disqualification. I then began a feud with Nikita Koloff, whose career I supposedly ended long ago. I didn't stay at TNA long, however.

I returned to WWE on a few occasions. On the October 31, 2005, episode of Raw they enlisted Goldust and me to be back up for Jonathan Coachman.

As the story goes, Jim Ross was fired leading up to a special stipulation match where he could possibly regain his job. Steve Austin agreed to face Coachman at *Taboo Tuesday* with the stipulation that Ross would get his old announcing job back if Austin won. However, Austin would lose his own job if he lost. I was excited to work with Austin again because Coachman was not a wrestler. Goldust and I were there to pretty much take all the heat for him – meaning we would work spots with Austin.

Austin never made it to that match and the job stipulation storyline was dropped.

Vince knew fans would be pissed. To explain such a huge name like Steve Austin missing from Taboo Tuesday, he said on Raw that Austin got in a bad car accident. Vince was smart. Fans couldn't really be upset with that. Therefore, Dave Batista was brought in to take Austin's place. In the end, Batista defeated Jonathan Coachman along with me and Goldust.

What really happened was Austin really hurt his back badly a few days before and just could not wrestle. Rather than to just cut the match altogether from the Tuesday PPV and have us lose a payday, Vince decided to still give us the work.

On the June 11th episode of Raw in 2012, I had another WWE appearance. This was for part of a great angle they were running with Heath Slater, where he took on a different legend every week leading up to the 1000th episode of Raw. What would happen was, Heath would come out every show and talk smack until a WWE legend would finally come out and beat him.

I had my turn with Heath Slater and defeated him in a singles match. It was just like the good old days.

Then finally the 1000th episode of Raw came, and the angle continued. I was a legend lumberjack of sorts, keeping Slater from leaving a match with Lita, which she went on to win.

CAMEO AT THE HALL OF FAME

One of my fondest cameo returns to WWE was when they booked me to be a guest at the Hall of Fame. Vince flew me out to sit in the audience and just have a good time to further add to the appeal and the overall feel of legitimacy of the yearly event.

Even though I really, really, really take it seriously and want to be included in it, some say the WWE Hall of Fame is not legitimate. They claim it is all a big money-making work and that they book it like a wrestling show. I don't care. I want in.

As far as the actual wrestlers are concerned, they induct a main eventer, a tag team, a female wrestler, an old timer and a minority every year. They also book a celebrity for the entertainment part of wrestling. I know – weird. The idea of who actually achieved the most or had the best in-ring ability has very little to do with it. Many believe that is just an attraction to hype WrestleMania each year, and that is it. However, it does still mean a lot to some of us old timers, and I hope they will include me anyhow one day. That ring would look awfully nice next to my Super Bowl ring. Just sayin'.

I remember walking in before it was open to the public. The vibe that was being set had a high school reunion feel to it. You wanted to feel like you were successful to everyone, and you had to be on your toes, ready to impress others. Nobody wanted to look like the welfare case that had nothing going on.

The director showed me where I was to sit, but I wasn't ready to do that. I walked around for some time and got to say hi to a lot of people who meant a lot to me. Dusty Rhodes and Jim Ross were the first ones I went to. They were always big supports for me, so it was great to catch up with them and thank them once again for all they had done for me.

I saw all kinds of faces I hadn't seen in years, and it was really cool to catch up with a bunch of them. In the twilight of most of their careers, a lot of the wrestlers I shared time in the ring with were now fathers and even grandfathers with new perspectives on life. Some were clearly less self-centered, while others were now totally living their lives for their offspring.

It was nice to mend some broken fences, as well. I talked to Flair a little and we let bygones be bygones. Though I know he was instrumental in holding me back from time to time, he also was a big part of my history, and there was no ignoring that. We shook hands, Flair can really be a class act when he wants to be. He is one of the truly very gifted athletes I have worked with, and I had to hand it to him.

After speaking with Flair, I saw another familiar face out of the corner of my eye. It was Shawn Michaels. I hadn't seen Shawn for some time, but believe me, hanging with him wasn't really my idea of fun. Even though that SummerSlam fiasco was years ago at the time, it was still always the big elephant in the room for us.

I held some resentment towards him, I cannot lie. I didn't want to even talk with Shawn. I saw him start to approach me, and I made a point to get tangled up with someone else to avoid him.

I remember I found myself talking with a producer I didn't even know, so as to not have to talk with Michaels. I wasn't really listening, however. What I was really doing was thinking about what I was going to say, and how I was going to react if I ended up having to talk with Shawn.

To look and see where Shawn had made it was a real surprise to me. By the way, he ran wild back with the women and the mischief in his AWA days, I actually thought he should have done twenty years ago. But there I was, wandering around confused at what to do with Shawn Michaels shadowing me at an event, clearly waiting for a word with me.

Shawn finally cornered me just before the event had started. He shook my hand, and I looked the other way. I was ignoring him and he knew it. I was short with him, and he wanted more, but I was saved by the bell. The show started. We took our seats and I know not giving him closure was bothering him.

After one of the guys was inducted, they broke for a period of time and Shawn came running right back over to me.

"Listen, Vader," he said. "I just wanted to say I'm sorry."

Oh, geesh. This is going to be good.

"I'm sorry for being an asshole," he said. "I'm trying to be a better person, now and I want you to know it bothers me that I wasn't the best I could have been." I listened to him continue. "I'm pretty surprised that you never just beat the shit out of me. Why didn't you just stop me from being an asshole?" Shawn asked, seeming to be the most sincere I had ever seen him.

I started to see him in a new light and it was good. He owed me nothing and didn't have to come humble himself to me, but he did. That took real courage and he instantly started getting some of my respect back.

I went on to tell him about the shopping center I was building and that I couldn't afford to lose my job for my family's sake, or else I would have considered kicking his ass.

Shawn looked pretty sad at what I had to say. He had a family now too and understood. He admitted that he was a different person back then and had since "seen the light." His faith really did do wonders for him.

"I'm sorry man," he said. "If I was someone who had to deal with the old me back then, I would have probably just punched me in the face." Then, he asked for forgiveness.

I suppose I could have said, "Too little, too late," but that would do nobody any good. I forgave him. The closure I felt immediately was real. Not wanting to forgive was an obstacle for me, but once I did, I wished we cleared the air long ago.

Everyone has been hurt by the actions of another. Not being able to move on and forgive someone creates permanent mental injuries. These wounds can leave you with lasting feelings of anger, bitterness, depression or even insatiable vengeance. I have been there and held onto bad stuff and it didn't help me in the least. Now, I'm working on overcoming these obstacles.

It's true. If you don't practice forgiveness, you hold onto bad energy and might be the one who pays for it in the end more than the person you resent. I've learned that forgiveness can lead you down a better path, just like Shawn Michaels said at the Hall of Fame.

CHAPTER 26 - THE COMEBACK

After my career slowed down, I started picking up some bad habits. I started doing some recreational drugs to pass time, and I also started to develop a really bad diet. A few drugs led to doing more and more illegal drugs and also drinking too much.

This really took a toll on my body and also my relationships. Eventually, all this bad stuff going into me led to something good going out. All that garbage was a major reason why my wife and I broke up. After she left, things only got worse.

Without a "better half" around to regulate things, I stopped taking care of myself. I was working out less and basically, started living off of dollar-menu fast-food shit. I never went to the supermarket to shop to try and eat right. No vegetables, no nutrition, just shit. Most every day for me consisted of me stopping by McDonalds for some McFilth. Sometimes three times a day I was pigging out on cheap greasy cheeseburgers and other bad, fried foods. Couple this with a growing addiction to illegal drugs, and it couldn't have been good for my body.

It wasn't good. I wasn't listening to the warning signals.

TOXINS

There was a guy in Oklahoma that owned a bar and started up a little wrestling company. I had worked with him a number of times, and he approached me at an independent show. He wanted to build a school into the side of his bar and charged students to take wrestling lessons. Then, to follow the typical independent wrestling model, he would also run shows there starring some of the students as talent.

He wanted credibility to draw money, so he asked me to come in and teach some of the classes and also take over the book on his shows.

At first, I figured that it would give me something to do. I would have less down time on my hands to continue to screw up my life up. I wanted the distraction, and I needed the money. This idea of moving to Oklahoma was also good because my son also lived there, and then I would get to see him more. I agreed and grabbed up a hotel room (not an apartment) nearby to give it a whirl. Eventually, I knew it would fold, but it was something for the moment when nobody else was calling.

The promoter did his job. He hustled some money and found some wannabe superstars with some cash to throw around. I showed up the first day and did a speech for a class of about 15 or so wide-eyed hopefuls. After my talk, I showed them the basics and ran the best drills I could for the first day. It started out pretty well, and the kids were buying it.

By the end of the night, however, the one factor that I hadn't thought of immediately came into play.

The school was in the same building as a bar.

One of the reasons I took the job was to stay busy and away from the bad stuff. It doesn't take a brain surgeon to guess what happened next. After a few hard hours of training, we got "thirsty." It didn't take long at all. The first day of training ended and we just moved from one room to the other. *Training Day One* quickly became sitting around with a couple of the boys, getting drunk and talking about wrestling.

After one really long day and a long night of drinking after that, that was it. The first flag was thrown.

I don't remember how it ended. I don't remember how I got back to the hotel or anything. The next day I woke up slowly. I tried to stretch my arms before opening my eyes, and it felt like I had been hit by a freight train. "What the hell?" I thought. As I awoke painfully, I heard some kind of beeping sound. I looked around. I was not in my own clothing, and I was not in my hotel room. I opened my eyes to see a drip bag and a heart monitor machine.

I was in a hospital.

In a panic, I tried to get out of bed, but I could barely move. My joints and everything ached and didn't work at all. Trying to jump out of bed looked more like a slow roll to my knees. Hearing the struggle, I remember a pretty nurse coming over to my bedside.

"Hold on there," she said, barring my way.

"What happened to me?" I asked.

"We are trying to figure that out right now," she replied. "Your buddies dropped you off. You couldn't move."

I didn't know if I looked worried, but I didn't say anything. *I still couldn't move.*

"It's okay, honey. You'll be alright." Seeing me in distress, she continued, "You just need to stay off your feet for a few days."

I stayed there off my feet for a few weeks in that very same bed, but not because I wanted to. I was hardly able to move and not even able to use the restroom by myself. Thank God I had insurance. In hindsight, I can't imagine what the bill would have been if I didn't have my own plan. At the time, however, I wasn't worried about money.

Somewhere into the second week of my stay, I was fed up with calling the nurse just so I could poop. Determined to walk twenty feet on my own two feet, I pushed myself out of the bed and pulled myself up. I took one step and immediately my legs crumbled under my own weight.

It was over. "This is it. I am an old man," I said out loud in teary eyes. I didn't know what was going on in my body. I figured it must have been all those bumps I ignored in the ring finally catching up to me, all at once. I felt like I had aged 30 years overnight.

I sat on the floor unable to move and shook my head in disbelief. I believed that my youth was finally gone and that I would likely never walk again. It was a very scary feeling and nothing like I had ever experienced before. Vader was supposed to be the man with no fear. Leon White was shitting his pants, both figuratively and literally.

After about twenty minutes of trying to pull myself back up onto the bed by myself, I gave up and tapped out. I called for the nurse, humiliated.

"Help," I said quietly first, defeated. "Help! Nurse!"

The nice lady came in and saw me on the floor. "No, no, Leon. Hold on." She ducked out for a moment and came back with a reinforcement.

"I'm sorry," I said choking down a sob, as the custodian and the nurse pushed me back up to the bed.

"It's okay, honey. This is what we are here for."

A few more days went by, and I did get a little strength back, at least enough to move a little. Eventually, my son came and helped me check out. He wheel chaired me out to his car.

I didn't talk much until we were on the road. I was too embarrassed to admit drugs and alcohol had done the damage, and I pretty much did all that to myself. "The doctors said I had an allergic reaction to something," I lied. "Hey listen, I may need some help getting to the airport tomorrow."

"Say no more," Jesse said, always there to help.

I stayed in the hotel room alone that night to really dwell on what the doctor told me on the way out. "Due to a lifestyle of drugs, alcohol, and beating on your body with wrestling, you have developed Rheumatoid arthritis."

I could walk, but barely. Every step was a battle and it hurt like hell. In the morning, I was spent. I had to be carried out of there for the flight home.

I finally got back home to my condo in Colorado, but I was really down on myself. This led to some more drinking, which I know didn't help. I didn't know if the "old man feeling" was permanent or not and started to accept the fact that the aches and pains in my joints may be a new constant reality for me.

Fortunately for me, I had time. I became a depressed detective. I made a lot of phone calls to see if someone could do something to fix what the hospital couldn't. After a lot of dead ends, I finally got a call from a doctor friend of mine who knew a specialist from Germany in the States who thought he could help.

I made the appointment. The specialist looked me over and in a few minutes, he seemed to know right away what to do. "You have a lot of junk in your system," he said. "If you eat clean and stay away from ALL the bad stuff, we can fix it."

A heavy weight was lifted off my shoulders. *We were going the cleansing route.* He gave me something to clean out the toxins in my blood and I soon learned that he was right!

A few days later, I felt much better. A few months later, I had done pretty well for myself. I was eating better and staying away from the bad stuff that knocked me out. I was working out again and slowly but surely, I finally started to feel like myself.

I accepted some bookings and was pretty excited to get to go back to my old stomping grounds where I would really feel alive again.

Flying to Japan was a long trip. It was something like 16 hours. Right before the flight, I had a good workout to try and wear myself out so I could sleep as I always did; that usually did the trick.

Excited to be back on the scene or something, it wasn't working this time. An hour or two after liftoff, I was still very alert. I knew I needed some sleep to be on my game in Japan with the time difference, so I reached above my head for my carry-on to look at some magazines.

Getting my groove back felt really good. I was on the road again after feeling like my life was over, finally back in a state of normalcy. I felt at home doing something again that felt normal. There was no pain, and I was in control. I flipped through a magazine and when I was done, I reached back into my trusty carry-on for another.

I remember looking at an older wrestling magazine that I had packed in there some time ago, but it didn't take long before I was getting sleepy. I had just popped a couple of sleeping pills that I had also found in my bag, and they were working fast.

"These are some pills," I thought to myself as I could barely hold my eyes open.

Everything went black.

The pills kicked in and my blood sugar went so high that I went into a diabetic-related coma for close to 40 days.

Now, I didn't even know I was diabetic.

I was out cold for over a whole month of my life.

OUT OF BODY EXPERIENCE

One of the oddest obstacles I have ever faced in my life was death itself. During the darkness period, I felt a vibration in my body. I heard the wind in my ears. The urge to move was tremendous, but it felt like a lead blanket was weighing me down. I couldn't move my arms or legs on my own, but I was still moving.

I was drifting.

I was floating.

It felt like I was stuck in a current, like in a river, I thought, but I couldn't see.

The darkness eventually lifted. It was hard to see at first. Everything was blurry, but my eyes slowly began to focus. Something square and white was below me. The center came to focus.

I was floating above a bed and looking down. There was that beeping sound, again. There was a heart monitor. "Am I still in Oklahoma?" I wondered. "Have I been dreaming the whole time?"

I started to panic. "Maybe I never made it home and never made it to that specialist," I thought. "What if I was still in pain after that first red flag and never well enough to get on that plane to Tokyo? What if that was all a dream?"

I was in a daze.

"Who is that fucking old bald guy?"

I looked down at the frail man, motionless. He was on his side lying in the bed. I was drawn to the body. "I can't see his face. I can't see his face. I need to see."

I hovered along the ceiling in a corner. I managed to swim and to pull my way over to the other side of the room.

It took a moment, but I finally recognized the face. It was very similar to the same one that always looked back at me in the mirror, but this one was more wrinkled... More sullen... More dead?

"NOOO! No, I'm dead!"

I tried to yell but nothing came out. It was like my vocal chords were locked. I wanted the nurse to come and tell me everything would be alright, but she wouldn't come.

"I am alone," I cried, but without hearing my own words.

I stared a long time at my own old, wrinkled body. It seemed alien to me like it wasn't even me, but I know it was. I tried to spin around. There was an urge to go up towards the sun. It was like the sky was pulling me and I was falling upward.

I held myself down and floated around the hospital room some more. I wanted to get out of it. I wanted to just go up and out toward the light above me. Sick of fighting the pull, I let the current take me out of the room. It pulled me higher and higher, then I stopped still in midair.

"Leon, it's not your time."

I don't know if I was imagining my dead aunts and uncles, or if I could actually see them in front of me. I saw what I believed was them and they were holding their hands up towards me.

I didn't want to go back to my body. I could sense it was painful being in that body.

"Leon, it's not your time."

I felt a new pull towards the bed. I swam away from it, but then it was too much. Suddenly I was back in my body on the bed. I felt all the pain at once again and it was horrible. My body ached. My head hurt. I didn't want to be there. I wanted to be back in the air. I pushed off the body, much like you would push off the wall in the side of a swimming pool.

I was back in the air. The pain was gone again, and I drifted back toward the sun pulling me above the room. The gravitational pull to the bed started again, so I allowed myself to be pulled to the doorframe and drifted out of the room.

Tokyo hospital. Long term care.

I was not in Oklahoma. I had been in this hospital before after some strong-style New Japan matches, but I was never in this part of the hospital before. I didn't know how to get out.

I floated down the hall. "Hello. Hello?!"

Japanese nurses and doctors were going about their daily businesses. They couldn't hear or see me. I drifted into a neighboring room. A family was gathered around a bed, crying. I circled around the bed and saw an empty shell in it. In the corner, an old man sitting in a chair looked at me and made eye contact. He shook his head. I stared at him for a few moments and watched him float quietly up into the ceiling and out of sight.

I tried to follow him but could not. The pull back to my room became stronger, but I didn't want to feel that pain again. Everything felt good outside of the body that was laying there in the bed. I fought the pull.

Panicking, I decided to plan an escape route out of the building. I started to really explore the hospital. After some detective work, I found there were about seven turns to get out. The final turn wasn't really an official exit, but rather a glass door that led you out into a beautiful Japanese garden.

I couldn't open the door, but I could see my way out. The garden had beautiful flowers and well-trimmed shrubs. It had Buddhist and Shinto statues. I wanted to be there. I pulled on the door again, but it wouldn't move.

Something told me I needed my body to open the door, so I followed the pull back to my room. After I made those seven turns back to my bedside, I could clearly see my body again. It was a wrinkled mess and scared me.

I tried to turn again and hoped to go through the ceiling but the pull was too strong.

I jumped in and out of the body. Each time I entered it, a wave of pain surrounded me and made me push away from it. I probably jumped back out of the body and back into it a dozen times. The last time, I fought to get back out and I couldn't.

Tokyo hospital. Long term care.

I finally woke up in my body. Everything ached but I could move. A bunch of things were anchoring my sore body down to the bed, and I needed to make it to the glass door. I needed to get out of that hospital.

I still had the urge to escape. I sat up and pulled a bunch of electrodes off me. I yanked an IV needle out of me and pulled an EKG monitor off me as well.

I made it to my feet for the first time in almost 40 days and stumbled in front of the mirror. I had lost 100 pounds or more and was down to 312. My skin was hanging off me. I looked in that mirror and started crying. My face looked like it was melting. I had skin hanging off my arms and chin and legs. "Everything is gone. All these years of hard work in the gym are gone," I said to myself. Seemingly only a few hours ago, I was flying to a Japanese wrestling event a big strong man, and now I could barely walk and looked like an old man.

It was scary, very scary, and I needed to get out of there.

With the last bits of energy I had, I ran as fast as I could on pins and needles. I followed the escape route I had planned exactly. After my seven turns, I landed in front of the glass door. I pushed it open and made my exit.

I was standing in the Japanese garden in a hospital smock with my naked wrinkled ass open to the world.

There were little flowers everywhere etching the slate walkway. A beautiful fountain poured out its contents into a stream. A lovely wooden bride arched over a coy fish pond. I looked down into the water, with all the beauty of nature around me and saw my reflection.

I looked like a dead Saint Bernard.

"Mister White. Mister White!" A Japanese doctor said in broken English, interrupting me. "Please come back inside."

I ignored him for a moment and turned around. He led me back to my room. Each step felt like hell. My knees were on fire.

"How did you find your way out of the hospital so fast?" he asked.

SLAYING MONSTERS

Arthritis really set in all throughout my body. The coma went from bad to worse with the new pain in my knees. I could barely get up to use the restroom. Not moving for so long had done even further damage to my already banged-up knees. The Japanese doctor told me I could go home, but that I had to have both of my knees looked at as soon as I got there.

He also told me that I was diabetic and that this was the cause of all this. I guess because I was so big and strong, I always just pushed through any symptoms, just thinking it was body aches from wrestling. While I knew that this illness was life-changing, I didn't much worry about it at the time. I really just wanted to get the fuck out of there.

After I returned to the States, I would basically find myself in bed for another year and a half after that coma.

I knew I had to do something, so I just said fuck it. No more alcohol and no more chewing tobacco.

I quit cold turkey.

Now, I know some people are probably thinking "both at the same time?!" What a stupid idea. You know what? You are right. It was one of the hardest things I ever did. I remember two or three nights after withdrawals, I was going nuts. I was shaking. I was breaking out in body sweats. I couldn't sleep because of withdrawals on top of already not being able to sleep very well.

I couldn't take it anymore. I mean, I know I always wanted to come off as the big strong monster, but killing two massive monsters off at the same time like this was impossible. I couldn't do it alone. I picked up the phone and asked for help. I called the ambulance when my heart was racing a million miles a minute. They came over and gave me IV fluids and sat with me, and things finally started to get better.

The toxins were leaving me. With me slaying the two monsters, I could finally attack the other problem.

I had insurance, but it didn't really cover lost income. Luckily for me, I had signed a deal with a Japanese company called ADK to allow them to use my likeness in commercials and promotion for their products. They honored their eight-year agreement with me even though I couldn't make any live appearances for commercial shootings. With their money, my insurance, and my savings, at least I knew everything would be covered.

I was tired of being in pain. My knees were hurting like nothing I had ever experienced before. I thought it was because of the arthritis, or maybe it had something to do with the 21 knee operations I had between my football and wrestling careers. I started taking four or five OxyContin just to get through the day and it worked, but I knew that this was something I didn't want to do forever. When I felt like I was getting addicted to guzzling down pills as a normal way of life, I knew I needed help.

I went to my doctor and started discussions about knee replacement. The doctor convinced me to get both of my knees replaced at the same time. I originally thought it was a great idea, but in hindsight, it is something I regret doing drastically.

The first surgery was a success. My son Jesse came home from college. He sat with me for days before and after the operation. In the hospital room, Jesse fed me, the same as I fed him as a baby. I eventually was discharged from the hospital and sent back home. There, Jesse helped me with my recovery and PT at home. He stayed as long as he absolutely could. I practically had to beg him to leave. He really wanted to stay and help but he had to go back to school. After he left, I went to my first follow up appointment to monitor my recovery. I thought everything was going well, but then the doctors said my wounds were not healing. After doing some tests, we learned that there was a horrible infection in both of my knees. I needed emergency surgery before things got worse. Little did I know, I would have a total of three surgeries over the next ten days.

After the second surgery, my knees were still infected. My body was rejecting the titanium and again I had to go under for a third double knee replacement. Yes, you read that correctly. They replaced both of my knees a third time! When they became infected yet a third again, I felt like the hospital was against me… like it had to be a plot against me. You could have told me any of the wildest conspiracy theories in the world and I would have believed them then. I started thinking they were doing something wrong on purpose to do me in, to save money for some rogue medical insurance company that made ends meet by faking operations and greasing the palms of dirty doctors to save a buck in the long run. It was driving me nuts.

I heard from the doctors that someone called them up and told them who I was. They pleaded to the insurance company to give me one more try with another operation, but the insurance company told the doctors that they were all done with the funding. They had given up hope, but I'm glad everyone didn't. My good friend Tom Perry, you remember, my old football teammate who got a hole drilled in his head to relieve the pressure, he came down and started raising hell. He went off on anybody who would listen.

"What do you mean the insurance isn't going to cover the fourth operation?!" he would say at the top of his lungs in every office in the hospital. Tom fought for me real hard. He brought an attorney into the insurance company and threatened them within an inch of their lives.

In the end, they decided to try one last technique to save my legs to shut good old Tom up. They opened me up and did like a power wash type thing. They cleaned out the whole area and scrubbed up all the muscles and the entire inner area of the prosthesis.

When I finally came to, Tom was there.

"They said you have three days to see if your knees will take this time, if not, there is some discussion about amputating your legs," Tom said. "But that's not going to happen. I'll be here pulling for you." And pull for me he did.

Let me tell you, boy. That was a very long three days to stabilize. I was under a lot of pain medication, but when I was conscious, I was praying to Jesus and I was scared to death. If the prosthetic knees didn't take, there was no way I was going to live with two prosthetic legs. I was actually praying for the worst.

After the operation, I was slammed with some more bad news. "Leon," the doctor said, "because of the high cost of these operations, your insurance is likely going to cancel you." And that they did.

After the three or four days I could stay in the hospital, they needed to send me into a homecare facility where I could get attention 24/7 and it wasn't going to be cheap.

I woke up for the start of a good four-month stay in Boulder Manor.

"Argh!" a phlegm-filled throaty voice bellowed by my side. "Arrrggghhh!"

I looked around and saw the really old, ugly, yellow wallpaper and my three new roommates. The air had the obscene, sterile, senile home smell that I just hate. While surveying the situation, I saw one of my new roomies bang out a deuce into his bedpan and pass out in a cloud of his own farts.

Because the state was picking up some of the bill for them, I was really sharing quarters with the cream of the crop, and none of them had any money. There was a crack addict, a deranged war vet, and someone who I think was legitimately just dead.

Without insurance due to being high risk, everything was out of pocket. Some days, some of the tests and services that they provided me with came to around $1,000. I remember one particular day, whatever they did was in the area of upwards $20,000!

It was during this time that today's medical system failed me. Rather than to address serious problems, they just doped me up on sleeping pills and painkillers and waited for me to heal.

Four months of excessive medicating created a new obstacle that I never thought I would fall subject to. Pumping me up with meds eventually turned me into a bit of a junkie for that crap – so much so I would actually have to go to rehab for it later on in life. I needed pills just to get by. At one point after all that, I was taking 240 Vicodins a month, like 100 more than was recommended.

The nights were tough. I would sometimes get wired up on something they gave me and actually couldn't sleep. I would get just too jittery. I would hear moans and screams somewhere down the hall. Then I would hear the crack addict snore like a hog. It would get quiet, and I would concentrate on the drip of a dangling bag of liquids somewhere above my head to try and fall asleep. I would feel like I was just about to finally get some rest when all the sudden, the war vet would jump out of the bed in some kind of post-traumatic stress fit.

"Nancy! Nancyyy!" he would yell at the top of his lungs dodging invisible bullets.

"Would you shut the hell up, Earl?" the crack addict would say. "She's not here. Now, get back into bed and get some sleep!"

It was like a scene out of *One Flew Over the Cuckoo's Nest*. I remember lying there at night and staring at the ceiling. I contemplated suicide. It was one of the darkest times in my life. It was then that I really started praying and talking to God. I mean, I always believed in God and had my faith, but when you are down and out like I was, praying all the time becomes a very easy habit.

After about four months of this living hell on a piss-stained mattress, they did some tests and told me I was good to go. Thank God, the prosthetic knees finally took, but I would soon learn that I didn't have very much time to celebrate.

Jesse was still attending college and couldn't be missing school to play nurse for me. So somebody else stepped up. Even though we had our differences, during this time my ex-wife went out of her way to take me in to help me during the recovery. She didn't have to do that at all, but this really speaks on the type of person that she is and I am still forever grateful.

Even though I made it out of the Cuckoo's Nest, my new knees were functional, but I couldn't really walk. I wasn't strong enough quite yet to use my new knees, and something else was really holding me down. Immediately after my knees seemed to be coming out from the darkness, my back started to fail.

My back became a big problem for about six months. The doctors said it stemmed from being forced to lie on it for so long while my knees were healing. During the recovery from the knee operations, I weakened my back so much that I couldn't rehab to learn how to walk again. Then, I had to go back into the hospital to have a very serious back surgery.

My breathing was down because of my back pain, and I went into critical condition. They rushed me into the emergency room and cut me open. Once they got in there, they found all kinds of stuff. I had wrestled for 30 years and my back was a mess. They kept me under too long trying to set things right and the alarm went off - *I was dying.*

Fortunately for me, they immediately said, "Quick. Just close him up!"

If I had been under for even a minute or two longer, I would have died right then. My breathing dropped down to three to four breaths a minute and there wasn't much they could do.

In the wake up room, they really had some difficulty trying to wake me up. They had a nurse in there for hours who kept touching me and talking to me. Eventually, I snapped out of it, but it wasn't over.

There was another whole year of rehab for both my knees and my back.

During this time, I decided to get my shoulder surgery done as well. I honestly didn't know if I was going to make it through everything so I figured I might as well get everything fixed at once. I had a lot of time. I couldn't use my shoulder very well, and when they finally operated, they took two thirds of AC joint out and replaced it with an artificial substance.

Fortunately for me, the operations took, but not without a cost. After the coma incident, I was smaller and weaker. I was also eating up pain pills like they were candy, and honestly got addicted.

CHAPTER 27 – SON, SLEEP, & THE LOVE OF THE GAME

My mother had a hard time disciplining us as kids. Our father had left us early. He left me even before I was even a teenager. This made things hard on us financially, as well as developmentally. While it isn't an excuse, I didn't have a great example to show me exactly what to do when my son came along. I had a job that really kept me away from him, but I always tried to do him the best I could.

THE SON OF VADER

For me and my son, I wasn't always in what you call a traditional relationship during his childhood. Before Jesse was born, I was always on the road. I was in a relationship with a really good-looking woman. She probably wasn't the best girl for me in the long term; a guy on the road so much who could get easily paranoid from the ins-and-outs wrestling business and think the worst. She may have not been the best for me as a wife, but she was the best mother anyone could hope for to raise my son.

Before I had a chance to break things off with her, the next thing you know she was pregnant with my baby.

I know it was possible I could have easily followed in the steps of my father, but I didn't want to do that to my baby. I refused to follow in the footsteps of my dad. I knew firsthand what it was like not to have that father figure in my life. I know I made some bad decisions. A good father could have helped me to refigure those moves before they could have even happened. I wanted to give my son at least that option.

So I had a come-to-Jesus moment with that baby before he was even born. I made a commitment to my unborn son, a child that I didn't know yet, that I would not be that guy and I would never leave him.

While the marriage didn't turn out the best, I think Jesse turned out pretty good.

I wanted the very best for the "Son of Vader." Growing up, Jesse always went to private schools. We could have sent him to a public school, but I only wanted the very best for him. I wanted him to get the best grades and be the best he could be. I didn't want him to have to endure the distractions that I had from a city school, but I still wanted him to have a good experience with sports. Therefore, the high school we went to was very good at football.

Around my WWF transition to All Japan, I had spent $200,000 on what was supposed to be a 2,000 square foot guest home. What a real good gym that turned out to be! I might have put the fear of God into Jesse about never missing a work out.

My buddy Dave Logan played football for The Cleveland Browns. He had a nine-season career in the NFL and continued on as a radio personality on AM radio as "The voice of the Broncos." He was also the football coach at Jesse's high school. He helped make my son an All-American. During Jesse's football days, he was a 6'1' center, benching 500 pounds. He had strength and skill. If he had been only two inches taller, he probably would have gone even further than he did.

I really loved the fact that Jesse came to me for advice with his football. Me being there for him helped him with his work ethic and also helped him to understand the importance of graduating with honors. He knew my backstory with the shortened football career and took my advice.

Jesse got a call from the University of Oklahoma and accepted a full scholarship to play for the Sooners.

After football was over for Jesse, my career was winding down. I no longer had a son to live vicariously through football, and I started feeling old. Maybe depression kicked in again, I don't know, but I was really starting to fall apart around this time.

I had let my marriage go. I had let my health go. I had let my body go. I honestly felt like I was dying. There was a period of time for about a year where I wouldn't even leave my little condo. I stayed home all day in the dark. I stopped working out. I wouldn't even leave the house to get groceries; I just had them delivered to the door.

Then one day something happened that changed my life. Hell, it saved my life.

"Dad, I think I want to wrestle."

While my knee replacements and my back surgery had eventually become successful, I was in no physical shape to train my son, but this request was the best thing that could happen to me. I needed to get back in shape and live again to help someone else.

No longer worrying about me, I started eating right. I got back in the gym. I started feeling the blood pumping through my veins again. I had a reason to live again.

I was back in the gym. I was back to eating right. It took a lot out of me to get back to trying to eat right and gain some muscle back, but little by little I saw improvement. My strength improved. My skin tightened up a little.

Despite the fact I didn't have a whole lot of motivation before, I did have a nice condo. I was fortunate enough to be able to get into my Jacuzzi every night as part of my own personal rehab plan before bed.

I remember sitting in the gym trying to come back, looking in the mirror at 2 AM.

"You have to be able to lift 50 pounds, I said.

I was speaking to myself. I was all alone.

It was a lot of hard work. All the while, I was doing it for myself and also doing it to be the father I never had growing up. The incredible journey was all putting one foot in front of the other, with baby steps, the entire way. The first night I was lifting 50 pounds on the bench. The next night it was 52 pounds. The next night it was 53, and so on and so on.

I came back from all of this, and I didn't just come back. I came back and excelled.

Once the timing was right, I had a promotion all set up in Japan, ready to go. The same Japanese media company that was paying me under contract during recovery of my knee replacements set up a whole wrestling promotion that was eventually to be focused around the Son of Vader!

They didn't want it to just be him, however. They wanted it to be a passing of the torch kind of thing over a period of time where I would actually tag team with Jesse to show him the rite of passage. It was a great idea. I loved it because it meant that Jesse would get a whole other style under his belt from working in Japan. This would make him super valuable in the eyes of American promoters.

I flew over to help get the company going and once we were ready, I told him to come live with me in Japan. On April 29th, 2010, I made a one-night return to wrestling at a wrestling event called "Return of the Emperor."

At the show, I teamed with my son Jesse and former tag-team partner Scorpio to successfully defeat Makoto Hashi, Tamon Honda, and Tatsumi Fujinami in the main event. Wrestling with my son was tremendous for me. He was the apple of my eye.

I would get to do it one more time in aftermath of the 2011 natural disasters in Japan. Jesse and I got to wrestle on some very special tribute cards for All Japan Pro Wrestling and Pro Wrestling Zero1. I stayed in Japan and started to make some deals that could have really panned out for the both of us. However, before we could do it again, and before I could really set up something big for Jesse, WWE called and booked him for a tryout.

Ten days after the tryout, Jesse was offered a contract. My idea was if I had just had a few weeks, I could have gotten my sponsor to make him an offer and get him going in All Japan's dojo, the same company that Giant Baba had put on the map.

I had everyone interested in the Vader & Son concept. New Japan, All Japan, NOAH, and others. I was paid $80,000 for one of their tournaments alone there and every show was sold out. Jesse would have been a star, but he was reluctant at first.

"Please Jesse, come to Japan first and train with our guys and then we can send you over to the WWE training camp. They will wait."

"But what if they won't Dad?" he asked me. "Dad, what if this is my only chance. I have to take it now."

It was tough to argue with him. I know the offer from WWE felt like winning the biggest football game ever to him. I really didn't want to piss on his celebration party, but I believed that having a little patience would have been a solid investment in his future.

"Jesse, they will eat you up at the training facility if you go now," I pleaded. "You can't show up with no training at all. It's super competitive. If you show up and need to be trained from square one, you will just get lost in the shuffle. They aren't equipped for that. You need to make an impact right away, or it's over."

I really wanted him to get all the styles and holds from the Japanese dojos and then have him head over to WWE's early version of NXT.

However, Jesse had inherited the stubbornness of his own father.

As any other kid would do who watched wrestling since he was a baby, he got all excited and wanted to immediately go to WWE before he was ready, in my opinion. I figured Japan would have been great for him on many levels. It would have cut his weight and give him a whole style that would a few years later give him the edge he needed at the training facility. It would have also given him invaluable experience and he would have learned how to really tell a story in the ring.

Instead of coming in on top to turn heads, Jesse wanted to go to NXT before he was ready at the risk of just looking average.

We bumped heads a bit and I feel bad about this even today. It is one of my very few regrets in life. A day or so later after that call from WWE, I called back and said, "Jesse it's final. You are going to Japan first. You need the experience first and the look of a wrestler."

"I can't miss this opportunity dad," he argued.

He gave it a shot and didn't do so badly. He became an NXT Tag Champion along with the now Monday Night RAW announcer Corey Graves. Wrestling as "Jake Carter," he was there for about two years or so and could have gone even further. But then he got hurt, and that slowed things down for him in WWE developmental.

Today, Jesse is doing very well for himself. Rather than continue his wrestling career, he followed my advice and got out of the wrestling business. He put his college degree to use and is doing great in health care sales. While he may have missed his wrestling calling due to circumstances, he doesn't have to take bumps at all and he doesn't have to live his life on the road. This gives me good peace of mind.

MODERN DAY GLADIATOR

I have never really told anyone this because it feels like a weakness, but I have a very difficult time falling asleep. For the past ten years of my life, I have had some kind of chronic insomnia. Until recently, whatever the problem was, I don't know, but I haven't had a decent night's sleep for years.

While writing this book with Kenny, a real bad spell came on and I couldn't sleep for four nights in a row. This happened often. Finally, I slept a little bit. Then starting the very next night, I stayed up for almost two weeks straight.

It may not sound like much to someone who has never experienced it, but a lack of sleep seriously messes with your overall health. For anyone who is struggling, I highly suggest doing the research on what a lack of sleep does to your body and also seeing a sleep specialist.

Out of desperation, I decided to finally admit defeat and I set up an appointment with a sleep institute.

I learned that sleep deprivation is horrible. It reduces performance and alertness. It affects your memory and your ability to think/process information. It causes stress on people's relationships. It increases your chance for occupational accidents and automobile accidents. It also creates a poor quality of life, due to a lack of energy.

I also learned that it physically is bad for your health. It leads to high blood pressure, Attention Deficit Disorder, stroke, and even heart failure,

Terrorists have found that sleep deprivation is an awesome form of torture. Some take their victim and hit them with an electric shock every two minutes so they simply cannot sleep. They also take your eyelids and stitch it to your eyebrows so you can't close your eyes.

Realizing I had barely slept in ten years, I identified the suicidal-type feeling I experience every time I lay down and know that I can't fall sleep.

Just to get by during the day and stay alert, I found in recent years that I needed a pick me up to survive the day. The lack of sleep makes you grumpy as hell. On days where I have personal appearances, I've found I need to drink two of those 5-hour Energy drinks. That is the only way sometimes that I would be able to be good to the people that come to see me at autograph signings, after a round of days with no sleep.

On literally no sleep again, I found my way to a real smart guy that I hoped could help me. I was told that this was the doctor to find. He had an IQ of 200.

I sat down in the office of Doctor Ricard. He was a compassionate man, but as he sat down I could have sworn I heard him laugh.

"What is so funny?" I said, acting a little on the defensive.

"Oh, nothing. Now, please. Tell me a little bit about your problems."

I went on to tell him about only getting a few hours of sleep a night and having to take sleeping pills. When I mentioned the frequent use of the pain pills due to injuries acquired from wrestling, he started to chuckle again.

"Doc, I don't find any of this funny," I snapped. "What the hell is so funny?!"

"Well, about your situation - absolutely nothing," he said. "However, about who you are as a person, that is why I may have laughed."

Before I just about stood and got up and walked out of there, the good doctor calmed me down.

"Please sit, Mr. White, or should I say Vader?" he motioned for me to switch seats to the more comfortable chair in the corner. "You don't understand, I am a huge fan of yours. I have been following you your entire career."

I cracked a smile. "Really?"

"I was hoping it was you when I took the appointment and I saw Leon White. I mean, I'm sorry you are having this problem, but I'm really selfishly happy to meet you."

I leaned back in the chair. Having a fan who was also a very smart man try and tackle my problem was ideal. "He might be a great person to have on my side," I thought. Sometimes super fans really went out of the way to help.

"I'm an older man now, but I'm not just a wrestling fan, I also love football. I remember watching you way back when you were an All-American," he confided. "I remember this one game where you were on the receiving team. Everybody had somebody to cover and it was clear you located the guy who was going to cover you."

"Okay," I said. "Sounds familiar."

"That game you went head on, face to face with that guy and hit him harder than anyone I ever saw get hit in football," he said reliving the moment. "They put the camera on you. You put that guy right out of the game, but you were out cold from hitting him so hard."

"If it's the play I think it was, we got the ball, right?"

"You sure did. Then, I was watching you intently on the sidelines to see what you were going to do next. One more play and you were right back in the game."

"Thank you, sir," I said living vicariously through the eye in his mind. "Those were the days."

"See I know who you are, Leon. I always looked you up after that. I watched you do the same type of thing in the NFL. I watched you do the same thing in wrestling with your eye and the other injuries. Then, the same thing in shoot fighting," he said.

"It's nice to hear you've been a fan all of these years, Doc, but I can honestly say I didn't expect all this." I was as polite as I could be with such little sleep, but I really wanted to say it felt like I just walked onto the set of *This is Your Life: Vader*, and I wanted to get on with my problem.

"I know you think I am just a crazy fan, but I am about to make a point," he said, "One that is probably leading to your sleep problems."

"I am all ears," I said.

"Before I tell you what I think the problem is, I need you to tell me some more about your past."

Doctor Ricard asked me various questions about my life.

I told him that at around 8-years old I was already playing 13-year-olds because of my size. They beat the bonkers out of me and made me a very mean football player. Then I explained how life for me turned into a food chain; I got beat up by the bigger kids, and I beat up kids who were younger than me.

I told him how the food chain continued. I explained falling victim to selfish coaches with agendas who had power over the players and the subsequent health issues in football. I told him how history repeated itself in wrestling and then I became the rookie once again and got my ass beat every day of the week in AWA by Bruiser Brody and Stan Hansen.

The doctor listened and shook his head in various places of my story.

Stan would never call anything with me before the match or even in the ring. Brody was the same way. They never wanted to call anything. They did this with me because they knew they could control me. They could beat the tar out of me knowing I had to listen because I was the new guy.

"Is that how it usually works?" he asked.

"No, not really. But that is all I knew back then," I said. "You can't do that today," I explained. "Today, you can fight your battle by negotiating well in the back before the match even happens."

"I see," he said.

"You have to predict the obstacles before they happen and set up a good plan in case they do," I said. "I learned the art of survival in the locker room way too late in the game. I know now I learned the hard way." I said.

"How is that?"

I admitted to self-medicating. I admitted to partying. I listed out almost all of the 50-some-odd surgeries that I had endured.

Doctor Ricard shook his head. After taking in the brutal moments of my life, he knew he was right all along. He seemed to know exactly what my problem was. He stopped taking notes and looked me right in the eye and said, "You are a modern day gladiator."

"Excuse me?"

"You are a gladiator. You can't sleep now because as you get older, all the pain from your crazy fights and surgeries comes back to haunt you at night. It is all coming back at once and now it is compounded and increased," he said. "My guess is, basically, you don't get any quality sleep because you have had so many concussions and your body is in shock from so many surgeries and injuries."

"Like a gladiator," I repeated.

"All the fights and operations have put massive stress on how your body operates," he said. "Leon, for the past 10 years, you also took pills that would have killed any normal man," he said. "The toxins, the coma, all of it takes its toll. You have fought your whole life and now you have to keep on fighting if you want to keep on living."

"Are you saying I could die?"

"It's possible, but I'm here to make sure it doesn't come down to that," he said.

His gladiator theory made a lot of sense. It was an "aha moment" for me.

"When the gladiators where on top, they would get it all," he said. "The women, the riches, the food. But once they got hurt and they couldn't fight anymore, they were just thrown away by society. This is also what society does to gladiators today, Leon. Seems like your situation a little."

The doctor set up an appointment to do a sleep test.

A few days later, I went to his lab to do the test. He realized right away that my blood pressure and heart were both out of whack. He had me do what I normally do when I can't sleep.

He wired me up to like 100 electrodes. I took a muscle relaxer and some sleeping pills to fall asleep.

They watched me sleep. They found out that I would be down for an hour or so then I would actually stand up while I was sleeping. I would get right out of bed for a moment, stand up and then lay back down.

"Wait no," I said. "I don't remember that."

He showed me the tape. He was right. It was sleep apnea.

"The reason you are doing this is your body is trying to get better air," he said. "It's subconscious."

He wrote me a prescription for a light pain killing agent and gave me a four day supply of sleeping medication. "Now stop taking that garbage you are taking," he said.

The next night they put me on an air mattress, and they had me sleep with an incline wedge pillow.

I slept right through the night for nine hours and didn't wake up once. That was probably the first real night of sleep I had had in ten years.

A lack of good sleep continued to be a massive problem for me.

FOR THE LOVE OF SPORT

If I had a time machine to go back to the young real estate agent Leon White standing before a crossroads before selecting wrestling, I don't know if I would do it again. Now, I love wrestling much more than real estate, don't get me wrong, but after 30 years, the bumps, being on the road, a massive list of injuries and a massive list of surgeries have all taken their toll. I cannot lie.

What people do not realize is that you sacrifice your body, your mind, your whole life. I have had relationships lost because, as a wrestler, you go away for 30 days at a shot and when you come home, you pretty much hibernate like a bear. You want to find the time to spend with your family, but you're tired, and you've got to get a workout in everyday to maintain your look and keep prepared just so you can go out and leave them once again for the road.

Wrestling really sounds glamorous, and it depicts you as being a rockstar when you are successful, but to the victor come the spoils.

Wrestlers don't often tell you the secret formula to success. *In order to gain fame, you often have to lose family and friends.*

The big names are on the road 300 nights a year. They are not around to see the first baby steps, to hear the first words. They are not there to see prom night or graduation.

When you live on the road, you don't know anyone. There isn't much socializing. You get dislocated from people. You lose friends on the road, and the road becomes your only friend, your only life.

It can become very lonely.

And then there are injuries. I've had I believe 48 surgeries to date. It seems one operation for one injury has never been enough for me. I've had several related to the patellar tendon injury from football and at least a handful of orbital socket repairs and eye surgeries. I've had nose procedures, shoulder repairs, rotator cuff surgery, knee reconstruction, collapsed ribcage repair, sternum surgery, arm/elbow surgery, the list goes on and on.

I played high school football, I played college football, but I'm pretty sure I never was taken out of a high school or college game with a concussion. I can't say the same with wrestling. Let's face it. It is entertainment and the show must go on.

Since this is the path I have chosen, I will not give up. I continue to wrestle and make appearances around the world to this very day. My work ethic will not allow me to quit.

I've been working hard in the gym every single day.

Right now, I feel like I'm in better shape than when I was world champ. I feel bigger and better than ever before.

At this point, it is not about wanting to be the champion again. It's about the journey, the climb, the wanting to be the guy on top again. Wanting to be the best and staying hungry until given the right moment to strike. I've learned to never put off until a later time what you can do right now.

TWO YEARS TO LIVE

This book was ready to go a year ago. When we finished and were finally ready to print, an unsuspected new chapter of my life began to write itself. I thought we had written every single word and paragraph we needed, until a "sentence" was written for me...

I was sitting on the stainless steel table in one of those hospital smocks at the medical center. My feet were dangling. Like any other checkup, it seemed like a lifetime for the doctor to come back to my room. I was anxious to hear the results of my sleeping tests, and why I was having breathing problems.

Only weeks before this visit, my regular doctor put me in the hospital. I was bloated, retaining water in the lower portion of my body like never before. They drained so much water out of me that nobody could believe it. That and going three or four nights with no sleep was really taking its toll on my body. I just closed my eyes when the door finally opened.

"Mister Leon White?"

"Yes, sir," I said, responding to the unfamiliar face.

"We've been looking at snapshots of your heart."

"Who are you?" I asked, not recognizing the face, because he was not the doctor I was there to see.

"I'm a heart specialist," he said, introducing himself. "Your doctor called me in to look at the results, and we frankly found something that's much more serious than we had hoped for… It's congestive heart failure."

"What does that mean?" Now, I had not come in to the doctor's office to hear any sort of new problem with my heart. That was the last thing on my mind.

"Leon, I'm sorry to tell you," he said, "with this condition, you probably only have about two years to live."

Two years to live?!

I had a hundred questions to ask him, but I could barely speak. I was in shock. Almost as soon as he had sat down with me, he was getting up and heading for the door.

"Wait a second. I'm going to die from this?! What about if I lose some weight?"

"Unfortunately, no. Your heart is just too worn out. My guess is that your lifestyle is finally catching up with you now," he said like he was preaching to me. "I understand you beat on your body for many years."

I nodded. Someone told him my background.

"From the looks of things, it's finally taking its toll."

That sounded completely out of line. Here the guy is the bearer of bad news, and he has to also kick me when I'm down? No. I wasn't taking it. I got up and walked out. I was pissed. As I stormed by the reception desk, my head was spinning in a million directions. I went in there looking for help and was blindsided by a judgmental asshole with no bedside manner.

I went straight to the hospital from the gym. I hopped on the bike and pedaled hard for a half hour. I got my heart rate racing as high as I could get it. I immediately climbed on the treadmill and ran my fastest. After 15 more minutes of cardio, my pulse was even higher. Nothing happened. I walked out of the gym, completely alive. I went home. I tried to take my mind off of what the heart doctor said, but it was impossible. I tried to get some sleep that night, but my eyes were stapled open, and I found myself just staring a hole in the ceiling. I had that "too tired to sleep" thing going on, where every part of my body screamed for rest, but I just couldn't shut off my mind.

Two years to live. Two years to live?

It was then that those four words started to haunt me. They repeated on a loop all through the night. Then, the next morning they were everywhere. They were in the kitchen. They were in the bathroom. They were in my front yard. They were in the closet. No matter where I went, those words were bouncing around every corner of my brain. Two… Years… To… Live…

I felt that those words were going to "earworm me to death" before I even made it to two years. I found myself crying at random moments. I felt helpless. I didn't know what to do. After days of wondering, I had enough. I decided to go to my regular doctor to see what she thought. When I got there, she confirmed that tests were not good. However, she said that his method of telling me the bad news was not very good, either, saying his diagnosis was also only his professional opinion, said in a "not-so-professional" way.

Hope was all I needed to hear. I wanted to prove that first doctor wrong. I started working out even harder. I went to another doctor; a well-known heart specialist who had a private practice with three specialists who all worked for him. In the end, all four concurred and had nothing really new to report. Still, no answers.

The next few weeks, I had my moments. Sometimes I felt like I was going to cheat death. I felt on top of the world and that I was going to prove them all wrong. I was going to eat better. Train better and lengthen my life. Other times, I felt like there was no point to even trying. I felt helpless, like death was coming for me and there was nothing I could do.

One evening, I had just picked up some healthy items from Costco; some nice vegetables, some clean protein. I was determined to make myself better. I had made that trip to the store probably a hundred times before without any incident and was pretty much flying on autopilot. I drove by a store window. It read "Buy 2, Get 1 Free." The hope of living left again, and the shadow of mortality crept in on me. *Two years to live…* Those horrible words haunted me. I painted a picture of my son, alone at my graveside. I saw my friends and family mourning. I zoned out, making the windy, back road turns out of instinct when I cut a turn too late.

WHOMP! WHOMP! WHOMP!

Everything around me spun. The vehicle was rolling. It felt like the most violent rollercoaster ever. My body was tossing like a ragdoll. My insides were rammed by the insides of the car, as well as my shoulders, my ribs, and my chest.

It flipped three full times around and slid on its hood and roof toward the side of the road. It all happened so fast. Finally, it slammed into a ravine to a jerking halt.

I opened my eyes. I tried to catch my breath. I panicked. I looked around the ruins inside my car. I was off the road and looking at grass through both sides of my shattered windshield. There was broken glass everywhere. The whole roof was caved in where my head was, mashed down, and on a tilted slant sideways.

The engine was revving up. I smelled sulfur and burnt rubber. I couldn't move. I was stuck there. It was crazy. I was shaking. I was crying. It was horrific. It was one of the worst moments of my life. I heard hissing. I smelled smoke.

Dear God! I can't get out and I'm going to burn to death. I'm going to burn to death! Nobody uses this road. Nobody is going to see me!

"HELP! HELP!!!" I was screaming. During the accident, I flipped over the front seat to the back. Both of my feet were pinched down hard in what was left of the back dashboard. I was screaming, crying and praying to hear the sound of another car.

Two years to live, my ass. I'm going to die right now...

Finally, thank God, I heard a sound beyond the madness of my motor out of control. They paused I think in shock, probably looking at the whole mess of a scene before someone came running. Then, I saw sneakers. I bit my lip.

One sneaker started kicking the window. It tried and tried with no success for what seemed like hours until eventually there was a tiny crack in the corner. It focused its attack on the growing crack. It stomped and stomped until finally, the glass gave out.

I looked at the opening. Exiting the window was not going to be an easy in and out like Dukes of Hazzard. It was all jagged along the bottom edge, like teeth. The boy crouched, then he tore off his shirt. He wrapped it around his hand and cleared the area the best he could, brushing the shards clean.

"Mister, there is fire!" he said, pointing at the hood.

Sure enough, black smoke. Engine parts were melting and I was still stuck inside. I knew there was a full tank of gas. There was light from the fire above what used to be the glove box. I knew I had to get out. My feet were still stuck. I wriggled like my life depended on it, because it did. Just like a fox who eats his own leg to get out of a trap, I yanked and pulled, no matter how bad my feet hurt. Just before I gave up, one foot finally freed. Then using it as a brace, I pushed the other free. Once I was no longer clamped in, there was just enough room squeeze my body out.

I dropped to the ground. I looked up to see the underbelly of the giant tin can that was holding me hostage. Its tires were a mangled mess. I was shaking and crying. I hugged that little kid. "Thank you so much," I said. "Please. I have to give you something. Take my number. Please."

"I don't want anything," he said. "It's ok, man. Really."

His sister had called the police. They came and put out the fire and brought me home. When I was finally home safe again, I looked at the reflection of who should have been a dead man in my mirror. It looked like I had just been in my worst fight ever. My face was a mess. My head was beat up. My eyes were black and blue. My nose was puffed up. My forehead was swollen.

I smiled for a second, thinking I had cheated death once again, just like all the times in the ring. Then, it hit me. There was still one more obstacle to overcome.

LIVING WITH AN EXPIRATION DATE

Living is hard. The diagnosis haunts me. Knowing your days are numbered changes the way a person thinks.

Reality comes back at you. You try not to think about it. No matter how hard you try, no matter how busy you keep yourself, it still comes back and hits you like a brick wall. Hopelessness. You are void. If I choose to believe the doctors, then there would be nothing left, so I try to stay positive, but I still wake up at four in the morning shaking. I struggle. Sometimes I feel like a little boy afraid in the dark, and I just want someone to hold my hand and tell me everything is going to be alright.

Sometimes, I feel like it's almost not worth it. With the meter ticking, it's like I am just watching, waiting for it to end. Sometimes, I go three or four days with no sleep and I just about go crazy. I want to live to be 90 to see my great grandchildren, but sometimes the struggle seems almost too hard. It's all moment-to-moment living now, and I hate knowing what my expiration date is.

I understand how it just could be easier to take a bottle of pills and stop all the pain. If I didn't have my son and it was just me, I can't say I wouldn't have considered that option. But then when I think about what "the easy way out" would do to the people I love... what it would do to my brother, my sister, my mother, my ex-wife and my son... I could never do that to the people I love.

Keeping myself busy is important. I recently took a booking in Japan where they dropped me on my head. Everything went black. I legit passed out because my body just couldn't take it anymore like it used to. I know this is going to sound very John Wayne of me, but I have decided that if I am going to die, I am going to do it doing something I love. If I am going to die, it is not going to be in a hospital bed, it will be in a wrestling ring.

Life is a gift. I have lived a life of ten men. I had a mother and father. I never missed a meal. I was healthy. I graduated. I was the first one in my family through college. I was able to get married to a beautiful woman and have a beautiful son. I've worked hard and been able to work hard. I've always had money and roof over my head. With all of the awards and everything that I have been recognized for, I couldn't ask for a better professional life. For everything, I'm thankful. No complaints on this end. So, if I do die tonight in my sleep, I don't want anyone to feel sorry for me.

I moved from the Rocky Mountains of Colorado to Dallas so I could spend more quality time with my son, and live life. I'm keeping busy now.

Now when I have those nights when I can't sleep and those days that I can't function, I try and focus on being positive. I find hope in thinking about all that I've done and all I have accomplished. I look at how I have defied the odds in the past, and I think about all the other big crazy obstacles that I've overcome. *Two years … my ass!* This diagnosis is just another obstacle to overcome, like all the rest.

The term "Vader Time" to me has always meant overcoming obstacles and steamrolling through anything that gets in the way of your dreams or goals.

My goal is to get healthy and live a long life. My final dream now is to be in the WWE Hall of Fame. I believe I can do this by continuing to work hard and be noticed.

In 2016, I was able to induct my friend Stan Hansen. What a great honor that was to give him his HOF moment. I had fun with it and wore a pair of slinky eye glasses at the end, but it was his time, and more than anybody, Stan deserved it.

Maybe this year, my legacy will be further secured in the minds of wrestling fans everywhere. Maybe this year, all the years of hard work and pushing past adversary and injuries will finally pay off.

If it happens or not, it will always and forever be…
Vader Time.

EPILOGUE – BY JESSE WHITE

On 6/18/18, my father died.

The doctors gave him "two years to live" back in 2016. Approximately 19 months after he made the announcement on Twitter, we lost him, just five months shy of two years.

Life is a bitch...

Back before the grim diagnosis in early November 2016, the phone rang. It was my father's primary care physician. He said that his tests came back and his health was a major concern. He strongly suggested that he check himself into the ER immediately.

Over the next week, they discovered some major health concerns. One, in particular, was a recent retaining of 40 pounds of extra water weight in his arms and legs. This is one of the first signs that his heart was not functioning well, and a symptom of Congestive Heart Failure.

"The doctor told me I have two years to live," he said, making his first call to me from the hospital. "They also said there's nothing I can do to change it."

"Wait, no. Bullshit, there's always something you can do. Can I speak to the doctor?" I didn't even believe the news at first. I knew my father was getting old, but growing up watching Big Van Vader do the things he did... There was nothing that he couldn't do. He was King Kong, he was Superman! I thought there was nothing that could bring him down. However, I was very wrong. There is one asshole who is very strong and also undefeated, and he is Father Time.

Things needed to change fast. I went to my dad's place for Thanksgiving, hoping to convince him to move to Texas with me. I knew that would be a tough sell because he loved everything about his home; the mountains, the weather, and the fact that he had been living there since the early 80's after his time with the LA Rams. During our talk at the dinner table, I almost insisted. I figured I had to flip the coin, become the man of the house, and take over. However, he saw absolutely no value in a move. We enjoyed our dinner and time together, but he refused my help making the move and retired off to bed.

In the middle of the night, my father woke up, remembering to close his garage door. At two in the morning, I heard a scream. "FUCKKKKKK! Jesse get down here!"

Walking through the pitch black garage, he skewered his leg on a sharp corner of an old bed frame. I found him hobbling to his bedroom and losing blood fast. I grabbed a towel and held him still. After a few minutes, I lifted the cloth to see how bad the hole was. Let's just say it looked like the Grand Canyon. I called the ambulance and he was off to the same hospital he just got out of.

There, they sedated my father. At about 4:00 am, he woke up. He didn't know where he was there or inside an MRI machine humming in his ears. He was pissed. He shimmied out of the MRI machine and tried to leave the building. He ended up fighting five or six security guards. I guess that "LA" inside of Pops never really left. He was ready to knock someone the fuck out. During the fighting, blood from his injury was pouring out all over the floor.

"Bull, Bull. Everything's Okay! Calm Down!" said a voice from behind. It was Coach Mike Metoyer, a guy who grew up and played college ball with my dad who randomly worked at the hospital. He eventually calmed him down, but it wasn't over. As my dad made his way back to the room, he slipped and nailed his head hard on the MRI machine.

During all of this, I was sleeping in the waiting room. Around 4:45, a guard woke me up saying, "There's been an incident. I need you to come with me." Confused, scared, nervous... I follow the guard into the elevator. He pressed Floor 6 - ICU. I walked into the room and see my father handcuffed to the bed and snoring his ass off. The hospital had to give him a strong sedative to knock him out. The puncture wound severed nerves in his left calf so badly that he was in danger of also losing the motor functions of his left foot. They soon rushed him off into surgery.

After a few days in the hospital, he was ready to go. I took off some time from work and made sure he got back to his house okay. Once all was good, I got ready to head back to Dallas. Before I did, he stopped me.

"I don't want to die. I am not ready."

There are very few times in my life that I can remember my father being scared and this was one of them. "Let's get you down to Dallas," I said. "I'll get you with my team of doctors. We will train, eat clean, get you back on track and get ready to knock some heads - like camp together. We will beat this."

Finally, he was ready.

THE MOVE TO DALLAS

After Christmas, we took the twelve hour drive to Dallas. I had an apartment waiting for him just minutes from my place as well as doctor appointments and a gym membership. Being in Dallas with me was a great help, but it wasn't the only "Dallas" that he would see help from. A few days after the move, my dad got a call from Diamond Dallas Paige. A week after that call, he was off to Atlanta to start the DDPY program which changed my father's life, as well as mine. Dallas and his wife Brenda spent hours educating us about the quality of foods we put inside our bodies. We both learned so much. For this, I am forever grateful.

Back at home, Pops settled in and developed a nice little schedule. As his new gym buddy, we created a routine that included his weight training and the DDPY program. Things were on the up and up. Every day we pushed each other and became even closer. We started doing stuff together that we never really got to do while I was growing up. From movies to museums, we had a lot of fun. I am also thankful for that because we finally got to make up for some lost time on the road.

My dad had a new energy about him. On the surface, he was doing well. He lost about 25 pounds, was eating regularly healthy, and following up with all of his doctor appointments, all except the cardiologist. Every time I tried to schedule an appointment, my father would cancel. He was scared - we both were. If we were to get some bad news, we both knew that everything was going to change. It was like we were on this little vacation. We didn't want it to end. We didn't want to face reality.

Against the advice of doctors and my own wishes, my dad took a wrestling booking over in Japan. Over the ten-day period, he fell off our schedule. When he got back, there was nothing left in his tank. He stopped working out, he started eating unhealthy again, and he started missing appointments with his doctors. I will always wonder... what if he had never gone? I'll never know, but I do know this; he loved professional wrestling and performing so much, he would do it at any cost.

TROUBLES

One day I picked my dad up for lunch. The restaurant was busy that day and there were literally no parking spots. I eventually found one a little ways out, about a three minute walk to the entrance. When we got to the front door, my father quickly sat down.

"Something's not right," he said, grabbing at his chest. I was scared, but he just shook it off. He took a couple of deep breaths and said everything was okay. We went in and grabbed a table. Our conversation started off with the usual BS stuff (work and girls) but he was clearly ignoring what just happened. He asked me a question and I ignored it, then hit him with another question of my own.

"Papa," I said. "When are you going to let me take you to the cardiologist?"

There was a long wait. I could see the sorrow in his eyes. "I am scared Jesse. I am not ready yet." My father really felt like his time was coming to an end.

I hated myself for the way I reacted but I was pissed. I felt like he was giving up on me and that was unacceptable. It turned into an argument. We were pretty heated and eventually started yelling at each other. Things were said by both parties that we regretted. Even though I am my father's son, an apple doesn't fall to far from the tree when it comes to stubbornness, but I knew this was not a time to stay angry. After a few days of calming down, we made amends and said our apologies.

BAD NEWS

I don't remember where it was but he went on another autograph signing. As soon as I picked him back up from the airport, he got in the car and said, "Make the appointment." His chest had been hurting him for three or four days consecutively!

I made the appointment and two days later, we were at the hospital for some tests. I was in the waiting room wondering to myself over and over again, "Good news, or Bad news?" When the nurse finally brought me in to see my dad, she had no answers for me. I still didn't know until I walked in the room and saw the look on my father's face. Then, I knew it was exactly what we had been avoiding. The cardiologists explained that his heart had over ten clogged arteries and that four need to be operated on immediately.

"Everything is going to be okay. We are going to get through this," I said, repeating lines I had rehearsed over and over in my head.

My father was scared. Two days later, he went off to an autograph signing in NY. That was his very last one. When he returned, he went to see one of the top Cardiovascular Surgeons in Texas and felt that he was our guy. Even though he was talking quadruple bypass surgery, he made my father feel comfortable and confidant; everything you could want when meeting with a guy who was going to cut open your chest and operate on your heart.

While waiting five days in the hospital to be clinically ready for surgery, my father received hundreds of calls from family and friends, many I didn't know. One old familiar friend stopped by as well; Steve Borden aka Sting. Between the calls and the visit from Steve, my father in good spirits and we all prayed together.

The night before surgery, my father told me exactly what he wanted to happen if something were to go wrong. At the time, I took that info and stored it way back in my brain refusing to believe I would need it soon. I focused on recovery and what we would need to do.

When the surgery finally came, six hours later the surgeon came around the corner with a big smile on his face. I immediately knew the surgery was a success. When I went in to see my father, it was scary. He had hundreds of tubes and wires coming out of him. I knew it would be a long road to recovery. While my father was still asleep, I called everyone to let them know the surgery was a success. Eventually, he woke up.

"Ughhh. I feel like I got hit by a truck," he said, opening his eyes. I laughed. "Actually, it feels like Mick Foley hit me with a shovel again, but this time on the chest." He was in a lot of pain, but at least he was in good spirits.

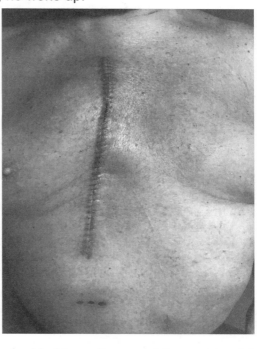

Over the next few weeks, recovery was okay. He was retaining some fluid in his legs, but he was eventually transferred to a short-term recovery hospital 15 minutes from my house. I remember one particular day there, I stopped over to cut his hair and trim his beard. We decided to walk around the parking lot for a little exercise. "Wow, Dallas is beautiful. The trees are actually really green." This was huge because my father wasn't a big fan of Dallas because he missed the mountains of Colorado. That moment reminded me of a Facebook video I saw where a son gifted his father a pair of glasses. When the father put them on, he started crying. You then learned that he was colorblind and the glasses allowed him to see in color for the first time. The surgery could have been my father's seeing in color moment making him look at life differently. There were so many things he still wanted to do. I wanted to help him with that and see another twenty years.

When he finally went home, he took to more walks outside and more cardio at the gym. He was eating clean. Things seemed positive. The next week we saw mostly good days, until… he stopped answering my calls. When that happened, I rushed to his place and put my ear to the door. I heard him snoring and, in a sigh of relief, decided to let him catch some ZZZs. Later that night, I returned. He was still snoring and something felt wrong, so I broke in. He wouldn't wake up and was nonresponsive. I called 911 and we got him over to the hospital. They put a tube down his throat. He had stopped breathing and we almost lost him.

That night a very serious case of Pneumonia took over his respiratory system. We had to put him into a medically induced coma to fight the infection. While he was asleep, they ran some tests to determine what his brain activity was like because when I found him his oxygen levels were so low it could have led to brain damage. Over the next three weeks, we finally fought off the infection in his lungs enough to wake him up. When he came to, he thought he just had his heart surgery. He had no idea what was going on but he saw my face and he recognized me.

The next three weeks were hard, because of a tracheotomy; a tube in his throat that didn't allow him to speak. We basically had to play charades to communicate. Besides that, everything else was going well and he started to recover fast. In fact, the doctor let me know that he was extremely happy with his progress and looking at having therapy start in a day or so. During my lunch break the next day, I stopped by my dad's room.

"Hey! My baby boy," he said. I was sucking back tears. It had been basically a month since he last spoke.

The conversation we finally had is one I will never forget. We hugged. We laughed. We said how much we love each other. I eventually had to leave to finish up some things at the office. About an hour later, I received a call from my father. He wanted to let me know how much he loved me and how much he appreciated what I was doing for him. He was grateful. We said I love you and said goodbye, and I told him I would see him in about an hour.

This was the last conversations I ever had with my father.

My father passed away on June 18, 2018, at 7:25 pm.

In death, there can be beauty, and for my father and I …there was. The last day I got to spend with him was a gift from God. We said everything we wanted to say and we were able to say our goodbyes. I am so fortunate to have experienced that time with my father and I will forever cherish those moments we had. There are people in this world who never get to experience what we did in those last moments with their loved ones and him and I were blessed enough to experience them.

My father gave his life to the sport of pro wrestling. It's something he loved doing. My father's resume is one of a kind. However, one accomplishment you won't see on this list is being a father. He often admitted that he probably missed half of my life growing up because of being on the road. But even so, he did more in that little time with me than any other fathers I knew, and they were around full time! From schooling to training to sports, he instilled in me early on what hard work looks like. He gave me so many blessings that I am forever grateful for. I am confidant when I say one of his greatest accomplishments of all was being my father.

I love you up to God and back.

TITLES

FOOTBALL: High School All-American, 2X College All-American, 3rd Round Draft Pick to the LA Rams (1978), NFC Champion (1978), Super Bowl (1978), Only professional wrestler to reach the Super Bowl and hold a heavyweight Championship.

WCW: 3X WCW World Heavyweight Champion, WCW United States Heavyweight Champion, Battle Bowl Winner 1993, Wrestler of the Year 1993 (Only Super Heavyweight Ever to accomplish) for both PWI and WON, Best Heel 1993

NJPW: 3X IWGP Heavyweight Champion, First Non-Japanese Wrestler to ever hold the IWGP Heavyweight Championship, IWGP Tag Team Champion, Super Grade Tag League

AJPW: 2X Triple Crown Heavyweight Champion, First Wrestler (Including Japanese Wrestlers) to ever hold the IWGP and the Triple Crown, World Tag Champion, Champion Carnival Winner 1999, Most Improved Wrestler Award 1999

UWFI: Pro-Wrestling World Heavyweight Championship, Best of World Tournament

CWA: Europe: 3X CWA Heavyweight Champion, CWA International Heavyweight Champion

UWA: Mexico: UWA Heavyweight Champion

NOAH: GHC Tag Team Champion

CREDITS

AUTHOR:
Leon White

CO-AUTHOR/GHOSTWRITER:
Kenny Casanova

**EXECUTIVE PRODUCER OF
LEGAL STUFF & EDITING:**
Marty Carbone

EDITORS:
Ian Douglass, John Cosper

FAMILY EDITS:
Jesse White

RESEARCH CONSULTANTS:
Rob Rosen, Bert Williams

WOHW WEB SITE STUFF:
Kerri Bevan

BOOK SOCIAL MEDIA:
Beth Kempf

BEHIND THE SCENES HELP:
Maria Bevan
Mike Johnson
Shockwave The Robot

**QUOTES &
CONTENT:**
Mick Foley
Dave Logan
Jim Ross
Jesse White

TEAM VADER:
David Schloss
Rob Naylor

COVER ART:
Iron Skull
Productions

**PHOTO COLLECTIONS &
PHOTO CONTRIBUTIONS:**
Tye Harris (Title Page Art)
The Whites (Family shots)
Wrestling Revue Archives (Rookie)
Chris Swisher (AWA & WCW)
Gernot Freiberger (CWA shots)
Dr. Mike Lano (Triple Crown)
Dick Bourne, Mid-Atlantic Gateway
(SuperBrawl V)
Jimmy Suzuki (Japan Shots)
Gary Michael Cappetta (Foley)
Diamond Dallas Page (Hall of Fame)
Andrea Kellaway (Comeback shot)

HELPFUL RESOURCES:
WOHW.com
KennyCasanova.com
VaderTime.com
ItsVaderTime.com
KamalaSpeaks.com
BrutusBeefcake.com
ECWsabu.com
DangerousDannyDavis.com
PWInsider.com
InsideTheRopesVIP.com
MemphisWrestlingHistory.com
Slam Canoe Wrestling
ObsessedWithWrestling.com
BETwrestling.com
Steve Austin Show Podcast
Keepin' It 100 with Konnan Podcast
Something To Wrestle With Podcast
Sean Mooney Prime Time Podcast

**A VERY SPECIAL THANKS
FROM KENNY CASANOVA:**
...I dedicate my work to my wife
Maria for putting up with all of my
nonsense and the four years spent
on this project! ...To Marty for the
pages of errors and edits (let me
finish!) ...My dad for taking me to
events as a kid ...And to anyone
else who supports these wrestling
books to keep the legends alive!

KENNY CASANOVA
CO-AUTHOR/GHOSTWRITER OF THIS BOOK

Kenny is a ring announcer, pro wrestling manager, wedding DJ, English teacher, and Fulbright Scholar. As the organizer of this project and other ones like it, his recent mission has been helping guys like Brutus Beefcake & Kamala get their stories out there for the appreciation of future generations.

Please email questions or promotional inquiries to Kenny himself at **ken@kennycasanova.com,** or find him on all social media platforms.

Walking on Hot Waffles is at WOHW.com
...with more books like this one including *Kamala Speaks, Brutus Beefcake, Mr. X: Dangerous Danny Davis,* and *Sabu: Scars, Silence & Superglue.*